# Charles N. Hunter
# and Race Relations in North Carolina

**The James Sprunt Studies
in History and Political Science**

*Published under the Direction of the
Departments of History and Political Science of
The University of North Carolina at Chapel Hill*

**Volume 60**

*Editors*

**The University of North Carolina Press**
Chapel Hill and London

J O H N     H A L E Y

# Charles N. Hunter
## and Race Relations in North Carolina

© 1987 The University of North Carolina Press
All rights reserved
Manufactured in the United States of America

Library of Congress Cataloging-in-Publication Data

Haley, John.
Charles N. Hunter and race relations in North Carolina.

(The James Sprunt studies in history and political science; v. 60)
Bibliography: p.
Includes index.
1. Hunter, Charles N., ca. 1851–1931.
2. Afro-Americans—North Carolina—Biography. 3. Slaves
—North Carolina—Biography. 4. North Carolina—Race
relations. 5. Afro-Americans—North Carolina.
I. Title. II. Series.
E185.97.H84H35   1987        975.6′04        86-11369
ISBN 0-8078-5061-6

*Designed by Chris Wilkinson*

# Contents

# Preface

                  At the outset of this project I intended to write a biography of the public life of Charles N. Hunter, who was born a slave and lived until the Great Depression. But as I began to place him within the context of his time and social milieu, what unfolded was a multilayered work that is also a study of race relations and black history in North Carolina. Hunter was an exceptional man if for no other reason than that he left an impressive set of papers, which contains an account of his struggle for dignity, equality, and acceptance in a society whose dominant members were committed to assigning blacks to an inferior position. During his lifetime he communicated with most of the major black personalities of his day, and he was involved in many of the important activities, organizations, and institutions that affected the black community in North Carolina. In addition to showing the frustrations and anxieties of educated and capable blacks who desperately wanted to be integrated into society as a whole and be in the mainstream of the great movements of their times, a study of Hunter's life is to a degree a study of the post–Civil War history of his race in North Carolina.

    Hunter also had important connections within the white community. His relationships with his former owner's family and a select group of native whites frequently resulted in personal favors or support for projects that benefited his race. He was always proud of his acquaintances with a large number of the "old school gentlemen" of the white race, and he claimed that "through all and despite all," they were his friends. Yet Hunter's mentality was also shaped by forces other than his contacts with native whites. When the Civil War ended, he cast his lot with northerners, and he received his formal education and a thorough indoctrination in Republican

## Preface

party politics under their guidance. Throughout his life, he praised the abolitionists and the Union Army, who "liberated a race and revolutionized the life of a Nation."[1]

When Reconstruction ended without achieving real equality for blacks, Hunter began to express the idea that a satisfactory adjustment of race relations lay in an alliance with the best white men of North Carolina. He defined these men as those who had once owned slaves, and who had lived in close proximity to blacks. He saw them as men of the "purest patrician strain" whose social status was so firmly entrenched in southern society that they did not fear contamination by, or competition with, blacks. Neither did they need the aid of legislation to preserve their social status, and they also knew that blacks had no intentions of overstepping racial boundaries. Hunter frequently contended that "Between such people and the Negro there has never been and there will never be any Negro problem."[2]

When he was approximately sixty-three years old, Hunter wrote that his whole adult life had been devoted to promoting a better understanding and a closer cooperation between the races. In working toward these goals, he embraced almost every philosophy of race relations except separatism and violence. At times he appeared as an avid accommodationist who advised his race to sacrifice certain rights and privileges common to other American citizens in favor of those more immediate and beneficial gains that whites were willing to grant blacks. Long before Booker T. Washington achieved renown for his Atlanta Compromise speech in 1895, Hunter had publicly advocated that blacks adopt a conservative approach in race relations, and he acknowledged the greatness and the superiority of the white race on the basis of its record of achievements. He also believed that his race had to attain a high degree of intellectual development and economic self-sufficiency before it could demand civil and political equality, and he thought that progress toward these ends could be hastened if blacks devoted their energies to industrial and vocational training, cultivated good habits of thrift and morality, and remained submissive and passive to the abuses of whites.

On rare occasions, however, Hunter's liberal and reforming impulses prompted him to pursue a radical philosophy of race relations, and he recommended that blacks adopt a militant program of incessant and uncompromising agitation to secure equality. His wavering stance on race relations gave him the appearance of inconsistency. But this was true of most black leaders, who were rarely frozen into either the accommodationist or

# Preface

the radical camp. They generally followed the most opportune course for the moment that offered the greater chance for success. Yet it also seems that Hunter was somewhat inconsistent and devious by nature. Part of this may be explained by the necessity of frequently having to alter a position on racial issues in the interest of economic security or self-protection. After making speeches or publishing articles, he was often pressured into recanting his viewpoints and explaining his motives in ways that were acceptable to whites. Nevertheless, an examination of his life also provides a much needed treatment of race relations in North Carolina during the late nineteenth and early twentieth centuries.

This is also a study in leadership styles, and although Hunter was not a leader of people, he was a leader in advancing ideas. With the exception of an occasional politician during the Reconstruction and the Fusionist eras, there were in fact few blacks in North Carolina who ever approached the status of a popular leader who commanded a large following, and who had the power to execute plans and programs. There were, however, many semiemancipated blacks, including Hunter, who led various religious, fraternal, professional, and social organizations. These men were generally torn between pursuing limited objectives to further the goals of their organizations and institutions and working to enhance their own personal status. If occasionally one came up with a plan that would benefit the masses of blacks, he was rarely able to achieve anything approaching a statewide consensus and obtain the support necessary to bring it to fruition. The majority of blacks in the state no doubt knew that these self-styled leaders were limited in their ability to produce results, and they were also aware of the fact that whites most often designated black leaders, allowed them to exist, and deposed them when they threatened the established social order.

At times Hunter and his black associates referred to themselves as leading or representative men of their race. In this they approximated the model of the "Race Man" or "Race Leader" posited by St. Clair Drake and Horace R. Cayton. The leading men in North Carolina, like the "Race Man'" in the North, for the most part tended to oppose all attempts to subordinate their race, and they generally supported activities that would benefit blacks. They always urged their people to exercise discipline and to take maximum advantage of their educational and economic opportunities. But in an attempt to improve their race and to stimulate it to even greater achievements, these men rarely missed an opportunity to "needle, cajole, and denounce blacks for their inertia, diffidence and lack of race pride."[3]

# Preface

Hunter, though a political activist and propagandist, claimed that he was not a politician. While realizing that blacks had made their greatest gains under the stewardship of the Republican party, he did not blindly support it. Instead he split his votes among Republicans, independents, and Democrats, and he generally favored those candidates who, he thought, were best qualified regardless of party affiliation. This eclectic approach in politics at times got him into trouble with black politicians, and occasionally he was accused of being disloyal to his race. Hunter constantly urged the Republican party to adhere to its original commitment to human rights and equality, and during the twentieth century he was a leading spirit in the fight to thwart the success of the lily-white movement in North Carolina. Hunter also believed that much of the race hatred generated in North Carolina during Reconstruction was a direct result of the political activity of blacks, and he felt that one of the lessons his race should have learned from that experience was that whites were determined to control governments at all levels. He also correctly predicted that the continued involvement of blacks in the political process would in time produce violence. Consequently, he recommended that blacks refrain from seeking public offices, and he saw this as a necessary prerequisite for the maintenance of friendly race relations and the material, moral, and mental advancement of his people.

On another level, this book is also a commentary on the role that Hunter and his associates played in giving sustenance and publicity to the social myth that alleged that North Carolina was the best place in the world for blacks. Inherent in this myth was the idea that race relations in North Carolina were better than in other southern states. In time this myth became a part of the historiography of North Carolina. For example, Frenise A. Logan, in the preface to his book *The Negro in North Carolina 1876–1894*, wrote that there was much "historical truth in the bold statement of Professor C. Vann Woodward that segregation and white supremacy as they pertain to North Carolina" were products of the twentieth century southern white mentality, and that from the end of the Civil War to 1898, the state witnessed "only a few of the policies of proscription, segregation, and disfranchisement" that later characterized race relations. There is also much myth in this "bold statement," and this study will show that, on balance, race relations in North Carolina were no better than in other states to the south. Blacks were the victims of the same types of injustices and oppression that were inflicted upon their race in other southern states, and they

# Preface

were hardly perceived as anything other than separate and subordinate members of society.[4]

Immediately after the Civil War, the leadership of North Carolina, supported by popular opinion, reaffirmed its historic commitment to white supremacy. It was agreed that blacks would have neither political nor civil equality, and this was an accomplished fact by the end of Reconstruction, which was a relatively brief period in North Carolina. Thereafter, although not always sanctioned by constitutional amendments or statutory enactments, racial segregation was pervasive throughout the state, and blacks were consistently deprived of human rights and dignity. They also suffered the effects of physical violence, a miserable education system, and civil and political inequality. The political activity of blacks in the famous Second Congressional District and during the Fusionist era, often cited as indices of good race relations, were aberrations in the history of North Carolina. Well before the turn of the century, conservative whites had decided to depoliticize blacks, and they were largely successful through the use of legislative decrees and unethical and illegal election procedures. When the established social and political order supporting white supremacy was threatened by the Fusionists of the 1890s, whites responded with legalized Jim Crow and disfranchisement.

Hunter and other blacks were never satisfied with the state of race relations in North Carolina, and they frequently conveyed this feeling to the white community. Yet the elites of both races paradoxically claimed that race relations were better in North Carolina, and that the state was the best place for blacks. One must certainly wonder what motivated such rhetoric when it was not substantiated by facts. The myth concerning the good race relations in the Tarheel State served a real psychic need for its proponents. Whites wanted the reputation of being good and just people, and at the same time they used the myth for purposes of social control: to pacify blacks, to prevent change, and to promote civil peace. The myth also enhanced the status and self-esteem of the leading blacks by convincing them that they had helped create, and were living in, the best of all possible situations. They too repeated the myth to escape greater oppression and to placate those whites who had the power to grant them favors or prestige.

Scholars have expressed ambivalent attitudes when dealing with myth and history. Some have noted that serious history is a critique of myths rather than their embodiment or destruction. Others claim that some myths

# Preface

can indeed be good things, which no person, including the responsible historian, would wantonly destroy. On the other hand, Pieter Geyl's interpretation of the relationship among myth, history, and the historian seems to me the most appropriate. He saw the historical spirit as "a force for truth and against myth." Geyl and others have warned that cultivators of the good or useful myth, including Hitler, Mussolini, and Stalin, have shown where history can land us when it is detached from truth. For years the social myth concerning the good race relations in North Carolina had either escaped the scrutiny of historians or was left unchallenged. But it did not get past William H. Chafe, who in his *Civilities and Civil Rights* identified the paradoxical nature of North Carolina's image and noted that by the late 1940s the state had "a reputation for social enlightenment and a social reality that was reactionary." Chafe steadily chipped away at the idea that North Carolina was "an inspiring exception to Southern racism." It had never been, and this was particularly true during the lifetime of Charles N. Hunter.[5]

I wish to record my sincere acknowledgments to a number of individuals who helped make this book possible. I am indebted to Professor Joel Williamson of the History Department of the University of North Carolina, who first focused my attention on Charles N. Hunter and guided me during the initial stages of this study. I am particularly obligated to a delightful colleague, Professor Carole Fink, who read my manuscript and offered valuable aid throughout the duration of this project. An especial thanks is due to Lewis Bateman, Executive Editor of the University of North Carolina Press, for his patience, encouragement, and assistance in bringing this book to fruition. I also appreciate the efforts of Pamela Upton of the UNC Press, who graciously guided me through the editorial process. Attendance at a National Endowment for the Humanities Summer Seminar helped provide the means for furthering my research. I am grateful for this assistance, and also acknowledge the sage counsel and encouragement of Professor George Brown Tindall, the seminar's director. Finally, my thanks are due to Catherine Talent, who typed and retyped my manuscript.

# Charles N. Hunter
# and Race Relations in North Carolina

# 1

## Friends or Enemies?

Charles Norfleet Hunter was born a slave in Raleigh, North Carolina, in approximately 1851. His father, Osborne Hunter, Sr., was the property of William Dallas Haywood, whose home was located on the northeast corner of East Edenton and North Person streets. Osborne was a slave artisan, skilled as a carpenter, wheelwright, and miller, and he was primarily employed in the making of cotton packers or screws. Hunter's mother, Mary, was not the property of the Haywoods. She was hired by Hunter's father, who paid a nominal sum for her time, and the couple maintained a residence at the northeast corner of Jones and Dawson streets. The Hunter family enjoyed the dubious distinction of being classed among the "aristocratic slaves" of Raleigh.[1]

Hunter's mother died when he was approximately four years old, and her children were moved into the home of their master and placed under the care of an aunt who was also the mammy of the Haywood family. The Hunter children lived most of the time at the fireside of their owner and were mainly cared for by his younger daughters. Hunter recalled that his brother, Osborne, Jr., was the special charge of "Miss Annie" and he of "Miss Maggie." His playmates consisted of children of both races and he could not recall a single undertone of racial consciousness on their part. When he was old enough to be of some service, he was placed in the home of Richard H. Battle.[2]

Hunter's childhood was certainly not typical of that of the ordinary slave, and neither were the relationships that he claimed existed between the Haywoods and their human property. This may explain his idealized and romantic impressions of slavery. He wrote that the Haywoods and their slaves constituted one big family whose white and black members regarded each other with mutual love and friendship, and that this arrangement made "life so far as it could under existing conditions ideal." Hunter insisted that "an injury done to a Haywood Negro was an injury done to a Haywood white and vice versa."[3]

Hunter's cordial relationship with the Haywood family did not end with his emancipation. Throughout his life he maintained contact with the Haywoods, and he frequently turned to them for advice and assistance. The Haywoods treated him with dignity and respect, and they seemed genuinely interested in his welfare. Hunter owed much of his success to the influence of the Haywoods, and he claimed that there was no member of that family who would not gladly render him any service. A half century after his emancipation, he wrote in reference to the Haywood family: "I have always been able to claim a friend in each generation." He constantly professed his love and friendship for the descendants of the Haywoods, and in the year of his death he wrote, "I learned early in my life to love them. The attachment was strengthened with the accumulation of years." Hunter summed up his feelings toward the Haywoods by citing the words of Ruth to Naomi in the Bible, "Thy people shall be my people and thy God my God."[4]

Unlike many other blacks of his generation, Hunter was never ashamed of his slave ancestry, and he held no ill feelings toward former slaveowners. It seems almost as if he admired the people who maintained and operated the peculiar institution, for he believed that among the slaveholders of North Carolina there were men and women of the "noblest type and tenderest sensibilities." He was proud of having been the property of the Haywoods, "a family distinguished for its intellectual culture, social refinement, and great wealth." He appropriated some of the status of the Haywoods, and he saw himself as a reflection of that family. He contended that he and the Haywoods were essentially the same in spirit. They shared similar thoughts, ambitions, and aspirations, and Hunter maintained that he even partook of their "likes and dislikes, their prides, passions and even their prejudices."[5]

In spite of their kind treatment, the Haywood slaves were far from satisfied with their condition. Hunter remembered that although they remained loyal and devoted to their owner during the Civil War, they prayed for freedom and a Union victory, because they knew that the outcome of the struggle meant the difference between perpetual bondage and liberty. When the war ended, the Haywood slaves were permitted to remain with their owner until they became adjusted to their new status. In this regard

### Friends or Enemies?

Hunter was indeed much more fortunate than many of the freedmen, who, once emancipated, were cast aside to shift for themselves in a hostile environment.[6]

The Union victory and the emancipation of slaves were traumatic experiences that created a major crisis in the lives of North Carolinians. Emancipation wiped out what many whites thought was an ideal system of race relations that had been carefully designed to control the lives and labor of the vast majority of blacks in the state. Suddenly, blacks were no longer slaves and property; they were human beings and free persons, and whites viewed this reversal with mixed emotions. They worried how blacks would act in their new status, and they pondered the future pattern of race relations.

Some whites stoically accepted the results of the Civil War and emancipation, and seemed genuinely interested in helping the freedmen. Though a small minority, this group attempted to persuade others of their race to adopt similar attitudes. An editorial in the *Raleigh Daily Record* of 8 June 1865 urged its readers to acknowledge the freedom of blacks, stay close to them, and encourage them to be frugal, moral, intelligent, and industrious citizens. It also reminded whites that, having always claimed to be the best friend of the black man, "let our conduct towards him now be such as to convince him of this fact."[7]

On the other hand, the majority of whites saw the destruction of slavery as being tantamount to the destruction of civilization itself. They believed that emancipation had "battered down and broken in" the door guarding the entrance into white society, leaving it wide open for the intrusion of blacks. Many were also anxious lest their former slaves be elevated to a position of equality. In September 1865 Jonathan Worth, soon to be the governor of North Carolina, wrote in reference to the future of race relations, that "the South is never again" and he thought that it would be best for every white man to leave the state. To Worth, blacks were an inferior race, and there was "no more supreme nonsense" than the idea of making them the equals of white men.[8]

Some whites also feared that emancipation had transformed the friendly relations that allegedly existed between slaves and masters to one of hatred and antagonism. They naïvely believed that the freedmen considered all whites their enemies, and especially wanted to seek vengeance upon their former owners in order to take their property, or to "extract a drop of white blood for every stroke of the whip they received in slavery." There were widespread fears throughout the state of black insurrections.[9] However, the hatred that whites assigned to the freedmen were probably projections of their own innermost attitudes. Whites probably felt guilty over their enslavement and inhumane treatment of blacks, and expected some sort of retaliation as a natural consequence. Then too, whites knew that the mutual friendship between slaves and masters was for the most part figments of their own imagination and that it never really existed to any great extent. A former slaveowner was honest enough to admit that "the average white man regarded his negro merely as a beast of burden and not his friend."[10] Moreover, it seemed that it was the white population who generally hated blacks after their emancipation. Responding to this sentiment, one white confessed that his race hated "'em because they's free." This attitude was not an isolated instance. A correspondent of the *Nation* on an extensive tour through North Carolina immediately after the war reported that everywhere there was evidence that whites, rich and poor, unionists and secessionists, "unaffectedly and heartily do despise the negro."[11]

The contempt that whites had for blacks manifested itself in negative attitudes concerning their efficiency, character, and intelligence. With emancipation, the alleged faithful, devoted, loving, and trustworthy slave was transformed instantly into a damned-no-account, lazy, vain, insolent, vicious, and brutal freedman, who, whites felt, would surely retrogress further down the scale of humanity. Some took consolation in the belief that blacks would gradually become extinct.[12]

Whites also had negative ideas about how blacks perceived their freedom. They mistakenly believed that, for the freedmen, emancipation meant insolence to old massa and missus, and the right to do nothing except roam about the countryside and lead a life of gaiety "unalloyed with visions of the hoe and cornfield." A white farmer and his wife were of the opinion that all the "niggers" they knew would rather starve to death than to work for themselves or others. E. J. Thompson of Orange County thought that following the Civil War blacks were more trifling than ever, "they laughed and talked and stole," and spent what little money they had on old finery. He wondered about the future of the freedmen and opined that if "they are not sent off to Liberia a few more winters will freeze them up."[13]

This latter attitude reflected the desire of some whites to get as far away from blacks as possible. The freedmen constantly reminded whites of their loss of power and status, and they were also living reminders of the "Lost Cause." Many whites probably thought as did an old woman in Robeson

County, who remarked in October 1865 that the "niggers is jest gone to ruin," and she wished that Sherman had removed them all when he freed them. In some instances whites forcibly drove blacks from their midst. The former owners of one Sandy threatened him with 100 lashes if he did not leave his plantation. A farmer's wife at Reidsville stated that her husband would have nothing to do with his former "niggers." He had run off two families and was contemplating dispatching the rest even though they all wanted to stay.[14]

Strangely enough, there were some whites who were reluctant to surrender their slaves despite the latter's alleged shortcomings. This was because many whites refused to believe that slaves were legally free, whereas others thought blacks would be reenslaved and would probably never be free. They deliberately refrained from notifying blacks of their freedom or kept them in a condition that closely approximated that of slavery. Two months after the end of the Civil War, blacks in Granville County did not know they were free and were working as usual. The blacks who labored for Donald MacRae of Carbonton, as late as September 1865 remained pretty much in the status quo ante. He imagined that they felt a little disposition to show their freedom, but this did not seem to bother him, for he stated that he would not let them do as they pleased.[15] A reporter of the *Nation* encountered an old black ferryman in Rowan County in the fall of 1865 and asked him if he were free. "I dunno master," he replied. "They say all the colored peoples free, but I'm a goin' on the same as I allus has been." Ironically, although this old black knew he was free and he wanted to be free, he explained that he was leaving it up to the honor of his mistress to so inform him.[16]

This man was an anomaly. The masses of his race were not disposed to remain within the institution of slavery any longer than their situation would permit. As early as 1861 slave refugees, primarily from the eastern part of the state, were enjoying freedom under the protection of Union armies, and by 1864 there were approximately 17,419 refugees under the control of the federal government. Many had been established in freedmen's colonies in the vicinity of New Bern, Beaufort, Plymouth, Roanoke Island, and the Hatteras Banks. By the close of the war they had proved to themselves that they could prosper and thrive in freedom.[17] Indeed, by 1865 the superintendent of Negro affairs in North Carolina reported that the freedmen were not as helpless or dependent as poor whites. They were more fertile in expedients, more industrious, more religious, and more vigorous in body and

## Friends or Enemies?

mind. Other observations showed them to be genuinely grateful for their freedom and without malice toward whites. Only occasionally was a freedman encountered who wanted to "put upon the white man's limbs the fetters which have dropped from his own."[18]

By the end of the Civil War these refugees had also established a clear set of goals and aspirations for the future. They simply wanted the same rights, freedoms, and privileges as other citizens to defend themselves: to enter into contracts, to litigate and implead one another, and to select their own churches, schools, and political parties. More than anything else they desired education and the ownership of land. If the freedmen were given legal equality and if the debilitating effects of race prejudice were removed, the superintendent of Negro affairs was confident that in time they would find their place in society. However, he was not overly optimistic about the possibility that native whites would let this happen, for he also recommended that the federal government assume the role of "godfather" and throw the "strong arm of its protection" around the freedmen until they were acknowledged as free persons and citizens by the dominant race. This recommendation was not just that of a northern radical. J. W. Payne of New Bern correctly perceived the situation when he wrote in June 1865 that in order to protect and establish blacks in their new status, "it would be necessary for the federal government to present a strong and determined front penetrating almost to the very household hearth of the white people of the state."[19]

On 29 May 1865 President Andrew Johnson announced his North Carolina plan for Reconstruction. Among other things, it called for the assembling of a state convention for the purpose of revising the constitution of North Carolina to make it conform with the results of the Civil War. Johnson appointed William Woods Holden provisional governor and gave him responsibility for preparing his state for restoration to the Union. In his first proclamation to the people of North Carolina, Holden outlined the extent of freedom for blacks. They were free to be happy and thrifty, to enjoy property, and to maintain a decent family life. They were told that above all they had to work and honor labor contracts. Otherwise they would become vicious, worthless, and friendless, and in the end perish as a race. As far as political rights were concerned, Holden informed the freedmen that they could neither expect to understand nor to enjoy the privileges of self-government.[20]

Thus the freedmen began their new lives by being officially informed

## Friends or Enemies?

that they were inferior creatures, and that they would not be allowed any political privileges to help them improve their status. They understood that they were poor and lacked the necessary resources for advancement, and they felt deeply the hatred of whites. In a petition to President Andrew Johnson in the spring of 1865, a group of North Carolina freedmen described themselves as being "poor and greatly despised by their fellow men."[21] The freedmen were also victims of an all-pervasive system of violence instigated by whites. This entailed overt physical assaults that seem to have intensified after emancipation. For example, the catalog of complaints filed at the Salisbury office of the Freedmen's Bureau by September 1865 shows the extreme measures taken by whites to impose their will upon blacks. For leaving a plantation, John's wife was whipped and Martha was tied with a rope around her neck and dragged back by a mule. For other distasteful acts, Dick received twenty-two lashes, Norris was struck in the head with a brick, Robert's sister was hit in the head with a fence rail, and Elias had his gun taken away and was told that "no nigger has a right to carry a gun." The assistant superintendent of freedmen in Salisbury reported that he received an average of twenty-one complaints a day from blacks during the month of August 1865. An agent of the Freedmen's Bureau in Greensboro noted that the first thing that came into the minds of many whites if a black offended them in any way "was to take a gun and put a bullet into him or a charge of shot." It was this agent's opinion that the withdrawal of federal troops would be the signal for a reign of violence and oppression against blacks.[22]

In addition to being victims of overt physical violence, blacks also suffered from the effects of a system of quiet personal and institutional violence that denied them human rights and dignity. Hunter recalled that following the Civil War the freedmen were objects of persecution, oppression, and tyranny, and that the very people who had acquired their wealth, education, and social status from the unrequited labor of the slave became his bitterest enemies and "employed every resource of their fertile ingenuity to obstruct his every approach to a higher and purer manhood."[23]

By the summer of 1865 blacks began to take collective action to protect themselves and to secure their rights. Some formed themselves into separate communities, and established local chapters of the Union League primarily in the eastern part of the state. In August the black citizens of New Bern held a mass meeting for the purpose of "taking such measures as will advance the welfare of the colored people of the state and to make known to each other and the world their desires." The rhetoric at this meeting was a clear indication that blacks were dissatisfied with their treatment and the general state of race relations.[24]

Resolutions denounced the atrocities of whippings, thumbscrewings, and cold-blooded murder that had been inflicted upon blacks in almost every part of the state. These acts were seen as evidence of the immense race prejudice and hatred of former slaveowners against the freedmen. The meeting also condemned the practice of keeping blacks at work until crops were laid by; then driving them away and refusing to provide them with food and shelter any longer. Objections were offered to the continued enforcement of the "old slave laws," particularly those that denied blacks the privileges of education, control over their families, and the right to give testimony in courts. As for their so-called white friends, blacks agreed that there were many who were perfectly willing to give them Bibles and spellers and at the same time keep them in a degraded condition by denying them the right to vote and other legal privileges. Abraham H. Galloway, the leader of the meeting, acknowledged that the rebels did not want his race to vote, and some had threatened to "quit the country and go to Europe," rather than to see this happen. Galloway thought it would not be such a bad idea if some whites did leave, and he announced that the black man was going to agitate until he got the right to vote, and the only way to silence him was by "throwing the ballot box down his throat."[25]

Before adjourning, the New Bern meeting issued a call for a state convention of blacks to be held in Raleigh in September. Blacks in the central and western parts of the state considered the call premature, impolitic, and unwise, especially because their convention would be held in the same city and at the same time as the state Constitutional Convention, which had been called by the governor in accordance with President Johnson's plan of Reconstruction. Holden instructed the convention to repeal North Carolina's ordinance of secession, legally abolish slavery, and repudiate the state's war debt. Nothing was mentioned concerning political and civil rights for the freedmen. This may have prompted militant blacks from eastern North Carolina, who thought that the constitution and statute books of the state contained "enough evils to be cured and there were others to be prevented from getting there," to overrule those of their race who opposed the date for the black convention.[26]

Although in publicizing their convention the blacks announced their desire for peace, freedom, racial harmony, and goodwill toward all humankind, some whites responded to the news with hostility and violence, suspecting that such a gathering was only a prelude to insurrection. When the blacks of Chapel Hill met to select delegates to the convention, students from the university broke into the meetinghouse and threatened to burn the structure down.[27]

On 29 September 1865 the first Freedmen's Convention in the South met at the Loyal African Methodist Church in Raleigh with approximately 150 delegates from forty counties and a host of black spectators of both sexes in attendance. The delegations represented a cross section of the population, including carpetbaggers, army veterans, ministers, waiters, barbers, mechanics, and plantation hands. Some were well educated whereas others were illiterate. However, most were described as intelligent and articulate men, who knew the purposes for which they had assembled. One delegate told a reporter that although he and many others of his race were often branded by whites as being ignorant, they knew enough to understand the meaning of justice, and "when a white man and a nigger" got on the scale, "don't I know the nigger is mighty light."[28]

Justice was exactly what blacks wanted. During the early stages of the convention, a militant faction from the eastern part of the state demanded the right to vote, to testify and act as counselors in court, and to serve on juries. But by the end of the first day, a conservative element had gained control by convincing the majority of blacks that they had to live in North Carolina, and that their best friends would be the intelligent white people of the state, not the people of the North. Thereafter, the tone of the convention became accommodationist and conciliatory. On the second day, ex-Governor Thomas Bragg, Governor Holden, Jonathan Worth, and other prominent whites were invited to join the convention and assist in its deliberations. None accepted the invitation and some presumably agreed with Jonathan Worth who, a few weeks earlier, had written that the majority of whites in the state were determined not to tolerate or get along with blacks as long as they insisted on equality.[29]

Denied an opportunity for face-to-face communication with the native white leadership, the delegates outlined their desires in a memorial address to the Constitutional Convention and the people of North Carolina. They seemed almost apologetic for having accepted their freedom, and stressed the point that although a few blacks in North Carolina had actively supported the Union during the Civil War, the majority had been passive, loyal, and obedient to their masters; some had even aided the Confederacy by serving in military camps, erecting fortifications, or raising supplies. Blacks professed their love for the people and the state and they saw no reason why their "God bestowed freedom" should sever the friendly ties that had for so long united the two races. They announced their intention to remain in North Carolina unless forcibly expelled by whites, and thanked those former slaveowners who had acknowledged emancipation and were inclined to help their former slaves.[30]

The freedmen of North Carolina understood that federal troops and agents would not remain indefinitely in the state to protect them against race prejudice and injustice. Indeed, they claimed no desire to look abroad for protection and sympathy in the belief that these would be granted to them by native whites. The blacks' requests in their memorial address were modest, and they asked for the absolute minimum consistent with decency and justice: friendly relations with whites, employment opportunities with just compensation, education, and the removal of all disabilities that discriminated against them on the basis of race or color.[31]

Hunter claimed that he was present at the convention, and insisted throughout his lifetime that it was one of the most notable gatherings ever assembled in North Carolina. He believed the delegates had displayed remarkable statesmanship, and their actions were characterized by calmness, dignity, and an absence of bitterness. To Hunter, the memorial address represented the "heart throb" of the blacks of North Carolina, and he was profoundly impressed by the portion that stated, "Born upon the same soil and brought up in an intimacy of relationship unknown to any other state of society, we [blacks] have formed attachments to the white race that must be as enduring as life. . . ." This statement later became the cornerstone of Hunter's philosophy of race relations.[32]

There were nevertheless indications that the delegates to the black convention suspected the intentions of their white friends. Before adjourning, they established a State Equal Rights League for the purpose of securing full citizenship for blacks and the repeal of all discriminatory legislation. The convention also formally petitioned Major General Thomas Ruger for military protection for those delegates returning to localities where bitter feeling existed against their meeting. Then too, while the convention was in progress, the initial issue of the *Journal of Freedom* appeared. This was the first black newspaper in the state, and it was dedicated to securing equal rights for all men and the building of a regenerated South on a firm and lasting basis of true Republicanism. The *Journal's* editor warned the delegates not to expect too much from whites. There were a great many who were superficial in their acceptance of the results of the war, and "it is a pity that the authorities cannot pierce through their skins and discover the rottenness beneath. . . ."[33]

This warning was unnecessary because in a very short time the white leadership of North Carolina let blacks know how they felt about them. Some of the delegates to the black convention, present as spectators at the Constitutional Convention, heard the menacing remarks on the subject of future race relations. David F. Caldwell of Guilford County wanted to see the blacks of North Carolina sifted and scattered all over the country. The delegate from Richmond County, Alfred Dockery, after professing his love and friendship for blacks and reminiscing about the slave mammies of his family, maintained that he had little hope for the elevation of the freedmen, because they were poor, demoralized, and degraded. He was of the opinion that whites had two courses of action in dealing with blacks. They could either enact a code that would regulate their conduct to prevent them from becoming a disgrace and danger to the community, or they could pursue the policy that Andrew Jackson used against the Indians. He preferred the latter course and recommended that blacks be isolated on government lands in the Southwest.[34]

Blacks were also present when their memorial was read, and they listened while John Pool, the chairman of the committee to which it had been referred, branded them as being ignorant of the operations of civil government, improvident of the future, careless of the restraints of public opinion, and lacking any real appreciation of their duties and obligations to society. Pool also proclaimed that whites had an inherent and universal prejudice against blacks that would probably exist forever and which should be respected by law. Hence he recommended that legislation on behalf of the freedmen avoid all theoretical schemes of political and social equality. Although Pool's report was unanimously adopted, Edwin G. Reade, the president of the Constitutional Convention, insisted that the native whites of North Carolina were the best friends of blacks and they would advise, protect, educate, and elevate them. However, with the exception of legitimizing slave marriages and requesting that the president of the United States remove all black troops from North Carolina, the convention referred all other matters relating to blacks to the next legislature for resolution.[35]

Of course, the actions of the convention were thoroughly consistent with the climate of public opinion in North Carolina, because no candidate dared go before the people as an advocate of equal rights for blacks. The former Confederate general, Rufus M. Barringer, noted that in the fall of 1865 the "public mind was lashed into a tempest of rage and fury against any man who advocated justice to the freedmen." A less articulate white told a reporter of the *Nation* that, in the selection of delegates to the convention, the people wanted men "that'll keep the niggers in their place. If we let the nigger git equal with us the next thing we know he'll be ahead of us." Sidney Andrews reported that the best men in the Constitutional Convention unblushingly repeated the creed, "I believe in the white man only. I believe that this country was made for white men only. I believe that this is a white man's government, and no negro should have any part in it."[36]

When the first postwar legislature convened in January 1866, the conservatives treated their black friends to some legislation subsequently known as the North Carolina Black Code. The code legally set blacks off from the rest of society, subjected them to disabilities that severely restricted their rights as citizens, and left them in the status approximating that of antebellum free blacks. Throughout its sessions of 1866 the legislature continued in its determination to keep the freedmen as separate and subordinate members of society. Conservatives denounced the Freedmen's Bureau and they were adamant in their opposition to the civil rights bill and the newly proposed Fourteenth Amendment. Moreover, at an extralegal constitutional convention, which assembled in Raleigh in 1866, whites wrote clauses into the constitution of North Carolina that restricted officeholding and suffrage rights exclusively to members of their race. However, this revised constitution was rejected by a slim margin when it was submitted for ratification. Objections were not raised to the provisions of the constitution, but rather, to the legality of the body that had drafted them.[37]

It was also clear by 1866 that whites had reneged on their promise to help educate the freedmen. There were no provisions in the constitution for the education of blacks, and in fact whites had destroyed the whole system of public education out of fear that the freedmen would gain admittance to schools. Indeed, the great majority of whites believed that the education of blacks would be useless, if not harmful. There was anxiety that schools would be racially integrated and this was sure to lead to social equality, immorality, and miscegenation. Furthermore, whites deliberately sought to disrupt or destroy the educational opportunities provided blacks by private or religious sources. Hunter believed that this was one of the great manifestations of cruelty toward his race. He was grateful for the educational opportunities offered his race by private citizens of the North and the South, and he was proud of the fact that Gertrude Trapiers of the Haywood family was a part of this process. He thought that she was perhaps the first southern white woman to undertake educational work among the freedmen. During 1865–66 she organized a school for freedmen in an old building on Salisbury Street in Raleigh, and Hunter claimed that her Sunday school for blacks eventually resulted in the founding of Saint Augustine Episcopal Church.[38]

Hunter equally praised the work of the brave northern educators who came to the South, "when ignorance reigned supreme and when blacks though nominally free were still the slaves of the degradation which ages of chattel slavery had fastened upon them." He recalled that the teachers and their families were made the victims of unchristian hatred on the part of southern people, who resorted to abuse, social ostracism, and even the most brutal violence in an attempt to halt the education of his race. In the year of his death, he wrote that blacks should be eternally grateful to those northerners who came to them "during the dense darkness of our intellectual night bearing the torch of Christian education. O what would we have done, what could we have done, without them."[39]

In October 1866 blacks held a second state convention in an attempt to deal with their white friends. For several days delegates from sixty counties met in the African Methodist Episcopal Church in Raleigh under the auspices of the State Equal Rights League. The meeting was held ostensibly for the purpose of discussing education, but it soon became clear that blacks had other objects in mind. Once again the native white leadership was invited, but, with the exception of Governor Worth and W. W. Holden, all the others declined. Some, however, did offer words of advice in letters to the convention. Their correspondence showed that whites were still unable to conceive of blacks as being anything other than a servile people, for they advised blacks to train themselves in ways that would promote good work habits and not to concentrate on higher forms of education. For example, former Governor William A. Graham suggested that if blacks learned how to work on a farm or in a trade, to obey and fulfill the terms of contracts, and to go to church, they could inexpensively acquire knowledge that was infinitely more important than any academic training. Moreover, blacks were told that they would in all likelihood have to bear the costs of their own education. The delegates dispatched their educational business with the founding of the Freedmen's Educational Association of North Carolina, charged with establishing nonsectarian schools thoughout the state that would be open to all people regardless of color or poverty.[40]

The convention then turned its attention to race relations and politics. Resolutions were adopted denouncing the outrages of murder, shootings, and robbery committed against blacks, specifically in Craven, Duplin, Halifax, Hyde, Jones, and Wayne counties. Whites were called upon to cease disrupting the family life of blacks by ruthlessly taking and binding out their children without the consent of parents. Blacks were urged to form themselves into local chapters of the Equal Rights League and collect and transmit to state headquarters all information concerning offenses against their race. The state office would in turn publicize this information so that the world could know the disadvantages under which blacks labored in North Carolina. Finally, the resolutions praised Congress for having passed the Freedmen's Bureau bill, the Civil Rights Act, and the Thirteenth Amendment, and urged it to continue to work until the rights of all Americans were protected. A vote of thanks was also extended to Charles Sumner, Thaddeus Stevens, Benjamin Wade, Lyman Trumbull, Horace Greeley, Frederick Douglass, and Henry Highland Garnet for their services and encouragement to blacks.[41]

Before adjournment, the convention published an address to the citizens of North Carolina. In a spirit of meekness, they asked whites:

> Can we look to you for protection or not, to shield us from the murderous hand? Oh! humanity, where is thy blush? Our defenseless wives and children, fathers, sons and brothers are beaten with clubs, robbed, shot and killed in various localities, and the authorities regard it not. We beg you as white men in authority to shield our defenseless heads, and guard our little homes, we appeal to your religion and humanity. We claim by merit the right of suffrage, and seek it at your hands. We believe the day has come when black men have rights white men are bound to respect. . . . Oh! North Carolina, the land of our birth, with all thy faults we love thee still, will you, Oh! Will you treat us as human beings.[42]

This address met with the same fate as that of 1865. According to Hunter, the prevailing sentiment among the masses of whites was "wrought up to the point of madness," and the rights that blacks had so humbly prayed for were made party issues. The leading whites declined the hand of friendship proffered by blacks and held that "This is a white man's country and that Negroes have no rights in it save such as in charity the white man may grant."[43] James H. Harris, who had presided over both of the black conventions, agreed. In 1865 and 1866 Harris was a conservative black, and he was primarily responsible for convincing his race that it should adopt a similar course. He believed at the time that the masses of blacks would have gladly returned the old native white leadership to power with full authority to conduct the affairs of state. But the conservatives refused to acknowledge and recognize blacks as full citizens, and instead of cooperating with them they drove a wedge between the races by raising the cries of "Negro domination" and "social equality."[44]

These two terms, which defy any accurate definition, would in the future prove to be effective and potent weapons against any attempt made by blacks to gain civil or political rights. If they sought to vote, hold office, or participate in the political process in any way, the cry of "Negro domination" reverberated throughout the state. "Social equality" was a highly emotional phrase that could evoke a savage response whenever raised. Whites interpreted every effort by blacks to secure equal opportunities as a movement for social equality. Although blacks could not define the term, they spent a considerable amount of time and energy in trying to convince whites that whatever it was, they did not want it either.

By late 1866 the freedmen of North Carolina were casting about for a new set of friends, and they could do so in good faith because they had offered the conservative white leadership of the state the first chance to prove their friendship. The new friends they found were men who promised them protection in the exercise of their freedom and rights of citizenship. Some were native whites who were Unionist during the Civil War, but most were northerners who professed allegiance to the Republican party. At the time it seemed perfectly natural to Hunter for blacks to ally themselves with the party that was responsible for their freedom. It was also logical for blacks to want to vote for members of that party, and elevate them to positions of leadership in the state. Hunter asked, "Is it conceivable that the Negro could have made any other than the choice he did make?"[45] Hunter also found himself a new group of personal friends. While serving as a messenger in the headquarters of Major General Nelson A. Miles, the commander of the Union garrison in Raleigh and assistant commissioner of the Freedmen's Bureau, he formed acquaintances with a number of Union officers who advised and assisted him. He also received most of his formal education under the influence of northerners at the Johnson Normal School

## Friends or Enemies?

in Raleigh where he graduated as valedictorian of his class. This school was rated as one of the best for blacks in the South, and it later became Kittrell College. Hunter also attended Shaw University for one year.[46]

William Woods Holden was also an early idol of Hunter's, for he was one of the few native whites who eventually came to the conclusion that Reconstruction could not be effective unless blacks were given some political and civil rights. Without these, Holden thought the freedmen would be left in the status of peons or serfs, and would never have received any justice. Holden's attitudes were no doubt prompted by political opportunism, which he justified by his desire to see his state escape the more extreme measures of a prolonged military occupation as proposed by Thaddeus Stevens, and the confiscation of property as advocated by Andrew Johnson.[47]

But to many blacks during Reconstruction, Holden was the hero of the moment despite his checkered career as politician and slaveholder. In January 1866 he told a group of blacks that he was truly sorry about his past and "had long ago reformed." At the Freedmen's Convention in the same year he insisted that he was and had always been a friend to blacks, and he desired to see the good feeling that had always existed between the races cultivated and strengthened. Moreover, Holden believed that the Union had to be restored on principles of truth and justice, and he assured the freedmen that the federal or state government would see to it that they obtained civil rights. Blacks believed Holden, and in the summer of 1867 the North Carolina Equal Rights League petitioned Congress asking for the removal of the political disabilities imposed upon him under the provision of the Reconstruction Acts. The petition praised Holden's record on behalf of the Union, humanity, liberty, and justice. It noted the fact that "his name and sufferings have become dear to us all. . . . There are so few in whom we can place confidence or who have been tried in the furnace and withstood the test." Hunter wrote Holden in 1876 that "no man has ever gained so full the heart of our people in this State as yourself."[48]

Hunter also became friends with two of the most prominent black politicians in Raleigh during Reconstruction, George W. Brodie and James H. Harris. Both were members of the Union League and founders of the Republican party in North Carolina, and their attitudes helped shape Hunter's early political philosophy. Brodie was described by the *Raleigh Daily Progress* as a "yankee negro of male persuasion" who thought he was the Joshua of his race. He was a carpetbagger preacher who had come to

Raleigh in August 1865 to assume the leadership of the African Methodist Episcopal Church. He later became a presiding elder of his church, as well as manager of the Raleigh branch of the Freedmen's Savings and Trust Company. Harris was basically a professional politician who at times taught school in Raleigh. It was alleged that he was a confidant and trusted adviser to Horace Greeley, Charles Sumner, Salmon P. Chase, Henry Wilson, Frederick Douglass, Ulysses S. Grant, and William T. Sherman, and that he deserved as much credit as anyone for founding the Republican party in North Carolina. Harris enjoyed a wide reputation even among some white conservatives as an intelligent, liberal, and eloquent man. Other whites viewed him as a dangerous man who thought the welfare of his race rested in his hands.[49]

The founding of the Republican party in North Carolina coincided with the demise of presidential Reconstruction. From its inception Congress and the president had constantly vied with each other for control of the Reconstruction process. Radical Republicans in Congress felt that Johnson's plan did not sufficiently punish unrepentant rebels, nor did it provide for the civil and political equality of freedmen. As a result of the congressional elections of 1866 radicals gained a majority in Congress, and they subsequently assumed total responsibility for Reconstruction. The effects of presidential Reconstruction were nullified in all states except Tennessee and the remainder of the former Confederacy was placed under military rule.

By March 1867 many blacks throughout North Carolina believed that they had to take an active interest in looking out for their own welfare. Spirited by the passage of the Fourteenth Amendment by Congress, and armed with political privileges under the Reconstruction Acts, they also thought they had a role to play in the reconstruction of their state. "You have to effect a great moral and political reform," were the instructions that James H. Harris received from James M. Edmunds, the Grand President of the Union League of America. Harris was advised to begin work at once by gathering his race into local councils of the league, and to initiate the first steps of their political education. Blacks flocked to the Republican party, which was organized in North Carolina on 27 March 1867. Its first convention was made up of approximately equal numbers of people of both races from across the state, and twenty-four whites and seventeen blacks constituted the party's first Executive Committee. The platform of the party was simply the endorsement of civil rights and suffrage without regard to color and an early ratification of the Fourteenth Amendment, measures that forced Governor Worth to conclude that the meeting was probably "the most radical which has assembled in the United States."[50]

The introduction of the Republican party raised fears of Negro domination and social equality, and many whites intensified their resistance to Reconstruction. Convinced that the party was out to destroy the social order of the state, many whites agreed they would rather live under a military despotism than accept Republican rule. Mary Ellen Hedrick of Chapel Hill was of the opinion that "all do object to any and everything that tends to bring the races into closer relationships." The people would never accept legislation "forbidding hotel keepers from making any distinction on account of color and requiring that all public schools shall receive black and white children alike and they shall sit side by side."[51]

Free schools, free labor, and free speech were the issues used by blacks in their vigorous campaign to elect Republicans to the convention called by General Edward R. S. Canby to draft a new constitution as required by the First Reconstruction Act. Passed by Congress on 2 March 1867, this act outlined the basic principles and procedures for radical Reconstruction. The black leaders of the campaign in Raleigh were politically astute men, all of whom were friends or later associates of Hunter. In addition to Harris and Brodie, there was Handy Lockhart, "a sensible and aristocratic man," and James H. Jones, "a clever fellow." It is interesting to note that Jones, a founder of the Republican party, had been the personal body servant of Jefferson Davis and had accompanied him throughout the Civil War. Republicans succeeded in capturing a majority of the delegates to the convention, and this resulted in a further deterioration of race relations. General Nelson A. Miles reported that the results of the election had caused a large portion of the white population to regard blacks with feelings of intense hatred. Evidence of their vengeance could be seen in the daily reports coming from all parts of the state.[52]

Blacks had a clear understanding of the work ahead of them at the Constitutional Convention, which met in Raleigh from 14 January to 17 March 1868. They had been advised by Senator Henry Wilson of Massachusetts that they held in their hands the fate of their race during a critical period. He hoped that the poor and hated black men united with loyal whites would have the honor of returning their state to the Union with the equal rights of all men restored. "Do not my dear sir fear Congress," wrote Wilson to James H. Harris. "Reconstruct your state, secure equal rights for all men, provide schools, equalize taxation, encourage industry, and you will shame us of the loyal North into doing justice."[53]

Conservatives, though a minority at the convention, made a concerted effort to write race distinctions and white supremacy into the constitution and attempted to draw the color line on every issue that held the slightest possibility of social equality. They offered proposals specifying that no one of black ancestry would ever be able to hold any state executive office, that blacks and whites would not serve together in militia units, that no white man would ever be required to serve under or take orders from a black officer in the militia, and that interracial marriages would be prohibited. None of these proposals was accepted, and the delegates proceeded to produce the most liberal constitution in the history of North Carolina. The convention did, however, adopt resolutions offered by a black delegate from Halifax County condemning marriage and sexual intercourse between races and reaffirming the idea that segregated schools were in the best interests of both races.[54]

The election of April 1868, called for the purposes of ratifying the new constitution and electing a new set of officials, was the first postwar white-supremacy campaign. Conservatives subordinated all other issues to that of whether whites or blacks should rule in North Carolina. Of lesser importance but equally emotional in their appeal to race prejudice were the issues of interracial marriages and schools. Racist rhetoric was not enough to prevent the adoption of the constitution and an overwhelming Republican victory. When the Republican-controlled legislature met, it ratified the Fourteenth Amendment, and North Carolina was restored to the Union on 20 July 1868. A month before he surrendered his office to William Woods Holden, the conservative Governor Jonathan Worth accurately predicted that the people would not readily submit to "numerous and important innovations of their ancient laws and customs." To him, "the present scheme of things will generate hatreds and damage to all people."[55]

Hunter's attitudes regarding Reconstruction changed radically over time. A half century after the advent of congressional Reconstruction, he stated with confidence that the black voters of North Carolina "were not enamoured of the graceless horde of vampires who got possession of the State" and despoiled it. However, during Reconstruction, Hunter was a supporter of these "vampires" and enjoyed whatever benefits he could obtain at their hands. While still in his teens, he secured an appointment as assistant cashier in the Raleigh branch of the Freedmen's Savings and Trust

Company. Chartered by Congress in 1865 as a private thrift institution for blacks, the company by 1872 had thirty-four branches in various parts of the United States. George W. Brodie was manager and chief cashier of the Raleigh branch. Hunter's friend Colonel Jacob F. Chur, a former assistant commissioner of the Freedmen's Bureau in North Carolina, advised him that his job in the bank provided an opportunity for self-development. What he learned in banking, bookkeeping, and general information would be of immense importance to him in later life. "My knowledge of you," Chur added, "convinces me that you will not lose your opportunities for advancement." Hunter became familiar with the operations of the bank and frequently managed the entire facility for weeks at a time while Brodie was away on political or religious business.[56]

Hunter believed that the Freedmen's bank exerted a positive influence on the black community of Raleigh. In addition to the normal functions of banking, it provided blacks with advice and counseling and taught them the value of thrift. However, the Raleigh branch was not without its enemies, who consistently circulated rumors designed to impede its progress. But they were not entirely successful, and in 1872 Hunter reported that the bank was "daily growing in popular favor and confidence and soon its deposits will be counted by tens of thousands." He thought that much of this success could be attributed to the powerful influence of many of the "staunchest conservative white citizens," who showed more concern and interest in increasing the number of black depositors than did the Republicans.[57]

However, in Raleigh's highly politicized environment, Hunter, firmly in the Republican camp, knew that many of the staunch conservatives were actively seeking to overthrow Reconstruction, often through violent means. Ever since the fall elections of 1868 a reign of terror instigated by the Ku Klux Klan and other secret societies prevailed in many parts of North Carolina. Some whites during and after Reconstruction viewed the Klan as a salutary agency and justified its outrageous activities as necessary and appropriate to the occasion. But the atrocious and almost savage behavior of secret societies in North Carolina was commensurate with some of the worst crimes in history. For example, the Klan's offenses ran the gamut from mere intimidation and banishment, to the burning of churches, schools, mills, and homes, to murder. Some of its victims were whipped, tortured, mutilated, shot, hanged, drowned, scourged, and in some instances the dead bodies of its prey were defiled. Both Governor Holden and Richard C. Badger, whom he appointed to investigate these outrages

## Friends or Enemies?

against blacks, concluded that blacks were treated with great barbarity, and that the Klan, the White Brotherhood, and the Stonewall Guard subjected many men and women to indignities that were disgraceful to civilization and humanity.[58]

Although some of the activities of the Klan were politically motivated, it is evident that the organization used violence as a means of social control. However, Hunter placed more emphasis on the idea that the Klan was a response to the political situation. On 21 October 1869 he observed that the Klansmen were "at their work of murder" in Jones, Lenoir, Chatham, and Orange counties, and that blacks in those areas were afraid to exercise the right of citizenship or to vote the dictates of their consciences. The situation was particularly bad in Orange County where "murder stalks almost un-rebuked by Democratic officials whose business it is to protect peaceful and law-abiding citizens." Many loyal black and white Republicans had been forced to leave the county and seek refuge in Raleigh or some other princi-pal town. Hunter was glad to report to his friend Colonel Chur that Gover-nor Holden had just issued a proclamation calling on all good citizens to uphold law and order and advising them that if the outrages of the Klan continued he would institute martial law.[59]

However, the activities of the Klan did not stop with the governor's proclamation, the Kirk-Holden war, or the Force Act of 1870. Indeed, the terrorism of the Klan was a major factor in the Democratic victory of 1870, which gave conservatives control of the legislature and a majority in the state's congressional delegation. Although the governorship was still in the hands of Republicans, for all practical purposes North Carolina was re-deemed within two years after its readmittance to the Union. Almost a decade later, the editor of the *North State* noted that beginning in 1870 the whole system of state government was influenced by the Klan: "The legisla-tion of North Carolina, so far as it affects the colored people and their interests, bears the unmistakable impress of the Ku Klux, and breathes the intolerant spirit of that bloody order."[60] There was also "a Ku Klux legisla-ture to make the laws, a Ku Klux solicitor to prosecute, a Ku Klux jury to try the case and a Ku Klux judge to pass sentence; men who have all taken a solemn oath to exert their power to keep down the colored people. When we add to this the notorious fact that these men and their friends believe that 'niggers' have no right to vote . . . we can see that the system is a far more formidable engine of oppression than any open violence, because *its work is done under the forms of law.*"[61]

During the 1870s Hunter's attitudes toward Reconstruction and the Republican party in North Carolina began to change. He understood that the Klan played a major role in the Democratic success of 1870, and he had nothing other than "words of severest condemnation for the inhuman wretches who committed hellish crimes against inoffensive blacks and white Republicans." But he was also convinced that corruption within the Republican party contributed to its defeat. To him, the Democratic victory was simply a "spontaneous uprising of an outraged and plundered people" who wanted to punish those who had ruined and discredited the state.[62] But he tended to sympathize with those native white Republicans who, he thought, were victims of social ostracism, proscription, and slander solely because they cooperated with blacks. Yet they too were condemned for their use and abuse of black voters and for their attempts to hold his race responsible for the "condition of affairs which has made the name of the Republican Party odious among the people of the State." Hunter assigned to white Republicans the total responsibility for the fraud and corruption in government in North Carolina during Reconstruction, and he also exonerated his race from any complicity in these crimes, because "not one dollar of this stealage was ever traced to the pockets of any Negro."[63]

Hunter erred in his contention that the Democratic victory in 1870 was a "spontaneous uprising." The idea of regaining control of the state at the earliest possible moment and undoing the work of Reconstruction was ever present in the minds of conservative whites. Furthermore, it was suggested that North Carolina was in the vanguard of a conspiracy to overthrow Reconstruction. John Pool, a former United States senator from North Carolina, alleged that the best minds of the South in concert had agreed to nullify Reconstruction by altering provisions in the constitutions that had been forced upon states as the price of readmission to the Union. North Carolina was selected as the pilot state for this general movement because its citizens were least likely to be suspected of extremism in opposition to federal authority and, therefore, "best suited to proceed by solidly effective, rather than impulsive and ostentatious steps." It was also believed that once North Carolina had taken the initiative, other southern states would follow with less fear of provoking a hostile response from northerners or the federal government.[64]

# 2

# Reformer and Accommodationist

Hunter matured during the 1870s, and during this time he developed many of the interests, attitudes, and personality traits that characterized his later life. He also achieved some notoriety as a journalist, reformer, and public-spirited citizen, and he set out to find a way to bring the races closer together. His first attempt took place in the summer of 1869 when he noted that no particular arrangements had been made to celebrate American Independence Day. He suggested to the editor of the *North Carolina Standard* that the citizens come together to plan a suitable celebration for the nation's birthday. The *Standard* responded by asking all, "without reference to politics," to meet and immediately arrange for this event. On 4 July 1869 blacks and whites held a celebration in Raleigh, and according to Hunter, "we had a very nice time." He wrote to his friend Colonel Jacob F. Chur that Joseph W. Holden delivered a very nice speech, which was possibly the best he had ever heard. Hunter neglected to tell his friend that the audience was segregated with seats on the right reserved for whites and the galleries on the left for blacks.[1]

Hunter's interest in public demonstrations and displays continued throughout his lifetime. He viewed these events as a means of bringing the races closer together on both a physical and a mental plane. He believed that the more blacks and whites saw and talked to each other, the greater the chance for the reduction of the prejudices that kept them apart and suspicious of each other. However, Hunter and other blacks had to find some occasion to celebrate other than the Fourth of July. By 1871 they had been publicly informed that blacks had no business commemorating the national Independence Day because it was a holiday for whites. Conservative whites

### Reformer and Accommodationist

maintained that blacks had no history until their emancipation, and that "any celebration or observance of any of the important events or eventful days of the past is gratuitous absurdity and disgusting mockery."[2]

Blacks and some of their white friends had already arrived at the conclusion that 1 January 1863 was of greater significance to their race than 4 July 1776. At their Emancipation Day celebration in Raleigh in 1870, Horace L. Pike, the editor of the *North Carolina Standard* and the principal speaker for the event, told blacks that the day of their emancipation would always rank among the great landmarks in the history of the world because it was the death blow to human slavery. He insisted that it should be "the dearest day of all the year to every colored man." Governor Holden, who was also present for the affair, agreed; and he hoped that "through all generations blacks would continue to celebrate the day of their Emancipation."[3]

For almost a half century Emancipation Day was the major secular holiday for blacks in North Carolina, and it was widely commemorated throughout the state. The most elaborate celebration was generally held in Raleigh, and it was attended by thousands of blacks including delegations from other areas. Parades, prayers, poetic orations, speeches, and singing were standard features of Emancipation Day celebrations. These occasions gave blacks an opportunity to commune together, to recount their past struggles during slavery, and to recite their progress since emancipation. Of major importance were the Emancipation Day resolutions, which articulated the hopes and aspirations of blacks and let whites know what to expect from them during the ensuing year.

Resolutions were voted upon by the audience before adoption and they tended to reflect a popular consensus and the prevailing climate of public opinion. Emancipation Day ceremonies were also a form of group therapy for blacks. In speeches and resolutions, the black community voiced its grievances against racial injustices and at times the rhetoric was quite militant. Indeed, it seems as if whites almost expected and were willing to tolerate some note of dissatisfaction from blacks on Emancipation Day. Selected whites were generally invited to attend and participate in the celebrations, and the ones who received invitations were those who momentarily enjoyed the highest esteem of the black community, or who had the power and influence to grant it particular favors.

For most of his life Hunter was actively involved in the Emancipation Day celebrations, and he was frequently called upon to speak or draft the resolutions. As secretary of the Committee of Arrangements for the festivi-

## Reformer and Accommodationist

ties in Raleigh in 1872, he extended invitations to two divergent personalities: Senator Charles Sumner of Massachusetts and Bartholomew F. Moore, one of the drafters of the North Carolina Black Code. Neither accepted his invitation, but each responded to it in ways that were indicative of his racial attitudes. Moore informed the Committee of Arrangements that the personal freedom of blacks was worthless until they had learned how to conduct themselves in an honorable, virtuous, and intelligent way. On the other hand, Sumner's advice was for blacks always to insist upon equal rights. "While others urge amnesty first," he wrote, "I begin with justice to the colored race. When this is assured, it will be easy to grant the other." Sumner advised blacks of a bill pending in the Senate that would secure equality for their race, and he asked for their aid in obtaining its passage.[4]

However, blacks in North Carolina could not give Sumner much help, for they were having enough problems of their own trying to hold on to what few rights they already had. They knew that their freedom was not yet assured, nor would it be if the state fell totally into the hands of the "old rebel leaders who would not be reconstructed." Then too, the impeachment of Governor Holden dealt a shattering blow to the morale of the black community. At their Emancipation Day celebration in 1872, blacks announced their continued confidence in Holden and they praised him as the "protector of the defenseless of both races."[5]

In the elections of 1872 Hunter joined with the majority of blacks in an attempt to prevent a total Democratic victory. At their convention in Greensboro the Democrats, in a move to attract black voters, endorsed the political and civil equality of both races. It was later predicted that with the aid of the more intelligent colored voters, the Democrats would achieve the largest possible majority against "Caldwell and corruption." Not many blacks were taken in by this strategy, and they believed that if the party were really sincere in its commitment to equal rights, it would have endorsed this measure in 1868.[6]

Hunter's estimate of the political situation in 1872 placed him philosophically in the camp of the liberal Republicans. He contended that setbacks in previous years had had a salutary effect on the Republican party. It was beginning to realize that to win elections, it would be to its own advantage to "unearth and denounce every specie of fraud whether in the pales of their own organization or any other." The party was greatly in need of men of unimpeachable integrity who could assume its leadership and purge it of every taint of corruption. Hunter thought that if Republicans would rally behind a "great reform movement prosecuted in every department of the state and federal government," it could be assured of victory. As far as state politics were concerned, Hunter thought that North Carolina was more solidly Republican than any other southern state and that the party was essentially healthy and "never in a better position to meet the enemy in open combat."[7] Locally, Hunter saw positive forces at work within the Republican party of Wake County, and he applauded the harmony and enthusiasm displayed at its convention. He believed the county ticket was made up of men of the finest character, and that its strength "struck terror into the ranks of the opposition."[8] Hunter's political predictions did not ring true, and, with the exception of the reelection of Governor Caldwell, the Republicans failed miserably in their attempt to regain control of the state. Hunter probably voted for the first time in 1872. He did not vote a straight Republican ticket, for he later recalled, "The first vote I ever cast was given to my former master who was a candidate for Mayor of Raleigh against Col. W. H. Harrison, Governor Holden's brother-in-law."[9]

Hunter was indeed moving closer to the old native white leadership, and by 1874 he was actively participating in various political and social reform movements that included many Democrats. In the spring of that year he joined a bipartisan and interracial movement led by Joseph W. Holden, Needham B. Broughton, and James H. Harris to clean up the government of Raleigh. Hunter stated that he supported this cause because public affairs in Raleigh had been greatly mismanaged and reform was necessary to save the city from total bankruptcy. He also felt that his status within the black community of Raleigh was such that he could successfully run for public office, and he offered himself as an independent candidate for alderman. During his campaign he promised to work for a thorough investigation of every aspect of city government, publicly to expose every instance of wrongdoing, and to serve as the representative of all the people. He also urged blacks to assume an independent attitude in politics and to release themselves from the clutches of "political wire-pullers, demagogues, and tricksters."[10]

Hunter probably had other motives in running for office besides reforming the city administration of Raleigh. He wanted personal recognition, and he realized that the most popular and prestigious blacks in the state were politicians. Although he would later denounce these men, in 1874 he was one of their admirers and aspired to join their ranks. He was particularly proud of the members of his race in the legislature, and believed they were

## Reformer and Accommodationist

men of intelligence and industry who deserved the respect of all the people of the state regardless of color or party. Hunter never succeeded in obtaining an elective office. During the campaign in 1874 his opponents alleged that he was really a Democrat running on a temperance platform. A. N. Upchurch, a leading white Republican in Raleigh, in a letter to George W. Brodie, wrote that Hunter was a Democrat who had actually remarked that he "would rather vote for a democrat in a ditch then [sic] vote for a whiskey man who sells whiskey." Upchurch instructed Brodie to fire Hunter immediately. Hunter publicly denied these charges but he also stated: "I have unloaded myself of dishonest, corrupt and drunken men of all parties and shall stand by my principles whether elected or not."[11]

During the campaign Hunter had received assurances that he was the choice of a large majority of the black voters, but this was not the case and he lost the election by two votes. He attributed his defeat to the work of professional politicians who succeeded in turning the black community against him. Thereafter, Hunter never missed an opportunity to denounce the professional politicians of both races as an unsavory group of men. Though defeated, he received some consolation from knowing that "eighty-three of the most prominent white men in his ward voted for him." He was also proud of the fact that the reform forces were victorious, and he later claimed the distinction of having been a leader in the "fight that dislodged the corrupt Republican administration and placed the city of Raleigh in the hands of the Democrats. . . ."[12] Nevertheless, this one foray into the political arena was sufficiently distasteful to deter Hunter from any future attempts for an elective public office.

More than likely there was some truth in the allegation that Hunter was running on a temperance platform in 1874, for he was very active in the postwar temperance movement in North Carolina. He was probably introduced to the movement by northern white educators who, in their instruction of the freedmen, never missed an opportunity to extol the virtues of sobriety and to persuade blacks to join temperance societies. Moreover, temperance was the one reform movement that native whites universally recommended to blacks. During the early years of Reconstruction, the temperance movement was an integrated effort and blacks and whites were often members of the same organizations. However, in time, possibly because temperance work frequently involved contact between black men and white women and raised fears of social equality, blacks were encouraged to form their own societies.

## Reformer and Accommodationist

On 29 August 1871 Hunter and several other blacks formed a juvenile temperance society called the Howard Band of Hope. This group was named after General Oliver O. Howard, and Hunter was its president and superintendent. Howard thanked Hunter for the honor of having named the organization after him, and he wished the society every possible success.[13] The constitution of the organization was later amended so as to admit all persons above the age of seven years. On 5 March 1873 Hunter and twelve other men, at a meeting in the office of the Freedmen's bank in Raleigh, organized the Queen of the South Lodge No. 6 of the Knights of Good Templars. Within a year's time, the membership of the lodge exceeded 650 persons, and it was presided over by Hunter. He thought that with the exception of the church no institution possessed a greater capacity for good, or enjoyed more success and acceptance among blacks than the Good Templars. Some whites also believed that the lodge flourished beyond anything they had ever known, and that it was working a reformation among blacks that was truly marvelous. They praised Hunter as a "most worthy and exemplary colored man," and they thought that a more zealous temperance worker could not be found in the state. These whites also agreed to do all they could to encourage and sustain temperance work among blacks.[14]

However, when Hunter and his fellow black Templars applied to the Grand Lodge of North Carolina for a charter, the password, and other essentials, they were promptly denied on the grounds that the International Order of Good Templars did not permit the initiation of blacks into their lodges. This prompted the black Templars to call a statewide convention for the purpose of petitioning the Grand Lodge of North Carolina for permission to establish a separate lodge for their race in North Carolina. In May 1873 the first black Templars convention ever held in the United States convened at New Bern, and Hunter was selected to deliver the opening address and serve as temporary president. The delegates to this convention constituted an impressive body of blacks. For the most part they were young and intelligent men, and according to Hunter's brother, Osborne, they were the "bone and sinew of North Carolina who had the best interest of their race at heart." The delegates included such men as James W. Hood, Joseph C. Price, John C. Dancy, and several others who would later become state and national black leaders.[15]

In his opening address Hunter stated that whereas previous conventions of blacks were held for the purpose of securing physical and intellectual freedom, the Templars had assembled to obtain the moral emancipation of their race. He congratulated them on being a part of that historic occasion, and alleged that the black citizens of North Carolina had always been in the lead of "every good work and new enterprise having for its object the uplifting and elevating of our long despised and persecuted people." As Hunter saw it, blacks with their limited resources could not afford to be anything other than a temperate people, and he asserted that alcohol was a "fateful destroyer, initiating misery, want, degradation, and death." Then too, he believed that sobriety was a way for blacks to show whites that they were progressing in their moral development, and it would also be "one of the grandest arguments that blacks are yet to exert a powerful influence as a Nation."[16]

A letter from the Grand Lodge of North America was read to the convention stating that the Grand Lodge of North Carolina had violated its rules by refusing to recognize black lodges. The letter also advised the Templars to petition the international order for permission to establish a lodge. However, the convention proceeded on its own to establish an interim Colored Lodge of the International Order of Good Templars, and Hunter was elected to serve as the Grand Worthy Secretary. The order then drafted its petition for a separate lodge and this precipitated an international controversy that eventually led to a schism within the International Order of Good Templars.

The Order of Good Templars was established in America in 1851, and its constitution affirmed allegiance to the idea of the universal brotherhood of men. Only one Grand Lodge was authorized in any state, and each was autonomous in its local jurisdiction. But the international order did have the authority to ensure that Good Templary was conducted worldwide in accordance with its constitution and laws. When the order was introduced into the South, its membership was generally confined to the white population, and this practice had not been questioned until the petition from North Carolina blacks came before the Right Worthy Grand Lodge at its 1873 meeting in London. The petition created a dilemma. The problem was how to secure maximum membership without sacrificing the order's historic commitment to human equality. Debates, proposals, and counterproposals relating to this issue ensued over a span of three years. One faction proposed to amend the constitution so as to permit the creation of separate lodges for individuals of different linguistic or racial backgrounds. Another group thought that the British should combine with former American abolitionists from the North and force southern lodges either to accept the principle of equality or to withdraw from the order. In all probability this would have meant the exclusion of southern white Americans.[17]

In 1875 the international order amended its constitution to provide for separate lodges for blacks in North Carolina and Maryland. This action in essence deprived blacks in other states of the privilege of membership in the order. At this point, part of the British membership raised cries of protest against the establishment of duplicate lodges in individual states. Others protested because of "an overwhelming desire to extend the principles of *'Liberty, universal brotherhood, equal rights of man, etc.'* to Negroes in the South and to show their detestation of whatever savors of caste and tyranny. . . ." Eventually expediency overcame principle, and the Right Worthy Grand Lodge at its meeting in Louisville, Kentucky, in 1876 adopted a resolution providing for separate lodges for blacks in any state. Immediately thereafter the British representatives and some of their sympathizers seceded from the order and formed the Right Worthy Grand Lodge of the World. In 1877 a special representative of this group came to North Carolina and organized several lodges among blacks.[18]

Hunter remained active in the temperance and prohibition movements in North Carolina for most of his life. Although he was an effective worker, one must certainly doubt his sincerity and question his motives. By 1900 a serious flaw in Hunter's character surfaced that later reduced his usefulness to the cause. He was accused of having a serious drinking problem. It is indeed possible that Hunter drank during his earlier participation in the movement and that he embraced temperance for reasons other than a moral objection to the use of alcohol. Of course, he seldom followed his own advice. It has also been noted that an individual's desire for status, respect, friendship, and recognition independent of a group's stated goals is often sufficient inducement to cause one to join a particular organization.[19]

Hunter indeed wanted social status, prestige, and public approval and he admitted as much. On being selected as temporary president of the temperance convention of 1873, he remarked that he "least expected to enjoy such a flattering exhibition of the esteem and confidence of my brethren from different sections of the State as has here been manifested." Participation in the temperance movement was also a way for blacks to sublimate their desires for political involvement and to exercise their leadership abilities in a way that was acceptable to whites. Following the convention of 1873, former Governor William W. Holden wrote to Hunter that he had been observing with interest and gratification the progress of temperance among blacks, and he was pleased to see that many of their leading men were at the forefront of the movement.[20]

At the same time that the leading black men were advancing to the front of the temperance movement, they were also retreating in other areas. In the early 1870s it seems as if they could almost sense an imminent end to Reconstruction. They prepared for this eventuality by adopting a more conservative stance in politics and race relations and by refraining from doing anything that would incur the wrath of whites. For example, in 1871 James H. Harris advised Moses Patterson, "a most respected colored man," not to run for the office of Wake County coroner because it would be "too much to ask for a colored man to go into the parlor of a white man to hold an inquest." Two years later when Harris was seeking the office of clerk of the Superior Court of Wake County he got a dose of his own medicine. Friday Jones, a prominent black of Raleigh, publicly campaigned against Harris and urged blacks not to support his nomination on the grounds that it would be detrimental to good race relations. Jones reasoned that many white women would never consent to undergo a privy examination before a black clerk of the court, and he suggested that Harris should seek reelection to the state senate where the "sensibilities and ideas of propriety of no lady can be wounded. . . ."[21]

By 1874 the Democrats had gained almost complete control of Wake County, and they let it be known that they had no use for black officeholders or public officials. In June of that year the *Weekly Republican* warned that the Democrats had drawn the color line in Wake County and that if they had their way, "the proscriptions against blacks would be so bad that within the course of a few months the whole colored population would be forced to leave the state."[22] The color line also extended beyond the limits of Wake County, and it was very much in evidence in all parts of the state. During the 1870s the physical distance between the races was widening, and everywhere there were segregated schools, churches, and fire companies, and even some newspapers separated their classified advertisements for laborers according to race. Not only this, but state institutions were almost totally segregated.

The constitution of North Carolina did not mandate a segregated school system, but according to State Superintendent of Schools Alexander McIver, no legislation in favor of racially mixed schools had ever been attempted. In 1874 McIver asserted that "opposition to mixed schools was so strong that if the people had to choose between mixed schools and no schools they would prefer the latter." There were also separate schools for the deaf, dumb, and blind, and by 1877 it was no longer acceptable for black and white mental patients to associate together. In that year the Board of Directors and the superintendent of the State Insane Asylum recommended that the black patients housed in the state facility be withdrawn as soon as possible in order to conserve the best interests of both races.[23]

The few blacks who were brave and assertive enough to enter public facilities and demand equal accommodations were either turned away or subjected to gross indignities. This was particularly true of eating establishments, because whites had a deep aversion toward dining with blacks. A Raleigh newspaper in 1870 applauded the fact that a white carpetbagger and his black companion who "called for crackers and cheese for two" in a Raleigh restaurant were promptly told that "colored people were not allowed to eat at tables." Some whites would not condescend to eat even with the best black men. In 1872 it was reported that Dr. Eugene Grissom invited his fellow colleagues on the State Penitentiary Board to dinner and then offered the lone black member his meal at a separate table in the same room. Two years later Representative Richard H. Cain of South Carolina announced to the United States Congress that he and Representative Robert B. Elliott had recently traveled through North Carolina, and they could not sit down in any restaurant from Wilmington to Weldon without entering into a contest. Because the two did not "desire to draw revolvers and present the bold front of warriors," they had their meals brought to them in their railroad car. Even then, whites objected because they thought the two black congressmen from South Carolina were "putting on airs."[24]

The intensity of the commitment of whites to a segregated society can be seen in their determined opposition to federal civil rights legislation. In January 1874 John H. Williamson, a black member of the legislature from Franklin County, introduced a bill in the General Assembly that would have instructed the state's congressional delegation to support legislation granting equal political and civil rights for blacks. Despite the fact that Williamson's bill contained instructions for the congressmen to vote "against all bills tending to an enforcement of social equality," it did not pass. Instead, the General Assembly approved a resolution petitioning the Congress of the United States not to pass the Supplemental Civil Rights Act because it would result in the suppression of public schools for both races, the closing of many houses of worship, the ruin of landlords and hotel proprietors, a thorough demoralization of society, and bitter strife between the races.[25]

## Reformer and Accommodationist

Hunter was lukewarm on the idea of a federal civil rights bill. As early as 1872 he was leaning toward the doctrine of separate but equal facilities for the races. In that year he seemed satisfied with the existence of segregated institutions for the deaf, dumb, and blind, noting that the "perfect impartiality" shown by the Board of Trustees in the administration of the white and black departments was "evidence of the progress of civilization." Two years later Hunter publicly asserted that if race relations were as good in other states as they were in North Carolina, there would be no need for a civil rights bill. Moreover, he contended that the friendly intercourse between the races in his native state convinced him that blacks in North Carolina lived among the best people in the world. He urged blacks to continue to strive by their "manly and upright bearing" to strengthen the ties that bound the two races together in the past.[26]

Hunter's statements did not reflect the realities of race relations, and one must wonder why he denied the necessity for a civil rights bill in the face of evidence to the contrary. Surely he realized that his race did not enjoy civil equality. He also knew that blacks in their desires to expand and grow were subjected to discriminatory limitations and disabilities. No doubt he hoped for full equality in an integrated society, but he was enough of a realist to know that this was not going to happen. Then too, none of the measures of Reconstruction had been effective in reducing racial segregation. Hunter probably understood that a civil rights bill would prove equally ineffective unless it was accompanied by a radical transformation of public opinion in its favor or enforced by the full power of the federal government. Searching for racial harmony, he was aware that whites tended to regard those blacks who demanded equality as antisocial persons, and they had proved their ability to suppress these types. In 1874 Hunter wrote that the prospect of a civil rights bill had triggered an intense emotional response in North Carolina and awakened some very unpleasant feelings.[27]

Hunter was not the only black in North Carolina who had misgivings about the effectiveness of a civil rights bill. In June 1874 the Republicans of Edgecombe County at their convention, after nominating a black for the state senate and another for the United States House of Representatives, adopted a resolution on behalf of 3,500 black voters disapproving of the "Sumner Civil Rights bill." These blacks also stated that they did not desire perfect equality, nor did they want any rights other than those guaranteed under existing legislation.[28]

Hunter's contention that blacks in North Carolina lived among the best

## Reformer and Accommodationist

people in the world can partially be explained by the fact that he was easing into the role of a passive accommodationist. Indeed, he became the model of the accommodationist described by John Dollard. This type idealized native whites, adopted their values, sentiments, and attitudes, and eventually professed love for those whom they at first feared and resented. The accommodationist also renounced militancy as a form of protest against the undesirable features of life and accepted the status quo. Hunter knew that if blacks were to remain in North Carolina in any peace, they would have to accept an inferior position in the social order and not give whites any trouble. By disclaiming the need for additional civil rights legislation and praising the existing state of race relations, he was catering to the attitudes of whites and at the same time letting them know that he was not an antisocial person. In his conservative approach to race relations, Hunter looked into the past for ways to live in the present. Like many others of his generation he fell back upon his slave experience. It has been noted that the education of slaves consisted primarily of lessons in survival and accommodation. They learned the techniques of masking their feelings and emotions and how to flatter the egos and placate the fears of whites.[29]

Being an accommodationist was not an easy task because it severely taxed one's psychic energy. It demanded the maintenance of a dual personality, the conscious playing of two roles and the spreading of two messages, one for whites and one for blacks. Hence it is no wonder that Hunter was an anxious and inconsistent person. He was frequently censured by his race for acquiescing in things that he knew were not true, and he must have suffered inner conflicts from the knowledge that he had consciously sacrificed his dignity and compromised his principles. However, Hunter was never locked into the accommodationist role and, in a fit of anger or in an occasional brush with reality, he spoke out against racial injustices.

When the Raleigh branch of the Freedmen's bank closed in 1874, Hunter worked for a while as chief clerk in the office of the Assessor of Internal Revenue for the states of Virginia, North Carolina, South Carolina, Georgia, and Florida. From this position he observed the political situation in the South during the elections of 1874, and was appalled at the outrages committed by white conservatives against inoffensive and peaceful citizens. He had hoped that the use of violence to carry elections was a thing of the past and that "Southerners would adopt a different and far more effective, if not to say legitimate way of acquainting the Nation with their grievances." He thought these acts of violence, particularly at election time,

## Reformer and Accommodationist

only showed the true feelings of native whites. Blacks were forced to believe, despite their desire to the contrary, that southerners still had hopes of "so nullifying the work of the Republican Party respecting the Negro as to place him in a condition little, if any better than that of a slave." Instead of whites accepting the results of Reconstruction and working to bring peace and prosperity to the region, Hunter maintained that they chose to "linger around the grave of their departed greatness, vainly hoping that by some means it may yet be resurrected." Hunter admitted that southern whites had suffered as a result of Reconstruction, but he believed they had been responsible for their own misery. Citing North Carolina as a case in point, he maintained that whites "must charge upon themselves the entire responsibility of whatever may have been the evil influences to which they have been subjected."[30]

Hunter also believed in 1874 that the question of whether the South would have its own way in determining the future of race relations would soon be settled. He appealed to whites to accept everything that had been done for the protection of blacks and to give up all hopes of depriving them of their just rights. If so, Hunter believed they would find in the black man a true and faithful friend. "I am a Southerner," he wrote, and "I feel for that section of the country. I want to see it prosper and its people happy." The Democrats of North Carolina in 1875 let it be known that their formula for peace and prosperity did not include equality for blacks. The Constitutional Convention of that year proceeded to curtail those rights that blacks then enjoyed and further to institutionalize racial segregation. Integrated schools and interracial marriages were prohibited by constitutional amendment, and the whole concept of popular government was altered so as to guarantee whites local control. County and township government was placed almost entirely in the hands of the legislature, and this in effect amounted to a partial disfranchisement of black citizens. The black members of the convention were so incensed at the extremism displayed by the Democrats that they joined with a few white Republicans in condemning it as "a revolution that had virtually overthrown the government of the people."[31]

By 1875 Hunter was no longer of the opinion that North Carolina had the best people in the world, and he contemplated leaving the state. He thought of going to South Carolina where there was some chance for a young man and where, unlike in his native state, a black could enroll in the state university. He also considered migrating to the North, and he asked a friend in Philadelphia about living conditions and the prospects of finding em-

## Reformer and Accommodationist

ployment in a "great metropolis." Hunter hoped that soon his life would be happier, nobler, and better, and he confided to this friend, "You cannot imagine how things have changed at Raleigh." Things had indeed changed for Hunter in Raleigh. His status within the black community had steadily declined since he began to associate with Democrats and temperance workers. Blacks also resented his contention that they should refrain from seeking political offices until they had advanced themselves educationally and materially, and that their continued insistence and overemphasis on the right to hold office would result in great harm to their race. Hunter felt that he was a victim of oppression and that almost every black in Raleigh, including his close friend George W. Brodie, had turned against him. Yet he was willing to bear this burden, for he believed that he was "battling energetically for himself, for God and the right. . . ." Hunter lost his job in the office of the Assessor of Internal Revenue, and he could not find another suitable one in Raleigh. In the summer of 1875 he asked the black congressman from the Second Congressional District, John A. Hyman, to assist him in obtaining employment, possibly as a route agent, on the railroad from Charlotte to Goldsboro. When this did not materialize, Hunter began to consider the possibilities of a career in public education.[32]

One of the reasons why blacks in North Carolina either favored or demanded a segregated school system was that it provided employment opportunities for the educated members of their race. Some were also of the opinion that the education of their children could not be entrusted to whites because they were incapable of understanding the emotions and attitudes of blacks. Responding to this attitude, James W. Hood stated in 1868 that it was "impossible for white teachers to enter into the feelings of colored pupils as the colored teacher does." There were also fears that white teachers would further perpetuate feelings of inferiority among blacks. The idea of white supremacy was so firmly ingrained in the minds of whites that some blacks believed that they would naturally transmit this to students during daily contacts in the classroom.[33]

Whites were also troubled over the question of who was going to educate blacks. Many believed that blacks were incapable of teaching themselves, yet they abhorred the thought of relinquishing this important task to northern whites, who would surely "instill into the simple minds of blacks doctrines that would subvert social institutions and tend to array the races in hostilities and perpetuate those antagonistic feelings which were prevalent after the War." In 1873 Alexander McIver, the superintendent of public

## Reformer and Accommodationist

instruction for North Carolina, admitted that the one great issue connected with the education of blacks was how to teach them to think and act like southern whites. He preferred entrusting this mission to whites, but it was "well nigh impossible in North Carolina" to find people willing to do the job. Hence he was forced to recommend that blacks who were mentally and morally well qualified be certified as teachers.[34]

One of the tasks of the black denominational institutions was to turn out safe black teachers who were morally and mentally correct and who would promote "right thinking" among the members of their race. It was for these reasons that native whites supported or tolerated such institutions as Biddle Memorial Institute, Shaw University, and Saint Augustine College. Biddle Institute was specifically established for the purposes of educating the most pious and talented of the freedmen so that they could take the lead in preventing the "retrogression in civilization and religion of four million semicivilized and partially Christianized freedmen." Reflecting on the history of Shaw University, the *Raleigh News and Observer* concluded in 1919 that the institution had exerted a wholesome influence and "right thinking" upon its students who, in turn, indoctrinated others of their race—and because of this, race relations in North Carolina were better than anywhere else in the nation.[35]

Hunter was an early supporter of education, and he believed that it was the surest and safest route for the advancement and progress of his race. He also knew that black teachers were esteemed members of the community and that they were charged with important responsibilities. His brother, Osborne, was supervisor of the Colored Department of the State Institution for the Deaf, Dumb, and Blind, and in 1874 he was one of four blacks who belonged to the Educational Association of North Carolina. This was a prestigious group whose membership included Calvin H. Wiley, William H. Battle, and Alexander McIver. Hunter was present when Osborne delivered an address at the second annual meeting of the association in July 1874. In the course of his remarks, Osborne recommended that blacks postpone classical education and concentrate on those studies that were of an immediate and practical benefit. He was not opposed to classical education per se, but he thought it would be better to "crawl before we walk." Hunter thought his brother's address reflected great credit on his race, and he was deeply impressed by the warm reception and approving comments it received from the white members of the association. He also interpreted the friendliness and respect shown by whites toward the black members of the

## Reformer and Accommodationist

association as "omens of better days." Hunter had Osborne's address printed and recommended that it be disseminated to black educators thoughout the state as a means of advancing the cause of practical education. Naturally, he inserted in the printed version some thoughts of his own, including the idea that "just in proportion as blacks become educated and refined and *learn to respect themselves*, just in proportion will they be respected by others."[36]

Hunter's experience at the convention probably convinced him that a career as an educator was one way for him to obtain the respect and friendship of whites. In 1875 he accepted a teaching position in the remote village of Shoe Heel in Robeson County, and embarked on a career that spanned more than a half century. In December of that year Hunter boarded a train for the first leg of his journey to Shoe Heel. Years later he recalled that there were no Jim Crow arrangements in those days, but he might have qualified this statement with the caveat "on this railroad." From Fayetteville he took a stagecoach to Lumberton, and in spite of the bitter cold he was forced to sit up front beside the driver. Only after the protest of an attorney, Neill A. McLean, of Lumberton, who wanted some company, was Hunter permitted to ride in the passenger compartment. The two men then wrapped themselves in the same blanket and conversed along the way. During a stop en route, the driver invited McLean into a house for coffee, and he in turn invited Hunter. The lady of the house gave McLean a chair and a cup of coffee, but she made no similar gestures toward Hunter. He remembered, "O, how I did want just a swallow of that coffee. However, I was glad to get warm." Once at Shoe Heel, Hunter secured his position in the community by placing himself under the patronage of McLean. This was aided by a personal letter from his former mistress to McLean commending Hunter to his interest. Afterward, McLean introduced Hunter to many of the gentlemen of the community, and he offered to assist Hunter at any time he could be of service.[37]

Hunter was definitely out of his environment in Shoe Heel. There was no schoolhouse and classes were conducted in the local Methodist church. He was surprised at the ignorance of the people and their general lack of culture and refinement, and he immediately set out to improve this situation. In addition to his school activities he taught two Sunday schools, but his work in the latter area was hampered by a lack of Testaments and other printed materials. He managed to obtain some Testaments from a friend, and he also asked William W. Holden to send him any printed matter of a secular or

## Reformer and Accommodationist

religious nature, because "a paper, a tract, or a testament is much valued by the people." Hunter also supervised a temperance society. He wrote Holden, "I am again battling in the cause of temperance. . . . Here as in Raleigh much of the earnings of our people are swallowed up in the dramshop." The majority of the black citizens of Shoe Heel did not belong to Hunter's temperance society, and it seemed to him that they detested any person or movement opposed to the whiskey traffic. However, he thought that his prestige as a temperance worker would be enhanced if Holden would write a letter "addressed through me to the colored people of North Carolina on the subject of temperance."[38]

Hunter was still involved in politics and actively working for the Republican party. He was obviously disturbed by the lack of political astuteness of the local citizens and the poor quality of black political leaders in Robeson County. As late as 1876 many people still thought Holden was governor of the state. With the exception of a few local politicians, Hunter claimed that the only others known to the masses were Holden and Ulysses S. Grant. "There is not a colored man in the County of any fitness for the work who takes part in the local canvass," wrote Hunter to Holden. He exempted himself from this characterization because he claimed that he was doing all he could to strengthen the party. Since the people did not subscribe to Republican newspapers or have access to campaign propaganda, Hunter tried to obtain these materials for them. The black congressman John A. Hyman sent literature, which Hunter read to the illiterate blacks of the community and passed on to those who could read, with instructions that they read it to their neighbors. In March 1876 Hunter predicted that with political education and a few energetic workers, Robeson County could be listed as doubtful in the fall elections.[39]

Meanwhile in Raleigh, Osborne Hunter was warning Republicans who hoped to get elected in November to prepare themselves for a hard fight. As a political observer, he felt the Republicans could no longer rely on their large majorities and that the Democrats would offer a determined resistance and even use force if necessary to protect their position. Neither could Republicans stand on their past record, which he thought was rather shabby. The party had to rally around principles and not men, and Osborne believed it was time to select new leaders who could deal with the great financial and economic issues of the day. He suggested that the party be purged of all men who were not dedicated to the spirit and principles of true Republicanism. Osborne also offered several recommendations as to how the party could reform itself. He thought that all nominations should be made in duly publicized open conventions, that only "SIMON PURE, RUM-PROOFED AND CLEAN HANDED Republicans" should be nominated for office, that nominations should be unanimous, and that delegates should be required to pledge themselves to support the party's nominees.[40]

Race rather than reform was the major issue in North Carolina during the campaign of 1876. Cries of social equality, black domination, mixed schools, miscegenation, and white-supremacy slogans that would become familiar Democratic shibboleths in future political contests came forth from all parts of the state. The Democratic rhetoric also gave blacks a chance to find out what their white friends thought about them. Typical of the oratory of the 1876 campaign was a speech made by Senator Matthew W. Ransom at Hillsborough. He prefaced his remarks by claiming that he was as good a friend of blacks as they had, but they were not qualified to rule or to control the destiny of North Carolina. This was a white man's job and, to prove this point, Ransom appealed to a perverted brand of history. He alleged that for 6,000 years whites had proved their superiority by being first in the assertion of liberty, the enforcement of laws, the establishment of schools, and the diffusion of the gospel. Moreover, he maintained that everything wrong in the world could be found upon the continent of Africa.[41]

Faced with such rhetoric it is no wonder that Hunter and other blacks perceived the Democratic party as the "embodiment of the worst hatred to the Negro and all his rights and privileges." Blacks understood the importance of a Republican victory, and they went to the polls and delivered to that party the largest vote ever. But this was not enough to counter the effectiveness of the Democratic racist campaign, and blacks were stunned when the Republicans went down in defeat. Five months after the election Osborne Hunter wrote that there were many blacks in the state who still doubted the reality of the Democratic victory.[42]

On the other hand, there were some blacks who immediately understood the significance of the Democrats' success, and they wanted to get out of the state to escape further oppression. In December 1876 John H. Williamson introduced a resolution in the General Assembly requesting that the state's representatives and senators in Congress assist blacks in obtaining land west of the Mississippi for the exclusive use of their race. The resolution stated that in North Carolina and other southern states, black voting and office holding had stirred up so much prejudice and animosity in the minds of trusted white statesmen that blacks believed it was no longer

## Reformer and Accommodationist

possible for the two races to live together in any peace. Blacks also resented the wholesale degradation and slander of their race and they stated they could no longer remain in North Carolina as long as the "origin of the Negro race, his color, physical formation, ignorance, and poverty is made a pretext, or forms a principal harpy for democratic politicians to indulge in during political contests." Williamson's resolution was eventually tabled without debate.[43]

Meanwhile, those blacks who were not contemplating leaving the state also feared that their rights as citizens would be further suppressed. In December 1876 the leading black men of Raleigh sought assurances from Governor-elect Zebulon B. Vance that this would not be the case. In speaking to the blacks of Raleigh, Vance emphatically disclaimed any desire on the part of the Democrats to deprive them of any rights they possessed under the law. The *Raleigh Observer* estimated that the applause that Vance received from the audience "indicated the confidence which his assertion inspired." Vance gave blacks additional assurances the following month during their Emancipation Day activities in Raleigh when he told them that his solemn oath of office bound him to respect their rights and he would be a "perjured wretch if any citizen, white or black should lose one jot or tittle of his rights," as long as the chief executive of North Carolina could defend them. Again, Vance's remarks brought forth frequent and hearty applause, and many of the leading blacks shook his hand as he retired from the hall. Such remarks on the part of the governor and the whites always had a tranquilizing effect on the leading blacks, and they also helped perpetuate the myth that all was right between the races in the Old North State.[44]

At least Hunter thought so, and in the spring of 1877 he contended that nowhere, North or South, did a more kindly feeling exist between the races than in Shoe Heel. He invited all those who doubted that they could live peacefully together to come to this community. However, he acknowledged that in politics and social life "the line of demarcation is as distinct here as anywhere, each seems to revolve in his separate orbit . . . , upheld and supported by the sympathetic influence of each other." Hunter also assumed the role of spokesman on behalf of the former slaves of North Carolina, and he was sure that he represented their sentiment when he stated that they bore no ill will toward their former masters. If blacks could only be sure that this feeling was reciprocated, he maintained, they would be willing to cooperate with their former owners in any work having as its object the "upholding of

our glorious old State." Hunter revealed this sentiment to John C. Scarborough, the newly elected superintendent of public instruction for North
Carolina, and advised that education was the key to peace and progress in
the South because "politicians will ever find in an ignorant people ample
means for their wicked and selfish ends." Hunter hoped that the day would
soon come when North Carolina would be blessed with a happy, contented,
industrious, and united people and when "strife and enmity between the
races will be entirely done away with—when the aim and end of both will
be the common good."[45]

The masses of blacks in North Carolina were not fortunate enough to be
residents of Shoe Heel, and they, including Hunter's brother, Osborne, had
a different view of race relations and seriously doubted the good intentions
of the Democrats, who controlled the state. In April 1877 Osborne wrote
that even though his race had received promises, assurances, and pledges
directly from the governor, his fellow officials, and the legislature, "anxiety
had reached its highest pitch among the colored population of North Carolina." Many of the blacks were thinking about leaving the state and Osborne
stated that the "subject of colonization is now undergoing a thorough
discussion among our people." He was right. The following month a state
convention was held in Raleigh for all blacks interested in emigration, and
the North Carolina Emigrant and Aid Society was established to facilitate
their removal from the state.[46]

One source of the anxiety that Osborne referred to was the fear that the
Democrats would attempt to separate the races further. Some blacks wondered if they would be set off by themselves, "in an isolated condition, in a
sort of political quarantine as if they had smallpox or yellow fever." Dis-
avowing any desire for social equality, these blacks pleaded for the maintenance of contact between the races because they needed the culture, experience, and sympathy of whites. The Democratic-controlled legislature in
1877 adopted a resolution that should have dispelled any doubts in the
minds of blacks as to their future status in the state. It was agreed that the
two races could live together in peace and harmony and that the constitutional rights of blacks would be respected. But the General Assembly
viewed with "repugnance the absurd attempts, by means of 'Civil Rights'
Bills to eradicate certain race distinctions, implanted by nature and sustained by the habits of forty centuries." The idea of white supremacy was
reaffirmed, and blacks were told to forget about political office, because
only men with the highest intelligence and the most experience could

provide the state with good government. The legislators also resolved to accept the duty of educating and uplifting their black brethren.[47]

This policy statement stirred the leading blacks. In the fall of 1877 they called a state convention to consider ways to advance the material, moral, and educational status of their race. Resolutions adopted at the preliminary conventions held to select delegates indicated that blacks intended to make education their first priority. The *New York Times* presumed that the proposed convention would be made up of the most intelligent blacks in North Carolina, and it advised them that "for the time at least, they should eschew politics. Just now there is nothing to be gained from political discussion." In October blacks from forty counties assembled in Raleigh and remained in convention for two days. Showing up were a number of politicians who immediately vied with each other for leadership positions. James H. Harris was eventually elected president in preference to James E. O'Hara. State Senator George L. Mabson and J. C. Price served as vice-presidents, and John C. Dancy won the position of secretary. Hunter was given the rather insignificant task of convention reporter. A newspaper article signed "Norfleet," which was Hunter's middle name, announced that a "political element gained control of the convention and with one or two exceptions shaped its actions to no general good."[48]

Norfleet hoped the convention would adopt a resolution or at least issue a statement proclaiming the withdrawal of blacks from politics. He felt this was absolutely necessary for the future progress of his race, because it had already paid too much attention to politics and politicians and "too little to the essentials of true greatness. We must have morals, mind, and money." The delegates did unanimously agree not to entertain any proposition that could be construed in any way as being political in nature and then proceeded to chart a course for their race that was accommodationist and unrealistic. They decided that henceforth education, morality, and industry would constitute the basis of their elevation and prosperity and that blacks had to support temperance organizations, purchase land, and become wealthy. Teachers and preachers and all good citizens were called upon to expose vice and immorality wherever found, and to help create a good moral climate conducive to the development of integrity. In what amounted to a lack of social consciousness and concern for the less fortunate members of their race, the leading black men resolved to subject "base and unworthy" blacks to "public odium and social ostracism."[49]

The issue of education received considerable attention. The delegates claimed the right of blacks to control their own schools, decried the practice of excluding them from representation on school committees and boards, and called for longer school terms and more normal schools for the training of teachers. The convention was also of the opinion that the aggregate wealth of blacks in North Carolina would be increased if young males turned their thoughts away from acquiring a professional education and concentrated on agricultural and vocational training. The delegates voiced their intentions to remain in North Carolina because it was their home, and they dismissed all emigration schemes and movements as impractical, inexpedient, and detrimental to blacks in America. While acknowledging that blacks in the state faced many obstacles and evils, the delegates oddly enough contended they were encouraged by the disappearance of race prejudice, the growing sentiments of friendship and confidence between the races, and the obliteration of the color line.[50]

Blacks thought they saw additional evidences of the friendship of whites when they assembled at Raleigh on New Year's Day 1878 to commemorate the fifteenth anniversary of their emancipation. Before the formal ceremony Governor Vance conducted a review of the black militia units from Wilmington, Raleigh, and Fayetteville. He complimented the troops on their fine appearance and on the good order and discipline they had displayed during their first visit to the city. The troops then paraded through the principal streets of Raleigh. Blacks liked to point to the militia as evidence of the good race relations in North Carolina, but the existence of black troops was also an indication that whites were firmly in control. Whites would never have tolerated the presence of black military units in the state as long as they were perceived as a threat to the social order. The formal celebration was opened with the customary prayers, songs, and the reading of the Emancipation Proclamation. But when Governor Vance spoke to the crowd, his remarks must have had a dampening effect on what had been a gala event. He told the audience that he could not celebrate Emancipation Day with them because he had done "all that mortal man could do to prevent the occurrence of this day in the history of the country, and that he and his party did not believe the reconstruction acts were constitutional, and therefore the negroes were not properly freed." However, he had accepted the results of the Civil War and the recent amendments to the Constitution of the United States, and he thought that blacks had a right to demand from him the equal protection afforded other citizens. The governor praised blacks for having made some progress in industry and education during the preceding year and for their good behavior. He was pleased over the fact that he had received no reports of riots or disorderly conduct on the part of the blacks and that kind feelings toward whites had manifestly increased. His instructions to the assemblage were simple enough: "train your children to labor and honesty is now your great duty. If you do this you may rest assured that all other temporal blessings will follow in due time." The secretary of state, John A. Engelhard, was also invited to make a speech, but he too did not think blacks were constitutionally freed, and he also thought it "would be doing violence to his conscience if he sanctioned the proceedings by his presence."[51]

Vance was the first Democratic governor to speak at an Emancipation Day ceremony, and he was censured for this by some of the major newspapers in the state. The *Charlotte Democrat* maintained that the sight of Vance addressing a black audience and professing "great love and respect for the negro" was indeed extreme. The editor of the *Raleigh Register* likewise believed that Vance's actions were extreme and were motivated for the sole purpose of courting the black vote. The *Register* hinted that Vance was guilty of practicing social equality, and this made him no better than the former Republican governors. Vance later confessed that he had to apologize to the white community for this unsavory behavior.[52]

By 1879 Hunter's philosophy of race relations was remarkably similar to the themes embraced by the romantic school of writers that emerged in the postwar South. He and these writers both found good features within the institution of slavery, and they tended to glorify selected plantation personalities: the kind master, the angelic mistress, and the faithful bondsman. They emphasized the close personal relationships that occasionally existed between slaves and their owners, and they also praised the loyalty and good conduct of slaves during the Civil War. White paternalism was accepted as a beneficial arrangement for both races, which involved reciprocal duties and responsibilities. Whites would govern by virtue of their superior intelligence, power, and wealth, but they were also obliged to protect and help elevate blacks. In return, blacks would accept their inferior position in society and always look to native whites for counsel and guidance.[53]

Hunter knew that the black model most acceptable to whites was the one that most closely approximated the old-time, deferential, and safe slave who loved his master and identified with his interests. There were many blacks with these characteristics in North Carolina after Reconstruction. Those who had acquired education, improved their material status in acceptable ways, and had not been guilty of agitating for social, civil, and political equality were the ones who enjoyed the patronage of whites. They were selected as teachers and heads of educational institutions, and charged with the responsibility of inculcating desirable traits in others of their race. Whites designated these blacks as the "leading" or "best" colored men. Through constant reminders of his slave heritage, Hunter subtly told whites that he knew how to act and that he was eligible to become a leading colored man. He also wanted to remind them of their heritage as slaveowners and thus revive their sense of duty toward blacks. Then too, Hunter always maintained that race relations could be improved by capitalizing on any residual good feelings emanating from the institution of slavery.

All the elements of Hunter's philosophy of race relations coalesced and were put into action with the founding of the North Carolina Industrial Association (NCIA). In early 1879 Hunter, his brother, Osborne, and a few of their associates gathered in the back room of Alexis Long's barbershop on Fayetteville Street in Raleigh. They decided that a blind devotion to politics and the "chasing of political will-o-the wisps" did not promote the true growth and prosperity of their race and would in the end prove a "disastrous disappointment." If blacks were to become a great and use-ful people, these men agreed that they would have to travel the same route that had been successfully pursued by other races. They had to devote their energy to labor and the improvement of their moral and intellectual condition.[54]

In furtherance of these goals, the NCIA was founded to "encourage and promote the development of the industrial and educational resources of the colored people of North Carolina, and to gather statistics respecting their progress in the various pursuits and customs peculiar to civilized and enlightened Nations, to hold annually an exhibition of the progress of their industry and education. . . ." Hunter drafted the legislation incorporating the NCIA, and he was associated with its activities for over fifty years. He and his brother, Osborne, both claimed credit for the idea of the organiza-tion, and they coedited the *Journal of Industry*, its official publication. In establishing the NCIA, the Hunter brothers sought the advice, direc-tion, and aid of the most prominent whites in the state, including Gover-nors Vance and Jarvis, and Leonidas L. Polk, the state commissioner of agriculture.[55]

Polk warned Osborne that if he expected the aid and sympathy of the

## Reformer and Accommodationist

intelligent and patriotic white men of the state, he had better ensure that the *Journal of Industry* refrain from any involvement in politics and sectarianism, and adhere closely to its stated objectives of inculcating ideas of modesty, economy, and honesty in the black population. Osborne later assured Zebulon B. Vance that this would indeed be the case; that the paper would be devoted exclusively to the moral and intellectual improvement of blacks and the "cultivation of those relations between the two races which are essential to the happiness and prosperity of each."[56]

The initial issue of the *Journal of Industry* appeared in April 1879 bearing the motto "God Will Help Those Who Help Themselves." The entire cover page was undoubtedly intended for a white audience. There was a reprint of the complete text of a letter written by Calvin H. Wiley in 1865 setting forth his ideas on the future course for race relations in North Carolina. This letter absolved blacks of any responsibility for causing the Civil War, praised their loyalty during that conflict, and told whites that they would indeed have opportunities to prove their assertion of being the blacks' best friend. Wiley asked whites to accept their Christian duty and assist in the mental and industrial development of blacks and their spiritual regeneration. The Hunter brothers commended the letter to their white friends with the comment that had Wiley's advice been heeded in 1865, the race problem would have been solved.[57]

The editors of the *Journal* addressed a letter "To the White People of the South," which was calculated to make them aware of their duty to blacks. It told whites that they owed a debt to blacks that had not been paid in full. Surely whites knew that, as both slaves and freedmen, blacks had always been loyal and faithful to them. They had even "gone down into the very jaws of death—into the mouth of hell" to protect their lives and property. Whites could begin payment on their debt by sustaining the NCIA, and they could rest assured that their own fortunes would be enhanced in the same proportion as that of blacks. The objectives and philosophy of the NCIA as expounded by its founders may have proved acceptable to whites, but they were totally unsatisfactory to some of the leading blacks, who condemned the organization as the "rankest political heresy." At a meeting of prominent blacks in Raleigh, Hunter and his comrades in the NCIA were accused of having sold out to the Democrats. They were branded as traitors to their race, and sentenced to a whipping unless they retracted their previous statements regarding the political activities of blacks. According to Hunter, a committee was appointed to "wait on us and demand that we recant. We treated the committee very cordially but pursued the even tenor of our way."[58]

The major activity of the NCIA was its sponsorship of the annual Negro State Fair, which later became an important component of the "show and tell" tactics for the improvement of race relations. Hunter believed that many whites felt that blacks would fail to measure up to the standards of citizenship or civilization, and that the whole world was closely watching his race, looking for signs of progress. He also felt that blacks had to prove themselves worthy of freedom and citizenship before they could demand greater equality. Hence the prime objective of the fair was "to place before the world every evidence of our progress as a race which it is possible to secure."[59]

Within a few years, the annual fair became the most popular social event for blacks in North Carolina. During fair week blacks poured into Raleigh to participate in various contests and exhibits or just to have a good time and relax. Fair week was also a time for blacks to commune with each other and to attend to the business of their race. Various educational, social, business, fraternal, religious, professional, military, and even political organizations scheduled their annual gatherings to coincide with the fair. The fair was also another point of contact between the races. Whites came as spectators and at times they entered contests or exhibited their goods. As on Emancipation Day, the most prominent whites who were currently in favor with the black community received special invitations to participate in official fair activities. This gave the leading black men an opportunity to show off, to reaffirm their status, and to gain some prestige through association while escorting white dignitaries or sitting with them on the speaker's platforms.

The white guests observed both the exhibits and the blacks. They commented on the personal appearance and behavior of the crowd, assessed the progress of the black race, and issued instructions for its future conduct. Hunter believed that whatever success the fair enjoyed could be partially attributed to the best white men who gave to its promoters "not only wise advice and cheering words but active help and generous financial support."[60] Some whites undoubtedly supported the black fair because it indirectly sanctioned racial segregation, and it kept large numbers of blacks away from the state fair. The favorable response of whites to the black fair

## Reformer and Accommodationist

helped increase the membership of the NCIA, and in time its rolls included almost every prominent black in the state. By the 1890s the NCIA was perhaps the only black institution in the state that cut across all lines of class, gender, and special interest.

On the opening day of the first fair, Governor Thomas J. Jarvis assumed he was talking to the better class of blacks. "I take for granted that you have classes among you," he said. "If you don't you ought to, white people have them." He then defined the better class of blacks as those who were attempting to educate their children, accumulate property, and make themselves intelligent and respectable. The governor assured blacks they were free and entitled to all the rights and protection that the best white men enjoyed, but if they wanted to elevate themselves to the plane occupied by whites, "the man who does right will be permitted to enter; the wrong doer will be excluded." Jarvis neglected to state what constituted right and wrong and who would be the ultimate judge in this matter. He also proclaimed North Carolina as being the best place in the nation for blacks, and it was his opinion that, "from the seaboard to the mountains in every county, and in every section, the most amicable and peaceful relations exist throughout our state between the two races." Jarvis had not only misrepresented the state of race relations, but had also miscalculated the attitudes of whites. Democrats chastised the governor for associating with blacks at public gatherings, and they accused him of reneging on his commitment to white supremacy by courting the political favor of blacks, and neglecting poor whites. The governor was warned that after advocating and voting for black normal schools and asylums, appointing black justices of the peace, and traveling in a "Negro carriage," and being orator of the day at a black fair, it was too late for him ever to try to get elected by crying, "Negro, Negro."[61]

The leading men liked Jarvis's remarks at the fair; they shouted, "Amen," and tried very hard to convince others of their truth. But, like Jarvis, these men were at times out of touch with reality, or they deliberately lied about race relations. For example, the Hunter brothers assured whites in 1879 that blacks were happy and there would be no significant migration out of the state. Yet, in that year alone, thousands of blacks decided that North Carolina was not the best place for them, and they left in search of a better life elsewhere. This migration, part of a larger movement of blacks from the South, attracted the attention of the United States Senate, which established a Select Committee to investigate its causes. During hearings, over one-third of the time was devoted to the migration from the Tarheel State. Testimony revealed that many blacks felt they were oppressed, and that their progress was constantly being thwarted by whites.[62]

One of the leaders of the exodus, Samuel L. Perry, claimed that he represented the sentiment of ordinary blacks, because he did not "have much to do with the big professional negroes, the rich men." He and others testified that blacks in North Carolina were confronted with severe problems. Black children were forced to attend inferior common schools, the crop-lien system locked sharecroppers and tenant farmers into a continuing cycle of poverty, and blacks did not get justice in courts. They were methodically excluded from juries, and defendants were convicted on half the evidence required to secure a judgment against a white. Once sentenced, blacks were subject to cruel and unusual punishments. Further, blacks resented the fact that they were partially disfranchised by laws that made the selection of men to fill the most important offices of local government the prerogative of the state legislature. This enabled Democrats to appoint whites to offices in areas where they could never get elected because of the existence of large black majorities. Moreover, it was alleged that the Democrats frequently packed Election Returning boards and stole elections.[63]

Perry maintained that the recent migration was not the result of a hastily made decision. As early as 1872 a number of blacks had contemplated leaving North Carolina, but by 1876 this sentiment had somewhat subsided when the legislature "gave us some schools and one thing or another, and we all got satisfied: that is the college you hear so much talk about and the asylum." As far as race relations were concerned, Perry stated that a major source of unrest among blacks was the feeling that their former masters would never recognize them as equals. If blacks accepted a servile status, some whites were inclined to help them, and "there are some colored people if he has got good white friends he will get along all right, but there are a few of that kind." Perry's testimony on race relations was corroborated by that of Richard C. Badger, a prominent white attorney of Raleigh. A former member of the state legislature and former United States district attorney for the Western District of North Carolina, he testified, "We have been living, you know with the races who were our slaves; the slaves that we could whip whenever we wanted to. . . . In all respects they are regarded now as a hired class of people, and any association between them

## Reformer and Accommodationist

and the white class is almost impossible." Badger thought that in time there would be amity between the races, but blacks would never have social freedom.[64]

Such disparaging remarks concerning conditions in North Carolina did not go unchallenged, and some of the leading men presented arguments in refutation. Their evidence is interesting because it offers some insight into how the myth concerning the good race relations in North Carolina was sustained. Excerpts from the Hunter brothers' *Journal of Industry*, which claimed that black mechanics, farmers, doctors, lawyers, and teachers had unlimited opportunity in North Carolina, were read to the committee. Some of the leading men who testified were friends or associates of Hunter, and the more influential belonged to the North Carolina Industrial Association. As if every black in the state spent his days roaming the midway, preparing for a teaching career, or awaiting some physical or mental infirmity, the leading men consistently praised the existence of the black state fair, a few normal schools, and asylums for the deaf, dumb, blind, and insane as gifts to blacks from the Democratic legislature and positive proof of the friendship of whites. The leading men testified that there was no valid reason for the migration, and the few blacks who were inclined to leave comprised the ignorant and shiftless element of their race that was caught up in a spirit of wanderlust. They claimed that the majority of the black population of North Carolina was happy and prosperous. It enjoyed perfect political and civil equality with whites, and labored under no oppressive conditions. After listening to James E. O'Hara testify in this vein, Senator William Windom remarked, "I am trying to find the paradise for the Negro, and I think I have found it at last. There is no race prejudice at all down there."[65]

Senator Vance of North Carolina submitted the majority report of the Select Committee, which was signed by all Democratic members. It concluded that the migration from North Carolina was not the result of any hardships. Rather, it was instigated by northern railroads and politicians and their black hirelings. The majority was convinced that the status of the leading blacks who testified during the hearings was "ample proof of the treatment of the colored people by whites, and their opportunity to thrive, if they were so determined." The leading men even succeeded in partially deceiving the Republican minority, who noted in its report that conditions for blacks in North Carolina were more fortunate than in other cotton states. The minority report did, however, cite the fact that "By the careful selection

## Reformer and Accommodationist

of a few well-to-do and more fortunate men from that state, the majority of the committee secured some evidence tending to show that a portion of the Negroes of North Carolina are exceptionally well treated and contented, and yet upon cross-examination of their own witnesses facts were disclosed which showed that, even there, conditions exist which are ample to account for the migration of the entire colored population."[66]

CHAPTER

# 3

## Leading Black Men

The opening year of the 1880s found Hunter back in his hometown of Raleigh employed as principal of the Washington Graded School. He and the other leading black men were caught up in the delicate situation of trying to convince their race that everything was good in North Carolina while at the same time attempting to correct injustices in a society that, according to their own rhetoric, was already nearly perfect. When Hunter and the leading blacks gathered on 1 January 1880 to celebrate Emancipation Day, there was a spirit of optimism in the air. It was a bright warm day, and the streets of Raleigh were filled with blacks from all over the state who came to witness the event.

Bands, fire units, and the leading black men with their invited guests in carriages constituted the parade, and militia units drilled in the streets. All received complimentary remarks from the white spectators. When the former slaves met their old masters, they greeted each other in a kindly and respectful fashion. A white reporter noted that "the behavior of blacks was admirable: no drunken men and apparently very little drinking; no fights, but everybody was good-humored, with friendly words for all."[1]

The orator of the day was Charles N. Otey, a lawyer, educator, journalist, and native North Carolinian then residing in the District of Columbia. Speaking in reference to the recent migration, Otey told the crowd, "I consider the Exodus a fraud. From some states it might be excusable but from North Carolina it is not." In his opinion, blacks were not oppressed, because "a better class of white people do not live on this globe than those that dwell in our native state." Moreover, he contended that whites in general were the greatest people in the world, and if blacks wanted to be like them they would have to acquire wealth, education, and self-respect.

# Leading Black Men

Whites thoroughly approved of what they saw and heard at the ceremony. The *Raleigh News* was glad to announce that none of the "soul harrowing brutalities that the Northern press takes such delight in publishing were visibly perpetrated," and that instead of the speeches advocating migration, it was "heartily denounced." The *Raleigh Observer* declared that Otey's remarks were "good advice," and its only regret was that they did not "fall upon the ears of all the colored people in the State." With such praise from whites, it is no wonder that within a few weeks Otey was called upon to testify before the committee of the United States Senate that was investigating migration from the South.[2]

At the same time the leading black men of North Carolina decided to conduct their own investigation into the causes of emigration, and in January 1880 they met in the senate chamber in Raleigh to discuss the matter. They found that blacks were indeed oppressed, and had just cause to complain of their treatment by whites and to demand redress. However, the leading men believed that migration was not the solution, and they felt that they were capable of handling the situation with a little cooperation from whites.

James H. Harris told the leading men that he thought the "minds of the better class of the dominant race" were beginning to realize the true condition of blacks, and would take steps to remove the causes of their dissatisfaction. The leading men hoped that this group would join with them in insisting upon the repeal of all legislation disadvantageous to blacks. Meanwhile, they would continue in their own efforts to convince the masses not to leave the state. But to do this, they thought the state had first to rid itself of those northern blacks who stirred up trouble and created unrest within their race. Equally repugnant was the existence of a group of black "political deadbeats and paupers" in Washington. This clique styled itself the leaders of their race, and assumed the right to speak and act for the black population of North Carolina. The leading men resolved to inform the president of the United States and his cabinet that no one but bona-fide colored citizens of North Carolina was authorized to represent their interests. Responding to this sentiment, the white editor of the *Raleigh Signal* announced that henceforth his paper would make no statements on the subject of emigration, because "the leading colored men of the State have lately issued a well considered address strongly disapproving the movement."[3]

On the opening day of the black fair in 1880, Frederick Douglass sat on the stage before a massive crowd that included Governor Jarvis and other state officials. There was probably some uneasiness when the "patriarch of the black race" rose to speak, but this was soon allayed, for Douglass proceeded to deliver a speech that could have been given by any of the "best white" or leading black men in the audience. He informed blacks that they were at the bar of world judgment and had to prove that, when left to themselves, they could prosper. They also had to overcome bias and prejudice, which was caused by their poverty and color. However, they should not expect any sudden change in the attitudes of their former masters, nor should they anticipate an immediate elevation to the status and dignity of a free man. Douglass declared that "a dog will scratch his neck even after the collar is removed. . . . The freedman still drags along with him something of the old servility of his slavery and the master . . . the arrogance and contempt with which he contemplated the slave."[4]

In 1880 Douglass, the famous runaway slave, could see both good and evil within the institution of slavery. It was good because it had taught blacks to work and this was essential for their progress as freedmen. In the finest tradition of any advocate of the Jeffersonian concept of the noble yeoman, Douglass contended that blacks were primarily an agricultural people; they should acquire and till small farms, be thrifty, educate their children, obey the laws, and accumulate property, because without it there could be no progress. He was not opposed to their leaving the South, but he wanted them to know that there was also racial animosity in the North. As he saw it, the major advantage that blacks enjoyed in the North was freedom from political persecution, and he hoped that in time this would also be the case in the South. He advised blacks to remain at home, and to remember, "You can more easily make North Carolina what it ought to be than to make yourselves in Indiana what you desire to be." Douglass admitted that he was not prepared for what he saw and heard on his visit to North Carolina, because it was widely reported abroad that a state of war existed between the races with "aggression on the one hand, oppression on the other." He announced his intention of correcting this false impression, by spreading the word to the North and West of "the visible good feeling and kindly relations between the white and colored people." Douglass did spread the word, and he later told a reporter of the *Indianapolis Sentinel* that his reception in Raleigh and Governor Jarvis's remarks at the fair convinced him that there was no conflict between the races in the South.[5]

Douglass's address at the fair expressed concepts that were so similar to those held by the leading black men that one could almost suspect he had received some prior coaching. It is also possible that he had been taken in by the superficiality of the occasion, since fair week was one of those times when whites and blacks donned their best masks and made sure that no feelings of ill will or discontent surfaced. Whites applauded Douglass for his conservative remarks at the fair, and his appearance also enhanced the image of the NCIA. The *Raleigh News and Observer* congratulated the managers of the fair on their fine efforts to improve their race, and urged them to continue with the full knowledge that they had the support and sympathy of whites.[6]

The professions of contentment and racial harmony that came forth from the leading black men on occasions such as the fair helped convince whites that they were fulfilling their duty toward the black race. If additional evidence were needed, they pointed with pride to the provisions made by the state for the education of children, and the care of destitute, deaf, dumb, blind, and insane blacks. During the decade of the 1880s some whites were even of the opinion that blacks received the same protection and treatment under the laws as all other citizens. They thought that surely blacks were satisfied and grateful, and if not, "What else did the Negro want?"[7]

It was hard for some whites to understand that many of the leading black men were dissimulators, who often expressed contentment but felt resentment. Displeased with their status, the leading blacks in the 1880s continued to press their demands for greater equality. Among other things, blacks wanted greater equality within the Republican party and a fairer share of the patronage positions in the state. Although black voters constituted the backbone of the party in North Carolina, the national Republican party had consistently pursued a policy of filling federal offices with white Republicans and Democrats to the exclusion of qualified blacks. The leading black men opposed this policy not only as discriminatory but as inconsistent with the party's principle of equal political privileges. At a meeting in January 1880 the leading men agreed that, because a national election was forthcoming, the time was ripe to protest against the inequitable distribution of patronage. They appointed a committee of five to go to Washington and inform the president and the various department heads that blacks in North Carolina desired an even division of patronage positions in recognition of the loyalty and devotion of 80,000 voters of their race.[8]

During their convention in 1881 the leading men complained that they had to contend with enough prejudice and discrimination in North Carolina, but it was particularly "galling" to them when their own political party excluded them from privileges solely on the basis of color. While voicing no intentions of quitting the Republican party, the leading men did serve notice that if they were to continue in the position of "hewers of wood and drawers of water," they would be forced to make such alliances as would best promote their interests. The following year J. C. Price warned that if the Republicans did not change their prejudicial policies against blacks, they could expect some very undesirable consequences.[9]

Hunter, who had previously advised blacks not to seek public office, joined in the agitation for more patronage. In the spring of 1881 he met with a representative of the United States Post Office, who was sent to North Carolina to inquire into the feasibility of retaining W. W. Holden as postmaster of Raleigh. Hunter turned against his former friend, and he opposed Holden's reappointment, not because of his inefficiency as postmaster, but because he, "like all other white Republican office holders, was opposed to the Negro enjoying official patronage. . . ." Holden was not reappointed, and he later stated that this was due to the fact that "I did not employ Negro clerks." In April 1881 Hunter received an appointment as a clerk in the Raleigh Post Office. He owed his position to the political influence of James H. Harris, who had also succeeded in getting John Nichols appointed as Holden's replacement. Hunter was the first black postal clerk in North Carolina, and the *Banner* in announcing his appointment thought that it would "call forth congratulations from a host of friends in all sections." When the first free delivery system was established in Raleigh in 1884, Hunter was one of the two black letter carriers, and in October of that year, Postmaster Nichols appointed him as chief of the Free Mail Delivery Service.[10]

Hunter's job in the Post Office improved his standing in the black community of Raleigh, and he was also soon recognized as being one of the black leaders in the state. For example, in September 1881 he was part of a committee appointed by Governor Jarvis to prepare suitable resolutions expressing the sentiments of North Carolina's citizens upon the death of President James A. Garfield. Included on this committee were W. W. Holden, Augustus S. Merrimon, L. L. Polk, and James H. Harris, the only other black member. During the 1880s Hunter believed that the leading blacks were not impotent, and could exert their power by respectfully protesting for the improvement of government. He felt that by focusing on specific injustices, blacks could hope to elevate the conscience of whites

## Leading Black Men

and transform public opinion in their favor. This would benefit his race because "just and equal laws were simply the index of the high and noble sentiment of the people." As a step in this direction, the leading men in 1882 issued a call for a convention to deal with the systematic exclusion of blacks from juries in many sections of the state. William P. Cannady, the white Republican editor of the *Wilmington Post*, specifically challenged Hunter and the other "leading colored men" to agitate this issue on every possible occasion, to assert themselves in the convention, and "to show the masses of their brethren in counties where they have no able leaders to look out for and defend their rights, they have friends in the State who will." Cannady, who was highly esteemed by blacks as an advocate for equality, also thought that it was time for the leading men to show the world that they could "stand up and fight for their rights as a matter of principle."[11]

However, conservative whites thought that blacks had no business protesting anything, and they certainly did not need to hold another convention. Charles H. Moore of Greensboro, who was a rising star among the leading black men, reported that a number of quasi Republicans did not think that the time had arrived when blacks could accomplish anything by holding a convention to agitate for equal rights. Moore had also interviewed a number of Democrats who thought that if blacks demanded anything in the way of equal jury privileges, it would do them more harm than good because it was sure to "stir up the bad blood of whites."[12]

Nevertheless, on 29 March 1882 delegates from fifty-three counties held a convention at Goldsboro. John C. Dancy served as chairman and, in his keynote address, he stated that the leading men had assembled because of their love for liberty and justice. They were concerned about the welfare of their race, and they especially desired that it have the right to pass judgment upon any citizen who was tried for breaking the law. According to Dancy, no man should question that right, yet "in sixty-one counties of our Old North State that right fails to be exercised." As usual, the leading men disclaimed any desire for social equality, and stated they only wanted equal civil and political rights. They unanimously adopted a resolution, offered by James H. Harris, that they would support any liberal man, Democrat or Republican, who was willing to "bury the dead past, in an earnest effort to build up our State and guarantee to all equal rights and privileges." The convention adjourned with the delegates feeling that their work would have a positive effect in providing the goals they sought. Three months later Hunter wrote that at last whites and blacks had "turned their faces towards the morning and are moving forward, and all things considered, I think we are moving on grandly."[13]

The *Wilmington Post* was also instrumental in prodding the leading blacks into accepting a more active role in matters relating to the education of their race. At their fair in 1881 Senator Zebulon B. Vance advised blacks not to place too much emphasis on education, but to learn how to work and to comply with the provisions of contracts. Strangely, blacks applauded the senator for these remarks. The *Wilmington Post* wondered why some leading black man in the audience had not challenged Vance on the spot, because his remarks were hostile to the education of his race. The paper noted, however, that it had doubts as to whether blacks would follow Vance's advice and be content with "any ordinary rough edge" of education. In 1881 the State Board of Education, which was chaired by Governor Jarvis, decided to discard those textbooks that were balanced and free of sectional bias, and to adopt a new series that were authored by southern men for use in the public schools. The *Wilmington Post* charged that both the State Board and Jarvis had either ignored the fact that there were intelligent black educators like Hunter, Charles H. Moore, Charles W. Chesnutt, John C. Dancy, James H. Harris, and others; or they did not feel inclined to seek the advice of "niggers" in matters affecting their welfare.[14]

Blacks were upset, for they had in 1881 established the North Carolina State Teachers' Association for the purpose of promoting the general welfare of their race, and it was not consulted on the textbook issue. The association was not exclusively for educators, and it admitted to membership anyone who was interested in the education of blacks. Lawyers, preachers, medical doctors, journalists, and politicians, many of whom were also affiliated with the NCIA, joined this new organization. The Teachers' Association was a group of elites who felt that teachers were "the shapers of men, women, nations, and therefore, the destinies of the world." The association did not favor racially integrated schools unless they would have integrated faculties. It did not agitate this issue, but contented itself in attending to the educational interests of black schools and securing uniformity of textbooks. Blacks protested against the decision of the State Board of Education to change textbooks on the grounds that it was an assault upon their rights and liberties. Edward R. Dudley of New Bern, speaking on behalf of the free people of North Carolina, contended that the action of the State Board was just another attempt to disfranchise blacks of the right to educate their children as they saw fit. According to Dudley, blacks objected

to the newly adopted textbooks because of their low scholarly level, prejudice, general political bias, and "misrepresentation of the men and measures to which the Negro owes his freedom, and which the country owes the
extinction of the foul blot of American Slavery." Blacks maintained that it
was all right if whites wanted to use the new textbooks, but they should not
be forced upon black children, who were already using the best books in the
country.[15]

Nevertheless, Hunter appeared satisfied with the status of black education in North Carolina. In the summer of 1882 he wrote that the best class of
whites was beginning to realize that it was in their own interest to educate
and elevate blacks so that they could have a better understanding of their
duties and responsibilities as American citizens. Educated blacks would
acquire land and property, and they would not be a burden on society.
Hunter believed that whites had also arrived at the conclusion that ignorant
black voters could never take a proper view of "men and measures best
calculated to promote good government and would always remain a dangerous element in politics." He welcomed this new interest in black education
on the part of the best whites and noted, "Our only regret is they were so
slow in coming to this wise and logical viewpoint."[16]

A myopic Hunter was shocked into reality in March 1883 when the
legislature passed the Dortch Act. This measure drew the color line in local
taxation for the support of schools by appropriating exclusively to white
education the taxes collected on the polls and property of whites, and to
black education the taxes collected from blacks. Ten voters of either race in
any school district could, by petition, call for an election to decide if the
Dortch Act would be placed in effect in their locality. If whites called for an
election, blacks could not vote, and the situation was reversed when blacks
took the initiative.

The Dortch Act was very popular among a substantial portion of the
white population. Some had always opposed any education for blacks, and
others felt that whites should not be obliged to educate blacks when they
could not adequately fund schools for their own race. Many whites contended that it was unjust to have to share their money with blacks, who, in
addition to receiving public funds, also benefited from the voluntary contributions of their northern friends. In addition, a group of whites in North
Carolina had always contended that neither race would benefit from educating blacks; it only destroyed their value as field hands and did nothing to
improve their moral standing. The Dortch Act was also an attempt to force

## Leading Black Men

blacks to obey and support the Democratic party. Aware of the emphasis that blacks placed on education, the Democrats consistently threatened to withdraw or curtail funds allocated for that purpose if they got out of line. In promoting the act, Democrats claimed they were tired of educating blacks, and then having to contend with their efforts to defeat every candidate that the party ran for office.[17]

Hunter vigorously and militantly protested against the Dortch Act, which he believed was based on that "blasting fallacy" that there must be ruling and subject classes, and the few must be educated while the masses are kept in ignorance. To him, the act conveyed the idea that blacks, who constituted one-third of the state's population, had no legitimate claims on the blessings and benefits of government, and that they should be "thankful and satisfied with any miserable pittance which in sheer charity may be doled out to them." He condemned the act as grossly unconstitutional and the most violent assault upon the genius of democratic government and public education that had ever been attempted in North Carolina. Hunter was also astonished when so many "good Democrats of whom better might have been expected" supported the measure. He called on all freedmen to use all possible means to defeat any political party that endorsed such measures such as the Dortch Act.[18]

The North Carolina State Teachers' Association at its annual meeting in 1885 announced that it considered legislation of the Dortch Act variety as acts of ingratitude on the part of whites. The association asked if whites had forgotten that it was blacks and their ancestors who for over two and a half centuries had labored to create the wealth and prosperity of the South. The association also told whites that prejudice rather than poverty motivated the passage of the Dortch Act. It offered as proof the fact that a newly arrived immigrant from Ireland, "who had never dug up a root or planted a flower in this beautiful Southland," could stroll into any town and enroll his children in a white graded school on the day of his arrival. Although the Dortch Act was eventually annulled through a series of decisions by the State Supreme Court in 1886, Hunter believed that it had reversed the progress of education, and that many years would be required to overcome its evil effects. But whites never forgot the idea behind the act and they constantly threatened blacks with its implementation.[19]

Hunter took an active role in lobbying on behalf of North Carolina's black population for the passage of the Blair Education bill, which would have provided federal matching funds to states for education. Funds would be apportioned on the basis of illiteracy rates and they were to be equitably distributed to white and black schools. The bill was approved by the United States Senate in 1884, but it was eventually killed in the House of Representatives. Hunter considered the Blair bill the most important piece of legislation that affected his race since emancipation. He felt that the bill was also of importance to the South because the bulk of the nation's illiteracy was in that section. As Hunter saw it, the South was not totally responsible for this condition. Ignorance was one of the necessary evils of a slave system that had been sanctioned and protected by the Constitution and the federal government. Holding "the North co-equal with the South in the responsibility for all the evil results of slavery," Hunter insisted that "Education was a debt that the Nation owed blacks." He believed that those who opposed the Blair bill and who sought to deprive blacks of educational opportunities were the greatest enemy of his race.[20]

Hunter "despised those mean little souls" who opposed the Blair bill simply because they thought that the South would be its greatest beneficiary, or out of a fear that southerners would not do justice to blacks in the distribution of funds. He also rejected the arguments of southerners who contended that the bill would either prove detrimental to states' rights or open the way for the extension of federal authority in the South. Hunter thought that surely there was enough wisdom in Congress to draft a bill that would not prove obnoxious to any section. He informed Senator Zebulon B. Vance of the importance of the Blair bill to blacks, because North Carolina lacked the resources to give all of its citizens a proper education. Without some educational assistance from outside the state, Hunter maintained that blacks would continue to suffer from poverty and dependence, and they would be "doomed to a slavery but a few paces removed from that which has already bathed the Nation in a flood of blood and tears." In 1885 the North Carolina State Teachers' Association adopted Hunter's resolution recommending that Congress immediately pass the Blair Education bill or a similar measure. It was also resolved to send a copy of the resolution to Senator Henry W. Blair and the members of Congress from North Carolina and to publish it in as many of the newspapers in the state as possible.[21]

Some whites in North Carolina also pleaded for the passage of the Blair bill because they thought it would ease their burden of maintaining a racially segregated school system. Reflecting this sentiment, Major Robert Bingham, the head of the Bingham School, in an address delivered before the Superintendents' Department of the National Educational Association

## Leading Black Men

in 1884 called for support of the bill. He claimed that segregated schools were essential for the maintenance of social order and that in every county in North Carolina the decision was "between two schools or no schools." Although Bingham believed that American blacks had made more progress than any other "savage race," he felt they were still inferior to whites and, because of this, segregated schools were in the best interest of the weaker race. He theorized that blacks were also aware of their own inferiority and knew that if schools were integrated, their children would never have a chance to excel and would always be uncomfortable "no matter what the teacher or other pupils think about it."[22]

Some blacks in North Carolina disagreed with Bingham, and they hoped that the Blair bill would contain provisions that would force the South to integrate its public schools. However, in an address delivered to the North Carolina State Teachers' Association in 1885, Sidney M. Finger, the superintendent of public instruction, told blacks to get that nonsense out of their heads. Advocacy of integrated schools was a sure way to get eliminated from the ranks of the leading men, and Finger claimed that anyone who favored this policy was a troublemaker who operated under the influence of northern ideas. Furthermore, such people enjoyed neither the confidence nor the respect of the community. Finger reminded the association that integrated schools would strip black teachers of their occupations and spirit of self-reliance, because only whites would be employed in racially mixed institutions. Therefore, he was sure that the most intelligent black teachers would agree with him that segregation was the best policy. Finger also believed that blacks were not sufficiently advanced to take complete control of the education of their race. Close and continuous white supervision was an absolute necessity to keep it from retrogressing. Black teachers did, however, have a grave responsibility to eliminate what Finger believed were the three great deficiencies of their people: improvidence, an aversion to work, and a propensity to immorality. The lack of morals was particularly serious, for it was endemic to American blacks whose ancestors in Africa lived in the worst state of barbarism. As a consequence, Finger maintained that blacks in America had inherited tendencies of meanness and immorality, and in many instances their moral development lagged behind their intellectual advancement.[23]

Most black educators, anticipating Finger's message, had already accepted segregated schools as an accomplished fact. They sought to improve their educational opportunities within the context of the separate-but-equal concept. Hunter believed that schools would never be equal unless blacks pushed the issue, and this was especially true of higher education. Ever since their convention in 1877 blacks had asked the state for an institution comparable to the one at Chapel Hill for whites. In 1885 Hunter published an article concerning the inequity in the state-supported system of higher education, noting that North Carolina was spending $70,000 to support its university at Chapel Hill and only $4,000 to maintain five normal schools for blacks. Though not challenging the blacks' exclusion from that white university, he did think it necessary for the state to live up to its constitutional obligation to provide a school which could be "to the colored people what Chapel Hill is to the whites." Hunter's article was possibly the strongest argument made by blacks for a state-supported college between the years 1877 and 1891.[24]

At the annual meeting of the North Carolina State Teachers' Association in 1886 there was some smoldering sentiment for the integration of the University of North Carolina. However, this was soon squashed, and the members agreed that segregated schools were a part of the "political organisms of the South." The association called upon the state to provide adequate facilities for the education of its black youth and their teachers. Recognizing that the normal schools for blacks did not justify the "educational boast of the State," the association appointed a committee to memorialize the legislature for the establishment of a school that would be "a reasonable offset" for the University of North Carolina.[25]

Hunter, the recording secretary of the Association, was selected by J. C. Price to prepare the memorial to the legislature. Referring to this, Simon G. Atkins, the organization's corresponding secretary, wrote Hunter: ". . . you know just how it should be done. . . . Make it strong and pointed." If the legislature ultimately received this memorial, it made no favorable response. In 1887 the black senator from Halifax County, Henry Eppes, presented a bill to the legislature that would have provided for a state-supported normal and collegiate institute for blacks. Speaking on behalf of this measure, Eppes reassured his fellow solons that the black of intelligence and character "spurns knocking at the door of any college or university where he is not wanted and opposes mixed schools and Negro supremacy." He only wanted equal privileges and a just educational system. Eppes said he knew there were many whites, including Republicans, who sneered at any form of enlightenment for blacks, and he warned that if his bill were rejected, and if the legislature failed to strengthen the existing normal schools for blacks, "we will come again bye and bye." Eppes's remarks did not impress his colleagues, who voted his bill down by a count of thirty-seven to one.[26]

The commitment of whites to the goal of keeping blacks in a separate and inferior position in society steadily increased during the decade of the 1880s. Yet when blacks established their own separate organizations and institutions they were frequently ridiculed, condemned, and viewed with suspicion. At their fair in 1883 blacks were told by the Honorable Ralph P. Buxton, a white Republican of Fayetteville, not to hold conventions or form separate political organizations exclusively for men of their race. Furthermore, they should by no means send black delegations to Washington on political errands, because they were usually regarded by whites as evidence of "sinister plots hatched by designing politicians who had political axes to grind." Buxton predicted that if blacks continued in their separate way they would be regarded with jealousy and distrust by whites of both political parties, and this would in time provoke "racial combinations in opposition."[27]

At the time of Buxton's warnings, a racial combination against blacks already existed in the form of the Democratic party of North Carolina. Politics was the one obstacle that prevented that party from having total control over the black population of the state. Democrats lamented the fact that blacks were perfectly willing to seek the advice and assistance of southern whites in everything except politics. While giving blacks no official standing or recognition within their party, the Democrats in the 1880s made a few feeble attempts to attract their votes. Most blacks, however, were not persuaded by these professions of friendship, and by 1884 most Democrats probably agreed with William H. Kitchen, who stated he was convinced that "appeals for the negro vote were worse than useless" and that he would make no further attempts in this direction.[28]

Thus Democrats continued in the 1880s to content themselves with winning elections through extralegal means and exploiting the issue of race. Referring to the politics of that era, Daniel L. Russell stated: "By and large Democrats relied mainly on terrorism and made race antipathies so hot that no white man dared to vote the Republican ticket unless he had some of the qualities of a hero."[29] During the campaign of 1884 Democrats exaggerated the themes of social equality, black domination, and white supremacy. Blacks had become accustomed to the seasonal tirades of degradation heaped upon them during political contests, but the campaign rhetoric of 1884, particularly virulent, was designed to conjure up the worst fears of whites.

Blacks favoring equal political and civil rights were depicted as a group of ingrates, who, instead of being satisfied with the blessings they already received from the state, would not rest until they had absolute political power in North Carolina. Democrats interpreted civil equality to mean mixed schools with black teachers controlling white children, and marriages between black men and white women. Moreover, political equality would surely lead to social equality, as witnessed by the example of Frederick Douglass. He was the leading advocate of civil rights, held a high government post, and was married to a white woman. If whites wanted to weaken the superiority of their race, Democrats claimed they could do this by simply voting a Republican ticket "so that miscegenation may come and degrade proud North Carolina to the level of barbarous Africa."[30]

In an attempt to subordinate class to race and to isolate blacks from any potential white supporters, some Democrats alleged that blacks were bent upon satisifying their insatiable desire for social equality. When this happened, poor whites would be the greatest sufferers because the best whites had enough money to erect walls between themselves and the black masses. The best whites were willing, however, to do their duty and help protect the less fortunate of their race against the menace of social equality. "We white men of one blood must stand together," cried the *Raleigh Register*, and the paper reminded its readers that any white man who treated a black as his equal was bound to lose the respect of the white community. Not only this, but the *Register* was sure that no self-respecting black would have any regard for a white man who treated him as an equal.[31]

The Democrats' strategy worked, and they succeeded in electing both their state and national tickets. Following the election of Grover Cleveland, Hunter wrote that the majority of blacks in North Carolina viewed the event as the "dawn of an evil day." He recognized the fact that blacks in the state had been living under Democratic rule since 1876, and he thought they had made substantial progress in the acquisition of education, social culture, and material wealth. They had also cultivated friendly relations with whites and had hopes of further improving themselves. But Hunter also thought that North Carolina blacks had enjoyed the psychological benefit of hope and security from the knowledge that the national government rested in the hands of the Republican party. The specter of a Democrat in the White House for the first time since the Civil War made blacks apprehensive.

Hunter wrote, "Just what turn sentiment with reference to the race question will take under the new circumstances, remains to be seen."[32]

Hunter soon found out that the Democrats did not have any use for his services in the Raleigh Post Office, and he lost his job after Cleveland took office. He was both surprised and disappointed, for he thought his position was safe because he had "secured the hearty support and thorough confidence of the people of all parties, both colors and both sexes." Once again, Hunter considered the possibility of migrating to the North, and in April 1885 he inquired into the prospects of finding employment in Ohio. He had also prepared himself for a government job in Washington. Hunter was one of the first persons in the nation to take a Civil Service examination. In the summer of 1884 he received notification that he had passed the test for Special Examiner in the Pension Office and had been placed on the register of those eligible for that position.[33]

Hunter was also offered a position in the Bureau of Engraving and Printing, which had been procured for him by General William Ruffin Cox. A Democrat and resident of Wake County, Cox represented North Carolina's Fourth Congressional District in Congress. He had formerly owned Hunter's cousin, Rufus Davis, who had accompanied Cox throughout the Civil War. According to Hunter, Cox brought his appointment to Raleigh and offered it to him. But he could not accept the "bestowal of this touching and beautiful sentiment" because of a prior commitment to the A. S. Barnes Publishing Company of New York. Hunter joined the company in 1885 and for several years he worked as a traveling agent. He was the only black employed in this capacity, and his work consisted primarily of selling books to black educational institutions. Much of his sales work was done on a part-time basis or during the intervals when school was not in session. In 1885 Hunter also reentered the teaching profession and reluctantly accepted a position as superintendent of the two black schools in Goldsboro. Hunter discovered upon his arrival in the city that the black school system had "broken down." It was without funds and the schools' doors were closed. According to Hunter, this state of affairs was brought about under the administration of a School Committee composed entirely of blacks. Hunter immediately went to the office of Julius A. Bonitz, the chairman of the white School Committee, and announced that his acceptance of the superintendency was contingent upon the willingness of the white gentlemen of the community to assist him in his work. Bonitz agreed, and Hunter later received similar commitments from the other members of the white School

Committee. During his conversation with Bonitz, Hunter also stated that he had no confidence in the administrative ability of the black School Committee, and that the only hope for bringing the black schools up to acceptable standards rested with the white people of Goldsboro. Hunter later claimed that this statement was not intended to cast disparagement upon his race, and that his ultimate objective was to achieve an integrated School Committee where one or two blacks could be trained by whites in the management of schools.[34]

Hunter was surprised at the positive response of the white citizens of Goldsboro to his suggestions. He persuaded the white School Committee to share its funds so that blacks could reopen their schools. With the support of whites, Hunter was instrumental in helping to establish a normal school that offered a complete program of classical education. He wrote, "I was not long there ere I found in the good white citizens of the place the chief support of the plans which were inaugurated for the good of the colored." He wished blacks would take the same interest in their own welfare as whites did. Whites liked Hunter's style and within a short time they placed him in the forefront of the leading black men of the community. The *Goldsboro Argus* announced there was "no more refined, educated, and courteous colored man in the State" than Hunter, who would "give a character to the schools which can but be beneficial to the colored people of the State." The *Argus* urged its white readers to support Hunter's educational work, secure in the knowledge that their aid would be faithfully applied and put to good use. Hunter was pleased to count among his many white friends in Goldsboro, Charles Brantly Aycock, Bonitz's successor as chairman of the white School Committee. He claimed that Aycock enthusiastically supported him in all of his efforts to uplift the blacks of Goldsboro. Furthermore, Aycock believed that Hunter had "done more to unite and promote kindly relations between the races than anything that had ever happened" in Goldsboro.[35]

Hunter's experiences in Goldsboro convinced him that there were thousands of good white men in North Carolina who were determined to strengthen the confidence between the races in every honorable way. Even though these men were for the most part Democrats, they did not let their party feelings come between them and the welfare of the state. Hunter was greatly disturbed, however, by the existence of unscrupulous politicians in North Carolina who were intent upon stirring up racial conflict "to the end that it may furnish an excuse for the repetition of the terrible tragedies of other days." If the state could only rid itself of these unprincipled men, "a few years would so strengthen the bonds of mutual good will among all our people as to defy all efforts to the contrary." Hunter called for good men, Democrats or Republicans, to come forth and take control of the affairs of government. "There should be reform, reform, reform," he wrote, until politics can be made to subserve the ends of general prosperity.[36]

Unfortunately for Hunter a segment of the black community did not have the same regard for him that the best whites had. For one thing, residents of long standing probably blamed him for the loss of control over their schools. The white School Committee, just as Hunter had suggested, eventually assumed the responsibility for administering black schools. Hunter was also active in the local temperance movement, and he edited and published a school newspaper, the *Appeal*, which made moral pronouncements on a variety of subjects in ways that were frequently unfavorable to blacks. In October 1887 Hunter was warned by a friend that some of the members of the community were prejudiced against him. By the end of the year his employment in Goldsboro had been terminated and he was without a job. Deeply hurt, Hunter regretted that the blacks of Goldsboro did not appreciate his many efforts toward their elevation. Once again he thought about leaving North Carolina.

His brother, Osborne, and his favorite nephew, Ed, had both migrated to Washington, and they urged Hunter to join them. Ed wrote that he could see no reason why Hunter should continue to sacrifice his own welfare for that of his race. In similar advice, Osborne told Hunter, "This business of destroying yourself in the interest of others and neglecting your own is suicidal," and he had better start looking out for himself. Hunter did not follow their advice, and decided to stay in North Carolina in the hopes of a brighter future. In 1888 Hunter was hired as a teacher in Durham, and he was also employed by Julian S. Carr to conduct a night school for his black factory workers. No doubt he was aided in obtaining the latter position by his public pronouncements in praise of Carr. In 1887 Hunter had proclaimed that Carr was the man best qualified for governor, and had urged the Democratic party to nominate him for that office. He estimated that Carr could "carry 30,000 more votes than any white man in the State," and that many intelligent blacks would second his nomination with their votes.[37]

Hunter had arrived at the conclusion that the best thing blacks could do to improve politics in North Carolina was to support good white men for office. Indeed, he contended that blacks in general had to give up the idea that they could hold public office because it was a right of citizenship. To Hunter, this was one of the bad lessons that blacks had learned during Reconstruction. Moreover, he now claimed that the political education that his race received during this era had sown the seeds of corruption among black politicians. However, blacks were not totally responsible for this state of affairs. The better-educated class of whites in the South refused to have any political relationships with blacks, and left the field wide open for bad white men who came among the freedmen with professions of friendship. According to Hunter, blacks received their political training and first experienced the duties of public office under the tutelage of inferior whites, and they "learned from them most aptly the art of subordinating every consideration to self and pelf."[38]

These corrupt and unprincipled black politicians did not fade away with Reconstruction, and Hunter maintained that the "pestiferous remains" of that era were still active. They had become a commodity for sale in the political market, and would gladly sell themselves to the highest bidder for the price demanded, which was "usually small." He believed that this prostitution of leadership had extended to the rank and file of black voters, and had done infinite harm to their race by creating the impression that politics was a game that every man played for himself. Because of this, blacks had no confidence in their leaders, and they no longer "rallied as one man at the sound of their bugle." Hunter stressed the need for black leaders who could guide and shape the destiny of their race, but he also felt that they had to be honest, intelligent, patriotic, and principled men who could not be bought or sold.[39]

Hunter's assessment of black political leadership appeared in an article entitled "Some of the Evils of Reconstruction," in the African Methodist Episcopal Church's *Quarterly Review* of January 1888. With the caveat that his article should not be taken as a wholesale and indiscriminate condemnation of all black leaders, Hunter also admitted that his race both in the past and in the present had produced many able leaders of whom all could feel justly proud. His aim was to stimulate blacks to support good men, and to "frown down" the self-seeker. "We should set our seal against incompetency, we should require strict moral accountability," he wrote. Hunter later named his brother, Osborne, Richard T. Greener, J. C. Price, T. McCants Stewart, T. Thomas Fortune, John C. Dancy, and Archibald and Francis

Grimké as models of the good young men who were dedicated to the elevation of their race.[40]

Hunter's article stirred up quite a controversy within the American black community. The editor of the *Detroit Plaindealer* thought that "Mr. Hunter's reasonings and convictions are the most clear and concise we have seen" and that many of the evils of which he spoke still existed, to the great injury of the black race. The *Plaindealer* recommended that the article be placed in the hands of every honest Afro-American in order to awaken them from the lethargy that had allowed "the scum of the race to force itself to the front; and there with poisonous fangs they have polluted public sentiment until in the eyes of many, the whole race is made to appear standing on the political auction block." On the other hand, the *New York Freeman* found Hunter's statements "rather severe" in their treatment of black politicians and voters, and the *Cleveland Gazette* noted it had stirred up many of the "old reconstructionists."[41]

The harshest criticism came from Bishop Henry M. Turner, who accused Hunter of defaming "a host of the grandest black men that ever figured in the Nation," and of grossly underrating those whom he should venerate. In reply, Hunter stated that he expected some criticism when he released his article for publication, and that Turner had obviously misread him. He did not intend to slander the "brave old heroes, who in the white heat of those terrible days of Reconstruction and before" devoted themselves to the cause of justice, humanity, and right. His target was the "fungus growth of Reconstruction," those bad men who had injured the prospects of their race, and who had so contaminated politics that the best men had "retired in disgust leaving the field open to men of insatiable rapacity." If Turner was offended by his article, Hunter told him that he could only conclude that his "arrow, sent without particular aim, did not fail to pierce at least one of the heavy helmeted 'Evils of Reconstruction.' "[42]

Hunter predicted in his article that if blacks did not retire from politics, they would provoke a response from whites similar to that of Reconstruction days. This was one of his more accurate predictions. During the political campaign of 1888 blacks in North Carolina were treated to an orgy of degradation the likes of which had not been seen since Reconstruction. Once again the most important issue between the two political parties was race. Democrats and white Republicans waged a contest around the twin themes of social equality and black domination. Republicans alleged that it was the Democrats who actually favored black rule in North Carolina. Democrats had gerrymandered the Second Congressional District into existence, thereby ensuring the continued election of a black to Congress, they had helped elect a black mayor in Tarboro, and Democratic governors had appointed black justices of the peace. White Republicans also claimed that in some sections of the state, Democrats were standing "cheek by jowl with the Negroes." This was particularly true in Craven County where a fusion of blacks and Democrats had taken control. Republicans reasoned that if the blacks of Craven County were good enough for Democrats to coalesce with, the principle must hold true for the entire state.[43]

Democrats were also indicted for doing more to break down the color line in North Carolina than Republicans ever had done. They were guilty of social equality and had to stand on their record. Republicans asserted that for years Democratic governors and lesser officials had been consorting with blacks. Jarvis spoke at black gatherings, and he even went so far as to assist J. C. Price in opening the Prohibition Ball in Raleigh in 1881. What was worse was the fact that Richard H. Battle, a former chairman of the Democratic party of North Carolina, and ex-Congressman William R. Cox had actually eaten with blacks at a social gathering held by Bishop Theodore Lyman of the Protestant Episcopal Church. Furthermore, white Republicans claimed that the Democrats of North Carolina by virtue of their endorsement of Grover Cleveland, gave their tacit approval to social equality, because he was as much of a "Negrophile" as Charles Sumner or Thaddeus Stevens. Cleveland had given government offices in North Carolina to blacks in preference to whites, placed black men in positions of authority over white women, favored mixed schools, and also had eaten with blacks. If additional proof of the president's advocacy of social equality were needed, white Republicans pointed out that Mrs. Cleveland had gone to the extreme of sending bouquets of flowers to sick blacks.[44]

The Democrats made no concerted attempt to deny these charges. Rather, they retorted by stressing the historical connection between blacks and the Republican party in North Carolina. Even though blacks tended to remain in the background in state politics, Democrats claimed that they were the leaders in district and county affairs. It was also an undisputed fact that a white Republican could never get elected to state office without black votes, hence his first loyalty would be to the people who elected him. Democrats reminded whites that if Republicans gained control of North Carolina, there was sure to be a repeat of the terrible days of Reconstruction, because there were not enough white Republicans to fill all the offices in the state and blacks would inevitably be placed in public positions. Josephus Daniels, the editor of the *State Chronicle*, warned whites not to forget that blacks were incompetent and totally unfit to rule, and that "whenever and wherever they were in power, corruption and ruin naturally followed."[45]

The election of 1888 was not without its violent aspects, and immediately after the voting was over there were fears of a race war in Durham. On election day a number of blacks in Durham had been challenged and declared ineligible to vote by Democratic election officials, and about 100 others with Republican ballots in their hands were kept waiting until after the polls had closed. As a result the Democrats carried the election by a slim margin of fifty-two votes, and thereby redeemed Durham County from Republican rule. This successful white supremacy campaign was directed by Caleb B. Green, the chairman of the Durham County Democratic Executive Committee. After the election Green's house mysteriously went up in smoke, and it was immediately charged that this was the work of dissatisfied black leaders and a few "miserable white scoundrels who urged them on." Simultaneously, rumors spread throughout the town alleging that blacks were buying weapons and dynamite, conspiring against the lives of Democratic voting registrars, and planning to burn the town. The white citizens of Durham took immediate action; detachments of military troops were activated, special police sworn in, homes and factories placed under guard, black leaders kept under strict surveillance, and people walked the streets under arms. In the midst of this crisis, Josephus Daniels recommended that the "hellish scoundrels who burned Mr. Green's house and their instigators ought to be hung if found."[46]

Overt hostilities were averted when Eldridge J. Jordan was apprehended and charged with the responsibility for the whole affair. A native of Freeport, Maine, and a white Republican, Jordan had been in Durham for about three years, and in 1888 he was the Republican candidate for constable. The Democrats claimed that ever since his arrival in Durham, Jordan had proved himself to be a man of bad character. An anarchist and a common nuisance, he had endeared himself to the black community by advocating social equality. It was alleged that he had even told blacks, "After the election we negroes will control this county." There was no doubt in the minds of conservative whites that Jordan had incited blacks to an incendiary course, and that his continued presence in Durham would surely result in bloodshed. The excitement abated when Jordan and his family were immediately banished from the town.[47]

Shortly after the campaign of 1888 a correspondent of the *New York World* asked Hunter to give his opinion on the use of intimidation as a means of controlling the black vote in the recent election. In the published account of this interview, Hunter denied any knowledge of the use of any such tactics. Immediately accused by Republicans of giving misleading statements as to the true condition of blacks in North Carolina, he was forced to publish a letter of explanation in the *Raleigh Signal*. Hunter contended that the correspondent of the *New York World* had so abridged his remarks that they could be easily misinterpreted. What he really meant was that he had no personal knowledge of any instances wherein the votes of blacks were controlled through a fear of harm to their persons, property, or fortunes. Hunter got off the hook by admitting that the votes of black citizens were systematically suppressed in North Carolina, and that this fact rather than intimidation reduced their effectivess.[48]

In the wake of the election of 1888 there were increased calls for disfranchisement. Democrats and Republicans alike renewed their contention that the chief prerequisite for an effective two-party system was the elimination of the black vote. Republicans claimed that the presence of blacks within their ranks impeded the progress of the party and kept away many potential white adherents. Others noted that the party did not really benefit from the black vote because the Democrats frequently resorted to corrupt means and stole elections in order to get into office. To purify elections these Republicans recommended that Congress either pass election laws to protect the ballot box and prevent corruption, or colonize black men. In the summer of 1888 Daniel L. Russell correctly stated that North Carolina was as much a part of the Solid South as any other southern state, and that it was thoroughly committed to "vitiating the war amendments which the South declared unconstitutional." The following year the *Raleigh Signal* announced that the Democrats had determined that "the Negro must be disfranchised as he is in the other States south of North Carolina." In 1889 Democrats moved toward this goal when the legislature passed an election law that, among other things, required voter registrants to give the date and place of their birth, their last voting precinct, and their correct residence. Voter registrars constituted the sole authority in determining the veracity of each applicant's information. A correspondent to the *Independent* (New York), in all probability Hunter, commented that the new election law was only a modification of the "South Carolina iniquity," with no purpose other than to suppress the black vote. He asked, "How many Negroes are there in North Carolina who can give date and place of birth?"[49]

The election law of 1889 effectively reduced the Republican vote. A number of blacks feared that the next move of the Democrats would be an attempt to disfranchise them through an educational qualification for voting, and by 1889 it was reported that blacks were preparing for this eventuality. They had ordered thousands of copies of Webster's *Spelling Book*, and planned to teach all voters how to read and write before the next election. Possibly the only thing that prevented the Democrats from the outright disfranchisement of blacks in 1889 was a fear of intervention by the federal government to ensure the legality of elections. Nevertheless, disfranchisement sentiment had taken deep root in the state, and during the 1880s the Democrats had conducted a rehearsal for the white-supremacy campaign of the 1890s.[50]

In May 1889 Governor Daniel G. Fowle announced that the race problem in North Carolina had been settled peacefully on the basis of white supremacy. There was no doubt in his mind that blacks were inferior to whites because of "the indomitable spirit, the tenacious self-reliance, the assertive power of strong manhood and conquering impulse implanted in the minds of Anglo-Saxons. . . ." Hence it was only natural that whites should occupy a position of dominance over blacks, and that socially and politically the two races would always be separate and distinct. Fowle was convinced that the "meek and lowly spirit of the Negro was not the most useful in the battle for life in North Carolina," and this could be seen by the fact that most were shiftless, indolent, and languished in poverty. In spite of this, the governor claimed that blacks were happy; they worked for fifty cents a day, did not complain about the laws or the administration of justice, and they were "mostly convinced that their interests are identical with those of whites." A considerable number of blacks were not happy in North Carolina, and although Governor Fowle maintained that the emigration movement was a failure because blacks were too poor to move, they had been leaving the state at an accelerated pace. In the fifteen months prior to March 1890, it was estimated that as many as 50,000 blacks had migrated from North Carolina.[51]

A month before Fowle made his statement on race relations, a group of leading black men held a convention in Raleigh to plan for the establishment of an agricultural colony in Arkansas. A circular published in advance of the meeting stated the reasons why these men wanted to get out of the state. They had labored for, and borne the abuse and ridicule of, whites for a quarter century, and their only reward was constant reminders that they were a disgrace to the country. It was clear that whites did not want them to remain in North Carolina as evidenced by the Dortch Act, the election law of 1889, and the starvation wages paid to black workers. The potential migrants stated they had had enough of North Carolina, and "as Israel under Moses we will start somewhere if we perish in the wilderness." The rhetoric and resolutions of the convention, filled with notes of dissatisfaction, caused the *Raleigh News and Observer* to comment that it would not be such a bad idea if the delegates did emigrate "to the greatest distance possible."[52]

In an attempt to ascertain how whites perceived the emigration of blacks from North Carolina, the *State Chronicle* asked a number of prominent citizens to respond to a series of questions on this subject. This survey, approximating a modern public-opinion poll, gives significant indications of what whites thought about blacks and how well they knew blacks. Captain Sydenham B. Alexander, the first president of the North Carolina Farmers' Alliance, thought that since the majority of blacks were familiar with cotton culture, they were moving to the Gulf States simply because that region was the most favorable for the production of that crop. The speaker of the North Carolina House of Representatives, Augustus Leazar, viewed the migration as a manifestation of the blacks' instinct to drift toward the semitropics of the South. He believed the migration would be a distinct advantage to North Carolina because it would afford more living space for the "superior race, the white man." The opinion of Dr. J. E. Person of Wayne County was that the migration was beneficial, and he also thought that if blacks were colonized or exported abroad, the whole nation would be more peaceful and prosperous. The secretary of the North Carolina Farmers' Alliance, Eugene E. Beddingfield, asserted that blacks were not "exodusting" far enough by going from one southern state to another. He would have been glad to see labor agents remove every single one if suitable white replacements could be found. However, if their removal was to cause an influx of "anarchists, socialists, and the scum of Castle Garden," Beddingfield stated he would prefer to keep blacks in spite of their superstitions and vices. The representative to the General Assembly from Carteret County, A. H. Chadwick, agreed that the black presence in North Carolina had kept out anarchists and other disorderly elements, but he too would have been glad to see most blacks leave on a voluntary basis. He would provide equal protection under the laws for those who remained, but they had to realize that they were inferior to the white man, and that they would always be ruled by him. The respondent from Warren County, B. M. Collins, acknowledged that blacks were the best available source of cheap labor and that he had always had kind feelings for their race, especially the older generation. However, he felt that blacks had to be "thinned out" because race relations were not getting any better. Colonel Joseph B. Stickney likewise wanted a reduction in the number of blacks and, when this happened, the rest would "readily fall into their true position—that of subserviency to that more intellectual race which is better adapted to the governing and directing."[53]

Thoughtful individuals wondered how some whites could claim that they were the best friends of blacks and at the same time wish them out of the state, or expect them to remain at home in an inferior and degraded condition. Blacks also wondered why the Democrats continuously waged a propaganda war against them, which seemed to intensify during election years. At such times the Democratic press delighted in magnifying the weaknesses and vices of blacks, to the neglect of their virtues and progress. A correspondent to the *Raleigh Signal* asked in 1889, "Is this friendship? Is this honest? Is that not hypocritical?" He wondered if it were not the intention of whites to crush totally the black race, which was damned if it stayed in North Carolina and damned if it left. An editorial comment agreed that the Democratic press constantly sneered at blacks, and held them up "as the most contemptible and disgusting creatures to be spit upon at will as occasion or spite may require." It did not matter if these verbal assaults on blacks were lies, distortions, or part of political strategies, because once they were uttered or printed, they attained a certain degree of psychological reality. They also served to reinforce certain basic beliefs held by whites regarding their own superiority, and prompted them to push blacks further down the scale of humanity. In 1887 Hunter wrote, "It is too often the case that our white friends in their sweeping denunciation of the senseless bravado and lawlessness of some colored people do not conceive of the hurt they are doing to a vast majority of the race."[54]

The whites' verbal abuse also created a heightened sense of their own inferiority among the leading blacks, and during the 1880s they constantly examined their relative position in society. Some thought that whites maligned them because they did not know blacks, or they were misinformed as

## Leading Black Men

to the true condition of their race. Many felt that if whites would only open their eyes and see their progress, they would cease to class them with the despised people who had never enjoyed the advantages of civilization. In 1889 Hunter suggested to the superintendent of the United States Census that his next report include several categories showing the accumulated wealth of blacks. He thought this would encourage his race to even greater achievements and help to reduce race prejudice. If the wealth of blacks were made public, Hunter felt that their enemies would not be able to depict them as drones, parasites, and pests to the industrial, political, and social systems. He also thought that this stereotype was all that many whites needed to justify the grossest injustices and the many wrongs heaped upon his race.[55]

Whereas Hunter stressed the acquisition of wealth as a means of improving race relations, his brother, Osborne, believed that blacks should improve their material status as a matter of economic self-interest. Osborne perceived that, in the future, economics rather than race would be the chief determinant of one's social standing, and he advised blacks to forget about laying up treasures in Heaven to the detriment of their welfare on earth. "Take all the world, but give me Jesus, has been the theme of the average colored American," he wrote in 1885. He thought that blacks had sung this song for so long that white Americans had taken them at their word, and accepted the proposition in good faith. They gladly gave blacks a monopoly in celestial things, while they set about acquiring a monopoly of this world's goods for themselves. According to Osborne, whites had done a pretty good job, considering their prodigious accumulation of wealth in the nineteenth century. He urged his race to do likewise: "Upon a proper disposition of this world's goods depends, in no slight degree, our future happiness."[56]

The leading black men at the end of the 1800s were in a quandary. They had tried to follow the advice of whites, and yet it seemed that both race relations and their status were not improving. In January 1889 the *Progressive Educator*, the official publication of the North Carolina Teachers' Association, which was edited by Hunter and Simon G. Atkins, announced a series of articles on the subject of "What Shall the Negro Do?" The editors noted that this question had reached a degree of urgency unequaled in the history of blacks as freedmen. A quarter century had elapsed since emancipation, but there was still "a great and powerful opposition" to their citizenship and equality. It is not known if any native whites responded to the

## Leading Black Men

query of the *Progressive Educator*, but Henry W. Blair of New Hampshire advised blacks to remain in North Carolina where they had plenty of room, good land, and a congenial climate. The state had been their home for generations and the senator believed that blacks could better conquer where they were. "In due time," he wrote, "you will get all your rights or your children will—sooner there than elsewhere." He told blacks to remain passive a little while longer. This was certainly no comfort to those who wanted immediate relief from oppression.[57]

Hunter seemed to think that the condition of blacks and his own fortune would improve with the advent of a Republican national administration. On the eve of Benjamin Harrison's inauguration, he saw an opportunity to recover his former position in the Raleigh Post Office. John Nichols, the Republican congressman from Hunter's district, advised him to wait and see who the postmaster of Raleigh would be, and then "Have your friends see him." Nichols also promised a personal recommendation for the job. Hunter then proceeded to collect endorsements to support his application for reinstatement. The A. S. Barnes Publishing Company "heartily endorsed" his application in the belief that Hunter was "an able and conscientious man of superior education" who was well qualified to perform the requirements of the job in an efficient manner. William Dallas Haywood of Raleigh noted in his letter of endorsement that "Hunter was brought up in my family," and that he was intelligent and well educated. In Haywood's opinion Hunter would make a good official if he got his appointment. Hunter also received a promise of assistance in obtaining the job from his friend Henry P. Cheatham, the newly elected black congressman from the Second Congressional District. This points out another characteristic of Hunter. He was generally prone to condemn black politicians, but he never missed an opporunity to avail himself of any services that they could render.[58]

When Hunter formally applied for reinstatement as chief carrier in the Raleigh Post Office, he got a refresher course in what it was like to be a black man in North Carolina. Colonel H. W. Shaffer, the Raleigh postmaster, informed him that although there were no other applicants, and there were no questions as to his fitness or qualifications, he could not recommend his appointment. Hunter then appealed directly to the postmaster general of the United States, and told him that his appointment was rejected *"for the sole reason that I am a colored man."* Hunter alleged that Shaffer did not want to have a black occupying a position superior to that of white mail carriers, nor one that involved official relations with white citizens. To make matters worse, Shaffer had decided to retain the services of the incumbent, who was not only a Democrat, but the same man who had replaced Hunter in 1885. As a "faithful, earnest, and loyal" Republican, Hunter reminded the postmaster general that Shaffer's attitude was repugnant to the party's principles and to all ideas of just government and equal citizenship. Futhermore, Hunter contended that in fighting Shaffer's decision, he was doing so "in behalf of the colored citizens of North Carolina whose cause this is." Appealing to the postmaster general's high sense of justice, he asked him to apply such remedies as were in his power.[59]

It is not known whether John Wanamaker, the postmaster general, ever received Hunter's letter, but Hunter did not recover his old job at the Raleigh Post Office. Shocked into reality, in November 1889 Hunter sorrowfully admitted that race relations in North Carolina were not improving, and that there was more bitterness between the races than at any time since the Ku Klux Klan era. This racial animosity was no longer the sole prerogative of the Democrats, because the Republicans had also commenced a "bitter proscription of Negro citizens." In his opinion blacks could not endure this severe and unbearable oppression, any more than a "magazine could stand the application of a torch . . . and they were determined under God to find relief." But Hunter was neither discouraged nor hopeless, and he suggested, "This may be the dark hour just before the break of day." This anodyne assessment of race relations in North Carolina appeared in the *Independent* (New York). Hunter asked the editor to "please guard my name against publicity." An editorial postscript mentioned that the writer of the article was engaged in educational work, and that he was fully aware of the consequences of such utterances because, "Free speech is no more possible for colored people in the South than a free ballot."[60]

On the same day that the article appeared in print, Hunter penned a letter to Governor Fowle, and its contents reveal the thoughts of an anxious, confused, and frustrated man. He asked for the governor's assistance in establishing a state-supported college for blacks with free scholarships for students, similar to those granted at the Agricultural and Mechanical College in Raleigh. Hunter also recommended that the complete management and direction of the institution be placed totally in the hands of whites. Although he did not intend to degrade the ability of his race, it was an established fact that blacks needed "the intelligent and sympathetic direction of the white race and the sooner we see this and act upon it the better for

## Leading Black Men

us—the better for all." He also offered for Fowle's consideration a program for race relations that would unite the better element of the people in a grand effort to promote the peace and prosperity of North Carolina. Hunter's proposal was simple: whites by virtue of their superior ability, intelligence, and experience would govern in a sympathetic and just way, and blacks would assume a position of subordination and docility. Such an ingratiating and accommodationist attitude on the part of Hunter merely served to reinforce Fowle's earlier remarks on white supremacy and black inferiority. It also proved that Fowle was right in his contention, "I insult a white man and he knocks me down. A similar insult offered to a colored man would be forgiven in the course of a few days."[61]

CHAPTER

# A Race Out of Place

The bright new day that Hunter predicted for his race arrived in North Carolina in the 1890s, but its stay was transient and by the end of the century blacks found themselves in the midst of the darkest of nights. Despite the severe national economic depression, the decade witnessed great progress by blacks, and it was truly their Progressive era. During this time blacks claimed that they were advancing educationally and materially at a faster rate than the masses of whites. There was extensive improvement in education, and in 1891 the long-hoped-for state-supported college for blacks came into existence. This plus the four state-supported normal schools and a number of colleges and universities, one of which contained law, medical, and dental schools, gave North Carolina the reputation of being an educational mecca. Blacks also acquired property at an accelerated pace, and their community intensified efforts to develop its economic base. There was the emergence of black-owned financial institutions, a textile mill owned and operated exclusively by blacks, and the foundations were laid for North Carolina Mutual Insurance Company which eventually became the largest and wealthiest black business in America.

In terms of personalities, North Carolina blacks claimed among the residents or natives of the state men who were leaders of national stature. James Walker Hood was the senior bishop of the African Methodist Episcopal Zion Church, and Bishop C. C. Petty presided over a district that included the states of Delaware, Maryland, Pennsylvania, Kentucky, and Ohio, and the District of Columbia. Until his death in 1892 the Reverend Joseph C. Price was a serious contender for the position later occupied by Booker T. Washington as the designated leader of the black race. North

Carolina blacks also boasted of the fact that they had the only black colonel in the United States Army during the Spanish-American War. The lone black member of Congress, who also represented the nation's blacks in that body, came fom North Carolina, as did the recorder of deeds for the District of Columbia. Within the state, the collector of customs for the port of Wilmington was a black man, and members of his race occupied a number of political offices at the state and local levels. Returning to North Carolina after an absence of several years, William V. Turner wrote in 1891 that he was delighted by the visible indications of progress. He was proud to see that those who in the past were hewers of wood and drawers of water were among the successful contenders for distinction, and black doctors, lawyers, and teachers were as efficient as any in the state. Hunter was cited as an example of the progressive black educators who were zealously and intelligently advancing the intellectual development of their race.[1]

Some blacks even let whites know that they were not particularly concerned about associating with them. There was an expanding number of men and women of culture, wealth, and mental and moral refinement within their own race. Indeed, they claimed that they preferred the company of their own learned ministers, capable lawyers, skilled physicians, trained educators, versatile and energetic journalists, and accomplished musicians.[2] The black community in North Carolina was conscious of its achievements, optimistic about the future, and for a while it enjoyed a greater sense of security than ever before. However, much of this dynamic and optimistic spirit rested on shaky ground: political power. Although Hunter and others would later try to disclaim this fact, the black community in the state thrived best when its political power was the greatest. During the 1890s, blacks retired the best white men of Democratic persuasion and replaced them with Republicans, who momentarily offered them greater encouragement and recognition as men and citizens. For a while North Carolina left the ranks of the Solid South, and blacks and whites came together in a new political coalition.

In the 1890s blacks in North Carolina were definitely out of their "place." They began to criticize and question the judgment of whites, to make political decisions, and to hold public office in increasing numbers. Such behavior did not fit the mental image and perception that whites had of blacks, and it ran contrary to the ideology of white supremacy. Whites could tolerate blacks as long as they accepted a position at the bottom of society. However, once they began to exercise the equal rights of citizenship, whites saw them as being "intolerably self-important and insolent," and a threat to the social order.[3] The problem for whites in the 1890s was simply to devise ways to put blacks back in their place, and herein lies the great tragedy of that era. Whites unmasked and openly displayed their true feelings as the race problem in North Carolina assumed the dimensions of a race war, culminating with the events at Wilmington in 1898 and the subsequent movement for disfranchisement. Afterward, whites were able to force into existence their oft-repeated prophecy that blacks were truly a retrogressive race.

At the beginning of the 1890s Hunter, in characteristic fashion, was considering migrating to the North, and again he was encouraged to do so by both Ed and Osborne. They advised him to take the Civil Service examination, because "appointments were going on every day and the Africo-American is holding his own" and enjoying the benefits of promotion and job security. Osborne was one of the highest-paid blacks on the federal payroll, and Ed saw no reason why Hunter, with his qualifications, could not obtain a similar position. But he warned Hunter that government positions in Washington involved a disregard for personal principles and the contact with many corrupting influences. In spite of an individual's inclination to do good, Ed wrote, "A man comes in contact with so much of the perverse and sinful side of human nature that he is more or less affected by it in spite of himself."[4]

This advice along with his love for North Carolina may have prompted Hunter to remain at home and work for a salary that during the decade of the 1890s never exceeded $600 a year. But there were other compensatory factors that made North Carolina attractive. During the decade, Hunter was employed as principal of the Garfield and Oberlin schools in Raleigh, and he enjoyed the status and prestige associated with this position. He was also registrar of the Vestry of Saint Ambrose Church, secretary of the Hesperian Literary and Social Club, and treasurer of the NCIA. Hunter had also been able to regain the esteem of the black community of Raleigh. For example, it was the honest judgment of the faculty of Saint Augustine College in 1892 that Hunter "as educator and orator has but few equals in the Negro race." He was distinguished for his high character and "heavy brain power," and the faculty designated him as the typical "Afro-Southron."[5]

In the fall of 1891 Hunter joined the staff of the *Raleigh Gazette*, and he served as assistant editor of this weekly for two years. Republican in its tenets, the paper was described as a power in North Carolina because it was

# A Race Out of Place

the accepted organ of the black community, who followed its advice in all matters pertaining to its welfare. John H. Williamson, the *Gazette*'s editor, announced that the addition of an experienced journalist like Hunter would surely "result in columns of increased interest and value to its readers." The importance of Hunter and Williamson to the black community can be seen in the fact that they were part of the official party that presided over the opening of the annual black fair in 1891. The new spirit of pride and confidence was very much in evidence among the many blacks who came to witness the achievements of their race. A newspaper reporter characterized the fair as "a great gathering of the great souls of the people," and he thought that a more representative group of blacks could not be found in any state of the Union.[6] There were "men of learning, men eminent in the field and in the forum; men whose names were widely known in every part of the civilized world; men who had been honored with high distinction by the government of the United States; men who are pushing forward into new realms and bringing new conquests of glory to their race, and not only men but hundreds of the most refined and cultured women of the race, graced the occasion with their presence."[7]

Whites were also at the fair, but they had no official part in the opening ceremonies. Hunter extended a welcome to the visitors on behalf of the city of Raleigh. In so doing he claimed that "no better city and no better people could be found anywhere on the face of the earth," and that a spirit of sympathy, friendship, and kind cooperation had always characterized race relations in Raleigh. Hunter was also pleased with the congenial attitude displayed by the thousands of blacks present at the fair. He noted that there was not a single frown on their faces, and he stated that this could not be said of a similar occasion in any city or country. Williamson agreed with Hunter's assessment of race relations, and it was his belief that "North Carolina was the best state in the Union and contains the best people in the world." He congratulated blacks on the fact that their exhibits far excelled those of whites. Williamson, a politician by nature, reminded the crowd that North Carolina was the only state that enjoyed the distinction of having a black congressman, and, if "the Democratic Party don't fight him too hard, it will have another in the person of himself." Delivering the annual oration, Congressman Henry P. Cheatham told the audience that there was no prejudice against them on account of their color. Race prejudice originated chiefly from the economic condition of blacks, and Cheatham maintained that his race had to have an economic base strong enough to support its claim to equality. In rhetoric typical of the New South oratory, he urged blacks to organize and operate factories, and to acquire bank and railroad stock as a means of "crowning themselves with glory," and adding to the wealth of the state and nation. Furthermore, Cheatham claimed that he had observed patterns of race relations all over the nation, but "In North Carolina he found a degree of good feelings painfully absent even in many states of the North." The distinguished visitor to the fair was P. B. S. Pinchback, the black lieutenant governor of Louisiana during Reconstruction. He remarked that he had been somewhat discouraged about the prospects of his race until his visit to North Carolina, but he had personally witnessed a friendly feeling of mutual cooperation between the races that renewed his hopes for a grander future and greater prosperity for blacks.[8]

The leading black men of North Carolina were less than candid in their utterances on race relations and this was even more true of Hunter and Williamson. Less than a month before the fair, the *Gazette* appealed to the "higher sentiments of our white people" in an attempt to mobilize public opinion against the many cases of lynching that had occurred in the past six months. It seemed to the editors of the *Gazette* that "Nowadays it was only necessary to raise a suspicion against a Negro, however groundless, in order to whirl him into eternity without the benefit of Judge or Jury."[9]

Proof that Hunter did not truly believe that race relations in the Tarheel State were improving can be seen in a series of editorials that he prepared for the *Gazette* in 1892 on the subjects of prejudice in America and the race question in North Carolina. As he saw it, the race question predated the founding of the American Republic. It was born with the enslavement of blacks, and it grew in strength and importance until it pervaded every aspect of life and threatened the very foundations of the nation. "In all areas of American life and thought," he wrote, "there is none other that enters so largely and so intimately into every consideration affecting the growth and greatness, the peace and prosperity of our common country." The basis of the race question lay in the extreme prejudice against blacks, which also originated with their enslavement and degradation, and it did not disappear with emancipation. Rather, it grew and thrived until it too had assumed a position of preeminence over every subject and issue of importance to the nation reaching "deep down beneath the foundations of our free institutions." Hunter had identified institutionalized racism in America and he was confident that blacks would have to contend with its effects for many years to come.[10]

# A Race Out of Place

Hunter was rather pessimistic also about the progress of race relations in North Carolina since the end of the Civil War. He pointed out that the very men who had led the state into that conflict were the same ones who in 1892 were trying to block the progress of blacks. They continued to proclaim that "this is a white man's country," and Hunter believed that they were still openly using the same "violent, inhuman, and fiendish" methods to deprive blacks of their just and legal rights. But he let whites know that blacks were not going to give up, and they still wanted the same things they had asked for at their first convention in 1865. They desired the same rights, privileges, and immunities enjoyed by other citizens, and they would settle for nothing less. Hunter asked, "Would not the patriotic white men of the State concede them this?"[11]

Hunter addressed two editorials to the white people of North Carolina. He told them that blacks had been faithful to the resolution that they passed in 1865, professing their affection for the white race and their love and loyalty to the state. There was no reason why whites should fear blacks, who wanted neither to dominate them nor to be their social equals. He suggested that they give blacks their rights, and "any designs which you may honestly fear from the exercise of those rights will disappear." Hunter asked for the repeal of all discriminatory and unjust laws in the belief that this would eliminate "a whole realm of bans, bars, and barriers" that prevented his race from realizing its power and ambition.[12]

Still, Hunter thought that there was a large number of good white men in North Carolina who would be willing to accord blacks their rights, but unfortunately they were not politicians, and they did not control conventions, platforms, and party sentiments. They had abdicated their responsibilities for public service, and turned the affairs of state over to the meaner element of their race. Hunter contended that it was the politicians of this latter class of whites who remained in power by stirring up trouble between the races and exploiting racial issues. He again appealed to the best men of both races to come together in a coalition to improve the human and material resources of the state. If the best white men of North Carolina knew blacks as well as they often claimed, then Hunter thought they must certainly be aware of the fact that the frequency of lynchings in all parts of the state was destroying life and liberty and the foundations of good government. He wanted the best white men to do their duty and speak out against this injustice. They could not afford to let their silence bear the implication of an endorsement of lawlessness. Hunter pleaded, "White men of North

# A Race Out of Place

Carolina you can do this, you should do this: humanity and Christianity demand it of you."[13]

In a subtle way Hunter was telling the best white men of the state that they were no longer deserving of that title. They had received a national reputation as being the best people of the South, and it was time for them to do justice to blacks; otherwise, his race would be forced to look elsewhere for new allies and new friends, just as it had done during Reconstruction. Hunter noted in April 1892 that the present political situation in North Carolina seemed favorable for a readjustment of party creeds in the interest of justice to his race. He begged whites to let blacks take every advantage of this new opportunity, and also to put an end to the "shameful crime by which the Negro vote has been deprived of its rightful power." Hunter might have been looking at the newly formed Populist party with its preponderance of Farmers' Alliancemen and sensed the possibility of some sort of political collaboration on the part of blacks with that movement. In 1890 the Colored Farmers' Alliance of North Carolina with its membership of approximately 50,000 had joined with the white Farmers' Alliance in electing legislators pledged to their principles. Thus the potential was present in the state for future cooperation with a third party movment.[14]

The leading blacks at the beginning of the 1890s foresaw a struggle between poor whites and the old and more affluent ruling class in North Carolina. They hoped to profit from this conflict because it would force to the front political issues of real substance that whites would have to address, and they could no longer get into office by simply exploiting the themes of black domination and social equality. Hunter's sympathies and those of a substantial number of other leading blacks were with the upper class of whites, "the noble sons of noble sires," who, they thought, did not as a general rule take part in election frauds and tended to uphold law and order. The leading blacks also mistakenly believed that only poor whites engaged in lynchings and other acts of violence, and that they alone did the "dirty work on election day." In 1892 Hunter advised blacks to stay away from the self-seeking and unscrupulous politicians and to help place the affairs of state in the hands of competency. His call was in vain because it seems that the good white men had indeed retired from the scene, and their place was taken by a type whom Walter Hines Page referred to as the "romantic race bully." Then too, by the 1890s some of the men whom blacks had earlier designated as "good" had assumed all the characteristics of the race bully.[15]

# A Race Out of Place

A case in point is that of Zebulon B. Vance who as governor in the 1870s promised blacks that he would protect them in the enjoyment of their rights as citizens. In January 1890 Vance openly admitted before the Senate of the United States that whites did use force, violence, and fraud to win elections. He intimated that this was nothing to be ashamed of, and was only additional proof that, after twenty-five years of freedom, the experiment in allowing blacks citizenship was a failure. If they were kept from voting by intimidation or were defrauded in the counting of ballots, then Vance believed that this was proof enough that they also lacked the capacity for self-government. He asked, "Are a people fit to govern themselves or others who would suffer themselves to be thus treated?" Furthermore, Vance rejected a basic premise of the American republican tradition when he stated that the superior white race by virtue of natural law had the right to govern even in those areas where they were a minority of the population. Collectively, the white race possessed superior knowledge, courage, and skill in the use of arms, and Vance was sure that any attempt to restrain them in the exercise of that superiority was unnatural. Whites would neither submit to black rule nor uphold racial equality, even if it meant the use of violence and the mutual destruction of the races.[16]

Statements like this forced Hunter and other leading men to question both the superiority of whites and their competency to govern. In 1891 Hunter wrote that the only hope for the development of the South and its advancement to a higher civilization rested in the application of Christian ethics to civil government. He also hoped that the white leadership would begin to apply the same code of ethics that governed their personal relationships to government and its subjects. The Reverend David Brown of Wilmington thought it was too late for this because whites, instead of being the most fit members of society, were a "fallen race," and had a greater propensity for immorality than did blacks. He also thought that whites had not proved their fitness and competency in establishing and administering just and equitable laws. The Reverend J. C. Price joined in the critique of the best white men by proclaiming them disturbers of society and obstacles to good government. To strengthen his argument, Price quoted a passage from Edmund Burke's *Reflections on the Revolution in France* as applicable to southern whites: "Those who attempt by outrage and violence to deprive men of any advantage under the laws proclaim war against society."[17]

The readjustment of party lines that Hunter predicted came in the elections of 1894 when a tenuous alliance of Populists and Republicans cap-

# A Race Out of Place

tured majorities in the state legislature and supreme court. During the campaign, Democrats were complacent as usual, expecting that racial slurs and cries of "Negro domination" and "social equality" were sufficient for victory. They never realized that a Fusion movement was abroad, nor did they ever dream that whites would divide their votes to any appreciable degree and support a political coalition with blacks. When the results of the election were announced, Democrats and many others were stunned and probably thought like David A. Schenck, who wrote, "It is wonderfully mysterious how this complete and dreadful revolution went on all unknown to the wisest men of the State. . . . God ordained it for some incredible purpose." The Fusionist victory of 1894 was indeed the revolution of the decade, and in many respects it was the Progressive era in North Carolina. The legislature of 1895 proceeded to reverse many of the conservative measures of the past and to enact progressive and beneficial laws that reduced interest and utility rates, increased appropriations for education and social welfare, reformed the electoral system, and popularized local government. Indeed, many of the laws passed by the Fusionists were the best the state had ever had, a fact that even some Democrats had to admit.[18]

In 1896 the majority of blacks supported the Republican candidate for governor, Judge Daniel L. Russell, in spite of his previous slandering of their race along with recommending that it be disfranchised.[19] However, he had succeeded in convincing blacks that he had reformed, and that he was indeed one of the best white men. He certainly fitted Hunter's description of that class. His family had owned slaves, Russell had his mammy, and he was raised among blacks. More important than this or his racist remarks was the fact that, as a judge, his decisions were often in favor of civil equality for blacks, and at times he had encouraged them in their political aspirations. Five years before his nomination for governor, Russell had informed the leading blacks, "Nothing that I might write or say could emphasize my adherence or devotion to the principles of human equality. . . . I have never surrendered to the tyranny of caste."[20] If Russell was not one of the best white men, he was perceived by blacks as a politician who would do them the least harm. Thus it was good interest-group politics for them to support him.

During the campaign of 1896 the Democrats used the silver issue in an unsuccessful appeal to blacks and Populists. Out of desperation they once again returned to their old standby, race prejudice, and attempted to turn whites against blacks. The Democrats tried to blame blacks for injecting the race issue into the campaign by claiming that they had drawn the color line against Populists and white Republicans. Blacks were the racists because they were trying to displace white officeholders through the nomination of all-black tickets. White men were called on to unite against blacks in an "irresistible phalanx of resistance." The *Raleigh News and Observer* warned that the honorable white men did not intend to submit to any outrages and would defend themselves with their lives, and that this "Comes not from the pen of the press per se, but it is burned in the hearts of the people."[21]

The Democrats did not want to give blacks credit for being astute enough to unite in interest-group politics, so they injected into the campaign two themes that were most offensive to conservative whites: northern interference, and the reemergence of corrupt white Republicans. It was reported that "Scouts of Marcus Auriferous Hanna" were present in the state, and that they were busily engaged in mobilizing blacks into a well-disciplined army in preparation for a political race war. The alleged emissaries of Hanna were described as a "new group of coons wearing stovepipe hats, yellow shoes and the loudest type of loud clothes." They had plenty of money to spend and kept the native blacks drunk and infuriated against whites. At night meetings and drunken orgies they campaigned on the issue of free silver or free blacks, and they "warned of trouble to come" if Democrats won the election.[22]

According to the Democrats, the work of northern Republicans was facilitated by Alfred E. Holton, the chairman of the Republican party of North Carolina, and Russell, both of whom were described as the "reincarnation" of Holden and Kirk. It even seemed to the Democrats that Russell had turned black and forgotten all about whites. He spoke mainly to blacks and appealed to their baser passions and their instinct to "rule and dominate." Furthermore, Russell was accused of having taught blacks that they were oppressed by whites, and thus "aroused their ambition to resentment and control." The white population was admonished that if Russell were elected things would be worse than during Reconstruction, because blacks were more assertive and more determined to have political and civil rights.[23]

Of course, not all blacks supported Fusion and Russell, and this was particularly true of a number of the leading men. Primarily educators, professionals, and businessmen, this group never forgave Russell for his racist comments, and they preferred to vote a straight Republican ticket, because among other things, they realized that Fusion was sure to produce a

# A Race Out of Place

backlash that would prove harmful to race relations. Though philosophically with this group, Hunter's political activities are hard to pinpoint during the Fusionist period. He consorted with Fusionists while at times working against them, offered his services to some straight Republicans, and conspired with and voted for some Democrats. Despite his past public rhetoric calling for full citizenship for his race, it seems that Hunter thought that the goodwill of whites was more important than political rights for blacks. Representative of this is his role in a conspiracy to thwart a movement for democratic reform in Goldsboro.[24]

In 1895 Hiram L. Grant, a Fusionist leader in eastern North Carolina, introduced a bill in the legislature that would have altered the charter of Goldsboro in the interest of popular government. This incensed the white residents of the city, who dispatched Charles B. Aycock to Raleigh to lobby against the measure. Aycock sought out Hunter, and told him that the good race relations he had helped establish while teaching in Goldsboro still existed. But if Grant's bill became law, "It would inaugurate an era of political strife and race rancor that would prove damaging to every interest of the city and especially to the Negroes. . . ."[25]

Aycock asked Hunter to contact James H. Young, the representative from Wake County, and solicit his aid in their conspiracy. Young was the most outstanding black politician of the Fusionist era, and one of the truly popular leaders of his race. In 1893 he acquired control of the *Raleigh Gazette*, which he used to wage political warfare against the Democrats, particularly Josephus Daniels and his *Raleigh News and Observer*. A shrewd politician who exercised real power, Young managed conventions, arranged tickets, struck bargains, and above all, he was extremely close to Daniel Russell, the most influential Republican in North Carolina. When Hunter asked for Young's help in defeating the Grant bill, Young was very bitter. He had just introduced a bill to amend the Charter of Raleigh, which his white colleagues would not support. According to Hunter, "Young seemed in the right mood to play any hand he could against them," and he agreed to help. The Grant bill was killed, and Hunter proudly claimed that "Aycock ever after that in speaking of the matter privately gave to Mr. Young and me the credit of having prevented the passage of that bill."[26] This was more than likely true, but the whole affair was nothing to be proud of, and Aycock cleared his conscience by shifting the onus onto the backs of his two black co-conspirators.

Hunter may have taken part in this scheme to get revenge on those blacks

# A Race Out of Place

in Goldsboro who were instrumental in terminating his employment as principal of their schools. No doubt he also wanted to stay in the good graces of Democrats and protect his reputation as a safe black. However, at the time of his involvement with the Grant bill, Hunter was not a leading black because he was clearly out of step with the prevailing sentiment of the masses of his race, which favored increased political participation. But Hunter did not trust his people's judgment when it came to politics, and he was sure that it would, in the end, be detrimental to their welfare. He understood the mentality of whites, particularly as it related to blacks and politics. Ever aware of the fact that they had certain "fixed ideas" regarding their own superior social and political status, he insisted they were determined to control and dominate blacks. When challenged on these points, Hunter wrote, "Whites would pour out blood as freely and as copiously as the Mississippi empties its waters into the Great Gulf."[27]

Since Reconstruction, Hunter had tried to warn blacks of the impending danger in vying with whites for political office. He was chastised by many of his race for his unsolicited jeremiads, but he continued out of a conviction that "Time, the great teacher, the wise unerring Judge would vindicate the wisdom" of his course. Like many whites, he drew an analogy between the Fusionist and Reconstruction eras and came up with the conclusion that any political alliance in opposition to the Democrats was transitory and dangerous. Hunter claimed that during the Fusionist era he was content to let blacks find out for themselves what he had personally discovered a quarter century before.[28]

If blacks were courting disaster by participating in politics, they certainly did not act like it during the election of 1896 when the Democrats were again defeated, and the Fusionists tightened their control over the state. Aided by recent electoral reforms, black Republicans were the decisive element in electing Daniel L. Russell as governor, and they also delivered to William McKinley what was probably the largest bloc of black voters in the nation. Blacks also elected a member of their race to Congress, and eleven others to the General Assembly. In Wake County, Jim Young won his bid for reelection by a margin of two votes over Hunter's friend and patron, Needham B. Broughton. Hunter probably voted for Broughton, for he supported some Democrats. Years later he confessed that he voted for William Jennings Bryan in 1896, "chiefly because of my admiration for Josephus Daniels who was my warm friend."[29]

Blacks were jubilant over the Fusionist victory, because they had accom-

# A Race Out of Place

plished a feat unique in the history of the state, and one that has yet to be duplicated. After years of seeing their votes nullified by Democratic election laws and fraud at the ballot box, blacks—particularly those in the Second Congressional District—perceived the victory as a final realization of their political power and the basic right to be represented by men of their choice. If North Carolina was a relative latecomer in the legal disfranchisement of blacks, it was not the result of any magnanimity on the part of Democrats. Rather, blacks had fought and won a successful delaying action in 1896, and they saw their victory as a temporary respite from disfranchisement. An editorial in the *Raleigh Gazette* stated that blacks should be proud of the fact that "we escaped at the last election such laws as the Democrats have in Mississippi, Louisiana and some other states." The writer of this was sure that had the Democrats won the election, "nearly every one of us would have had our right to vote taken fom us."[30]

Celebrations were staged throughout the state in honor of the Fusionist victory and successful black candidates, and this was true even in those areas where there were no black officeholders. There were parades and banquets in Tarboro, Louisburg, Halifax, Chapel Hill, Goldsboro, and Raleigh. In light of his previous remarks concerning black politicians, it is indeed strange that Hunter served as chairman of the Committee of Arrangements for a reception in honor of the black members of the General Assembly. One of the most elaborate of all victory celebrations, it was considered one of the historic social events in Raleigh, bringing together a magnificent array of representative characters from all walks of life. "Youth and beauty in all its loveliness were there. High intellectuality shone out on all sides. The dignity of maturer years graced the occasion. . . ."[31]

Black North Carolinians received congratulations from members of their race in other states, and the Tarheel State was cited as being the best in the Union for the advancement of blacks, and the abode of the "best specimens of Negro manhood anywhere in America." It was even predicted that the state would be to the South what Massachusetts had in previous years been to the nation, the leader for freedom, equal rights, and educational opportunities for all people. A letter to the editor of the *Gazette* from a black in St. Paul, Minnesota, noted: "The people of the West and North are turning towards North Carolina as an escape from long frigid winters, high taxes, and poverty." Blacks outside the state were making superficial judgments concerning conditions in North Carolina, not understanding that the recent gains of their race were aberrations. Like others, including some later

# A Race Out of Place

scholars of race relations, they mistakenly believed that what was, had ever been. Yet it also seems that the masses of blacks in North Carolina were not aware of the fact that their rejoicing was a bit premature; their new political status had not been consolidated, nor had any substantive changes occurred in the racial attitudes of most whites. Maybe they knew this, and were just enjoying a brief respite from oppression.[32]

The heightened spirit of the black community and the esteem that it had for its political leaders were evident at the Emancipation Day celebration in Raleigh in 1897. Metropolitan Hall was filled with "a well dressed high-toned, intelligent audience which was just overflowing with the spirit of the day." Hunter read the Emancipation Proclamation, but the hero of the hour was Jim Young, who had been chosen to give the annual oration. The crowd demanded that he tell them about his recent campaign and, after he obliged them, the applause and cheers nearly disrupted the affair. "Old and gray-haired mothers and fathers as did the young shouted Amen! Amen!" wrote a reporter to the *Gazette*. Young did not, however, deliver a political speech. Instead he focused on the need for his race to correct certain social ills and he called for a general reformation of his people to begin first "around the firesides and in the homes." At the close of the celebration, Hunter and Young were unanimously elected to serve as president and secretary, respectively, of the Emancipation Association.[33]

Besides their political achievements, blacks had other reasons for feeling proud. In late 1896 the state auditor announced that the aggregate value of real and personal property owned by blacks had increased between the years 1891 and 1895, whereas that of whites had shown a remarkable decline. The black community had also made substantial progress toward the reduction of illiteracy; and in less than a quarter century after emancipation its rate had declined by approximately 39 percent. During the same period the illiteracy rate for whites had actually increased, and in 1897 it was announced that the white people of North Carolina were the most illiterate of all in the nation except those in New Mexico, while blacks in the state had more education than those in several other states. Furthermore, the superintendent of public instruction recognized the fact that blacks were taking better advantage of their educational opportunities, and were less content to let their children grow up in ignorance than whites. Blacks were also elated when the State Board of Education in 1897 provided them with a textbook on the history of their race. This eliminated a great concern in the black community, for it was aware that its children "learned all about white

# A Race Out of Place

historic figures but knew very little about the Noble persons of their own race."[34]

The Fusionist legislature in 1897 also sponsored one of the most progressive educational laws that the state had yet witnessed. This measure was designed to strengthen public education by giving local townships the option of levying a school tax to supplement funds received from the state. The North Carolina State Teachers' Association endorsed this proposal, and Hunter was chosen to serve on an ad hoc committee to ensure that the tax went into effect in all parts of the state. Hunter worked enthusiastically for the implementation of the school tax because it was a safe, nonpartisan endeavor that had the backing of many of the best white people. He published an appeal to the black voters of the state asking that they approve the enactment of the school tax because it was the most important proposal ever submitted for their consideration, and he cautioned them to be on the lookout for the many people who still opposed free education for blacks. These "selfish, ignorant, and unworthy citizens" would surely try to persuade blacks to vote in the negative on the grounds that the measure would double their taxes and be of little benefit to them. A vote in the affirmative would be a vote for the progress, prosperity, and posterity of blacks, and Hunter hoped that voters of his race would not be responsible for the proposition's defeat.[35]

During the fair in 1897 it was evident that blacks were fully enjoying their historic moment, and they were highly visible in Raleigh during the week of this event. There was the usual great parade, and black troops drilled daily in the streets. Governor Russell had ordered the Charlotte Light Infantry, which was Company B of the state militia, to Raleigh for a week's encampment. The governor and the state adjutant general inspected this unit at a full-dress review, and pronounced it one of the best drilled in the state. Other events during fair week included Education Day (which brought together representatives of all the black schools, colleges, and universities in the state), Mechanics' and Farmers' Day, Women's Day, the annual meeting of the black Press and Authors' Association, a grand ball, and a football game between Shaw University and Saint Augustine College for a purse of $50. Hunter was forced to content himself with supervising the display of Garfield School, because he had resigned his position as secretary of the NCIA the previous year.[36]

The main event of the fair occurred during its formal opening when Jim Young escorted to the platform and introduced to the crowd a new set of

## A Race Out of Place

"best white men." Included in this group were William H. Worth, the state treasurer; Cyrus Thompson, the secretary of state; Hal W. Ayer, the state auditor; Charles H. Mebane, the superintendent of public instruction; James M. Mewborne, the commissioner of agriculture; and Zeb V. Walser, the state attorney general. This was the Fusion ticket of 1896, with the exception of Governor Russell who was absent because of important business in Wilmington. The *Charlotte Observer* alleged that Russell did not have any important out-of-town business, and that he offered this excuse, in order to avoid walking with blacks in the procession to the fairgrounds.[37]

Mewborne and Walser spoke to the crowd, and it had been a long time since blacks had heard addresses by whites that did not focus on the evils of their race, or damn them with faint praise. Mewborne attested to the fact that after 250 years of slavery blacks had made progress. Thousands of them worked daily in agriculture producing the essentials of life, and others were attaining intellectual heights as orators, lawyers, and politicians. In consideration of their rapid progress in "mental culture" within the short span of thirty years, Mewborne asked them to consider what they would be after a hundred years of free existence, and he advised his black friends to unite as a race and do good, pure, and honest things. If so, "there is no power on earth that can impede your onward march." Zeb Vance Walser must have shocked the crowd when he remarked, "I look around me and I see a great coming race. You haven't been a race long, you've been dogs." He claimed that blacks were still behind Anglo-Saxons, but they were fit for something else besides laborers. Moreover, they had helped his race for 250 years, and Walser wanted whites to help blacks attain their goals for a similar length of time: "Let's go along together like men and women—like brothers." Some whites believed that the remarks of Walser and Mewborne were "disgraceful admissions of social equality." But then, what else could be expected from white men who associated with blacks in political activities? If a refined and educated gentleman like Walser would make such a speech, the *Charlotte Observer* wondered, what in the world would the ordinary politician of Fusionist persuasion do?[38]

During fair week a number of leading men held a convention to protest against the Republicans' patronage policy. Only a few people showed up and they were for the most part opponents of James Young, Governor Russell, and Fusion politics. They were also friends or associates of Hunter, but there is no evidence that he was in attendance. The delegates thought that blacks in general, and the leading men in particular, were not getting a fair share of the patronage positions, and that Republicans were appointing inferior men to office. They also claimed that they did not want appointments solely for their material benefits, but for the moral influence they could exert upon their race. What this group of educators, professionals, and businessmen really wanted was personal recognition, for they had experienced a sudden loss of prestige, having been eclipsed by the politicians of their race. The delegates also formed the Lincoln Republican League for the purpose of promoting the interests of the Republican party. Although open to all Republicans, the league specifically advised black voters neither to nominate nor to support any candidate who was opposed to giving them full recognition. This policy was to be even more applicable to "colored men who are willing to trade off their race for office."[39]

Perhaps unknowingly the league may have contributed to the movement to disfranchise blacks. Its members voiced a sentiment in favor of an educated black electorate that could stand up for its political rights and know how to use them. For all their trouble, the leading men who staged the convention in November 1897 were condemned by whites and blacks alike. "Dubbed the Democratic Aid Society" by the *Gazette*, its editor warned readers that Dr. Aaron M. Moore and the forty-seven other blacks of unsavory political record were conspiring against their rights and liberties, and that they had no real standing among loyal Republicans. "They were wolves in sheep's clothing and emissaries of the Democratic Party. Keep your eyes on them," was the advice the *Gazette* gave its readers. But the Democrats did not think too much of that "disgraceful assemblage of sable-hued politicians" either. According to the *Biblical Recorder*, it was a "shameful affair of motley, blood-thirsty office seekers," and the paper noted that had Abraham Lincoln seen them, "he would have issued a new proclamation of deliverance."[40]

Instead of worrying about patronage and squabbling among themselves, the leading men should have been trying to devise strategies to deal with the Democrats who were about to settle the whole business of blacks and politics. To do this the Democrats had to unite the majority of whites around them, and they planned to separate the Populist party from its Republican ally and then weaken or wipe it out. This would reduce the possibility of whites dividing their votes among three parties, and it was believed that most would return to the Democratic fold. Democrats had no expectations of destroying the Republican party, because they had not been able to do so

# A Race Out of Place

since its emergence in the state. They were content, however, to let it exist as the party identifiable with blacks, but it too would be weakened by the disfranchisement of the majority of its supporters.[41]

The increased assertiveness of blacks during the 1890s only made Democrats more determined to strip them of their political privileges, and in the process break the spirit of the black community. Thus a new wave of violence was instituted against blacks, which included a campaign to cast them in the most unfavorable light by refuting all claims that they had made any progress as a race. During the last years of the nineteenth century, whites showed their true feelings and exposed to the world the myth that they were the best friends of blacks. Furthermore, they no longer claimed that North Carolina was the best place in the world for blacks. As a matter of fact, neither did many blacks.

Democrats claimed that instead of progressing, blacks during the 1890s had actually lapsed miserably into their natural savage condition. Their moral condition had not improved, and it was alleged that black males had become more addicted to rape because their concept of right and wrong was so low that they could not recognize the offense as a crime. Whites began openly to advocate lynchings in preference to orderly hangings in order to shock blacks and awaken them to a realization that rape was a crime. However, some whites had doubts that this would work, because blacks would be too ignorant to understand that lynchings were not injustices, but wholesome events.[42]

Naturally Democrats argued that black politicians and officeholders exerted a corrupting influence upon the morality and behavior of their race. It did not matter how docile or meek blacks were as private citizens; once invested with a little authority they became insolent and overbearing, and this had a dangerous effect especially on black youth. After seeing men of their race in positions of authority, young blacks soon developed a fresh hatred for whites, thought they were their equals, and proceeded to act in ways that were mercenary. It was also charged that blacks had not really improved their material condition, and they had not even come close to the basis of manhood or citizenship. They produced nothing except their young, and the masses of their race were fed, housed, and clothed primarily at the expense of whites. In return for these kindly acts, Democrats stated, they were constantly confronted by groups of ingrates asking for citizenship and public offices. Until such time as blacks attained the ability to support themselves, the *News and Observer* thought they should not consider themselves as citizens. Furthermore, the paper suggested that as a remedy for unruly and ungrateful blacks, whites should terminate their employment.[43]

Whites also threatened to terminate all educational assistance to blacks. Some felt that thirty years of public education at the expense of Democrats had only elevated blacks to the point of voting the Republican ticket and asking for public office, in the expectation of becoming rulers over their benefactors. An editorial in the *Biblical Recorder* in 1897 advised whites to forget about religion, brotherhood, and duty as excuses for educating and elevating blacks, if the only result was the production of postmasters, congressmen, and legislators. Besides, everyone knew that educated blacks were the worst of their race. Educated teachers and preachers were malicious demagogues, and the educated politician was naturally corrupt. It was also common knowledge that the more education blacks received, the more criminals they produced. The *Biblical Recorder* had also arrived at the conclusion that blacks needed "ten times as much religion as education" for their own good. The new air of insolence within the younger generation of blacks had to be curbed, and more institutions like Shaw University were needed. Shaw was praised for providing blacks with the proper religious training and the kind of education that would enable them to live in the "land of cotton and corn."[44]

Some whites even thought they saw signs that blacks were retrogressing physically and mentally. Bolstering this sentiment, Dr. John F. Miller, the superintendent of the Eastern Hospital in Goldsboro, reported that blacks could not adapt to their new social and political status and had been retrogressing ever since their emancipation. Licentiousness had caused many cases of lung degeneration, tuberculosis, and consumptive diseases, all of which, he claimed, were rarities during slavery. Insanity had also dramatically increased due to economic problems. Even though he thought that blacks were the mudsills of society and could exist on less than whites, Miller thought they suffered more during economic depressions. He was not referring to any physical suffering. Instead, he argued that the nervous system and mental equipoise of blacks were less sophisticated than those of whites, hence they were less able psychologically to sustain themselves during a depression. Because of this, Miller asserted that there were just as many insane blacks outside of asylums as within.[45]

Blacks had enough sense to wonder what had happened to the good white people of North Carolina. They could not understand how whites could

## A Race Out of Place

encourage lynching, lawlessness, and economic reprisals against their race, and the "starving to death of the children of faithful parents, who, as slaves," had ministered to them and their families. The leading blacks were divided in their response to this latest assault on their race. Some argued that blacks, grateful for the assistance of whites, had proved this by being peaceful, kind, obliging citizens, who were content to work for starvation wages. James H. Young agreed that blacks were appreciative of the help of whites, but he reminded them that true charity was never given and talked about "to the chagrin and shame of its recipients." He also thought that it would have been much better never to have received this assistance if it meant the sacrifice of one's manhood and citizenship. Other leading blacks used stronger words, claiming that it was nothing other than the "basest ingratitude" for whites to recommend withdrawing their support from a race that had labored for them for two and a half centuries for only food and clothes.[46]

Whites turned a deaf ear to these arguments of the leading blacks. By 1897 they were increasingly comparing conditions in the state to those that existed during Reconstruction, and recommended that the proper cure was the one applied during the redemption campaign. In February the *Raleigh News and Observer* called on all just white men to rally around the Democratic party and apply the remedy of 1876 in 1898, and "unless they be bastards and not sons, they will repeat the scenes, the incidents, and reap the glories of the campaign of 1876." The *Biblical Recorder* thought that stronger measures were needed, and in October it called for the outright disfranchisement of blacks by way of a constitutional amendment. The rhetoric of the Democrats either overly upset Hunter or he wanted to lead some whites into believing that he shared many of their attitudes concerning blacks and politics. Regardless, in 1897 he dusted off a copy of his article "Some of the Evils of Reconstruction" and sent it to an unidentified white person along with the notation that he might be interested in "reading the views of a black Republican along these lines."[47]

By December 1897 blacks sensed that their heyday in politics was drawing to a close, but they were determined to stay its occurrence. In announcing the Emancipation Day celebration for 1898, the *Raleigh Gazette* asked blacks not to forget that suffrage was one of the results of their freedom, and, "In the name of God and humanity, let us do our duty in the struggle to preserve that right." On New Year's Day 1898, Hunter, James H. Young, Henry P. Cheatham, and Governor Russell sat on the stage in Raleigh's

# A Race Out of Place

Metropolitan Hall as blacks and whites gathered to observe Emancipation Day. In speaking to the crowd Hunter and Cheatham tried to refute the recent negative statements about their race. Hunter tried to assure whites that blacks, who had not assembled in any spirit of hate, had nothing other than the kindest of feelings for the race that once held them as slaves. He was also sure that there were thousands of whites in North Carolina who reciprocated this attitude.[48]

Hunter also contended that, since their emancipation, blacks had not lapsed into any state of barbarism, but had made progress and were steadily advancing in all fields of human activity. Nevertheless they were conscious of their limitations and weaknesses, and acknowledged the superior power of whites. He also informed whites that his race still valued their aid and sympathy, but regretted that "some whites still linger at the tomb of the effete dogmas of a degenerate system piteously invoking their revitalization in the form of political despotism." Hunter, chairman of the Committee on Resolutions, presented its sentiments, which tried to reassure whites that blacks had no intentions of encroaching upon the "sacred precincts" of their social lives, nor did they seek to dominate the government of the state. Furthermore, there had never been anything in the history of North Carolina that would lead whites to think otherwise. Blacks desired only just laws equally applied, and an end to all discrimination based on race. Finally, Hunter solicited the support of all people of just judgment and Christian character in an effort to promote mutual progress and eliminate all forms of racial antagonism. The resolutions offered by Hunter were enthusiastically adopted by the audience. Governor Russell thought they were excellent. He congratulated blacks on their spirit of amity and friendship toward the race of their former enslavers, and promised that his administration was ready to encourage and recognize everything to promote their progress. Cheatham also commented on the good feelings between the races, and he asked that they come closer together instead of drifting further apart. He felt that North Carolina could not afford to follow the example of South Carolina and Mississippi, which had disfranchised half of their worthy citizens. He also warned his people to be alert and always to remember that "eternal vigilance is the price of liberty."[49]

The attention of Cheatham and other blacks was momentarily deflected from their impending disaster by the Spanish-American War. Following the declaration of war, Cheatham, Congressman George H. White, and other leading men from North Carolina called on President McKinley and offered him the moral and physical support of nine million blacks. Other black Americans doubted the wisdom of running off to fight for a nation that denied them their constitutional rights and subjected them to humiliation, maltreatment, and lynching. But the leading men of North Carolina followed Congressman White, who believed that despite their sufferings, blacks had a duty to defend America's honor. Some also saw the war as a great opportunity to reaffirm their manhood, and strengthen their claims to citizenship on the basis of military service. More importantly, they thought the war would awaken the sense of justice and morality of whites and help unite the races in a spirit of goodwill at home.[50]

Black North Carolinians pressured both Governor Russell and President McKinley for permission to participate actively in the conflict. In May 1898 Cheatham again visited McKinley and requested that North Carolina be authorized to raise a regiment of black troops for immediate federal service. Referring to this, the *Washington Bee* commented, "The more you kick the Negro, the more he likes to be kicked. Recorder Cheatham is anxious to convince the President that North Carolina is willing to send a black regiment to invade Cuba." The leading men were delighted and their white counterparts disgusted when McKinley took the unprecedented step of authorizing a regiment of black North Carolinians, led and commanded by men of their race. However, this decision also had a detrimental effect on the black community. The men who were selected to man and staff this unit were in many instances the civic and political leaders of their communities. Thus blacks were stripped of a portion of their most capable leadership at a time when it was most needed. James H. Young was chosen to command the Third North Carolina Regiment. Prior to Young's assuming his duties, the *Raleigh Gazette* suspended publication indefinitely, and this deprived the black community of its chief source of information as well as its main weapon in the propaganda war with Democrats.[51]

Hunter, anxious to do his part in the war, unsuccessfully sought a military appointment. Senator Jeter C. Pritchard, Congressman George H. White, and Representative William F. Strowd all promised to see the secretary of war or General Nelson A. Miles on his behalf. At home, Logan D. Howell, the Raleigh superintendent of schools, and John C. Dancy, the collector of the port of Wilmington, agreed to visit Governor Russell for the same purpose. But Dancy did not think he could do much good because Russell had not honored any of his requests. He wrote Hunter, "I know that you will not wish that I be turned down again and to your disadvantage." It is not known exactly what kind of position Hunter wanted, but it might have been in the nature of a war correspondent. At the time, brother Osborne was leading a movement in Washington to send "a competent Afro-American journalist to the seat of war to collect and preserve the glowing record of our soldiers." His choice for this position was T. Thomas Fortune of the *New York Age*, but Hunter might have thought he also merited consideration.[52]

Those blacks who were naïve enough to believe that the war with Spain would result in an improvement of their status at home were dreadfully disappointed. The war involved the nation in an imperialistic endeavor with clear racist undertones, and it spread more prejudice at home than civilization and Christianity abroad. The result was a convergence in the racial attitudes of southern and northern whites, or as Tom Dixon remarked, "The bloody shirt was buried at San Juan Hill. The Negro must stand alone."[53]

CHAPTER

# 5

## "Like a Devil Turned Loose"

As the Spanish-American War neared a close, Democrats in North Carolina accelerated their war against blacks. The white supremacy campaign of 1898–1900 is often referred to as a revolution, but it was a counterrevolution. The revolution occurred in 1894 when the Fusionists took control of the state. Thereafter the Democrats launched a reactionary movement to erase not only the results of Fusion government but of Reconstruction as well. In race relations and many other areas, Democrats wanted to return North Carolina to its antebellum condition. The only thing new about the white-supremacy campaign of the late 1890s was some of its personalities. The objectives, logic, and rhetoric used by the Democrats had a continuity that reached back into time, through the days of Reconstruction, to the Constitutional Convention of 1835 and beyond.

The Fourteenth and Fifteenth amendments to the Constitution of the United States had erased the adjustments made to the constitution of North Carolina in 1835, which had disfranchised all blacks in the state. Democrats had been dissatisfied ever since Reconstruction; they had never accepted the idea of black suffrage and were determined that it would not stand. The senior bishop of the African Methodist Episcopal Zion Church, James W. Hood, had been in North Carolina since the early days of Reconstruction, and he was a keen political observer. According to Hood, the Democrats had always hoped that a "state of affairs could be brought about which would give them an opportunity to undo the reconstruction work."[1]

This "state of affairs" occurred in the 1890s when blacks appeared assertive, progressive, and politically active, and it required no great deal of intellectual creativity for the Democrats to draw an analogy between the

Fusion and Reconstruction eras. Moreover, part of the mental baggage of most whites in North Carolina included a twisted version of Reconstruction, which also affected their views on race relations. Josephus Daniels, one of the leaders of the white-supremacy campaign of the 1890s, recalled that Reconstruction had bred resentment, violence, and a bitterness between men and races. It was also a "time when reason had lost its base, when men almost forgot God, when they became familiar with death and blood, and slaughter, and lay down with hatred in their soul," so said the biographers of Charles B. Aycock. They argued that the Reconstruction experience was deeply embedded in Aycock's psyche and influenced every moment of his private life and public career. More than likely, this was also true for many of the other leaders of the Democratic party.[2]

The propaganda themes of the Democrats in the campaign of 1898, though simplistic, had a strong emotional appeal. They alleged that the state was chafing under black domination and that conditions would further deteriorate if the Fusionists remained in power. Aycock's compelling argument was that the issue was not over the large number of blacks in office, but that the basis of Fusion government, especially its Republican faction, rested upon the strength of black voters. He reasoned, "It is the Negro behind the officer, and not the officer only, that constituted Negro government."[3]

Every good Democrat knew that black government was bad government, so it was only necessary to arouse the indignation of the masses of whites by parading before them a distorted record of corruption and maladministration on the part of the Fusionists. Furthermore, the Democrats claimed that they were white men, and implied that members of their race who belonged to other political parties were somewhat less than white. They asserted that Democrats had always ruled in North Carolina, and if whites permitted others to do so, they were neglecting their historic and racial duties. Whites had to come together to save "the State, their sisters, mothers, wives and children, their homes, altars, firesides and all that was dear and sacred to them"[4]

Ironically, the leaders of the propaganda war were the very men whom Hunter idolized and claimed as friends. This was particularly true of Josephus Daniels and Aycock. Daniels, the editor of the *Raleigh News and Observer* and a member of the Democratic National Executive Committee, was without a doubt the most effective propagandist of the printed word. Daniels's racist paper appealed to people's basest passions, and by his own

## "Like a Devil Turned Loose"

admission it was "fierce and vindictive." He further confessed years after the campaign was over that the terrible part of the whole affair was the effect that it had upon the law-abiding "respectable Negro who was caught in the middle of this great upheaval."[5]

Although designed primarily for white consumption, Democratic campaign literature directly affected the black community. Never before had there been such a wholesale assassination of the character of the black race in general and of black leadership in particular. Democratic propaganda was also intended to discredit the black population of North Carolina in the eyes of the world. The leading men, many of whom had consistently praised the virtue and friendship of the good white men of the state, were singled out by the Democrats for public vilification simply because they voted or held public office. Blacks across the nation considered men like James H. Young, Abe Middleton, James E. Shepard, Willie Lee Persons, John T. Howe, Isaac Smith, John C. Dancy, and George H. White to be among the leaders of their race. But to the Democrats of North Carolina in 1898 they were "nigger savages, lusty brutes, and rascals" who thirsted for white women, social equality, and political domination of the state.[6]

Hunter's other Democratic idol, Aycock, excelled in oratory, and he focused his attention primarily on the white people of the state. He extolled the disgrace and the sorrowful plight of whites who suffered under Fusion rule. Aycock's technique was that of an evangelical preacher and a great revivalist who was bent upon arousing feelings of sin, guilt, repentance, and the hope of salvation among his audience. Whites had to feel guilty for the sin of allowing Fusionist rule in the first place. Repentance and salvation lay in a return to the Democratic party, and the restoration of white supremacy.

A witness to one of Aycock's speeches in 1898 recalled: At one point in Aycock's speech that night, after graphic narration of harrowing conditions in the State, he paused and said he was not yelling "Nigger! Nigger! Nigger!," and then, striding forward to the front of the stage with stalking gesture, in the voice of a father speaking in reproachful shame to an offending child, cried out loudly, "White man! White man!! White man!!!" It was indeed a climax. That great audience, as if riding on a groundswell, arose as one, with frenzy of repentance. For several minutes the speaker could not proceed. Quiet from exhaustion came for an instant and then that call to manhood seemed to increase in force and intensity and again the heart of that crowd gave way to powerful sense of guilt and degradation; and after another pause, for the third time that consciousness of guilt in permitting such things to be done swept through the multitude, and all present were visibly and audibly enthralled.[7]

The best white men of North Carolina masterminded, financed, and directed the white supremacy campaign, but after stirring up racial hatred, they tended to rely upon poor whites to carry out acts of physical violence. Votes and violence were about the only things that poor whites could contribute to the campaign of 1898, and they were ready and willing to do their part. The condition of poor whites in North Carolina had never been good, but they were generally content to remain at the bottom of their race in the consolation that they were in some way better than blacks. The progress and assertiveness of blacks in the 1890s, along with a decline in the servile and deferential behavior that was expected of them, made poor whites anxious. They felt that their relative position in the social order was declining, and that the distance between them and the black masses was narrowing. Hence they were vulnerable to Democratic propaganda, and enthusiastically joined in the effort to put blacks in their place.[8]

It was almost certain that the intense hatred and emotionalism generated by the Democrats would result in racial violence. One of the first clashes occurred in September 1898 between members of the Second Regiment of North Carolina Volunteers and blacks of east Raleigh. Ever since the regiment had returned to Raleigh, its troops were nightly engaged in confrontations with blacks. Soldiers paraded through the black section of the city openly brandishing daggers and bowie knives and abusing blacks, whom they accused of insolent and offensive behavior. On the night of 17 September 1898 fights broke out between soldiers and blacks, who were armed with sticks, stones, knives, pokers, and brooms. The whites were defeated, and, although there were no serious injuries, the *News and Observer* reported that "the soldiers were getting a taste of real warfare."[9]

Violence erupted the following day when a large number of soldiers congregated on Hargett Street to get liquor. Several drunken whites and a few blacks fought, and once again the whites were defeated. Both sides went off for reinforcements. At length a riot broke out, and this time both groups were armed. The soldiers emptied their revolvers into the crowd without doing any serious damage, and they retreated with a group of

## "Like a Devil Turned Loose"

blacks in pursuit. Two whites and several blacks were wounded in this skirmish. At this point, military and civil authorities took immediate action to restore order and to prevent the spread of violence. Soldiers were ordered back to their camps, and Mayor William M. Russ and Colonel William H. S. Burgwyn went to East Hargett Street and attempted to reassure blacks that the situation was under control. They also expressed their regrets over the incident and asked that the better element of blacks counsel their people and urge them to return to their homes. A tense calm prevailed over the city amid rumors that both sides were arming in expectation of renewed attacks. Naturally, the *News and Observer* attempted to blame blacks for the entire affair, and told them that if they minded their own business they need not fear further violence. The paper also proclaimed that the patience of whites was rapidly being exhausted, and it would not be long before they would have to take the law into their own hands and force blacks to behave. "A clash is surely coming between the races," warned the *Observer*, and blacks had better believe that "in such clashes the white race is always victorious."[10]

During the rioting, Hunter saw two soldiers being fired upon and he reported the matter to the authorities. He knew the blacks involved, and announced his intention to swear out a warrant for their arrest. He also gave a statement to the press concerning the recent violence. Hunter denounced the conduct of irresponsible elements in east Raleigh, and stated that their action did not meet with the approval of the better element of his race. The good blacks of the city had always been willing to cooperate with all good citizens in the preservation of peace and the punishment of those responsible for outbreaks of disorder. However, he wanted whites to understand that members of his race also wanted protection under the laws and respect for their rights as citizens. For his actions, the *Raleigh Morning Post* lauded him as "one of the best colored citizens of Raleigh." In essence, Hunter had only been following the advice offered to blacks by the *News and Observer* when it reminded them that "Whites had a proper regard for good Negroes who know and keep their places, but only the meanest contempt for the impudent and unruly ones."[11]

It was probably a coincidence that the violence in Raleigh occurred within days of the Wake County Republican Convention, but events at this gathering indicate that blacks were beginning to believe that the Democrats were dead serious in their commitment to a total war for white supremacy. The situation was of sufficient gravity that James H. Young had to take leave from his regiment, return to Raleigh to help manage the convention, and devise a new political strategy. It was agreed to run only white candidates for office, and Young believed that this would deny the Democrats an opportunity to exploit the race issue effectively. He explained, "The men we've put up can't be cartooned by the *News and Observer* as niggers." Young also thought that too many blacks had been nominated for office in other parts of the state and some should be withdrawn. This was particularly true of eastern North Carolina. Abe Middleton, the black Fusionist leader in that section, agreed, and at the Wayne County Republican Convention in September 1898, he declared, "We don't want any more Negroes in office right now, cause we want to stop the Democratic cry of 'Nigger.' "[12]

The withdrawal of candidates did not pacify the Democrats, who probably would not have been satisfied if every black in the state agreed to stay away from the polls on election day. Democrats were out for blood, and the first appearance of the Red Shirts at Fayetteville on 21 October 1898 symbolized their commitment to terrorism. Overt physical violence broke out the following day in Robeson County, and thereafter there were racial skirmishes in the counties bordering South Carolina. A week after the Red Shirt demonstration in Fayetteville, at the Great White Supremacy Convention in Goldsboro, William O. Guthrie delivered what was in substance a declaration of war against blacks. He declared that whenever Anglo-Saxons were in conflict with another race, they had always asserted their supremacy and either conquered or exterminated their foe. With the Bible in one hand and the sword in the other, "We say to the nations of the world, 'Resist our progress and civilizaton and we will wipe you off the face of the earth.' " After cheering and applauding Guthrie's remarks, the convention had the temerity to resolve that they contemplated no violence and meant blacks no harm.[13]

Blacks, however, got the message, and by the beginning of November 1898 it was clear to some that they could not withstand a white assault. The very threat of a race war was sufficient to force a number of them to modify their stand on political rights. On 3 November James H. Young capitulated when he counseled a crowd of nearly 1,000 blacks not to involve themselves in anything that would provoke trouble with whites. Qualified blacks had a right to vote, but "if this matter of Negro office holding was to set the races in deadly enmity to each other . . . , then the Negro had better say to the white man 'Here take your political offices and let me live in peace and quiet and prosperous contentment among you as a citizen and fellow man.' "[14]

Whites were determined to end their campaign in a blaze of glory, and Wilmington, the largest and most prosperous city in the state, was selected as the site for the decisive battle of 1898. The city was publicized to the world as the home of the most insolent blacks and the most abused whites in the state. It was alleged that blacks had taken control of city government, and had thoroughly demoralized and totally subjected the white population. The homes of whites were threatened and their women abused, business and industry had stagnated, and a black editor of the city had publicly insulted the white women of the South. Indeed, conditions for whites were described as intolerable, and the liberation of the city from the throes of black rule became the cause of all Democrats in North Carolina. Prior to election day, the whites of Wilmington collected weapons, brought in reinforcements, formed an insurgency committee, organized for combat, and in defiance of federal and state authority announced their intentions to overthrow violently a legally constituted government. The feeble attempts of the Russell administration to maintain public order, and the unwillingness of the federal government to intervene to protect the rights of its citizens, left the blacks in Wilmington isolated and totally at the mercy of native whites.[15]

Even though their candidates had withdrawn from the campaign, some blacks in Wilmington were determined to exercise their rights of citizenship, and claimed that they would not humbly submit to coercion and intimidation. They too saw their cause as the cause of their race. The Saturday before election day was set aside as a day of prayer and fasting, and blacks prayed for courage and inspiration to meet the impending crisis. Later, at a mass meeting, John C. Dancy announced that the question of white rule had to be settled "now and forever, at the ballot box or afterwards by stronger measures." Blacks certainly were in no position to take any "stronger measures," and Governor Russell, who was in the city on election day, accurately described their plight when he reported, "There may be a massacre, there could not be a battle." If this was the case, why did not the governor intervene to protect them? Part of the answer rests with the possibility that he was in sympathy with the objectives of the white-supremacy movement. At least this was true some ten years earlier when he had recommended that the Republicans surrender all state offices to the Democrats. Russell thought that this was somehow benevolent because it would relieve whites of the fears of black rule, and thereby reduce passions, bitterness, violence, and dangers of racial conflict.[16]

Democrats were not content to settle the issue of black political activity at the ballot box, even after achieving a decided victory on election day. In fact, it seems that political victory was only an intermediate objective of the Democrats. Blacks had to receive an object lesson in white power that would put them in their place once and for all. The day following the election, whites adopted the "Wilmington Declaration of Independence," which freed them from all restraints under the Constitution of the United States. The authors of this document reinterpreted the meaning of black citizenship by reverting to a logic amazingly similar to that used by Chief Justice Taney in the *Dred Scott* decision. After probing the minds of the nation's founding fathers, the Democrats agreed that it was not the intention of the framers of the Constitution to subject their descendants to domination by an inferior race. Neither did they intend to enfranchise an ignorant people. Having admitted as much, Democrats were frustrated and clearly in a dilemma. They could not remove the objectionable portions of the Constitution, particularly the Fourteenth and Fifteenth amendments, and as a way out they chose a course of reactive and compensatory violence by striking at blacks. This gave them the means to vent their accumulated hostilities by displacing their aggression from an object that was too strong to be attacked to one that was too weak to resist. In the process they could also demonstrate their superiority and punish blacks.[17]

On 11 November 1898 the white insurgents staged a coup d'état in Wilmington and proceeded to wipe out the remnants of Fusion government while executing a punitive expedition against the black community. However, the violence was generally controlled, and a damage and casualty analysis indicates that it was mainly directed at educated and progressive black males. John C. Dancy, Jr., later recalled, "The main targets were men like my father, whose crime was that they were successful and prosperous beyond the condition of the average white man." The incident was also a reaffirmation of the power relationship between the races, and blacks not only in Wilmington but throughout the state learned a lesson they would not soon forget. If they could be openly driven from their homes and murdered in a city with the largest black population in the state, in the hometown of the governor, and with the prior knowledge of state and federal governments, then they were not safe anywhere. Blacks simply had two options for survival; they could get out of North Carolina or they could accept a positon as semiemancipated members of society.[18]

In the immediate aftermath of the violence in Wilmington, no white friends of blacks could be found. Not a single white man in the state publicly condemned the incident, and very few citizens of Wilmington echoed Jane Murphy Cronly, who on 18 November wrote, "For the first time in my life I have been ashamed of my State and the Democratic Party." She thought she would always remember the event with indignation and sorrow because there was no excuse for it. "The oft repeated cry it was necessary is false, utterly, entirely false." Two weeks after the affair, the *People's Paper* of Charlotte, which was one of the few publications that did not glorify the violence, announced that what had happened at Wilmington was sad commentary on the state of civilization in North Carolina, where the majority of the people claimed to be not only white, but Christian. The editor correctly noted that if one examined the events in Wilmington in light of divine truth and Christian ethics, then one could only conclude that the church and Christianity were both signal failures.[19]

Necessity, Christianity, and civilization were the very points used by whites to justify what happened at Wilmington. Explanations ran the gamut from the necessity to overthrow Fusion rule, defend the property and honor of whites, punish a black newspaperman for questioning the virtue of white women, and preserve civilization and Christianity. Colonel Alfred Moore Waddell, the leader of the white-supremacy movement in Wilmington, thought that the incident was necessary to shock blacks into reality, because they were temporarily insane and acted unnaturally. It was just not their nature to insist upon political power, but their minds had become so badly perverted that they could not understand that the white-supremacy move-ment was the salvation of their race. To him, violence was a necessary form of therapy to correct the situation.[20]

Strangely enough, the religious leaders of Wilmington, who were sup-posed to be the moral and spiritual guardians of the community, were among the strongest defenders of the use of force and violence. The Rever-end Calvin S. Blackwell of the First Baptist Church compared the event to the situation before there was a Heaven, when "God and his white robed angels fought against the devil and his black robed angels and God pre-vailed and banished the black leader and his deceived ones; and there was peace in Heaven." Similarly, the pastor of the Brooklyn Baptist Church,

## "Like a Devil Turned Loose"

James W. Kramer, proclaimed that God from the beginning of time intended that white men should lead and rule. The white men of Wilmington had only done God's work and helped fulfill his prophecy. Less esoteric was the interpretation offered by the Reverend Peyton H. Hoge in a sermon delivered on the Sunday after the election. He defended the use of violence as being necessary to teach blacks respect for white women, and he also saw it as an act of charity that the more affluent whites performed for their poor brothers who had to live in close proximity to undisciplined black men.[21]

The religious press of the state agreed with the arguments of the Wilmington clergy. The *Biblical Recorder* affirmed the righteousness of the white citizens' cause, and absolved them from all guilt or sin by placing the blame on blacks, who should "lay the bodies of their dead" at the feet of Alex Manly and those politicians who humiliated the white citizens of the city. The *North Carolina Presbyterian Review*, edited by Alexander J. McKelway, justified the Wilmington affair by its results and by appealing to the scriptural reference, "He who haveth the sword." McKelway thought whites had a right to use the sword to govern, because back of it lay the forces of intelligence, education, courage, capacity, character, and morality. Reflecting on the events of 1898, Bishop Robert Strange commented, "We saw what was needed and what could have happened, and when we think of what did happen, we all know that it was the best managed thing that ever did happen."[22]

Whites had no rational explanation for murder and arson because they could not see them as part of a continual pattern of violence against the black community. The root of this violence was an intense race prejudice that resided within individuals at the preconscious level. Though dormant, it could under the proper stimulus consciously express itself in violent and hostile ways. Such responses cannot be explained by logic because prejudice is essentially an affective rather than a cognitive process. The idea that blacks should not approach the political and social status of whites was an important part of the prejudice of white North Carolinians. When they perceived that this was about to happen during the Fusionist era, whites reverted to their preconscious, which functions as a sort of mental data bank, and retrieved the one proved method of keeping blacks in their place: violence. Walter Hines Page, in his novel *The Southerner*, captured the mentality in North Carolina during the white-supremacy campaign. Speaking of this movement the leading character remarked: "I did not know till now the hidden fury that lay in race hatred. Race-difference, which may be ever so friendly in the even course of events, seems to hold a latent quality that may on occasions flare into the fiercest hate. . . . This fanaticism seemed to be something that had simply been talked into activity, but if it could be talked into activity, it must have lain dormant all the while, it must be there at all times, ready to be talked into activity when needed." The leading blacks of Wilmington probably understood this and, immediately following the violence, those who were still in town resurfaced and cautioned their race not to do or say anything that might inflame new passions, and above all to remember that "words have created more trouble than anything else."[23]

The black leaders of Wilmington who dared to offer an explanation for what had happened showed a reasoning power similar to that of whites. They too blamed anonymous black politicians and their white cohorts, and the Manly editorial; and a few ministers even stated that the catastrophe was a mark of God's wrath. On the Sunday after the violence, black preachers obtained permission to hold religious services, but they were told by whites to exercise moderation and caution. A correspondent of the *Baltimore Sun* visited nine black congregations of various denominations, listened to sermons, and interviewed several pastors and deacons. An analysis of his report reveals that black religious leaders had stoically accepted the situation and were indeed counseling their people to submit totally to white authority, obey the law, and be peaceful. In turn, God would protect them and punish those who had committed wrongs against them. Judging from their rhetoric, it seems that these leaders were far better Christians than their white neighbors. The minister at Christ Colored Congregational Church, Fountain G. Ragland, preached a text of "love your enemies, bless those that curse you, do good for them that hate you, and pray for them that despitefully use you." At Saint Luke's African Methodist Church, Deacon Briscoe Harris, after drawing a parallel between the situation of blacks and the fiery trials of the Hebrew children, urged his people to trust in God and mind their own business. If not, he warned that "terrible consequences would follow." This was good advice because it was no time for blacks to assert themselves or to agitate any issue. They were alone and without the prospect of protection from any quarter.[24]

The more violent aspects of the white-supremacy campaign constituted a traumatic experience for blacks, not only in Wilmington but throughout North Carolina. They were shocked by the brutality of the best white men, and stunned by the sudden and complete collapse of black politicians. John Merrick recalled that following the Wilmington violence, black men's hearts stood still. "They pondered and shuddered and hugged close to the few white friends they trusted." The blacks who assumed the leadership of their race were accommodationists who were willing to assent to racial inequality. They also hoped that race relations could revert to its pre-Fusion status. The Reverend Joseph Perry of Raleigh summed up this attitude when he declared, "Let the white people have the campaigns and offices and let us get what we can of education, money, and Christ."[25]

Evidence of how quickly blacks got back into line can be seen in the events surrounding their annual fair, which was held the week following the Wilmington violence. Governor Russell was scheduled to open the event, but on the morning of the fair the Reverend R. H. W. Leake visited Josephus Daniels and asked him to serve in this capacity. Daniels was hesitant to do this in the belief that his activities during the white-supremacy campaign had made him unacceptable to blacks. Leake assured him that this was not true, and that blacks really disrespected the "old rascal who is up in the Governor's mansion." Furthermore, he claimed that they knew Daniels was their friend, and they needed someone who was a leader in the white-supremacy movement to give them assurances of friendship and protection. Daniels accepted and during his remarks he spoke of the friendship that the leaders of the white-supremacy campaign had for blacks. He also pointed out that the campaign was directed not at law-abiding blacks, but at the "Negro slave drivers of which Russell was the head."[26]

The managers of the fair also appealed to the white community to attend and give blacks encouragement in their efforts to improve the educational status of their race. Hunter was present at the fair lobbying for the incorporation of industrial-education courses in the public school curriculum. He contended that this would prevent black children from growing up in idleness and crime because they did not know how to do anything useful to earn a living. A reporter of the *News and Observer* thought that Hunter's ideas were worthy of serious consideration by the best minds of the state. Hunter also had a few other ideas he wanted to share with the *News and Observer*. On 19 December 1898 he sent a copy of his ten-year-old treatise "Some of the Evils of Reconstruction" to Fred L. Meritt, the managing editor of the paper, and authorized him to use any portion of the document in any way that he desired. He also sent Meritt a copy of a card that he had published in 1874 when he was a candidate for city alderman and a leader in the fight "against the corrupt Republican Administration" that controlled Raleigh. Hunter wanted Meritt to know that he had predicted the outcome of the white-supremacy campaign twenty-five years earlier, and that ever since that time he had been abused for taking a logical view of the relationship between blacks and politics in the South.[27]

Hunter was just one in a long line of leading blacks who tried to protect themselves by nestling close to the coattails of Democrats, and sought refuge under the umbrella of Booker T. Washington's ideology. In their haste to secure the approval of whites, accommodationists vied with each other in denouncing politics and extolling the virtues of the best white men. For example, the Reverend Samuel N. Vass, secretary of the black Baptist Sunday School Institute, wrote Josephus Daniels that it was the opinion of some of the leading blacks of Raleigh that "notwithstanding the sad conditions in other places, we are still in the midst of some of the best white people in the world." James B. Dudley, the president of the Agricultural and Mechanical College of Greensboro, who was in his hometown of Wilmington during the violence, later wrote to the editor of the *Wilmington Messenger* that the late campaign "had forcibly impressed and thoroughly convinced" blacks that it was imperative for them to maintain friendly relations with whites. They had finally learned that these relations would not exist as long as they remained politically active. Dudley admitted that he and a few others had long agreed that blacks in some parts of the state had enjoyed a political influence that was disproportionate to their intelligence and worth. "We knew that the Negro politician must be eliminated."[28]

Dudley somehow thought the violence at Wilmington was salutary, and he foresaw the dawn of a brighter day for blacks. "Foolishly and stubbornly we have lingered in the quagmire of stupidity, idleness and degradation," he wrote, but blacks had "learned in the inexorable school of experience that politics is not the star to guide us by night, nor the sun to warm us by day." Dudley must have forgotten that he had been deeply involved in Republican party politics, and that less than five years earlier he had been a delegate to the convention that nominated President McKinley. The editor of the *Messenger* must have forgotten this too, for he characterized Dudley as a clear disciple of Booker T. Washington who had imbibed "much of the wisdom of that ablest leader and teacher of his race."[29]

Democrats and the leading black men changed their assessments of each other at the same rate of speed. The Reverend R. H. W. Leake, who during the Fusionist era was designated by the Raleigh press as that "little nigger preacher," suddenly became "Dr. Leake" or the "colored Presiding Elder of the Raleigh District." This happened after Leake delivered a speech on 12 December 1898 blaming the Wilmington incident on the Russell administration. Leake, always a vocal opponent to Fusion politics, Russell, and Jim Young, noted that had his advice been followed in 1896 "the Negroes that now lie in silent graves would be living and those that are outcasts and fugitives would be at their own firesides and among their own people." According to Leake, Josephus Daniels should not be blamed for the excesses of the white-supremacy campaign, for he had only done his duty to protect blacks from themselves and Russell. Leake recommended that blacks should stay in politics and ally themselves with the best elements of the white population as a means of safety and protection. The good Reverend Mr. Leake also endorsed the enactment of Jim Crow laws to segregate the races in railroad cars, and he did not blame Democrats for not wanting to ride with blacks after their recent association with Russell.[30]

Even black politicians who were elected to the legislature in 1898 joined the accommodationists' bandwagon and tried to reassure whites that they would not give them any trouble in the General Assembly. Isaac Smith, who was elected to the house from Craven County, issued a statement two weeks after the Wilmington affair that accused Alex Manly of slandering white women in his newspaper and the black ministers of the city for passing resolutions approving of the editorial. Smith asserted, "White men appear on the scene as gods to uphold and defend their pure and unadulterated women," hence their activities at Wilmington were godly acts. For this bit of reasoning, the *News and Observer*, which during the campaign had called Smith "a black Shylock," now described him as a "colored banker" who gave sound advice to his race. Thomas O. Fuller, the senator-elect from the Eleventh Senatorial District, announced that he would go to the senate not as a politician, but as a Christian citizen. He voiced agreement with Booker T. Washington that the black man must first make himself a strong and reliable factor in his own community before he would have any influence in the political affairs of the state and the nation. Therefore, Fuller asserted, "I shall DEMAND nothing, but gently and earnestly PLEAD for a continuance of the sympathetic and friendly relations, which have been the proud boast of us all."[31]

The white-supremacy campaign of 1898 had further widened the rift in the state's black political leadership. Prior to the campaign the vast majority of black Republicans had supported the strategy of Fusion, while a vocal minority had opposed this concept. However, during the campaign a group of blacks emerged who either voted for or sympathized with the Democrats. Afterward, this group was frustrated because it was not the policy of the Democratic party to reward black men with offices or official recognition. To satisfy their desire for leadership and power, the collaborationists with the Democrats tried to take control of the black community. Black Republicans had similar ideas because they too could no longer sate their cravings for power and prestige by openly participating in state and local politics. Thus a contest developed between these two elements, and partisan politics were injected into every institution within the black community.[32]

The leading blacks of Raleigh were generally supporters of Jim Young or of the Reverend R. H. W. Leake. In preparing for the Emancipation Day celebration of 1899, the Young faction excluded the "Leakites" on the grounds that they were Democrats. Leake, on the other hand, believed that his group represented the best interests of his race, and that Young and his followers might say something during the celebration that would result in further harm to blacks. Accordingly, Leake organized a rival celebration. At length a compromise was reached between the two factions and a single celebration was staged, but in the meantime Hunter had been identified by the *News and Observer* as being in Young's camp. As secretary of the Emancipation Association and chairman of its Committee on Resolutions, Hunter felt compelled to explain his involvement in the Young-Leake controversy. He published a card in the *News and Observer* stating his hope that no one would be influenced by any false reports concerning him. Denying any attempt to ostracize black Democrats, he announced the inclusion of Brother Leake on the Emancipation Day program. Hunter also claimed that he had been "making every possible effort to stop this foolishness and have the people come together as of yore."[33]

The Emancipation Day celebration in Raleigh was an occasion for serious and sober reflection. Gone were the boasts, militancy, and jubilation of years recently past. Blacks also realized how alone they were because there were no whites in the audience, nor did any show up to address the crowd in the customary friendly terms. President of the Day William M. Graves, reflecting on the events of the previous year, concluded that the future of blacks in North Carolina was indeed dark, and about the only thing they could do was to stand still and wait for the salvation of the Lord. In presenting the resolutions, Hunter first affirmed that there was no spirit of hatred among blacks. They still had nothing but the kindliest feelings for whites, but they did condemn mob violence as unnecessary and brutal. He also acknowledged the dim future of blacks and the anxiety that existed within them. Their salvation was not in the Lord, but in the white people of North Carolina. He exclaimed, "The great white race to whom we must look for justice and protection cannot afford to be unjust. They cannot afford to degrade us any more than they could the erection of a pest house at their door." He called on the rich and powerful white race to point out in friendly manner the mistakes of blacks and lend them a helping hand. [34]

On the eve of the Emancipation Day celebration, other blacks from North Carolina appealed to the sense of justice of the president of the United States. Congresssman George H. White, Henry P. Cheatham, John C. Dancy, and Bishop George W. Clinton, along with members of the Executive Committee of the National Afro-American Council, called on McKinley at the White House. They asked that he use his and Congress's influence to ensure that the persons responsible for the outrages against their race in North Carolina be apprehended and brought to justice. Not surprisingly, McKinley ignored this request, whose fulfillment would have entailed rounding up most of the Democratic leadership of North Carolina. [35]

Hunter and the rest of the blacks in North Carolina soon found out that the great white race could afford to be unjust and further degrade them. Democrats had some unfinished business, and the relative calm that prevailed in the wake of the election of 1898 was just a lull in the campaign. Any perceptive observer could see that the next battle would be over the issue of disfranchisement. Democrats had promised that they would restore and perpetuate white supremacy, and party strategists realized that the best way to do this was through a constitutional amendment that would disfranchise the masses of blacks. "There is no half-way ground in a revolution such as we have passed through," wrote Josephus Daniels; "no election law can permanently preserve white supremacy." Charles B. Aycock reduced all controversy to its simplest terms when he stated, "We say the Negro is unfit to rule. We carry it one step further and convey the current idea when we declare he is unfit to vote." [36]

The leading blacks should not have been surprised when on 6 January 1899 a proposed amendment was introduced in the legislature prescribing an educational qualification for voting. Included was a provision for a grandfather clause, which served as an escape mechanism for illiterate whites. Some of the leading black men, particularly educators, had actually encouraged the disfranchisement of the illiterates of their race, and this facilitated the job of the Democrats. Hunter claimed that he had "long questioned the wisdom of conferring upon the ignorant freedmen the vast powers of the elective franchise," and he believed that the mass of blacks was not sufficiently intelligent to participate in politics. Hunter's friend Simon G. Atkins, the president of the Slater Normal and Industrial School in Winston, likewise regretted the fact that universal suffrage had been granted to blacks, because he believed in the "supremacy of intelligence and character and government by the most capable." In December 1898 James B. Dudley acknowledged that any legal and nonviolent movement to disfranchise blacks would be earnestly favored and supported by many intelligent and influential men of his race. Parson Leake agreed, and he thought that everybody would benefit if a large number of the illiterate voters of North Carolina were disfranchised. During his remarks at the 1899 Emancipation Day celebration in Raleigh, Professor Lovelace B. Capehart told blacks that the results of the white-supremacy campaign of the preceding year clearly indicated that suffrage and political equality were abstract rights that could no longer be maintained or defended. Governmental authorities, including the national administration, did not protect and uphold blacks in the enjoyment of these rights, nor did they give them their moral support. Capehart believed that it would have been far better had these rights never existed than to see them blatantly disregarded.[37]

The leading blacks who advocated an educational qualification for voting hoped it would eliminate all illiterates, and place government in the hands of the best men of both races. They probably did not anticipate the grandfather clause, but even after this device was included in the proposed amendment, the leading blacks still supported an educational qualification in the belief that it was the easiest of all disabilities to overcome if the state continued its support of popular education. Black educators also had selfish motives for supporting a qualified suffrage based on education. They could visualize a larger role for their schools and greater prestige for themselves within the black community. Furthermore, they knew that they could pass an educational test and thus claim membership in a select group who had earned the right to vote by virtue of their own merits. They could even feel that they were better than the masses of poor whites who did not vote as a result of their own personal accomplishments but on those of their "granddaddys."[38]

The Democrats blundered by linking suffrage to education. If a sufficient number of blacks became educated, the way would be opened for their reemergence in politics. As a way out of this dilemma, the Democrats announced their intention to restrict the education of blacks by withdrawing the financial support of whites. There was also widespread support for a constitutional amendment that would apportion educational funds on the basis of taxes collected from each race. In January 1899 Representative D. R. Julian introduced a bill in the legislature to amend the state constitution along these lines. Whether Julian realized it or not, this was an act of grand strategy. It forced the leading blacks, who had always believed that education was the first priority for their race, to focus their attention on education instead of disfranchisement. At the call of Congressman George H. White, a group of leading blacks from thirty-six counties hastily assembled in Raleigh in January 1899. After suppressing a faction that wanted to issue a radical and sensational statement that among other things called for a wholesale migration from the state, this group adopted a conservative memorial to the General Assembly. The leading men asked the legislature to continue its appropriations for black educational and charitable institutions and not pass any laws to reduce their aspirations, manhood, and usefulness as citizens. They hoped that whites would remember the faithfulness of their race as slaves and give blacks an equal chance to work out their destiny.[39]

Those blacks who sympathized with the Democrats even came out into the open and joined in the effort to preserve the educational opportunities of their race. They reminded the Democrats that many educated blacks had supported them, and as a reward the party and its press should put forth their best efforts to prevent any radical legislation to curtail the educational advancement of their race. The editor of the *Union Republican* (Winston) admonished blacks not to expect too much from the Democrats because it had always been their policy to bar blacks forever from enjoying the rights of free citizens. Blacks were also told to reexamine the claims that Democrats made about being their best friends. The editor thought that "If it was friendship to the Negro to keep him illiterate and compel him to serve only in the capacity of political and menial slaves," then the Democrats were indeed friends.[40]

On 13 January 1899 a delegation of leading blacks appeared before the General Assembly's Joint Committee on Constitutional Amendments. The Reverend R. H. W. Leake apologized for the sins that blacks had committed by exercising their political rights, and recommended that the legislature do whatever it thought was best regarding the disfranchisement of his race. Professor John O. Crosby, the former president of the Agricultural and Mechanical College at Greensboro, in a rash display of elitism, contended that out of the 125,000 black voters in the state, only 20 percent were capable of forming any political opinions. The remainder were a public menace who always blindly voted the Republican ticket. Crosby and Representative Isaac Smith both attempted to persuade the legislators that educated blacks were not opposed to white people, and that the state would actually gain by continuing its support of black education. Smith argued that education was the only way to produce good blacks, and if the masses remained illiterate the state would have to spend a lot of money prosecuting criminals. Furthermore, ignorant blacks were a danger to public safety because it was very hard to control them.[41]

Smith's argument pointed out another problem that Democrats had to face. They wanted to reduce educational opportunities for blacks in order to keep them out of politics, but at the same time they feared the potential dangers of an ignorant black population. Stephen B. Weeks got at this problem when he wrote, "No man can have less love for the Negro race, as a race than I have," but "a city cannot afford to allow a dead carcass to lie on the streets because of the disease it brings to its citizens." The same principle held true regarding the education of blacks. Whites had to provide for it, not out of love, but for their own safety. Weeks also believed that whites no longer had to worry about the possibility of blacks staging a political comeback once they became educated, and advised that "The history of Wilmington was proof of why blacks would not rule in North Carolina." In the end whites decided to continue the education of blacks as a matter of self-interest and protection. However, they would closely supervise the process and guide it along the lines of industrial and vocational training.[42]

The testimony of the leading blacks before the legislature came back to haunt them during the debates on the proposed suffrage amendment. Senator George Rountree cited the fact that they had acknowledged that their race had made little progress after thirty years of freedom and "were but a few years out of savagery." Therefore, he thought it was logical to conclude that the experiment in universal suffrage was a failure in North Carolina, and that immoral, criminal, unpatriotic, improvident, and ignorant people should have no voice in goverment. Rountree made these remarks in the House of Representatives in the presence of a large audience of blacks. He wanted these people to know that their disfranchisement was legal and humane, and that whites had always been just to them.[43]

Although they knew they were fighting a losing battle, the four black members of the legislature put up a last-minute fight against disfranchisement. This was also an attempt on their part to salvage some measure of self-esteem. They begged, pleaded, and appealed to every sentiment of justice and decency in an effort to defeat the amendment. They told whites that blacks had been slaves, they knew what it was like to be free, and the ballot was the earmark of that freedom. If whites wanted control over local and state government they were asked, why not obtain this by legislative action and permit blacks to vote in federal elections. This would preclude the possibility of having the state's congressional delegation reduced in the proportion to the number of blacks disfranchised. Moreover, by totally depriving blacks of their ballots, whites were told that they would be rejecting their Anglo-Saxon and Revolutionary heritage as well as their liberal tradition, which had always been in the direction of freedom. On a more personal level, the black legislators advised the Democrats that the passage of the amendment would be an open admission that whites were inferior to them. In this regard, Senator Fuller remarked, "You tell your children that they cannot keep pace with the Negro unless they are given eight years' advantage under a grandfather clause." Worse still, Democrats would also be guilty of admitting to the world that they were liars, because in the campaign of 1898 they had promised not to disfranchise blacks.[44]

The black legislators also saw the proposed amendment as an open refutation of the Democrats' claim that they were the best friends of blacks, especially of the older generation who had been slaves. Many young blacks, whom Democrats considered the "most obnoxious" element of their race, were literate and would qualify to vote, but the faithful old slave who had served whites in both peace and war would be disfranchised. When this happened, Isaac Smith warned that "it will take you and your sons 100 years to make the colored people believe that you and your fathers were their friends." Smith also announced that the saddest of all thoughts was that the very people whom he had held up to his race as their best friends were about to disfranchise them. According to a reporter, the white members of the legislature laughed as Smith made these remarks. Whites also cheered on the day the legislature adopted the amendment. This made the black spectators uncomfortable, and one by one they left as the state senate by a vote of 42 to 6 approved the measure. The General Assembly was not through with the debasement of blacks. Three days after the passage of the suffrage amendment, a Jim Crow bill requiring racial segregation on steamboats and railroads breezed through the legislature.[45]

These actions by the Democrats in February 1899 caused some of the leading men to conclude that it was not the intention of that party to control blacks politically, but to humiliate them as human beings. Bishop James W. Hood thought that if whites wanted to dominate the black electorate, all they had to do was to invite it into the Democratic party. Most blacks would welcome this because they had always desired a political alliance with the better class of whites, who already completely controlled and dominated every other aspect of the black community. Hood should have known Democrats claimed that, as decent white men, they did not enter into political relationships with blacks, and that, as Locke Craig remarked, "If you want to find the lowest type of white man, look for the one who associated with blacks on terms of political equality."[46]

The militant campaign of 1898 was revitalized by the Democrats in order to drum up support for the ratification of the suffrage amendment. Though accompanied by less physical violence than the campaign of 1898, the renewed effort employed the same tactics, techniques, and personalities. This movement to strip blacks of the right to vote also had a continuity equal to the political history of North Carolina. In 1899 Albion Tourgée wrote that the arguments used to support disfranchisement were identical with the ones to defend slavery, the slave trade, nullification, secession, rebellion, and Ku Kluxism. They were all based on the same basic premise, which was that whites were inherently superior to blacks.[47]

The rhetoric and reasoning used by the Democrats in 1899 and 1900 was indeed essentially the same as that used in 1835 to justify the disfranchisement of free black voters. During the latter occasion, whites argued that blacks came to America debased and worthless, and they would always remain that way because no amount of education or anything else would improve them. Black voters even then were perceived as a dangerous political factor that used its ballots to swing occasional elections. Worse still was the fact that blacks had the idea that political equality meant social equality, and whites claimed that the simple act of voting would surely lead to interracial marriages. The arguments of the Democrats also paralleled those used by radical racists during Reconstruction, and may well have emanated from the pernicious pen of Hinton Rowan Helper, who in 1867 wrote, "The Negro because of his natural inferiority, his despicable charac-

## "Like a Devil Turned Loose"

teristics, his gross stupidity, and his brutishness, he ought not to be allowed either to vote or hold office, nor to fill nor perform any other high function which appertains exclusively, to the worthy and well-qualified white citizens of our country."[48]

The fact that no new ideas of substance were added to the justification for the depoliticization of blacks in 1900 can be seen in a speech made by Locke Craig, which was typical of the oratory of the day. He admitted that the disfranchisement of blacks would merely put into law what had already been determined in the hearts of every white man in North Carolina, and it would also make the organic laws of the state conform to moral and divine laws, which were determined when God created the races of men. To him, blacks were the lowest group on the scale of humanity, whereas Anglo-Saxons stood at the top. This was true even of the poorest and most illiterate white because he had in his veins the blood of fifty generations of slave-owning ancestors who had proved their ability to govern and conquer savages. Blacks, not born to govern, had never possessed any right to vote either by law or by inheritance, and Craig maintained that the white people of North Carolina were determined that they would never again assert any claim to rule. If they did, whites would be "like a devil turned loose," and the issue would be settled by bloodshed. Speeches like this appealed primarily to mass emotions, but they were also applauded by educated whites.[49]

The idea of assigning races to inferior and superior categories based on inherent attributes, and maintaining that those at the top should govern, was intellectually acceptable in late nineteenth-century America. Additionally, T. Thomas Fortune, the editor of the *New York Age*, wrote Hunter in March 1899 that North and South were more united than they had ever been, and that there was little inclination on the part of the northerners to interfere with southern affairs. "The deuce of the matter is that Southern white men had educated Northern white men so that they have no faith whatever in black men." This troubled Hunter, for it did indeed seem that when whites in North Carolina assigned blacks to the depths of humanity, there were no escape clauses for leading men.[50]

In the spring of 1899 Hunter revived a ten-year-old project to improve his race's image through the publication of statistical evidence demonstrating its progress. He urged the superintendent of the Twelfth Census to collect and publish data on the amount of property owned by blacks, their religious, educational, business, and fraternal organizations, the total amount of their savings and investments, the inventions patented by blacks, the total amount of taxes paid to governments at all levels, and statistics relative to their criminality. The director of the census found Hunter's suggestions interesting. He promised to include some of the requested data in the next census, but also noted it would require special authorization to gather information on the remainder. This scheme of Hunter's was also motivated by a bit of self-interest, for he hoped that his proposal would generate a good government job for someone to supervise the collection of data. If such a position were forthcoming, he planned to fill it, and his nephew Ed advised him to submit an early application for the post. Despite promises of support from Senator Jeter C. Pritchard, Representative George H. White, and Henry P. Cheatham, nothing resulted from his proposal for a more accurate and detailed census of the black community.[51]

As the campaign for ratification of the suffrage amendment rolled into high gear, Hunter agonized over the fact that some of his white friends were leading the assault on his race. He deplored "the bitterness of that bitter contest," and was particularly hurt because his friend Aycock was in the vanguard of the movement. He was no doubt disappointed when his patron and confidant, Benjamin R. Lacy, revealed his racial attitudes by publicly stating, "God slanted back that brow and thickened that lip," and made blacks inherently inferior to whites. Hunter hoped to defuse racial passions by asking leading whites for some "friendly advice to the race as to the best course for it to pursue in view of present conditions." Failing in this, he delivered an eloquent address, "To the White People of North Carolina," at the Emancipation Day ceremony in 1900. He stated that his race had believed that the results of the Civil War had finally settled the status of its citizenship, and that the subject would never again be questioned. Because of recent events, blacks thought it necessary to express their viewpoints and invoke the best judgment of the entire nation.[52]

According to Hunter, there was no middle ground between slaves and freedmen, and men were one or the other. Blacks could not resist the conviction that the proposed suffrage amendment was the initial step toward nullifying both the Reconstruction amendments to the Constitution of the United States and the Emancipation Proclamation. Though anxious, they could not really believe that the disfranchisement amendment would actually be ratified. Blacks still had faith in the Christian character of the good white people of North Carolina and hoped they would use their influence in favor of right and justice.[53]

## "Like a Devil Turned Loose"

If the frequent allegations that blacks were unfit for citizenship were true, Hunter asked, "Who was to blame?" He reminded the best white men that blacks had first appealed to them for guidance during their convention in 1865. The best whites of the state refused and had "assembled themselves into an organization whose platform held that our emancipation was unwarranted by the Constitution of the United States." Thereafter whites resisted with every means at their command all attempts on the part of blacks to gain civil and political equality. It was at this point that blacks turned to white Republicans who sympathized with them in their aspirations for complete liberty. Hunter challenged the best white men to "review our relations with each other and ask yourselves the question, 'Would we have not done the same?' Could Negroes with self-respect have done otherwise?"[54]

If blacks had acted irresponsibly in the exercise of their political rights, Hunter claimed that disfranchisement was not the solution to this problem. "We cannot see that the best way to make a good man is to unman him," he exclaimed. He avoided calling attention to the fact that there were just as many ignorant and irresponsible whites as blacks by focusing on voters of foreign extraction. Hunter maintained that there were millions of these people in the nation who were illiterate, who knew nothing of the genius of American government, who could not speak English, and who came to the United States bringing "all sorts of isms out of which have grown strikes, destruction of property and murders." Because no one questioned their fitness for citizenship, Hunter asked if blacks were less fit than these immigrants. For those whites who deemed the race problem insoluble, Hunter advised acceptance of the teachings of "the Lowly Nazarene" on this subject. All they had to do was to look into their hearts and consciences and ask, "What would Jesus do?" Would he have heaped indignities upon blacks, encouraged lynchings, gloated over their ignorance, driven them from their homes and loved ones and virtually confiscated their property, deprived them of the right to vote, and then say that it was just and legal? In summation, Hunter told whites that if they wanted to reject the Christian way, and "do that which we so much dread," then blacks had no power to prevent it. Their only recourse was either to remain in North Carolina under conditions that no self-respecting people could endure or to leave the state. He added, "It will be the saddest day in the History of our race when the decree goes forth that we must turn our backs upon the land of our nativity: the land that has been enriched by the sweat and blood of our fathers, and mellowed by their dust, and seek homes in a strange land and among strange people. . . . We speak these words because we know of the unrest, the anxiety, and fears of our people."[55] Hunter admonished those blacks who intended to remain in the state that they could no longer look to political parties for protection in the exercise of their rights and privileges as free people. The best thing they could do was to educate their children, obey the laws, develop habits of morality and industriousness, and above all, "cultivate the confidence and seek the advice of the best white people."[56]

Hunter's address shows that at least for the moment he was face to face with the realities of the social situation in North Carolina. He also presented a rather ingenious argument. It placed the blame for the past political activities of blacks on the shoulders of the best white men of the state who refused to give aid and counsel to the freedmen. It also gave whites two choices; they could affirm their Christianity by refusing to ratify the suffrage amendment or they could pursue an opposite course and risk the odium of being an unchristian people. Henry P. Cheatham thought the address was a powerful statement of the case for blacks in North Carolina, and that it should be printed in pamphlet form and sent all over the South. However, some blacks thought that it would take a little more than speeches and pamphlets to prevent their disfranchisement. B. A. Johnson, the financial secretary of Livingstone College, in January 1900 suggested to Hunter that the friends and leaders of blacks from all walks of life come together on J. C. Price's birthday to discuss the condition of their race and develop a suitable response to the proposed amendment. Johnson thought that "we cannot well retain our self-respect nor the respect of the Nation if we sit quietly by and make no protest such as the Negroes of Georgia did." He also believed that many whites in the state opposed the amendment, and that through a manly, consistent, and vigorous appeal, blacks might enlist their support in a united effort to defeat it.[57]

Hunter and those other leading blacks who already accepted a limited disfranchisement were on precarious moral ground. Indeed, many of the leading blacks in North Carolina had become prime candidates for that class of blacks whom T. Thomas Fortune described as "new good niggers." He believed that there was a new group of southern blacks who were very much like the good "old niggers" of antebellum days, the meanest creatures on the plantation. The essential difference between the old and new "niggers" was that the latter class was generally well educated and its members held responsible positions. They apologized for whites and lauded them even when blacks were lynched, disfranchised, and thrown into Jim Crow cars, and they joined in condemning those of their race who had the courage and self-respect to exercise their rights as citizens and protest against these outrages.[58]

Although they knew the course of events could not be reversed, the leading men tried to recapture some of their self-respect and that of the black community by putting up a feeble resistance. Part of this included a last-minute attempt by Hunter to secure congressional protection for black voting rights in North Carolina. He contacted Senator Jeter C. Pritchard, who agreed with Hunter that there were many obstacles in the way of federal enforcement of the Fourteenth and Fifteenth amendments in the South. Pritchard nontheless promised to use every available means to protect the poor and illiterate of both races against disfranchisement. He told Hunter that blacks in North Carolina faced the most critical period in their lives, and unless their actions were characterized by prudence and forebearance, they "will receive a blow from the effects of which they will not be able to recover for the next century." Pritchard further agreed with Hunter that blacks should refrain from running candidates for local office during the campaign of 1900, because he thought "it would do more to assist the Democrats in their unjust and unwarranted assertion than all other causes combined."[59] Paradoxically, Hunter actively supported some Democrats during the campaign of 1900, and in July he volunteered to work on behalf of Needham B. Broughton, who was the party's candidate for the state senate from Wake County. Broughton graciously accepted Hunter's offer, and told him that he could much better serve the blacks than another candidate who knew nothing of them. Further, he claimed that Hunter and every other intelligent black in Raleigh knew that he had always been their friend and had assisted them in every possible way. They could now reciprocate by casting their ballots for him on election day.[60]

On 2 August 1900 the depoliticization of the black masses in North Carolina was assured with the ratification of the suffrage amendment. Whites rejoiced because they had at last reversed the work of Reconstruction and ended that troubled period in the history of their race. Lee S. Overman noted that whites were finally calm, and they rested in "that satisfaction which only comes of permanent peace after deadly warfare." White supremacy had been established for all time, and Overman naïvely believed that no intelligent white man of any political party, and not many blacks, would seriously wish that it be any other way.[61]

## "Like a Devil Turned Loose"

Although Hunter admitted that Aycock rode into office on the crest of the white-supremacy campaign, he voted for him anyway because of their personal friendship. He also claimed that Aycock was one of the "best and truest" men whom he knew, and that he had complete faith in "his wisdom, integrity, patriotism, and greatness of heart and soul." The day following the election, Hunter wrote Aycock that for the first time in his life he had cast a vote for the Democratic nominee for governor. He hoped that Aycock's administration would inaugurate a new and splendid era in the affairs of state, and bring to all people peace, security, liberty, and law. He told the governor-elect, "This is the ardent hope of the race to which I belong." Hunter later confided to Aycock that he believed his election was the work of God, and that the "Great Head" of affairs had called this wise statesman to assume leadership during a critical period in the history of North Carolina. "I hoped and I prayed that through your instrument race estrangement and bitterness would subside and that all people would unite themselves in a movement for liberty and law."[62]

Aycock was elected at a time when race relations were strained to their limits, and there was indeed the possibility that a radical racist such as Cole Blease or James K. Vardaman could have gained control of the governorship. According to Clarence Poe, Aycock came into office during a time of bitter hatreds and passions, and his call to idealism, "like the sound of music in an unexpected hour," turned the energies of North Carolina into generous and constructive channels. Poe also thought that his father-in-law, Aycock, had stood magnanimously, heroically, and unyieldingly for a generous attitude toward the black. This is a somewhat skewed version of Aycock, and if he ever inculcated such lofty principles, they were subordinated to the ideals of white supremacy. No one could have been elected governor of North Carolina in 1900 by espousing such principles. Closer to the truth is the fact that Aycock was swept into office because of the commanding and aggressive role that he played in the white-supremacy campaign. His appeal was to white men and his loyalty was to that group. Like others of his generation, Aycock firmly believed in the inherent inferiority of blacks, and he liked to refer to them as the weaker-child race. To him, whites were the elect of God, and that was why they held the title to rule. While their first duty was to their own race, they also had a God-given duty to aid blacks, and he urged them to shoulder their burden and help the weaker one progress along acceptable lines.[63]

As a religious person Aycock certainly must have known that his attitudes and pronouncements during the white-supremacy campaign deviated from Christian ethics, and he may have felt some remorse over his transgressions against his black brothers in Christ. Hence his advocacy of a charitable attitude can be seen as a form of guilt reaction that was purgative in nature; a reduction of aggressive attitudes following a successful act of aggression frequently produces a catharsis effect. Once the right to vote was separated from their rights of citizenship, the masses of black North Carolinians were left in a state of political dependency. They were hardly in a position to give anybody any trouble, so whites could afford to be generous, and before long blacks were back in their old place. Then the two races settled down in a tenuous state of peaceful coexistence. Robert Watson Winston alleged that this condition was brought about by the bloodshed and rioting of the white-supremacy campaign, as well as a gentleman's agreement between whites and blacks. The latter agreed not to vote, and the former assented to providing them with better schools, asylums, and orphanages. Winston stated that his pact held up for forty years, "after a fashion."[64]

Hunter could not enjoy any of the immediate benefits of this "era of good feelings," nor could he collect any rewards for having supported selected Democrats for office. The public became aware of the fact that he had a drinking problem. It is not known whether Hunter had been drinking all along, or if the habit was brought about or intensified by the stress generated by the white-supremacy campaign. He did claim illness as a reason, and there were some references to anxiety, strain, and a weakened nervous condition. When Hunter's drinking posed a serious threat to his continued employment as a schoolteacher, he sought the aid and protection of his white friends. Needham B. Broughton, a partner in the Edwards and Broughton Printing Company and senator fom Wake County, was particularly interested in Hunter. The two men had worked together in local politics, and for years they had been associated with the temperance movement. Broughton, thoroughly disappointed in Hunter, wrote him, "The early days of our friendship and the after years of your useful life in our school work gave me such regard for you that your falling away was indeed grievous." If Hunter could offer assurances that he had stopped drinking, Broughton promised that he would speak to Professor James B. Dudley and the Wake County superintendent of schools on his behalf.[65]

In June 1900 the matter of Hunter's drinking was discussed by the

Raleigh Township School Committee and referred to a subcommittee for investigation. Hunter was summoned to appear before this committee, and he was told to bring along his physician if necessary. In the meantime, Professor Edward P. Moses, the superintendent of Raleigh Township Schools, wrote Hunter that he hoped the matter would be resolved in his favor, and, "I shall be glad if I have been able to prove of any service to you." He advised Hunter not to push for a speedy settlement because his salary would continue until the School Committee resolved the case. On 28 June 1900 the secretary of the Raleigh Township School Committee wrote Hunter that it was his disagreeable duty to inform him that the position of the principal of the Garfield School had been declared vacant. Moses regretted this action, wishing that the decision had been in Hunter's favor. He advised Hunter not to act rashly and promised to assist him in getting reinstated in his old position or placed in a different one. Hunter faced certain financial ruin without steady employment. He was constantly hounded by his creditors, the mortgage on his home was on the verge of foreclosure, and his family was suffering from economic privation. In essence, Hunter was personally experiencing his earlier theoretical beliefs on the evils of drink. What was probably much worse than all of his hardships combined was the revelation of a flawed character and the accompanying loss of the esteem of the best white men of Raleigh.[66]

Nephew Ed, the black Puritan of the family, offered Hunter advice and assistance during his crisis. He went to see Henry P. Cheatham, the recorder of deeds for the District of Columbia, and found him willing and anxious to assist in finding Hunter a job in the government. Ed thought that the time was particularly auspicious for securing Cheatham's aid, "for he is looking after his own fences and will be only too glad to do favors that might in some remote way even help him in defending himself in his position against the numerous aspirants for it." Hunter in his hour of need once again turned to a professional black politician for help; he asked Cheatham for a job. Cheatham promised to try to get him a temporary position in the Bureau of Printing and Engraving, and he wrote Hunter that "once here with something to do, you can more leisurely and effectively plan for getting into a better place." This prospect fell through when the chief of the bureau told Cheatham that the only way Hunter could get a job in his office was through the Civil Service system. Finally, in the spring of 1901 Hunter packed his bags, turned his back on North Carolina, and headed north. After a temporary sojourn in Washington, D.C., he wound up in Trenton, New Jersey. He later tried to explain his reason for migrating by the fact that he could not stand the "inflamed state of dominant sentiment" in North Carolina. But it is clear that economic factors played an equally important role in forcing this decision.[67]

C H A P T E R

# Down and Divided

The white-supremacy victory, which did not produce any improvement in race relations, was viewed by some as a signal for a general onslaught against blacks and a license to take their property. Disfranchisement had also legislated the masses of blacks out of existence as freedmen. Their position in society was so precarious that even a few whites doubted if blacks could ever maintain a satisfactory condition without some political power and influence. However, most whites agreed that blacks deserved to be in a semiemancipated status, and during the opening decade of the twentieth century they launched a propaganda campaign to prove this point. This new assault against blacks was much harder to combat than overt physical violence because, with its trappings of intellectualism, it struck at the heart of a people's spirit. Moreover, it was not propagated exclusively by politicians and sensational journalists. Scholars, clergymen, and medical doctors all provided an intellectual justification for white supremacy. In reference to this, Congressman George H. White told the House of Representatives on 29 January 1901 that "at no time in the history of our freedom has the effort been made to mold public sentiment against us and our progress so strongly as it is now being done."[1]

At the core of the arguments presented against blacks was the idea that slavery had been good and freedom was bad. Racial theorists maintained that the masses of blacks in North Carolina in 1901 were worse than slaves because they were actually retrogressing and lapsing into a condition of savagery and barbarianism. The reasons for this were simple enough. In slavery blacks, reared under the influence of white men, had learned three things essential to the development of character: good work habits, obedience, and respect. Thus slaves were seen as better educated than twentieth-century blacks. They had worked hard, did not lie or steal, and had good morals, manners, and religion. Slaves were also viewed in retrospect as being happy, contented, and perfectly lovable creatures. Some whites thought that the only thing wrong with the peculiar institution was that it did not last long enough to effect any inherent changes in blacks, and it was also argued that each succeeding generation would be infinitely worse than its predecessors.[2]

Whites perceived young blacks as having been allowed to grow up like weeds. They were unrestrained, shiftless, roguish, insolent, and idle specimens who were primary candidates for the penitentiary or a lynch mob. This was particularly true of black males who, though childlike, had also developed an alleged mania for rape and criminal assault. It was claimed that these "lustful fiends and brutes" were a menace to society and terrorized whole communities in search of white females. If there was a respectful element among the younger generation of blacks, whites attributed it to the influence of a few former slaves who managed to retain traces of the dignity, conservatism, and decency that they had acquired in bondage. However, this minority was not enough to prevent the majority from deteriorating, and as a compensating factor blacks needed those frequent contacts with good whites that had been so beneficial during the days of slavery. These relationships ceased within a generation after emancipation, and thereafter the only social intercourse existing between the races was among blacks and the most depraved and degraded whites. Even these contacts could no longer be taken for granted, because not many whites of any class were interested in associating with blacks.[3]

At the dawn of the twentieth century, it was claimed that for the first time in American history blacks were friendless, and if they did not regain the affection of whites it was predicted that the current generation of both races would continue to be separated by active hatred and hostility. This was especially applicable in the case of blacks and poor whites who had never gotten along well together even during the days of slavery. The leading whites warned that one day their poor brothers, acting under the influence of race prejudice and political and economic antagonisms, would declare a general race war to settle their accumulated grievances. When this happened, it was predicted that blacks would meet the same fate as that which the Celts, French, Spanish, and Indians had received at the hands of Anglo-Saxons. Blacks were also told that they were indeed fortunate because their former masters were still able to exercise some restraining influence over

# Down and Divided

poor whites, but it was not known how long they could be held at bay. Although some focused on the savage instinct of poor whites, others claimed that southern society in general possessed the capacity for lapsing into temporary insanity. At the least provocation it took speedy revenge upon the violators of its laws and customs, and this could best be seen in the actions of the lynch mob where the ruling passion was a "savage diabolical bloodthirstiness" or a "fiendish bullyism."[4]

Along with violence and threats thereof, whites agreed that education was still a useful instrument for social control. The vast majority still maintained that education could not change the savage nature of blacks, but they thought that it would have a temporizing effect on the brutish and lustful male. It was also realized that blacks were determined to be educated, and that the best white men of the state had to continue their supervision of this process, or else schools would be maintained by militant blacks and their foreign and fanatical sympathizers from other parts of the country. The end product would be not fewer educated blacks, but fewer blacks educated under the proper influence, and native whites alleged that this was bound to result in civil strife and social disorder. By controlling the education of blacks, they hoped to produce a type they could tolerate. They would also determine which kind of education was best for blacks, and who was going to teach it. As Clarence Poe suggested, whites would "select the worthiest and safest black men to direct the education and influence the principles of the young negroes."[5]

The leading black men responded to this latest assessment of their progress and character in a variety of ways. Some went to the extreme and agreed with whites that their race was morally sick and depraved, "to the disgust and disgrace of civilization." They also believed that friendly relations had to be established with whites because that race had the "light" to keep blacks on the right path. Others thought that in applying a host of negative characteristics to their race, whites were guilty of distorting the truth. Even if their race was criminal, immoral, and unethical, blacks had acquired these traits from their masters during the days of slavery, and therefore whites had to accept some of the responsibility for these conditions. Furthermore, blacks had no problem in North Carolina except that of trying to make an honest living in the face of an organized opposition. If they had not made more progress it was only because whites had failed to deal with them on terms of absolute fairness and justice.[6]

While the debate on the character of blacks was raging in North Carolina,

Hunter was trying to return to the state and he asked the state treasurer, Benjamin R. Lacy, about the prospects of employment. Lacy promised to do anything he could to assist Hunter, and said he would contact Aycock, Senator Broughton, and the State Board of Education in this regard. Hunter had discovered that conditions in New Jersey were not much better for a black than those in North Carolina. In Trenton he had hoped to resume his work as an educator, and he had arrived with letters of recommendation from some of the "best black and white men" in North Carolina attesting to his good character and excellence as a teacher. The endorsers of Hunter's good character had apparently overlooked the reasons for his leaving North Carolina. The Reverend J. E. King, the rector of Saint Ambrose Episcopal Church in Raleigh, certified that Hunter was one of the best black educators in the state, and a communicant in good standing in the parish who "enjoyed the respect of all our people both white and colored." Likewise, Professor James B. Dudley regarded Hunter as one of the most talented, accomplished, and experienced leaders of the black race. Hunter even had a letter of introduction to the governor of New Jersey from James E. Boyd, the judge of the United States District Court for Western North Carolina. Boyd wrote that he personally knew Hunter, and thought that he was a man of the "highest character and most exemplary habits," who was thoroughly qualified as an educator. He also hoped that Hunter would be well received among the people of New Jersey, and that he would have the success that "his sterling worth entitles him to."[7]

In spite of these flattering letters, Hunter soon found out that the state of New Jersey did not need the services of a black educator from North Carolina, and in a short time he wound up destitute and desperate. "It is cold here and I have no winter clothes," he wrote to his daughter in November 1901. He feared that he would not be able to withstand the cold and would contract a disease that would disable him forever. Two months later he sought charity from the Protestant Episcopal Church of Trenton. In a letter to the rector, Hunter wrote, "I am actually suffering for food and cannot have shelter longer than the present week." He denied that he was a beggar, but he hoped that the church would give him some kind of aid and assist him in finding employment. Hunter explained that he turned to the white church for help because he could not stand the thought of seeking aid from black denominations.[8]

At length Hunter found employment as a farmworker, a waiter, and a common laborer in the coalyards and sewers of Trenton. He eventually wound up as a partner, general manager, and field agent of the Inter-State Real Estate and Employment Agency. Among other things this agency was involved in the procurement of southern black workers to fill jobs in the North. By the spring of 1902 the labor business was booming, and according to Hunter there was a great demand for black workers. They came north from all parts of the South, and he placed them in jobs as soon as they arrived. At this point Hunter returned to North Carolina to recruit more migrants and to plan for the movement of his family to New Jersey. Back in Raleigh he discovered that the sentiment against him had subsided, and that his prospects for reentry into the education field were favorable. He decided to remain at home and abandoned the idea of returning to New Jersey.[9]

Hunter's white friends in Raleigh viewed his activities as a labor agent with mixed emotions. Needham B. Broughton approved because he had long believed that the best solution to the "Negro Problem" was to scatter blacks all over the country because their congestion in the South impeded their political, social, commercial, and religious advancement. On the other hand, Attorney Richard H. Battle was sorry to hear that Hunter was enticing blacks to leave the South for more remunerative wages elsewhere. He believed that Hunter might not be doing his race any favors, for the "necessaries of life" were cheaper in the South, and its climate was more congenial to the good health of blacks. Hunter soon came up with a philosophical justification of migration as a solution to the "Negro Problem."[10]

As Hunter saw it the race problem was based on both the previous enslavement of blacks and their presence in the South in large numbers. The former gave rise to the idea of black inferiority and the latter raised fears of black domination. The fact that blacks had been slaves could never be erased, but Hunter maintained that ideas of inherent superiority and natural inferiority were mere assumptions growing out of slavery. It was true that at the moment the Caucasian race was the greatest on earth, but it would not always remain so; in a proper environment blacks could rise to a level of equality with whites. To reach this, however, blacks, like whites, had to relate to the world as their home. They could no longer afford to remain fixed in the South but should move to those areas that offered them the best opportunities. To stay in the South, work for low wages, and complain about disfranchisement, Jim Crow cars, lynchings, and unemployment was indefensible when they could escape these conditions by moving a few miles away.[11]

Hunter also argued that the only excuse for the social and political conditions that had prevailed in the South since Reconstruction was that large numbers of blacks had endangered good government. The attempt to govern the South on the basis of a large black electorate was both a "failure and a farce," and wise men should have known better than ever to have tried such an experiment. It only intensified racial antipathies and resulted in terrible consequences for blacks. If blacks intended to stay in the South, they would have to accept white rule. If they could not it would be best for them to go some place where they could enjoy equality of citizenship and the benefits of a government run by responsible intelligent citizens. Hunter also thought that a significant reduction of the black population in the South would remove the only excuse for disfranchisement, and in time the ballot would be returned to those who remained.[12]

Southern whites would also benefit substantially from a reduced black population. Hunter reasoned that race agitation had completely diverted the best minds of the South from the problem of economic development, and the region had become a profitable market and dumping ground for northern manufactured goods. This condition would rapidly change once blacks were scattered from "Maine to Manila." Hunter thought that southern whites, relieved of the fear of black domination, could then turn their attention to development and thereby free themselves from economic domination by the North. But the North would also gain from the orderly movement of blacks into its section. Hunter alleged that "The Negro is docile, easily controlled, and free of isms," and once trained in northern habits of life and labor, he would become the most efficient worker in the country.[13]

Hunter's views on migration were published in an article in the *Raleigh Morning Post*, and the day after it appeared in print he forwarded a copy to Senator Jeter C. Pritchard. He informed the senator that the article had the approval of many of the best white people. Hoping it could be put to political use, he wrote Pritchard that it was "the best campaign document our party can issue." If people followed his ideas the Republican party would profit. Blacks would be removed as active and prominent factors in party policy and management, and many white men who acted with the Democrats solely out of duty to their race would join the Republican ranks. When this happened, the South would be turned over to the government of its "intelligent class as completely as the North."[14]

Hunter told Pritchard that he was willing and anxious to promote further

## Down and Divided

migration, but he had already sacrificed two years of his life to that effort, neglecting his family and the education of his children. "With a little money at hand to meet current expenses and afford me some little help," Hunter wrote the senator he could "do the work magnificently." He hoped that Pritchard, as chairman of the State Republican Executive Committee, could spare at least $100 to promote such an important cause. Denying the role of a beggar, Hunter requested the funds out of "a deep sense of duty and devotion to the best interest of my race, party, and State." He added that if the Republicans of North Carolina were not disposed to retain his services, "The party will have ample need for me in New Jersey and other Northern States when the time comes." Pritchard was satisfied that Hunter's concept had merit, and he wrote him that he too believed that if blacks adopted the policy as set forth in the article, they could certainly improve their condition. He promised Hunter that when funds became available to the State Republican Executive Comittee, he would take great pleasure in assisting in the work that Hunter was doing so effectively.[15]

Meanwhile, Hunter also was using his Democratic friends to assist him in finding permanent employment. Benjamin R. Lacy, Richard H. Lewis, and the Raleigh superintendent of schools, Edward P. Moses, all favored rehiring him. Needham B. Broughton, who had seen "sudden destruction rapidly approaching Hunter," also agreed after being assured that he had been "cleansed of the terrible monster drink." Even the governor took an interest in finding Hunter a job. Aycock had corresponded with him while he was in New Jersey and, upon learning that he was back in Raleigh, the governor went to Lacy's office and told him that Hunter "is too good and too valuable a man to be allowed to leave the State." He suggested to Lacy that a sufficient inducement be offered to Hunter to persuade him to remain in North Carolina. Naturally, Hunter got a teaching position and within a matter of months was appointed principal of the Oberlin School. Hunter's case is a typical example of the power of whites to make or break leading black men. The people who fired Hunter in the first place were the very ones who restored him to the ranks of the leading men. Grateful for the assistance of his white friends, Hunter wrote Lacy that he would dedicate his life to justifying their confidence in him. Furthermore, he was "perfectly sensible of the high and solemn obligation which such a distinguished favor imposes."[16]

It was probably for these reasons that Hunter refrained from taking an active part in the political campaign of 1902. During the first statewide election since disfranchisement, blacks soon discovered that the race issue was still very much alive, and the Democratic party was as opposed to their participation in politics as ever. Its leadership claimed that it would not be satisfied until all blacks were out of politics forever. The problem of black voters worried Cyrus B. Watson so much that he wrote, "I have asked myself at midnight upon my bed, 'What of the constitutional amendment? Does it settle it? NO!' The race question is still the greatest question." Watson, like others, was troubled over the possibility that with the masses of blacks out of politics, whites would evenly divide themselves on issues and a true two-party system would develop in North Carolina. This would be a terrible tragedy, because the small group of blacks who could vote would be able to swing an election and consequently would still dominate. Moreover, whites were sure that blacks would vote for the party that offered them the best chances for political and social equality.[17]

Thus it seems that the Democrats who in 1900 wanted to remove only illiterate blacks from politics, had by 1902 decided to get the rest. Responding to this sentiment, Furnifold M. Simmons advised that until the elimination of all blacks was "unfeignedly and without reservation accepted by all whites as a finality," his race would have to stick together behind the Democratic party. Republicans knew this, and by the fall of 1902 they too were well on their way toward making their party an all-white organization. Leading this movement was Hunter's confidant, Jeter C. Pritchard. During the Republican state convention whites denied black delegates any voice in the proceedings, and eventually ousted them from the floor. The black delegates were not even allowed to remain in the convention hall as spectators. While they were being expelled a band played the song:

Coon, coon, coon,
I wish my color would fade,
Coon, coon, coon,
Quite a lighter shade
Coon, coon, coon,
Morning, night or noon,
Its better to be a white man,
Than a coon, coon, coon.

The humiliated delegation of blacks included some of the "most representative and substantial" men in North Carolina, among whom were the former congressmen James E. O'Hara and Henry P. Cheatham.[18]

## Down and Divided

With blacks out of the way Pritchard intended to offer a slate of white candidates who would run under the label of "Independent." He hoped that this would attract to his ticket, and eventually to a new lily-white Republican party, the remnants of Populism along with thousands of Democrats. This lily-white movement was certainly not hurt by the assertions of Hunter and those other leading blacks who had earlier claimed that politics was harmful to their race. Yet when Republicans tried to help by taking them out of politics, they became indignant and struck back. The leading black men condemned Pritchard as an ingrate who had used their race as a stepping stone to prominence and then turned against it. These blacks, including Hunter, did not easily understand that disfranchisement had destroyed the base of the Republican party in North Carolina. Without the masses of black voters, the party had no use for a few educated blacks. In terms of real politics the Republicans' only chance to construct a viable party rested on their ability to attract white voters, and they could not do this as long as blacks were active within their ranks.

The leading black men, viewing the lily-white movement as a flagrant violation of the historic principles of the Republican party and the Fourteenth and Fifteenth amendments, were determined to remain within the party and fight Pritchard's movement. In October 1902 James E. O'Hara, Henry P. Cheatham, W. Lee Persons, and R. H. W. Leake signed a call urging teachers, preachers, farmers, lawyers, and all who could qualify to vote to meet at Raleigh and nominate a ticket that could be supported by all intelligent blacks of North Carolina. Their call stated that it was time for black Republicans to assert themselves and show that they were men; otherwise they must "abandon all hope of ever getting any recognition as men or citizens worthy of respect." Blacks had worked hard to build the Republican party in the state and they wanted a heritage for their children in that organization. They also believed that by combating the lily-white movement they could build "a bridge of manhood and true racial pride" upon which their children could stand. Every voter, and especially those who could qualify under the grandfather clause, was urged to come together and show Pritchard that he could no longer traffic in black votes. Thus by the fall of 1902 the Republican party in North Carolina was firmly split along racial lines.[19]

Democrats relished this rift in the Republican party, and Furnifold M. Simmons agitated the issue by announcing that Pritchard and his associates had consorted with blacks until they had contracted "Negro Cholera

Morbus or to be more accurate what the doctors call 'black vomit.'" Simmons suggested that they try the same remedy that the Democrats used in 1898 and 1900 to rid themselves of negrophobia: "the White Supremacy cure." The Democrats also argued that the expulsion of the leading men from the Republican convention would have no effect on black voters, who would continue to support Pritchard's ticket. Accordingly, Democratic registrars were instructed to prevent as many blacks as possible from registering or at least to keep their number to an absolute minimum. "A Negro not registered is certain to give the Democrats no trouble," stated an editorial in the *Raleigh News and Observer*, and the paper also advised blacks to register their protest against Pritchard by not registering to vote.[20]

The effectiveness of the disfranchisement amendment and the vigilance of Democratic election officials can be seen in the fact that on the eve of the election of 1902 there were only 6,145 black voters registered in the entire state as opposed to 234,678 whites. Some eligible blacks may have remembered the violence of past elections, or they believed the statements of their leading men alluding to the fact that politics was not in their best interest. At any rate, the *News and Observer*, commenting on the low number of blacks registered, stated that in most of the counties they had shown no interest whatsoever in the election and had made no attempt to register. The results of the election proved disastrous for Pritchard and his lily-white Independent ticket. The overwhelming majority of the Democrats was enhanced when the 6,000 blacks who did vote cast their ballots against Pritchard.[21]

Assessing the results of the election, Josiah W. Bailey, the editor of the *Biblical Recorder*, announced, "The war is over." Blacks were out of politics, and they had better stay out for their own sake. Politics, the curse of blacks, was the only thing that stood between them and progress. It had engendered hatred, contempt, and prejudices and deprived blacks of the friendship of whites. Now that blacks had retired from the political scene, whites were no longer bitter. They valued the black man's labor, respected him as a human being, and understood that his faults were those of a lowly and misguided race. Bailey called for an era of good feelings between the races, "in Christ's name."[22]

Events would soon prove Bailey's assessment premature. Blacks remained in politics. They were elated when President Theodore Roosevelt on 26 November 1902 announced his refusal to draw the color line in the South and his determination to appoint colored men of good reputation and standing to office. Further, he could not consent to the idea that the door of hope and opportunity should be closed to any man purely on account of color. "Such an attitude would according to my convictions be fundamentally wrong," said the president. White North Carolinians of both political parties were upset by Roosevelt's remarks, and they thought that he had missed a "bully opportunity" to acquiesce in the accomplished fact of white supremacy. They suspected that Booker T. Washington had prodded the president into making this statement as a means of retaliating against Jeter C. Pritchard. During the campaign of 1902 Pritchard had visited Alabama, and his rhetoric appeared to have led to the expulsion of blacks from the Republican convention and the institution of a lily-white movement in that state. It was alleged that this so infuriated Washington that he used his influence in the White House to have Roosevelt denounce the lily-white movement and to insist that the constitutional rights of blacks be respected throughout the South.[23]

Washington temporarily fell from grace in North Carolina amid accusations that he had forsaken his role as an educator in favor of that of a partisan Republican politician. The *Raleigh Morning Post*, although rejoicing in the fact that there was no Booker T. Washington in North Carolina, warned that his attention would be directed to the state, "for he is said to be very bitter against Senator Pritchard." In a public statement denying these charges, Washington explained that although his position regarding blacks and politics had not changed, he would use his opportunities to improve their political condition. He also stated that he was compelled occasionally to speak out, honestly and truthfully, on fundamental issues that affected his race.[24]

The leading men were stimulated by the remarks of Roosevelt and Washington. They interpreted the president's actions as a signal that the federal government had finally awakened to their plight. At their Emancipation Day celebration in 1903 black North Carolinians heartily endorsed the president's stand on equal rights for all citizens, and the Committee on Resolutions, of which Hunter was a member, presented proposals calling for the same. The resolutions also advised blacks to go out of their way to show their white neighbors that they did not hate them but actually wished them well. However, their white friends should also realize that blacks were not happy with their condition since disfranchisement. They reminded the Democratic party in particular that during the white-supremacy campaign it had promised fair treatment and justice for blacks. Race relations had in fact deteriorated, Jim Crow cars were unequal, and blacks were still systematically excluded from juries even when their liberty and property were involved. Mob violence had actually increased, and several blacks had recently been "shot down in cold blood by parties well known, but still went unwhipped of justice." Whites were asked to remedy these evils and the leading men were confident they would because the "white race was too proud to do otherwise."[25]

Ironically, while calling for the equality of all people, the leading blacks were also making a concerted effort to divide their own race into superior and inferior elements on the basis of wealth and education. Like whites they too appealed to Social Darwinism as a means of justifying their claims to superiority. At the annual meeting of the State Teachers' Association in 1901 it was announced as fact that in the struggle for all life only the fittest survived. The leading blacks had proved their fitness by taking maximum advantage of the best educational opportunities available, and assuming the important responsiblity of "making the weakest struggle successfully so as to become the fittest." Their record clearly contradicted the assertion that blacks were retrogressing and were a menace to the State of North Carolina. Moreover, as progressive blacks, they had a special mission to watch over the destiny of the lower classes. Because they constituted the basis of black leadership, the leading men thought they deserved the support and encouragement of the best whites. They also hoped that whites would stop grouping them with the criminals, vagrants, and unproductive elements of the black race.[26]

Some whites who viewed these class divisions as healthy signs urged the leading men to continue in this direction. However, Governor Aycock believed that the leading men were a little too late because whites had already separated blacks into the classes of the "old time darkey and the present day negro." Regrettably, the "old darkey," the preference of most, was nearing his end. Whites would have to choose between that small group of quiet and sensible blacks or those who were retrogressing. Accordingly, some whites agreed to assist the leading men in sifting their race by giving some recognition to those of superior education, wealth, and character. They also hoped that this would serve as a pacifier and the leading men would suppress their desire for political and social equality in the knowledge that they stood at the head of their own race rather than at the rear of the white. Naturally, the leading blacks were warned that if they expected any recognition or assistance they would definitely have to accept racial

# Down and Divided

segregation as a fact of life. Indeed, it was claimed that whites had argued among themselves on many issues but all agreed "never to even consider the suggestion of social equality or social intercourse with the negro."[27]

The issue of social equality continued to plague the leading blacks throughout the twentieth century. Whites still refused to define the term out of a fear of boxing themselves into a narrow interpretation. But the leading blacks knew that it was a convenient excuse for denying them opportunities for advancement. They also wished whites would try to understand that self-respecting and educated blacks actually deprecated every attempt made by anyone of any race that had the remotest possibility of promoting social equality. They nevertheless did not want to be separated from whites and hoped for a union of the best classes of both races in an effort to preserve peace and prosperity. Hunter certainly did not want to be separated from whites, and he thought that "For their own good blacks had to be kept under the guiding genius of the best sentiments of the best people of the white race." He opposed any direct communication between the best whites and the black masses. Rather, he argued that whites could assume the leadership and direction of his race by exerting their influences on the leading black men, which in turn would filter down to the masses. In 1903 he wrote, "I am anxious to promote this end," and "I feel that the Divine hand is upon me and that I am called to preach this Gospel." He warned against expecting any immediate results because blacks had to start again at the bottom of society and gradually pull themselves up under the guidance of their leading men, who possessed innate qualities of leadership.[28]

Part of Hunter's gospel included a reversal of his earlier position concerning the desirability of blacks migrating from the South. By 1903 he decided that it was best for them to remain at home and become faithful and efficient workers, but this would not be an easy task, for they had threatened their position in the labor market. He claimed, however, that this situation was not irreversible, but blacks had to change their work habits immediately because their "unreliability, inefficiency, and downright dishonesty was rapidly approaching a climax." Hunter may have derived these ideas from the political rhetoric of 1902, when blacks were warned that if they did not improve their performance as laborers and domestics, they would suffer increased violence and hatred. Whites would rally around a political party that would "sweep away his schools, his orphan homes, and his hospitals," and they would either expatriate the black man or make him a chattel. It was also argued that the unsatisfactory position of the black worker was a major cause for the deterioration of race relations; it caused him to be talked about and kicked around by white men, and shunned and hated by white women.[29]

Hunter responded to this critique by publishing his own statement on black workers and their habits. He asserted that low wages were no excuse for inefficiency on the job, nor did they justify quitting one job for another with higher pay. There were other benefits more important than monetary considerations. Long and faithful service to an employer would help blacks develop good character and responsible manhood, and would dispel the notion that blacks were unreliable and shiftless. Once whites had established faith in them, black workers would receive the highest possible wages, and they could then begin to advance to a higher plane. He neglected to predict when this would happen or how blacks were going to survive until whites arrived at this state of mind.[30]

Hunter took the totally illogical position that he was eminently qualified and thoroughly justified in offering this advice to his race because he himself had risen from the ranks of the common laborer to his current position. As proof he cited his work experience in New Jersey. In fact, he had dropped from the professional class to that of a laborer by virtue of his own personal shortcomings. Nevertheless, the editor of the *Raleigh Morning Post* took pleasure in commending his advice to the blacks of North Carolina. Hunter believed that by calling attention to the undesirable traits of black workers, he could motivate a positive change. In a letter to the editor of the *Independent* (New York), he denied any intention to slander his race or to support the derogatory statements made about it by politicians. His race was not made up of vagabonds and criminals, and its progress and achievements under trying circumstances had been marvelous. But he did want to alert blacks to the current demand for workers who were honest and efficient. "We need a great 20th Century movement among blacks to develop these qualities," he wrote; otherwise his race would be forced out of the labor market.[31]

Hunter's observation of the character of black workers closely matched those of white North Carolinians. In 1905 the State Department of Labor reported that, in all but two counties, "It is boldly declared that Negroes as laborers are unreliable." The cause of this defect was presumed to lie in the tendency of blacks to leave the countryside for cities and towns in search of an easy life. Hunter had also written a few words on this subject, and he maintained that the desire for an easy life was not peculiar to blacks but was common to all southerners. He traced its origins to the institution of slavery, which had bred a distaste for all labor. Centuries of forced labor under a class that lived in luxury caused the slave to regard his work as a mere drudgery fit only for those who could not escape it. The slave envied the lifestyle of his master and looked forward to a similar one if ever he became free. Hence it was not strange to Hunter that upon emancipation, those blacks who had the opportunity rushed out and became professionals, while others just "hung around and did nothing."[32]

Some whites claimed that black professionals "hung around and did nothing," or at least had never done anything to help themselves. Governor Aycock for one thought so, and in 1903 he told a gathering of distinguished blacks, "You have had everything done for you by whites. They worked out your emancipation and have carried forward the work of your education." It was time for the leading men to shoulder their burden and help elevate their race. Hunter tried to use his position as principal of the Oberlin School for this purpose. He contended that black schools were agencies for uplift and they had an important role to play in inspiring people to "higher purposes, nobler ambitions, and a purer life." These lessons, far greater than what could be obtained from books, were to be instilled in his students and the black community at large. Whites approved of Hunter's ideas concerning the role of the school in the community, and the *Raleigh Times* hoped that they would find universal acceptance among blacks.[33]

In 1903 Needham B. Broughton appealed to the leading blacks to use their influence to improve the moral condition of their race and join hands with whites in a crusade against "Sin and Satan." Specifically he wanted their wholehearted support for the temperance movement. Apparently forgetting Hunter's earlier bout with booze, Broughton asked for his aid in solidifying Raleigh's black vote against saloons. He confided to Hunter that the "saloon men were bragging that they were going to vote the Negro," and he thought that the election would be the grandest opportunity for them since disfranchisement to show that they could vote responsibly. The election would test the influence of the leading men in their community because it would show the public where they stood on the saloon issue. Hunter accommodated Broughton by publishing an article in the *Raleigh Morning Post* calling on blacks to remove the stigma of being the chief supporters of the liquor traffic. He asked those who could vote to cast their ballots for "God and right." In personal letters to blacks requesting their support, Hunter noted that "the white people of the community who are our best friends are anxiously looking to see where we stand. Can we afford to disappoint them?"[34]

Hunter soon found out that his past reputation as a drinker was still alive in the black community. Henry Gaston Otey, accusing him of appearing ridiculous, counseled Hunter to be silent about the spirit of reform, and to remember that some blacks did not need reformation. Furthermore, he did not need advice from a man who had "caused his family trouble and his friends disgust." If the "wets" intended to carry the election by voting blacks, they failed; the "drys" won out as voters rejected the continuance of saloons in Raleigh. It is unknown if the influence of the leading blacks was a contributing factor to this victory, but at least they did not suffer a decline in status.[35]

The image of the leading men received a boost when Booker T. Washington visited the North Carolina Industrial Association's annual fair in 1903. Washington, the principal speaker on Education Day, treated his race to what whites thought was "wholesome advice," by urging blacks to remain in North Carolina and content themselves with being an agrarian people. They could progress in that status if they received the kind of education that would promote morality, patience, industry, frugality, self-help, self-reliance, and a desire to discharge public duties faithfully. Seated on the platform with Washington were the former politicians James H. Young and Abe Middleton, along with the leading black educators, including Simon G. Atkins, James B. Dudley, John R. Hawkins, Alfred W. Pegues, and James B. Shepard. The prevailing mentality of the leading men can be seen in their remarks. Atkins had clearly adopted the role of an accommodationist when he stated that if anyone conspired to deprive his race of the blessings of law, government, and the opportunities of life, blacks should only "strive harder to prove worthy of these rights and leave the issue to humanity." Alfred W. Pegues of Shaw University urged blacks to pay their poll taxes whether or not they could vote. This was necessary because part of the tax was applied to education, and "the better educated the white people are the more safety, protection and encouragement" we will receive from them.[36]

The *Raleigh Morning Post*, which had a year earlier castigated Washington for his alleged political activities, commented favorably on his address and announced that he was truly a sincere and great leader, and "the most distinguished and ablest man of his race to speak truths applicable to whites and blacks. . . ." The *Post* thought that the interest shown by the more intelligent blacks in Washington's remarks signaled a turning point in the direction of good work that would benefit the people and the State of North Carolina. The warm reception that whites accorded Washington during his visit to the state caused the leading men to promote his philosophy with renewed vigor. They praised the friendly race relations in North Carolina and advised blacks to be grateful for their schools, churches, and the kindly thoughts of white men. They told the black masses to stop complaining and learn to accept struggle, because adversity, rigorous treatment, and severe discipline made great individuals, races, and nations. Furthermore, they contended that no race had attained any success or commanded greatness through morbid reflection upon the disadvantages of its environment. Above all, they cautioned the black masses to be polite, civil, and courteous to whites and not attempt to push themselves any further into the society of the dominant race than that which was compatible with common sense.[37]

Shortly after Washington's visit, former Governor Daniel L. Russell gave blacks some realistic advice on race relations. He believed that they might as well accept the fact that they were not going to be elevated, and would always remain an inferior race. According to Russell, it was just simply not the nature of his race to allow them to rise above their current status. Booker T. Washington's philosophy was not realistic because financial and industrial equality was just as bad in the eyes of whites as social equality. If a black rose above his ordained status in life, Russell thought that he would surely invite assassination. "Let him own a fine farm, blooded horses and cattle and dare to ride in a carriage and if I were an insurance agent I wouldn't make a policy on his life."[38]

Incensed by Russell's statement, Hunter attempted to defend whites against what he considered to be a "horrible impalement and withering indictment" of the Anglo-Saxons in America. In an article with a strange mixture of fact and fantasy, which was published in the *Raleigh News and Observer*, Hunter poured out the basis of his current thoughts on race relations. He could not believe that the mighty, proud, Anglo-Saxon race, "descended as it were from the Gods," would harbor attitudes and treat blacks as Russell alleged. Neither would they surrender to a prejudice that had no basis in right, reason, or religion. Hunter conceded outright that there could be no social equality between the races, nor would blacks ever exercise any controlling influence in government. But his personal experiences and those of thousands of blacks constituted "an overwhelming refutation of the assumption of a steady, united, implacable, hatred of the Negro, simply because he was a Negro."[39]

Whites were not out to oppose or thwart the moral, material, and intellectual advancement of blacks, and this could best be seen in the lives of Aycock and former Governor Jarvis. Hunter considered these individuals honest, courageous, sincere, and wise men, who expressed the best sentiments of the best white people of North Carolina. He boldly asserted that outside his immediate family, the best friends that he had anywhere on earth were the white people who knew him. "They have aided me by their private and official influence, by their money, and by their personal sympathy. Whatever I am today, whatever may be my prospect in life, I owe to them." There were hundreds of blacks in the state with similar experiences, and Hunter cited the fact that Robert B. Fitzgerald of Durham, Berry O'Kelly and Edward A. Johnson of Wake County, and he himself could all prove that Russell was wrong. Blacks had received all the help, encouragement, and good advice they needed from whites. Hunter wanted it understood that he was not "palliating in the least to the many and great injustices to the Negro which have outgrown from his present condition." There were mean and vicious white men who inflicted crimes against blacks and were doing all they could to foster a spirit of hatred, oppression, and bitterness. "I feel it. We all feel it," he wrote. But he believed that whites at heart were good and would in time atone for and correct their own injustices. Hunter was not thoroughly convinced of the truth of his own statements. He confided to former Governor Jarvis that if one assumed that Russell's allegations were premised on the fierce assault that had been made on blacks since 1898, he could conclude that "it meant the utter and complete damnation of the race so far as it could be accomplished within the reach of the white race." He thought that Russell's assessment was indeed applicable to many whites, but not all, and Hunter was glad to inform Jarvis that he was in the latter category.[40]

If the benefits of friendship between Hunter and the best whites had extended to all blacks, there would have been no race problem in North Carolina, but such was not the case. Whites were just as determined as ever to keep blacks at the bottom of society, and even Aycock admitted as much. During the last year of his governorship he voiced an opinion somewhat similar to that of Russell when he stated, "I am afraid of but one thing for my race and that is we shall become afraid to give the Negro a fair chance."

## Down and Divided

When Aycock was about to leave office, Hunter informed him that his administration was one of greatness and glory, and it had constituted a "beautiful boon of Promise. God grant that it shall remain, every tint growing brighter until the whole State shall give back the reflection and the splendid era be inaugurated." Hunter was sure that men of both races and both parties were proud of the distinction accorded Aycock's name, which they shared as part of their common heritage. He also believed that his sentiments reflected those of the majority of the intelligent blacks of North Carolina.[41]

Aycock appreciated Hunter's kind words, and he told Hunter that he was glad if he had done anything to improve race relations. There was still a lot to be done. He wrote Hunter, "I verily believe that the conferring upon the Negro race the right to vote has retarded and injured them and created unfriendliness on the part of white people that will take years to get over." The governor hoped that the best people of both races would work together to shape the destiny of the state, and asked that the leading black men constantly point out to whites the need for friendly race relations.[42]

One of the whites who saw this need was the Episcopal coadjutor of North Carolina, Robert Strange, who in 1904 publicly called for equal educational, civil, political, and economic opportunities for blacks, and their equal protection under the laws. However, he emphasized the need for racial purity and emphatically announced that he was not advocating social equality. Whites could meet his demands because they involved civil privileges and did not open the door for social intercourse. Strange's thoughts on race relations attracted the attention of President Theodore Roosevelt. During a speech delivered in New York in commemoration of Lincoln's birthday in 1905, Roosevelt commended to the nation "the principles laid down by this North Carolina bishop." Roosevelt told southern whites it was time for them to prove the sincerity of their claims that they were the best friends of blacks and begin doing their duty by giving them equal opportunities and exact justice.[43]

Hunter was so carried away by Roosevelt's pronouncement on race relations that he designated it as a historic incident in the life of the nation. He thought that the president had risen to "the proud heights of Christian statesmanship" by recommending a policy that was the only basis for an equitable adjustment of the race problem in America. On behalf of America's black citizens, he drafted a letter to Roosevelt expressing their approval and support. Hunter was wrong again. He did not even speak for the black citizens of his own state, many of whom castigated Roosevelt's tolerance of lily-whitism in North Carolina. In 1905 the Republican members of the General Assembly resolved not to recommend any black as a delegate to any political convention or for appointment to any public office, and they also agreed to push for the removal of all blacks who held patronage positions in the state. Some black North Carolinians thought that this action on the part of lily-whites was a bold affront to Roosevelt, and if he allowed them to get away with it his racial policy would definitely fail. The president was called on to help blacks in North Carolina "rout out the rascals" and reorganize the Republican party of the state on the basis of its historic principles.[44]

Roosevelt's decision in 1906 to administer immediate and exact justice to 167 black members of the Twenty-fifth United States Infantry stationed at Brownsville, Texas, incurred the wrath of the nation's black community, including that of North Carolina. In meetings across the state, the leading men condemned the president for summarily ordering the dishonorable discharge of these troops, and Hunter publicly branded Roosevelt's decree an "executive lynch law" that violated every right and tradition of English jurisprudence. It had shocked the moral sense of the nation and deserved the severest words of condemnation. The Brownsville incident came at a time when blacks and some whites agreed that race relations in North Carolina were worsening. In August 1906 there was a nasty lynching in Salisbury that claimed the lives of two black men and a boy, and this event caused Willis G. Briggs, the former editor of the *Raleigh Evening Times*, to have some serious doubts as to the future of North Carolina and its Christian civilization. He thought that the lynching proved that "we have not as a people eradicated the lingering savagery," and whites still possessed the "elements of rashness and cruelty of primitive man."[45]

At the black fair in the fall of 1906 two whites who were highly regarded by the black community both noted the decline in friendly race relations. James Y. Joyner, the state superintendent of public instruction, and Charles F. Meserve, the president of Shaw University, also agreed that this was partially due to the breaking of the "tender old ties" that had bound the races together during slavery. Indeed, Meserve thought that there was more race friction than ever before, and he placed upon blacks the responsibility of correcting this situation. Since relatively few people of both races under the age of thirty-five knew each other, he suggested that race relations could be improved if blacks conducted themselves properly in public and were polite to whites, especially white women. What he really wanted was for blacks to recapture the deference and servility that characterized the slave. Meserve reminded his black audience of their slave heritage by stating, "You do not live in the houses of white people as your fathers and mothers did when the white race was the owner, the master race and the colored the owned, the slave race." Whether he knew it or not, Meserve also captured the essence of white supremacy when he warned blacks not to forget that whites were still the master race, who could destroy them whenever desired.[46]

The blacks of Raleigh and Durham, among the most intelligent and conservative of their race, were upset and anxious over the declining state of race relations. This was clearly demonstrated in the rhetoric of the speeches and resolutions of the 1907 Emancipation Day activities. The celebration in Durham was dominated by the class-conscious black bourgeoisie of the city, who adopted mild resolutions protesting Jim Crow cars, mob violence, election frauds, and voting irregularities. Oddly, it semed as if the black Bourbons believed that the conditions against which they protested did not apply to them, because they also adopted resolutions commending the fact that in Durham the laws were impartially administered, and race relations had always been friendly. Furthermore, the leading men asserted that the honest and progressive black man had always secured the sympathy and assistance of his white friends. The crowd resolved not to do anything to upset the peace and harmony between the races, and all blacks were urged to go out and "scatter seeds of kindness and flowers of love."[47]

Such verbiage was characteristic of the leading men of Durham, who were among the most pacified blacks and accomplished accommodationists in the state. They naïvely believed that their own individual progress was indicative of the potentialities of the black masses, and that their personal friendships with whites were accurate gauges of race relations. In concert with their white patrons, the leading men helped make Durham the showplace of the state, the South, and the nation. The experience of Durham's black capitalists also helped promote the myth that North Carolina was the best place for blacks. If anyone doubted this assertion, Durham was held up as proof positive that the two races could live together in harmony in the South, and that blacks could indeed prosper under the guiding influence of good white men. By 1906 Hunter had managed to affiliate himself with the black business community of Durham. He was hired by the North Carolina Mutual and Provident Association to manage its Raleigh office, and although still teaching in a public school, he was rather effective as an insurance man. He increased the strength of the concern in the Raleigh area, improved the efficiency of the office staff, and constantly tried to impress upon the home office the value of advertising. Hunter thought of taking a permanent position with North Carolina Mutual, and he wanted to use his power and influence to make it the chief financial institution of his race in America. In this regard, he wrote to C. C. Spaulding, the vice-president and general manager, "I want to devote my life to it."[48]

Hunter was eventually promoted to travelling agent for North and South Carolina with authority to visit and inspect local agencies, and to assist them in expanding their operations. He was also granted permission to write insurance anywhere in the state of North Carolina. Despite his promising future, he eventually resigned from the business because he could not get along with its management. There was constant bickering over personnel matters and local policies, and he was frequently absent from the Raleigh office attending to other affairs. Then too, Hunter did not fit the image of the North Carolina Mutual man. For example, he delivered a rather militant and controversial address on New Year's Day 1907 in Raleigh, before an overflowing crowd at Metropolitan Hall. The occasion was Emancipation Day, and Hunter's speech shows that he had been shocked into reality by the events of the preceding year. As he saw it, race estrangement, prejudice, and hatred had steadily worsened. Stripped of political rights, blacks had become impotent, helpless, defenseless, and the "inviting victims of every brutal caprice." Mob violence against blacks was no longer the work of masked men at night, but was conducted openly and boldly in flagrant defiance of the law. Through all of this, blacks had remained passive and cautious, and they had "sedulously sought to avoid any act or word that might be construed as provocative of race antipathy."[49]

Hunter asserted it was time for blacks to speak out on the issues that plagued them. For one thing, they had long boasted that they lived among the best white people of the nation, but they were beginning to see that this was not true. The white men who excelled in their "vile abuse" of blacks, and who were the most ingenious in "inventions of wrong, humiliation, indignity, and oppression of the defenseless race," were the very ones who enjoyed the highest esteem of the white community as well as the rewards of public office. These same whites also used every conceivable means to prove to the civilized world that blacks were "a race of brutes so deadly dangerous as to justify the most summary and drastic measures of repres-

# Down and Divided

sion." In the face of these facts, Hunter asserted that blacks could only conclude that it was the determined and persistent purpose of whites to nullify the Emancipation Proclamation and the Reconstruction amendments, and to prove that slavery for blacks was right and freedom was wrong. The blacks' only response was to appeal to the fair-minded Christian southern white men in the hope that they would correct racial injustices and "make the boast that North Carolina blacks lived among the best white people in the country come true."[50]

Hunter's address shows that it took him exactly three years to get around to realizing the truths contained in former Governor Russell's 1904 statement on race relations. Hunter was also following the advice of Aycock, who asked that blacks use every occasion to point out to the best white men the need for friendly race relations. Although Hunter's speech was unanimously approved by his black audience, he soon found out that whites felt otherwise. He was denounced as a firebrand, and the press thought that his speech was a definite deterrent to friendly race relations. It was considered ill-founded, hostile, and incendiary and had no other purpose than to encourage lawlessness among blacks. Not only this, but those blacks who approved of Hunter's remarks were branded as the worst enemies of their own race. The *Salisbury Post* reminded "the Wake County Negroes" that they were right about one thing, which was that they would never again be able to control their political destiny, and "no amount of incendiary talk would bring about a reversal."[51]

# We Are Your Negroes and We Are Here to Stay

Hunter was the least likely candidate in North Carolina for the reputation of a radical or a troublemaker, for if his latest scheme were to succeed, he needed the full support of the best white men. In 1907 the nation held the Jamestown Tercentennial Exposition in commemoration of the founding of the first permanent English settlement in America, and the several states including North Carolina prepared exhibits for this event. The national director of the exposition wanted to include blacks in the celebration, and Congress appropriated $100,000 for a separate exhibit showing their progress in America. To oversee the erection of their exhibit, and to dispense the funds allocated by Congress, blacks organized the Negro Development and Exposition Company of the United States of America with headquarters in Washington, D.C., and Richmond, Virginia.[1]

The idea of a great exposition that would give the nation's blacks an opportunity to show their material and intellectual achievements captured Hunter's imagination. In the summer of 1906 he and about two dozen other leading blacks, who were primarily stockholders in the NCIA, formed the Negro Development Company of the United States of America. The Reverend Charles H. Williamson served as the company's commissioner-general, and Hunter was selected as its secretary and state organizer. Hunter's administrative ability no doubt was a major consideration in awarding him this position, but he was also selected because of his capacity to garner support from the white community. The leading blacks believed that their venture would prove "an utter and complete failure" unless they received the sympathy, advice, and cooperation of whites, and Williamson wrote

## We Are Your Negroes and We Are Here to Stay

Hunter that "you know much better how to get to Mr. Daniels' folks than I do." Hunter obviously agreed, for he wrote to Giles B. Jackson, "I have many strong personal friends among the leading and most influential men of the State. These must be reached and their active support engaged."[2]

By August 1906 Hunter had established an office in Raleigh, and he requested authority from the head of the Negro Development Company to begin work at once in training a staff and making plans for the state exhibit, as it would require considerable time to assemble a representative display. Blacks did not have access to any state museum from which they could obtain materials, nor could they use the public press to inform citizens of the exhibit and solicit items for display. Instead, the exhibit's organizers had to contact blacks personally in their homes, workshops, schools, and businesses and urge upon them the importance of selecting the best and most creditable products for the exposition. This necessarily involved considerable funds for travel, postage, and printing, and Hunter considered asking the state for monies to supplement the congressional appropriation. He thought his efforts in this direction would be facilitated by the fact that some of his "strongest friends" from Wake County were running for the legislature on the Democratic ticket of 1906, and he wrote, "I must place myself in a position to command them when in the legislature."[3]

The activities of Hunter and his associates in securing an appropriation from the state are a good example of how they manipulated whites through flattery and appeals to their sense of pride and duty. Whites were told that black North Carolinians were determined to have the best exhibit in the nation, but they lacked sufficient funds to accomplish their goal. Where this was also true of their race in other southern states, whites had come to the rescue. White North Carolinians had to do the same, and they also had to understand that any advancement made by blacks reflected "honor upon the white people among whom they had lived and under whose fostering care such progress had been made possible." In a letter to Senator John C. Drewry of Wake County, Hunter contended that blacks reflected the character of whites. This was certainly true in the days of slavery when whites took pride in the character of their slaves, and although relationships had changed since then, he wrote that "in a peculiar sense we are your Negroes. We are just what you have made us. . . . If we have made progress that progress was made possible by your friendly interests and contacts." Blacks were a part of the state's resources and should not be neglected in its

## We Are Your Negroes and We Are Here to Stay

display. They wanted to stand "head and shoulders" above all their brethren. Hunter asked Drewry to help them do this by using his influence to secure an appropriation.[4]

In January 1907 Representative William C. Douglass of Wake County introduced a bill in the legislature authorizing an appropriation of $5,000 to aid blacks in collecting and establishing their exhibit at Jamestown. In lobbying for the passage of this bill, Hunter wrote Senator John W. Graham of Orange County that he had known his family all his life and that "his honored and courtly father was the embodiment of life so lofty that he dwelt in an atmosphere too pure to be tainted by anything sordid or mean." He implied that some of these good traits had been passed on to Graham, and solicited the senator's support for the pending appropriation bill. Hunter's lobbying activities paid off when in February the General Assembly by joint resolution approved the bill. He was elated by this action. North Carolina was the only state whose legislature made a special appropriation for blacks, which indicated the fine spirit that had always dwelt within the hearts of whites. He also believed that the blacks' request for funds had allowed whites an appropriate medium through which to display their cordiality, friendship, and sympathy toward his race. The governor of North Carolina, Robert Glenn, shared a similar opinion, and he saw the appropriation as a means whereby whites could give encouragement to progressive blacks and at the same time stimulate others to habits of industry and thrift.[5]

Neither Hunter nor the General Assembly thought progresssive blacks were capable of managing the monies appropriated by the state. The appropriation bill placed funds under the control of Colonel Joseph E. Pogue, the commissioner-general of the North Carolina Commission, Jamestown Exposition. Hunter stated that his experience with "Negroes in the management of money" sugggested the propriety of including these safeguards in the bill. He also feared that certain "Negroes at Washington" would try to gain control of the state funds and warned Pogue that he would probably be approached in this regard. Nephew Ed was very glad that Hunter had the good sense to get the appropriation "fixed so as to be out of the reach of vultures," but he was not averse to his uncle sharing in the largesse. Ed had earlier written that Hunter, who had contributed the most "energy and brain" to engineer the bill through the legislature, was entitled to a corresponding amount of the credit and emolument incident to its passage.[6]

Hunter certainly thought so. He took a leave of absence from his work, pleading illness, and in April 1907 he resigned as principal of the Chavis School in Raleigh. In his letter of resignation to the School Committee, he stated he had been engaged in educational work for thirty-two years and had devoted his talents to the great task of the educational uplift of his race. He had also sacrificed many opportunities offering a much greater remuneration. However, his age and the rising cost of living convinced him of the "unwisdom of further self immolation," and he was forced to enter a field that offered the best returns for his service. Hunter probably felt some remorse over walking out on his white friends who had given him a job and protected him in his position. Though he had achieved some success as a teacher, this could not have been possible without the help of good white gentlemen. To Needham B. Broughton he wrote that "you have stood by me and with me all along the years and I shall treasure your devotion to the cause and your personal interest in me as a priceless souvenir."[7]

When Hunter began working full-time on the Jamestown Exposition, the "vultures," to whom his nephew Ed had referred, surfaced in the form of the Executive Committee of the Negro Development and Exposition Company in Washington. Just as Hunter feared, the national committee on learning of the state appropriation tried to gain control of the expenditure of these funds, and it later attempted to deprive North Carolina blacks of a fair share of the monies authorized by Congress. This precipitated a sharp debate between Hunter and the members of the committee. He finally won out after warning them that the white people of North Carolina would not stand idly by and see their blacks mistreated, and they would take the matter up with the Tercentennial Commission, which consisted of the secretary of the treasury and other members of the president's cabinet. In Hunter's words, "They would appeal to Caesar and unto Caesar the case would go if necessary." Hunter claimed that this threat forced the committee to agree to give North Carolina blacks their proportionate share of federal funds. However, this actually happened only after Pogue met with the Executive Committee regarding the matter, and he later informed Hunter that whites would do anything possible to ensure the success of the black exhibit, and that "we are going to stand by you in every particular."[8]

Hunter was interested in gaining access to all funds possible because, in addition to a salary of $25 a month plus travel expenses, it seems as if he and Williamson would receive a share of any funds left over when the exposition terminated. Hunter was not pleased with his salary because Williamson's was twice as high. Yet he was willing to accept it because it

## We Are Your Negroes and We Are Here to Stay

had been fixed by the good judgment of white men, and also because he was anxious to see the exhibit installed and supported in a manner comparable with the dignity of North Carolina. But he also wanted whites to know that he was making a tremendous sacrifice in view of the fact that his services were in constant demand at better pay.[9]

Hunter energetically canvassed the state speaking in support of the exhibit and collecting materials that best represented the progress of blacks. He thought that the exhibit should also show the condition of black workers in North Carolina, and he visited or corresponded with Julian S. Carr, the Biltmore Farms, the Ashley Mill, and the R. J. Reynolds Company. When he visited the Reynolds plant at Winston, he was particularly impressed by the efficiency and loyalty of its black hands. He urged Reynolds to sponsor a display as a means of showing what labor conditions were really like in the state, thinking this would attract to North Carolina "a most desirable class of Negro workers." He also wrote Reynolds that an exhibit by his company would provide a great opportunity to advertise its products. Hunter was very interested in obtaining the participation of the Ashley silk mill in Fayetteville, which was the only textile plant in the state run exclusively by black labor. He realized that very few people in America were aware of this mill, and he thought that capitalists in particular needed to know that blacks could be developed into skilled operatives.[10]

A considerable part of Hunter's time was spent in journalistic activities. He edited and published a Jamestown edition of the *Journal of Industry*, and distributed several thousand free copies as a means of advertising the exhibition. He also planned to issue a booklet on "Negro Life in North Carolina Illustrated." This publication would show the daily life of blacks and would also contain valuable information and statistics pertaining to their past and present condition. His travels throughout the state and the materials he received for display convinced him more than ever that blacks were making tremendous progress and accomplishing great things. Yet he wondered, "who will know of these, a hundred years to come?" Hunter also wanted to expand the booklet into a general history of his race in North Carolina. He believed that blacks needed a history or a pedigree if they were ever to attain any standing among the great races of the earth. If it was important for "horses, mules, and cows and hogs and sheep and dogs and cats" to have a history, Hunter thought it was much more important for a race to have a history. Moreover, a good history would also be an indispensable means of giving hope and inspiration to black youth.[11]

## We Are Your Negroes and We Are Here to Stay

For information on antebellum blacks, Hunter requested materials from Professor Kemp P. Battle of the History Department of the University of North Carolina. He told Battle that it was important for blacks to know of the many noble people of their race who were able to attain a high standard of Christian character under the adverse condition of other days. "The memory of these times should be kept fresh and green," he wrote, and "their children should be taught to emulate their noble virtues." He was particularly interested in obtaining information on the black preacher John Chavis and on George Moses Horton, North Carolina's slave poet. Hunter's attempt to write a history apparently failed because blacks did not cooperate by responding to his requests for materials. Disappointed and greatly disturbed, he wrote to the president of Livingstone College, William H. Goler, that it was inconceivable that his suggestions on the subject of history hardly elicited a thought from the most intelligent blacks of North Carolina. Though he was unsuccessful in his first attempt, the idea of writing a history of blacks remained with Hunter until his death.[12]

The Jamestown Exposition ran from April through November 1907, and the highlight of the occasion for most American blacks was Negro Day. Held on Saturday, 3 August, this event featured a massive celebration with a parade, a military drill exhibition, a fireworks display, a grand concert by the Fiske Jubilee Singers and the Hampton Institute Band, and a visit by Booker T. Washington. A luncheon for 1,000 guests was staged in Washington's honor, and for his speech there were seating accommodations for 10,000 people. It was expected that large numbers of black North Carolinians would attend this event, and the Seaboard Air Line Railway offered them special excursion rates. However, enthusiasm for the occasion declined when reports filtered throughout the state alleging that black visitors to the exposition had been subjected to unjust, unreasonable, and humiliating discrimination on trolley cars and were denied equal privileges, treatment, and access to facilities except those on their own reservation.[13]

Hunter wrote to Henry St. George Tucker, the president of the Jamestown Exposition, that these reports caused many blacks in North Carolina to feel that there would be no pleasure in going to the exposition and that it would indeed be "a self infliction of hardship which they should seek to avoid." He insisted, however, that these reports were ill-founded and so senseless that it would seem unnecessary to treat them seriously, but they were having an effect on a certain class of people who were easily influenced by such information. He was still planning to bring up 25,000 blacks from North Carolina and was doing all he could to dispel their fears by telling them that they were welcome at the exposition and would enjoy the same privileges as whites "barring such race distinctions as are maintained everywhere in the South." Acting on information from Hunter and Tucker, the director of publicity for the exposition, J. W. Bolles, began a publicity campaign in North Carolina that was intended to remove any misrepresentation as to the condition and treatment of black patrons. Press releases announced that blacks would have access to every portion of the exposition and that every building would be open to them on equal terms with all other visitors.[14]

For Hunter and many other blacks of North Carolina, the big event of the exposition occurred during the period 12 to 18 August, which was designated North Carolina week. He wrote Pogue that blacks wanted to have a part in the program for this week because they also wanted to give as much glory as possible to the Old North State. They also thought that the occasion would provide a good opportunity for white North Carolinians to obtain for them national recognition for their achievement. Hunter wrote Pogue that "we want a speech from the governor and others at the auditorium of the Negro Building and we want you and the entire commission together with the governor's staff to be present." Pogue, agreeing with Hunter's requests, advised him to confer with Governor Glenn. Hunter wrote the governor that he rejoiced over the fact that North Carolina had a wise, patriotic, and fearless chief executive in the person of Robert Glenn. Glenn seemed glad to know this, and he infomed Hunter that he was sustained in his work by the encouragement he received from all the people of the state.[15]

Hunter's letter produced the desired effect, and Glenn was the only governor of any state who visited the Negro Building in conjunction with celebrations honoring specific states. On 11 August, addressing a crowd of blacks at the exposition, Glenn spoke of his kind feelings for their race, and how he as governor had endeavored in every "proper way" to show his interest in their progress. Glenn also alleged that his state was solving the race problem, and that blacks were given full protection under the law. Well-behaved, industrious, and law-abiding blacks knew that their greatest source of encouragement and their best friends rested among the white people. Good blacks in North Carolina had no complaints against the government or the white population, and Glenn contended that if anyone doubted the veracity of his remarks, he would refer them to Charles H. Williamson and Hunter for proof. Glenn's visit and speech overjoyed

## We Are Your Negroes and We Are Here to Stay

Hunter and he thought they were signs of better times for both races not only in North Carolina, but in the entire South. Referring to these events, he wrote Josephus Daniels that nothing could have given him more pleasure: "To me it means much." Hunter must have conveyed this same sentiment to Glenn, for the governor wrote him that he too was pleased to have been present at the Negro Building, and "I meant every word I said, and am glad that you think it will do some good."[16]

The show put on by North Carolina blacks at Jamestown excelled that of all others, and according to Hunter it attracted the attention of the whole country and "evoked the highest encomiums." He and the leading men believed that the Exposition gave them a universal respect "at the hands of the nation" that could not have been brought about in any other way. Hunter received his share of recognition for his work and was praised by the press and the best white men. Pogue lauded him for his faithful, efficient, and conscientious discharge of duty, and told him that the "colored people of the State owe you a debt of gratitude that they ought not forget." Some blacks were not all-thankful for the exposition, and probably wanted to forget the entire affair. Disgusted with its Jim Crow cars, widespread discrimination, and inferior accommodations for blacks, they, unlike Hunter, began to doubt if expositions showing their progress were really helping to solve the race problem.[17]

They were right, and the better times that Hunter predicted would follow the exposition did not materialize. As soon as the event was over, it was clear that the actions and rhetoric of the leading whites from North Carolina at Jamestown were nothing more than propaganda for outside consumption. Once back home, they took off their masks and reverted to their old pattern of behavior. For example, at their fair, held two months after the exposition, the leading blacks continued to praise Glenn as their best governor and their best friend. Though the governor appreciated this and told them he would always be their friend, he made no comment on their achievements, nor offered any words of encouragement. Rather, he lectured them that blacks in general had to develop good character and become respectful citizens and they could do this by refraining from "watermelon festivals, excursions, the flourishing of razors, and cakewalks." They would all have to work because North Carolina did not need "drones, idlers, and thimble headed dudes." It seems as if the character of the audience could stand some improvement because at the end of Glenn's remarks it gave "three rousing cheers for the governor," and the band played "Dixie."[18]

## We Are Your Negroes and We Are Here to Stay

While working at Jamestown, Hunter learned of an important position in Raleigh. In July 1907 he received word from a friend of the death of Professor Williams, the supervisor of the Colored Department of the Institute for the Deaf, Dumb, and Blind. Urging Hunter to apply for the position, his friend told him to contact Pogue, the chairman of the school's Board of Directors. He also thought it would be a good idea for Hunter to see his friend Benjamin R. Lacy and that the two of them together contact the governor. Hunter's friend advised him to "wait no longer than the funeral of Williams is over then go to work."[19]

Hunter went to work, and his efforts, though unsuccessful, were another example of the way he attempted to manipulate whites. He created a fictitious bandwagon composed of the leading white and black men of the state, all of whom allegedly favored him for the job, and then privately invited other whites to join the movement. Included in this group were the former mayor of Raleigh, William M. Russ; Needham B. Broughton; William Guthrie, the Populist nominee for governor in 1896; State Treasurer Benjamin R. Lacy; former Governor Aycock; and Dr. Hubert Haywood, a member of the family who had owned Hunter as a slave. In separate letters to these gentlemen, Hunter expressed his desire for the job but told them that he was averse to making any "spirited contest" and that he was perfectly willing to let them judge his qualifications. They knew him, had always shown an interest in his welfare, and were in some way responsible for his success. He wanted their endorsement and influence in securing the job, but only if they thought he was the best man. Hunter told Haywood that he was particularly anxious for an endorsement by a Haywood, and he had never called on "the old family for any help within their power that they have not cheerfully given." He also felt that an endorsement from Aycock would be a personal compliment from an "honored and distinguished North Carolinian," and that it would be of great value in furthering his ambition.[20]

Hunter then wrote to the superintendent and chairman of the Board of Trustees of the Institute for the Deaf, Dumb, and Blind and reminded them of the necessity to fill the vacancy in the Colored Department at the earliest possible date. He informed them that a number of the best citizens had urged him to apply for the job, and that he had in hand, and also the promises of, any number of strong endorsements which may be "seen if desired." Declining to influence the decision by long petitions and personal pressure, he hoped his application would receive a favorable consideration.

## We Are Your Negroes and We Are Here to Stay

If not, he would "rejoice if the position went to a better man." Hunter did not get the job or rejoice. Strangely enough, he blamed his rejection on the influence of black politicians who, he claimed, had conspired against him, rather than on the good white men who had the power to give him the job.[21]

Hunter and these politicians did unite in a movement to defeat Theodore Roosevelt during the campaign of 1908. As early as January 1907 Hunter had seen presidential qualities in Senator Joseph B. Foraker of Ohio. He praised the senator's attempts at securing justice for the Brownsville soldiers, and recommended that North Carolina blacks give Foraker a vote of thanks for his efforts to preserve "those sacred remnants of the constitution and law, so dear to every freeman." Blacks of Wake County agreed, and Hunter conveyed these feelings to Foraker along with his personal comment that they would be satisfied with nothing less than simple and exact justice. In February 1908 Hunter confided to Foraker that though blacks in North Carolina intended to assert their rights in the upcoming campaign they wanted to act sensibly and conservatively. They also intended to reward him for his stand on human rights, and they wanted Foraker to advise them as to a suitable course of action.[22]

Realistically, Hunter knew that Foraker had little chance of defeating the Roosevelt-Taft combination, yet he agreed with his nephew Ed that blacks had to show their gratitude and encouragement to the Ohio senator for his manly stand on human rights. He and Ed eventually concluded that the best strategy was to fight Roosevelt at the national convention by sending as many unpledged delegates as possible. Ed thought that "the Negroes hold the key to the situation as far as the election is concerned," and could use this advantage wisely at the convention "to alleviate much that is now a burden."[23]

It was impossible to select black delegates to the national convention through the machinery of the lily-white Republican party. When their delegates to the state convention were turned away, blacks formed a shadow organization composed of men dedicated to the true principles of the Grand Old Party. This new group held its state convention, and accused the white Republicans of North Carolina of trying to destroy their own party by discouraging black participation. Indeed, blacks asserted that it was far better to have the Democrats control the state than lily-white Republicans, who were no more than "an aggregation of time servers, tricksters and ingrates." They castigated Roosevelt and Taft for their passive acceptance of lily-whitism, and condemned the national Republican party for contain-

## We Are Your Negroes and We Are Here to Stay

ing elements who were determined to "chain the American Negro to the wheel of political adversity and grind out of him every spark of civil and political liberty." Unless the party was purged of such attitudes, blacks would be consigned to a physical, moral, and intellectual debasement unparalleled since the days of slavery. A reporter of the *News and Observer* thought that the rhetoric of this convention included perhaps the bitterest pronouncements ever made by North Carolina blacks. It even shocked some of the more conservative delegates, who urged their comrades to tone down their speeches by reminding them that "there was a time in North Carolina when such stuff as that meant death." The convention also selected six blacks and two whites who were to go to the Republican national convention as a contesting delegation, and present themselves as representatives of the true Republican party of North Carolina. The convention also established a permanent organization called the North Carolina Republican Executive Committee, which in time became the focal point of black political activity in the state. Hunter later joined this group and became a district committeeman representing the Fourth Congressional District.[24]

In 1908 Hunter was also affiliated with the National Negro American Political League, U.S.A., a Washington-based organization dedicated to mobilizing the political power of blacks to advance the interest of their race. Formed in Philadelphia in May 1908, the league was controlled by some of the most radical blacks in America, including Archibald H. Grimké, William Monroe Trotter, George H. White, and Hunter's old adversary, Bishop Henry McNeil Turner. The league believed it was time for blacks in the North and the West to use their political power to destroy lily-whitism and disfranchisement in the South, to force a reversal of Roosevelt's Brownsville decision, and to oppose Jim Crow laws. Meanwhile, the league hoped that blacks would support the presidential ambitions of Senator Foraker and oppose the Roosevelt-Taft combination.[25]

At the Republican national convention in 1908, the contesting delegation from North Carolina was rejected, but the National Negro American Political League was represented by approximately 100 members who lobbied for its objectives. The league pressured the Republican party to reaffirm its historic commitment to civil and political equality for blacks. Although the league was unable to prevent Taft's nomination, it did establish an anti-Taft committee to prevent his election. The league claimed some success in impressing upon everyone the fact that blacks would no longer blindly follow the lead of the Republican party.[26]

## We Are Your Negroes and We Are Here to Stay

When Taft was elected, blacks were a little uneasy because they did not know how the president-elect would respond to their earlier actions. Ed wrote Hunter that he was trying to suspend judgment until Taft "showed the real intent of his heart which he claims to be all right." In his inaugural address, the president stated that he was free of race prejudice and desired to see "intelligent and well-to-do blacks" vote. He also recommended the judicious appointment of distinguished blacks to offices as a means of recognizing and encouraging the continued progress of their race. Ed later confided to Hunter that the president's attitude had opened up for him "the Pandora's box of trouble." He was referring to the determined opposition of lily-whites to the president's racial policy, but Ed had also received private information that Taft was becoming disgusted with some of the "representations made by visiting Southern delegations."[27]

In April 1909 Hunter attempted to attract the attention of the president. In what may have been a veiled attempt to retaliate against the lily-whites of the state, he sent Taft a letter recommending the appointment of Frank L. Fuller, a white Democrat, as judge for the Eastern District of North Carolina. He claimed that Fuller was from one of the best and oldest families of the South and was highly esteemed by all citizens regardless of race, class, or partisan bias. Hunter also wrote, "I am a negro, came up out of slavery, and am now and have always been ardent Republican," and he advised Fuller's appointment because it would serve "to cement and strengthen the bonds of friendship between the white people of his class and the Negroes of the state upon whom much depends." Hunter hoped that his letter would be considered by the United States attorney general and Taft, and he asked Lee S. Overman, the Democratic senator from North Carolina, to see that it got into their hands. Overman agreed to do this, but he thought that the president would appoint a Republican to the position "if he could find one who was competent." Hunter's recommendation was entirely unsolicited by Fuller, who wrote that he was also "exceedingly gratified by the kind interest which my colored friends have taken in my candidacy for this position." Taft's appointment of Fuller and other Democrats to federal judgeships shocked the lily-white Republicans of North Carolina, but blacks were pleased. Hunter and many others probably agreed with the editor of the *New York Age*, who wrote that blacks would rather see a good old-fashioned Democrat made judge in North Carolina than one of the lily-white Republicans who were the most "asinine enemies of the negro race in the South."[28]

# We Are Your Negroes and We Are Here to Stay

Hunter was also after a federal appointment and he tried to procure a position with the Census Bureau. Because 1910 was a census year, he wanted the bureau to establish a special agency to compile accurate statistics concerning the black population. In characteristic fashion he wrote the director of the Bureau of the Census that "a large number of our most influential and thoughtful citizens, white and colored, of both parties" were deeply interested in securing an accurate census of blacks in North Carolina. Naturally, he hoped to occupy a prominent position with this special agency because for fifteen years he had been collecting and collating statistics pertaining to the growth and progress of his race. Hunter also appended to his letter a number of endorsements attesting to his qualifications for census work. He informed Senator Lee S. Overman of his plans, asked that he deliver this letter to the Census Bureau, and reminded him that an accurate census might mean the gain or loss of one or more members of Congress. Overman agreed to help promote Hunter's plans. However, the whole scheme fell through when the Census Bureau disapproved of a special agency for blacks.[29]

In the fall of 1910 the Negro Business League of North Carolina sponsored a statewide tour by Booker T. Washington in an effort to improve race relations. Hunter, a charter member and corresponding secretary of the league, formed during the black fair of the previous year, advertised Washington as a "great leader, a magnificent organizer, and a man with a masterful mind." Because Washington refused to charge people for the privilege of hearing him speak, his expenses were defrayed by the local business leagues in areas where he appeared. C. C. Spaulding, a member of the Executive Committee of the North Carolina Business League, wrote Hunter that "we do not intend for Dr. Washington and his party to have to spend one cent of their money" during their stay. Blacks in other states had entertained him at their expense, and Spaulding was anxious for North Carolina to accord Washington the same treatment. Washington's tour was a great success, and he spoke on an average of five or six times a day to racially mixed crowds. He told blacks to continue to improve themselves, and he urged whites to do their duty by encouraging, uplifting, and protecting his race.[30]

In the wake of Washington's visit, the leading black men launched a new wave of praise for the friendly relations between the races in North Carolina. They also intensified their efforts to pacify the black masses and to

## We Are Your Negroes and We Are Here to Stay

stimulate them to improve their moral, mental, and material conditions. The leading men seemingly tried to outdo each other in this regard. At times their rhetoric was totally inconsistent with reality and it certainly must have confused most blacks. James E. Shepard announced to a crowd at the fair of 1911 that black workers received better treatment and wages than any other class of laborers in the world and then proceeded to deliver a lecture on the immorality and criminality of his race. In his opinion the greatest need of blacks was not the vast accumulation of wealth but morality. His race's deficiency in the latter came from the bad influence of "moving picture shows, ignorance, superstition, and the use of cocaine or dope by youth." Not only this, but Shepard claimed that the black church was not helping the situation because it contained 27,000 ignorant or immoral ministers who largely held in their hands the destiny of their race. The time had arrived for blacks to drive the immoral preacher from his pulpit and demand that ignorant ones be sent to training school. The fact that Shepard was head of the National Religious Training School in Durham no doubt prompted these latter remarks.[31]

Hunter, who had on occasions chastised whites·for their biased observations pertaining to his race, joined in this most recent critique of blacks. In 1912 he was selected by the Emancipation Association to deliver the annual oration for its celebration at Raleigh, and his address was a mixture of praise and condemnation for his race. "Let us become a clean people," he told his audience, and he called for an end to idleness and the banishment of black criminals. In words similar to those of the leading whites, he advised blacks to build good character, obey the law and, above all, seek in every honorable way to cultivate the friendship of whites. Conversely, he asserted that in spite of their faults blacks should not be discouraged, because in freedom they had made progress and refuted the prediction made by many whites that once away from the "watchful eyes and directing hands of the master," they would soon lapse into barbarism, become extinct, or constitute a great class of criminals.[32]

Returning to an old theme, Hunter maintained that southern white society was not fully aware of the blessings it enjoyed from an adequate supply of black workers who had kept a whole host of evils out of the region: "There are no negro anarchists, nihilists, or socialists, there are no dynamiters with their bombs. Negroes do not have Black Hand organizations. He is not given to strikes and the wide range of destructive lawlessness that prevailed

### We Are Your Negroes and We Are Here to Stay

in the North. He does not organize robber bands to hold up trains, rob banks, loot post offices. From such menaces the South is practically free."[33]

Hunter also wanted the powerful white race to know that it would always have to contend with the weaker black race in spite of segregation laws, disfranchisement, and caste lines. "We are here to stay," he declared. "This is our country. We know no other," and the only things that blacks wanted from whites were equal and just laws applicable to all citizens. The press praised Hunter's speech. The *Raleigh Times* commented: "There was no bitterness in his address and there was much in it that both races could cultivate to advantage." The *Searchlight* agreed, and proclaimed that the speech was "excellent, safe in its teaching," and one of the best ever delivered at Emancipation Day celebrations.[34]

By 1912 Hunter had momentarily arrived at the conclusion that if blacks were to work out their own destiny, and ask for the correction of injustices, then it was necessary for them to become involved in politics. He realized that politics were the source of many of the problems facing blacks, and he felt that if whites can "make politics let us alone, then it will be more in order for them to advise us to let politics alone." However, he did not advise blacks to involve themselves in any political contest with the Democrats of North Carolina. Instead, Hunter and other leading blacks targeted the Republican party of North Carolina which they now saw as nothing more than an "organized band of office holders" held together by the cohesive power of federal patronage. They were determined that it would never be a viable political entity until it returned to the fundamental principles of freedom, equality, and justice.[35]

On 31 March 1912 Hunter signed the call for a meeting of the black Executive Committee of the Republican party of North Carolina to discuss the current political situation and decide upon a course of action. The *Raleigh News and Observer* interpreted the call as a sign that black Republicans "desired to warm up the present campaign." Meeting at Raleigh on 1 April 1912, the Executive Committee praised the Democrats of North Carolina as better than Republicans, because the former still permitted thousands of blacks to vote while the latter had "disfranchised us all." Refusing to remain political outcasts, they demanded their reenfranchisement within the Republican party. Hunter was among the signers of a "Letter to the Republican Voters of North Carolina" that outlined strategy for the upcoming campaign. Black voters were urged to meet all the

## We Are Your Negroes and We Are Here to Stay

requirements of the plan of organization for the state Republican party as stated by its chairman, John Motley Morehead. They were to register, attend all precinct meetings and, if possible, elect black delegates to all conventions. Blacks were cautioned to expect stiff opposition from white Republicans, who in many counties might exclude them from conventions. When this happened, they were to organize separate district conventions and elect delegates to a black state convention that would meet in Raleigh on the same day as the lily-white convention. There they would select a contesting state delegation to the national convention, which would be unpledged to any man despite rumors that blacks intended to rally around Theodore Roosevelt in order to prevent the renomination of Taft. Finally, the letter called on all white Republicans to join with blacks in an attempt to rejuvenate the original principles of the Grand Old Party.[36]

In Wake County a group of white Republicans, led by the old radical J. C. L. Harris, joined with blacks, and they succeeded in defeating the lily-whites and electing a liberal ticket in the primaries. In reference to this, the *Raleigh News and Observer* reported that the black voter was in his glory, and there was evidence that he was once again back in Republican party politics. However, the paper thought that whites should not feel threatened by any fears of black domination because the Democrats could "give the knockout to the whole push." Nevertheless, the issue of black domination did appear in the campaign when Senator Furnifold Simmons was challenged by a liberal element that tried to prevent his reelection. To solidify support, the Simmons faction returned to the central experience of the Democratic party and reminded whites that it was he who was most responsible for their present state of civilization. In the terrible days of 1898 and 1900, Simmons delivered them from the "Black Peril" and securely established white supremacy, and voters were advised, "We do not know how sorely we shall need him or how soon." Not to be outdone, supporters of Locke Craig, who was running unopposed for the Democratic nomination for governor, also reminded voters that he too was one of the "great defenders of the white race at a time when it was humiliated by blacks and deeply distressed."[37]

Not many North Carolinians were surprised over the victory of Simmons and Craig in 1912, but the election of Woodrow Wilson was an occasion for white rejoicing and black anxiety. Hunter was not upset over the election results because his political activities during the campaign were directed against white Republicans. He was especially delighted when the newly elected president selected Josephus Daniels for secretary of the navy. Hunter tendered Daniels his "hearty congratulations" in the belief that his appointment conferred honor upon all the people of the state, and he wrote, "I appropriate a part of the distinction to myself and to the race to which I belong. We are all North Carolinians." More than likely Hunter was sincere in his words to Daniels because he genuinely valued his relationships with the best white men. Yet his status as a leading black could no doubt be enhanced by associating himself with the best whites of North Carolina, past and present. For example, in 1912 he sponsored a memorial in honor of Aycock and delivered the oration for that occasion. After professing his love for the people and the State of North Carolina, Hunter went on to note that "Her honor is my honor, whatever tends to give her prestige and power among her sister states is cherished by me as deeply as any of her sons." Blacks should also be proud of the men who shed immortal luster on the state: the Gastons, Grahams, Haywoods, and Badgers, plus Vance and Aycock. Hunter had obviously erased from his slate of immortals his former hero, William W. Holden, as well as those blacks whose names he once thought should never be forgotten.[38]

Hunter recounted the privilege of being the personal friend of Aycock, who during his governorship "responded readily and gladly to every request of blacks." He wanted his listeners to know there were thousands of white men in North Carolina who "think like Governor Aycock thought." One wonders if Hunter forgot or ever realized that the lamented Aycock thought blacks in North Carolina were merely an inferior childlike race. However, he should not have forgotten that he had called out for an end to disfranchisement and "Jim Crow," and Aycock never responded. Hunter's audience was made up primarily of black schoolchildren who obviously internalized his conception of Aycock and race relations. The *Raleigh Times* reported that these children were singing patriotic songs and giving recitations from Aycock's speeches. In fact, they even donated $2.15 for a monument to him.[39]

While Hunter was extolling the virtues of Aycock, the late governor's son-in-law, Clarence H. Poe, launched an attack against blacks. In 1913 he proposed a scheme for racial segregation that excited widespread support not only in North Carolina, but throughout the South. Poe, the editor of the *Progressive Farmer*, envisioned a system of rural apartheid, and for North Carolina he also favored racially homogeneous communities in urban areas. In advocating this system of segregation, Poe insisted that in his

## We Are Your Negroes and We Are Here to Stay

heart he meant neither harm nor injustice to blacks, whom he was actually trying to help. He also hoped that people would not class him among the "bitter or destructive type of negro agitator." The response by whites in North Carolina to Poe's ideas shows that they were more than the musings of a half-baked racist. Thousands embraced his concept, even agitating for a constitutional amendment to bring it into effect. The legislature debated the issue and some of its members lauded Poe's scheme as an affirmation of black inferiority and the fact that whites would "never at any hazzard admit the negro on a parity" with them. Though the legislature rejected the idea, it eventually found its way into the platform of the Democratic party of North Carolina only to be removed when William Jennings Bryan refused to speak at the party's state convention until it had divorced itself from Poe's program. Still the concept did not die. The municipality of Winston-Salem adopted a system of residential segregation that divided the city into black and white sections, and in 1914 the convention of the North Carolina Farmers' Union unanimously adopted Poe's plan on behalf of its 40,000 members.[40]

The popularity of Poe's scheme frightened the leading blacks, for it was a clear indication that relations between the races were still not all that friendly. They realized that if the condition of blacks were ever to improve, they must abandon their policy of passive and total submission to whites and wage a modest protest against racial injustices. Hunter's friend James B. Dudley, the president of the Agricultural and Mechanical College at Greensboro, began by speaking out against residential segregation in 1914. Recognizing that black residential sections generally were devoid of pure water and sewer systems, he claimed that whites had no moral right to force his race into these areas until they had extended to them every facility necessary for the maintenance of good health. Even though he made no mention of integrated neighborhoods, Dudley was promptly branded an advocate of social equality, an idea that the *Greensboro Daily News* believed "remains in the mind of the average negro, especially the superficially educated negro, the greatest obstacle to segregation."[41]

Dudley was also upset over the segregated conditions for railroad travel. Blacks were forced to ride in old wooden Jim Crow cars, which were sandwiched between the engine and modern steel coaches for whites. There were frequent accidents, and in many cases the wooden coaches were crushed like eggshells. He was disappointed that the leading white men or some major newspaper had refused to fight against these "death traps" that were forced on blacks. Nevertheless, Dudley wrote that blacks "tried to be cheerful and believe that someday the view will be brighter." When a friend of his was killed in a train wreck while riding in a Jim Crow car in 1913, Dudley concluded that blacks, particularly the educators, had to take responsibility for the general welfare of their race and that the North Carolina State Teachers' Association was an ideal vehicle for this movement. He asked Hunter to assist him in mobilizing the support of teachers and in the collection of funds for a fight against Jim Crow cars.[42]

The Teachers' Association supported Dudley, and it appointed a committee on Equal Passenger Accommodations on Railroad Lines, charged with preparing a definitive case for presentation to the State Corporation Commission and, if necessary, the Interstate Commerce Commission. In October 1914 Dudley and an impressive contingent of blacks representing the State Teachers' Association, the Odd Fellows, the Masons, the Lott-Carey Foreign Mission Baptist Convention, the State Baptist Convention, and the black Methodist, Episcopal, and Presbyterian churches appeared before the State Corporation Commission. The petitioners argued that blacks had always remained passive and patient in the face of unjust and dangerous discrimination, but it was time for them to protest against Jim Crow travel on railraods. They did not ask for integrated travel, but only for equal accommodations. They might as well have, because the State Corporation Commission refused to honor their request.[43]

Hunter claimed that he could not understand the aversion that whites had toward associating with and living among blacks. He recalled that this certainly was not true during the days of slavery, and he felt that one of the better features of that institution was that blacks and whites lived together on the closest of terms, and with the tenderest of attachments. These were not wiped out with slavery and could still be used to improve the current state of race relations. He personally attested to the fact that the whites who knew him as a slave were always his friends, and that "we have no negro problem." Translating this experience to society at large, and in an apparent disregard for the indignities heaped upon his race during the half century since emancipation, Hunter publicly announced in 1913, "Today the Negro's heart beats as one with his former owners," and he was certain that this feeling was reciprocated. As a member of the Exslaves' Association of North Carolina, Hunter called for a reunion of these "old-timers" complete with a banquet, speeches, and songs in a grand effort to renew the kind sentiments between the races, "wipe out the sophistries of self-seeking

# We Are Your Negroes and We Are Here to Stay

political demagogues and give us clearer views of each other." Whether he realized it or not, he had committed the former slaves to the task of reprogramming the mentality of the leadership and the majority of the white population of North Carolina. There was a reunion of former slaves and their former masters during the black fair in 1913. The white community of Raleigh furnished the food and many of its ladies assisted in preparing and serving the dinner. Whites also provided the former slaves with free railroad and automobile transportation for the event. Hunter later wrote of the reunion that "we were all very happy," but it was not accompanied by any positive changes in race relations, a fact that he was forced openly to admit.[44]

A few months after the reunion, an anonymous southern white woman published an incisive article in *Outlook* magazine reflecting on the race problem in the South. She admitted that friendly relations between the races frequently existed on a personal level, but blacks as a class were subjected without distinction to the debilitating influences of segregation, and lived in constant fear of violence. These factors had created a climate of distrust that affected every aspect of race relations, and she correctly noted that to live in such an environment without moral deterioration required a "strength of character rare in men of every race." In words that were quite appropriate to Hunter and other leading men, she stated that it was no wonder that blacks had become "shifty and time serving," because they were forced to subordinate every plan or desire to improve themselves and get along with the better class of whites, to the more important goal of avoiding the wrath of the most dangerous class.[45]

Hunter was so impressed with this article that he recommended it for reading by the general public. It also provided him with an opportunity to get a few things off his chest. He agreed that the races were growing further apart, and that an air of mutual distrust and suspicion existed between them because whites and blacks really did not know each other. He urged whites to find out more about the family, educational, and religious life of blacks, and to develop the capacity to see them in light of their progress and poverty, rights and wrongs, and strengths and weaknesses. Whites also needed a better understanding of the activities of the leading blacks and they had to give them greater recognition for their efforts to improve their race. Above all, whites had to stop raising the cry of social equality as a pretext for denying blacks justice. They knew better, and Hunter claimed personal knowledge of the fact that the best white men who knew blacks

## We Are Your Negroes and We Are Here to Stay

were also aware of the fact that they had no intentions of "over-stepping racial boundaries and encroaching upon their social rights." He also felt that there were many whites who desired to help blacks, but refrained from doing so because they feared a "cold reception." On the other hand, many of the most thoughtful blacks were afraid to seek from white people "that friendly help, that community interest, that uplifting power which they alone could give," for fear of being repulsed.[46]

In essence, Hunter admitted that the best men of both races did not pay much attention to the messages they sent back and forth. They did not know each other, and they doubted their mutual professions of friendship. Yet he still claimed to believe that within the hearts of the masses of southern whites there resided a sentiment of justice, truth, honesty, and Christianity that would "ere long come to the surface in effective power." He was also convinced that there would be a revitalized Christianity among whites, and that in time they would attain a higher regard for the ethics of their religion. Then there would be no "Negro Problem" because nothing involved "subtleties so stubborn" that it could not be solved in light of Christian ethics.[47]

# 8

## A Dreamer and a Schemer

Hunter continued to appease whites and cater to the substance of accommodationist racism because he needed the aid of the white community for his educational work. In 1910 he was hired as school principal in Method, a small black settlement three miles west of Raleigh. Arriving at Method, he found the school closed because of low attendance, the black School Committee factionalized, and the people "in a state of confusion." The physical facilities of the school consisted of two small, poorly furnished rooms. He earnestly began work, determined to change these adverse conditions, and "erect a school of high grade such as could afford the needed facilities to the residents of the district and attract outside patronage." To do this he had to reassure whites that he was a safe educator, and he announced a policy that was sure to meet with their approval. The mission of black schools was to prepare youth for the work they were destined to do by virtue of their social status, and he saw the essence of real education as the "development of power—the ability to do things the world wants done and to do them in the best way."[1]

Within four years after his arrival, the Method school had earned the reputation of being one of the best in Wake County, and the *Raleigh Times* noted that it was presided over by Hunter, an "esteemed Negro." The school's physical facilities were vastly improved, and attendance had reached approximately 200 students. In 1915 an inspector for the General Education Board reported that the progress of the school was largely due to the work of the principal, "an old man." Hunter was able to improve the school with monies from the Slater and Jeanes funds, the General Education Board, and donations from patrons. With the aid of Berry O'Kelly, a merchant of Method and reportedly one of the wealthiest blacks in the state, he was also able to secure the moral and material support of the black community.[2]

In 1914 Hunter decided to erect a new industrial and training school, possibly with assistance from the newly established Rosenwald Fund. He asked Booker T. Washington to use his influence with Rosenwald to get the needed funds. Washington replied that he was "seeking to get all the light I can in order to help Mr. Rosenwald spend his money in the most helpful way," and he would keep Hunter's request on file. But he did not think it would be honored, because Rosenwald wanted to concentrate on building small, one-teacher schools in rural districts. At this point the black community of Method decided to raise $5,000 for the construction of the school, with assurances that a matching amount would be granted by Wake County. Hunter used his extensive contacts with blacks and whites to obtain donations, and both responded liberally to his requests. By 1915 blacks had raised $2,000 and wanted to begin construction. But Wake County was hesitant to commit its share, pleading hard times and poverty even though the state superintendent of public instruction had made it possible for the county to borrow the money from the state. The fact was, as an inspector of the General Education Board reported, that "the school authorities were simply timid about actually assuming the obligation of putting up so good a school building as they promised."[3]

Upon the insistence of Hunter and Berry O'Kelly, who was also chairman of the Method School Committee, blacks decided to start construction in the hope that it would stimulate increased community interest, and speed up the delivery of county funds. Through letters and reports, Hunter kept the school officials and leading white men apprised of every aspect of the school's progress and its beneficial effects on the black community. He placed great emphasis on the annual school closings or commencement exercises. These were another example of the "show-and-tell" tactics that blacks used to drum up support from whites, and they were also part of the legacy of Reconstruction. During that time educators staged public exhibitions and student examinations as a means of giving both the critics and the patrons of black education a chance to see for themselves the salutary effects it was having on the race.[4]

Hunter always believed that school closings, complete with exhibitions, speeches, and musical concerts, were events of the highest importance to the black community. Parents had an opportunity to see the progress of their children, who were eager to show through displays, recitations, and songs

## A Dreamer and a Schemer

what they had achieved. More importantly, these events enhanced the prestige of black educators, who were generally complimented by parents and white citizens on the effectiveness of their school work. At times a consolidated commencement was conducted at the county seat for all black schools. These nonpolitical and nondenominational events brought together all classes of people from all sections of a particular county. White county officials, educators, and private citizens attended these exercises, and blacks turned out by the thousands. The program often included parades, prayers, concerts, singing, games, banquets, student recitations, displays, and speechmaking. The white state agent for rural schools, Nathan C. Newbold, thought that county commencements did his race as much good as blacks, and that they were one of the principal agencies in bringing about school improvements. County commencements were also an important point of contact between the races, giving whites an opportunity to scrutinize blacks as well as to instruct and indoctrinate them regarding their duties and responsibilities. Newbold maintained that an additional benefit was that these ceremonies demonstrated to all people that large crowds of blacks could assemble in town and behave themselves in an orderly manner.[5]

Because black principals were also on display, Hunter always made extensive preparations for school closings and tried to ensure that the best white men showed up at his school. For example, the 1916 closing at Method was a grand affair. Among the invited guests present were Dr. James H. Dillard, director of the John H. Slater Fund; Professor Jackson Davis of the General Education Board; James Y. Joyner, the state superintendent of public instruction; Nathan C. Newbold, state agent for rural schools; Denison F. Giles, Wake County superintendent of schools; Professor Lautree C. Brogden; and other white men and women who were "glad of the opportunity to show their interest in the school." Preceding the formal exercises was a dinner for the white invited guests, which was prepared and served by students. The menu, hardly standard fare for most blacks, consisted of strawberries, broiled chicken, fluffed potatoes, asparagus tips served in Swedish timbales, tomato cup salad served with mayonnaise dressing in cucumber baskets, ice cream, and sponge cake. These viands showed that black girls were learning to cook not for themseves but for whites, and the partakers of the meal praised it as proof of the effectiveness of the domestic science department. Following dinner there was a round of speeches and singing, and the *News and Observer* reported that "the Raleigh delegation returned to the city much gratified at the evidence of good work at Method."[6]

While Hunter was building up his school at Method, he tried unsuccessfully to get a new school for blacks in the city of Raleigh. In 1915 the city proposed a $100,000-school-bond issue, and he succeeded in registering a number of blacks who would vote for this measure. In return they wanted a new school situated in the northeast section of Raleigh where none was available for blacks, and the general renovation of other facilities in order to make them safe for their children, particularly the Crosby school, which had been condemned as a safety hazard. Hunter and a number of leading blacks petitioned the Raleigh Township School Committee for these improvements, offering to support actively any measure promoting the progress of the city and public education. They were also confident that the School Committee was equally interested in improving the educational facilities of both races.[7]

Hunter forwarded the petition to B. F. Montague of the School Committee, who agreed with its rationale and thought that it had particular merit because it came from Hunter, "a man of intelligence and ripe experience." Montague promised to use his influence to support the cause of blacks, and he hoped they would also do their part by helping to pass the bond issue. However, he later informed Hunter that he believed any discussion of the subject of improved educational facilites for blacks, "no matter how meritorious," must await passsage of the bond issue, for "certain citizens that you or I might mention would vote against bonds for this reason if no other." One can only speculate over the probability that Montague was either trying to avoid being publicly identified as a friend of education for blacks, or he was trying to trick them into voting for the bond issue. One thing is certain, however: the measure passed, but blacks did not get a new school.[8]

Afterward, Hunter again voiced misgivings over the friendship of the best white men. While not doubting their sincerity, he thought that their efforts were hampered because they lacked "community expression," and that their influence and power as an agency for positive social change would not be felt until they had become an organized and unified force. This was absolutely necessary because the enemies of blacks were organized, active, industrious, alert, and resourceful. Hunter also recommended that the best whites identify themselves as friends of blacks, otherwise they could not escape being grouped among their enemies.[9]

## A Dreamer and a Schemer

Hunter's success in mobilizing the Method community and erecting its school helped stimulate a larger effort on the part of blacks thoughout the state to use their own resources in the development of rural schools. In May 1915 Dr. Aaron M. Moore, the secretary-treasurer of the North Carolina Mutual and Provident Association, wrote Hunter that he was determined to do something to uplift black youth in rural areas. After hearing of Hunter's success, Moore had become "doubly determined to make the thing succeed." He asked Hunter to help him realize this goal by "sending a communication to white and black newspapers introducing the rural school movement" and calling upon friends of the race to contribute their support. Hunter obliged Moore with an article telling the friends of education throughout the state that they would be glad to know that blacks, following the lead of whites, had finally acted on their own initiative to make rural schools more efficient. Calling attention to Moore's plan to raise an initial fund of $1,500 immediately, he requested that 100 black men and women contribute sums of $10 and $5 respectively for the nucleus of a rural education fund. Contributions from black citizens and institutions were generous, and within a year's time, thousands of dollars had been raised to supplement funds appropriated by the state for the education of blacks.[10]

The special effort to improve rural schools was carried on under the auspices of the Rural School Extension Department of the North Carolina State Teachers' Association, and Professor Charles H. Moore was appointed as full-time field organizer and inspector. Within a year, the Rural School Department had assisted in erecting a number of new schools, helped local school committees secure funds from the Rosenwald Foundation, forced the state to equalize the length of school terms for both races, and prevented the levying of taxes on the property of blacks for the support of schools for whites. During his first year of travel throughout the state, Charles H. Moore determined that North Carolina was woefully derelict in the education of its 200,000 black children who resided in rural areas. This only confirmed what Nathan C. Newbold, the state agent for rural schools, had found out two years earlier. In his report to the superintendent of public instruction for the year 1913–14, Newbold noted that "the average negro school house is really a disgrace to an independent civilized society," and it told in "unmistaken terms a story of injustice, inhumanity, and neglect on the part of white people." He contended that these schools were "intolerable, indefensible, unbearable and above all un-Christian." If whites were

## A Dreamer and a Schemer

really honest with themselves, they would have to admit that these conditions were caused by prejudice and neglect because they had really not tried to give blacks justice.[11]

The most serious deficiency discovered by Moore was that thousands of dollars earmarked for black education had actually been spent to build schools, hire additional teachers, or increase the school terms for whites. He reported his findings to the State Department of Education, which promised to remedy the situation. Moore did not know how long whites had been appropriating black school funds for their own purposes, but some blacks believed it had been going on for quite a while. Since 1909 they had also begun to suspect the truth of the frequent assertion that whites were financing the major portion of the cost of black education. In that year Charles L. Coon, the Goldsboro superintendent of schools, created a sensation by producing statistics to show that black schools in North Carolina were not a burden on white property owners, and that blacks were more than paying for the cost of their own education. The treasurer of Granville County confirmed this. Using Coon's method to determine who paid for the education of blacks in his county during the year 1908–9, he discovered that if the funds earmarked for education were distributed on the basis of population, blacks would have more than paid for their own schooling. Moreover, if revenues were distributed for education exclusively on the basis of race, blacks would actually fare better. Coon's findings provoked a bitter response from James Y. Joyner, the state superintendent of public instruction. Josephus Daniels's *News and Observer* branded Coon a "sensationalist," announced that his statistics were erroneous, and accused him of committing a crime against the state. However, Charles B. Aycock was so sure that Coon was right that he went to see Daniels, and "took him pretty severely to task about the matter." He also proposed to censure Joyner who, while serving as superintendent of public instruction in his administration, had used the same type of statistics as Coon when arguing against the division of school funds on the basis of race.[12]

Coon's revelation of 1909 and Moore's report of 1916 helped release blacks from generations of fears and threats that the education of their race would suffer if color was used as a basis for allocating school monies. They were also additional proof of the fallacy of the statement that whites were the best friends of blacks. But Hunter remained silent about Moore's findings, because at the time of their release he was riding the crest of popularity as a leading man and did not want to jeopardize the white community's support for his school at Method. The death of Booker T. Washington in 1915 provided him with an opportunity to enhance his status as a leading black. At his insistence the black teachers of Wake County sponsored memorial services and adopted resolutions declaring that Washington had done more than anyone "to assuage racial asperities and promote friendly cooperation between the two races in all good works." The teachers resolved "that in our humble way and in our limited spheres we will seek to keep aglow the spirit of Washington." Hunter forwarded the resolutions to Mrs. Washington, who asked him to thank the Wake County teachers for their kind words of comfort. She also wanted Hunter to urge the teachers to rededicate themselves to the principles of her late husband, whom she viewed as a martyr, and she was sure that "all of our people everywhere realize that Mr. Washington laid down his very life for the people."[13]

The egotistical Hunter might even have believed that somehow the mantle of Washington's leadership, at least as far as North Carolina was concerned, would be transferred to his shoulders. In a lengthy article entitled "Booker T. Washington and the White People of the South—A Word of Advice to Negroes," Hunter called upon whites and blacks, North and South, to rally around the life and principles of Washington in a grand effort to improve race relations. He also attempted to appropriate for himself some of Washington's prestige by drawing a distinct parallel between himself and the departed race leader. They were former slaves who owed their success in freedom to the good white men of the South. As educators, they advocated industrial training and the beneficial effects of manual labor. Each had counseled blacks to be patient and remain in the South, to practice good habits of thrift and morality, and to cultivate the friendship of their white neighbors. Both men also realized and had stated that the political ambitions of blacks had impeded their progress and increased race antagonisms.[14]

Hunter admitted there were many blacks who misconstrued Washington's motives and "interpreted to him sycophantic severity to conditions which he was trying hardest and in the most successful way to remedy." However, Hunter claimed he understood that Washington's motives were positive, and that he was not an enemy of his race. Like Washington he knew from personal experiences that the role of a race leader was not an easy one. He too had to contend with opposition, petty jealousies, all sorts of crazy notions, and selfish prejudice "emanating from his own race." Then too, the present system of race relations imposed hardships upon

# A Dreamer and a Schemer

blacks, which he and Washington felt as keenly as any member of their race. Yet he believed the Christian whites of the South were not the enemies of blacks, for they had understood the good intentions of Washington and himself and had given them encouragement and support. An editorial comment in the *State Journal* noted that Hunter's article was "wise and helpful," and it announced that "a great opportunity awaits the author of this article and other leaders of his race in carrying on the great work inaugurated by the founder of the Tuskegee Institution."[15]

Hunter's chances of becoming another Booker T. Washington or even the foremost black leader in North Carolina were slim indeed. He had to contend with too many other leading black men in the state who advocated and closely followed the Tuskegee line. The white men who praised Hunter's policy of race relations were little men in comparison to those who had supported Washington, and he also lacked a secure institutional base from which to assert his leadership. True, he was an educator, but only a public school principal who was firmly controlled by local white school officials. Then too there was a great divergence between the personalities of these two men. Hunter was rash and inconsistent, and at times he engaged in the very things that by his own admission tended to disturb or upset racial harmony.

Moreover, Hunter could not stay out of politics, and during every election year he was locked in battle with the lily-white Republicans. In June 1915 Alex J. Field, the editor and owner of the *State Journal*, announced with "profound regret, not unmixed with alarm," the Supreme Court's ruling that grandfather clauses were unconstitutional. He hoped that blacks would not try to reassert themselves politically, because it would disrupt racial harmony and be like "lifting off the lid of hell." Field also reminded his readers that when blacks enjoyed universal suffrage, whites "lived in this state for over thirty years in a hell of corruption and discord and strife, culminating in the Wilmington riot." In spite of this warning, blacks prepared for the 1916 political campaign. Hunter was still secretary and a committeeman of the North Carolina Republican Executive Committee, which decided to conduct a massive voter-registration campaign throughout the state. He signed the call for all "true Republicans of whatever race or class or previous conditions" to meet in convention at Raleigh on 24 April 1916 for the purpose of restoring the party to its original principles and securing for all citizens their rights and privileges. Blacks had to unite in a continuous demand for these great and fundamental issues, and they could

# A Dreamer and a Schemer

"no longer afford to be made the football of the bosses and designing politicians."[16]

The Democrats delighted in agitating the friction between Republicans, and on the day of the black convention the *Raleigh News and Observer* announced, "The G.O.P. is placed in a new role. Its disowned child is about to hit back. The worm has turned." The paper reminded blacks that they had traditionally been the strength and backbone of Republicanism in North Carolina, but they had also been used and abused by that party and were now considered as "squeezed lemons dumped on a trash heap." They therefore had every right to feel aggrieved and were thoroughly justified in their revolt against lily-whitism. At their convention, blacks once again selected a contesting delegation to the Republican National Convention. The chairman of the North Carolina Executive Committee, Harrison H. Taylor, later advised blacks "as a matter of good politics" to split their votes by supporting the Democrats' state ticket and the national Republican ticket. Taylor's strategy was good politics because it was easier for blacks to register and qualify as voters if Democrats were convinced of their support. Blacks also realized they did not have enough voters to swing a state election, but they could make their influence felt in closely contested local campaigns, particularly for offices of a nonpartisan character.[17]

As early as January 1916 the blacks of Wake County laid plans for the general election by announcing the formation of the Wake County Twentieth Century Voter's Club. This was a nonpartisan organization dedicated to registering every qualified voter to support the best "men and measures." At the Emancipation Day celebration at Raleigh in 1916, Hunter recommended that all blacks support the Voter's Club, and he served as its first secretary. Although the plans for the organization were made public, whites really knew of its existence only one month before the election when the *Raleigh Times* reported that "some Sherlock Holmes" had discovered a circular letter, a plan of organization, and some resolutions passed at a meeting of black voters and taxpayers. According to these documents, blacks agreed that they would have to unite and reassert themselves in politics, "otherwise the day would soon come when property rights so far as we are concerned will pass away and we will be reduced to a condition of vassalage."[18]

Whites believed the existence of the Voter's Club was a signal that blacks were once again in politics after an absence of sixteen years. They were not sure how many could qualify as voters, but the editor of the *Raleigh Times*

# A Dreamer and a Schemer

thought they were "equipped in large numbers." He doubted, however, that the influence of the black electorate would be felt in North Carolina because no political party wanted its votes. Nevertheless, the uncovering of the Twentieth Century Voter's Club surprised and troubled Republicans and Democrats, and they suspected that some type of plot or conspiracy existed among the black voters of Wake County. Both parties threatened to challenge the eligibility of black voters and called for the dismissal of registrars who placed them on the books. Neither carried out their threats because the blacks who registered were thoroughly qualified. The Republicans were especially upset, and the *Raleigh Times* reported that it did not "detract from the humor of the situation that the struggling lily whites are deeply disgusted" because they were bound to lose some black voters, "a circumstance about which . . . Hunter and the other 'signers' are worrying as they would about a 'possum up a tree.' "[19]

At first the Democrats were upset because they did not know for sure how blacks would vote. However, their fears were later calmed after learning that blacks intended to support the Democratic candidate for governor, Thomas W. Bickett. Following the election, Hunter wrote Governor-elect Bickett that "as a negro Republican I voted for you because of my confidence in your ability, your integrity, your patriotism." Hunter also wanted Bickett to know that many other blacks had also voted for him and they hoped his administration would serve the best interest of all the people of North Carolina. Bickett assured Hunter that he would indeed endeavor to see that every man in the state "gets an absolutely square deal regardless of condition or color." Hunter also congratulated the state treasurer, Benjamin R. Lacy, upon his reelection and also reminded him that he was not trying to "masquerade as a democrat. I am not. I am a Republican." But he had always voted for Lacy in every election because it was his way of paying personal tribute to an "able, patriotic and pure North Carolina gentleman." Lacy appreciated these remarks especially because Hunter was only the second person to congratulate him on his victory. He was also glad that his "course in life has commended itself" to Hunter's good judgment.[20]

During the campaign of 1916 Hunter learned of an underground plot, centering in the black churches and secret societies of Method, to oust him from his job because of his age and the fact that he was a former slave. He was able to hold on to his principalship temporarily when his white friends came to the rescue. Frank P. Haywood, a member of the family who had owned Hunter, had a high opinion of him and other former slaves, and he

# A Dreamer and a Schemer

feared that "these fine old types are not being reproduced in this rapid driving age—a condition to be sadly deplored." He wrote of his regard for Hunter in a letter to D. F. Giles, the superintendent of Wake County schools. Giles informed Haywood that he also considered Hunter "a leader in the best class of the Negro race," but it seems that he too was not overly enthusiastic about retaining him as principal of the Method school. Giles, who planned to make the school at Method an important educational facility, wanted a man who was thoroughly modern and proficient in the manual arts. He probably also wanted one he could control and who did not have Hunter's connection with the best white men. But he agreed that Hunter would prove satisfactory if "I can get him adjusted to our viewpoint." Haywood sent Hunter a copy of Giles's letter, with the postscript "Charlie, I hope this means favorable action." It did indeed, for when Logan D. Howell visited the superintendent on Hunter's behalf he found it unnecessary to say anything because Giles had decided against any action. Bolstered by his white patrons, Hunter wrote Giles that he could not help having been born a slave, and had no apologies for it. Furthermore, he thought if "some of those who are making that charge had been born slaves they would have a great deal more sense than they now show."[21]

Hunter's school progressed despite the local opposition to him, and by 1917 this institution, then named the Berry O'Kelly Training School, received national recognition as the "finest and most practical rural training school in the entire South," because its mission was to teach students how to make a living by working. The school provided students an academic background along with training in the industrial and vocational arts. It also contained a farm, gardens, and facilities for boarding students. An article in the *Manufacturer's Record* stated that the O'Kelly Training School was "a real county training school precisely the things negroes need, and it was no wonder whites showed so much interest in an institution which was designed to provide for them real workers, laundresses, seamstresses, carpenters, and other types of skilled laborers." Dr. James H. Dillard of the General Education Board was so impressed with Hunter's school that he commented, "If I had my way I would put it on wheels and carry it all over the South as an object-lesson to the colored race."[22]

Yet Hunter was not satisfied with being the principal of a rural training school, and he had his eye on a higher position in education. The legislature in 1917 established a State Board of Examiners and Institute Conductors. The members of the board were appointed by the governor and charged with the responsibility of testing and certifying prospective public school-teachers and directing teacher institutes at various locations in the state. Hunter hoped to receive an appointment as one of the black members of the board. Though lacking a college degree, he thought an appointment to the board would be a "very desirable one and quite agreeable to his nature and aptitude." The Wake County superintendent of schools, D. F. Giles, received an appointment to the Board of Examiners, and indicated to Hunter that he would recommend and support his nomination as a compliment to Wake County and a distinct benefit to the state. Giles also suggested that Hunter's chances for appointment would be enhanced by recommendations from some of his white friends.[23]

Accordingly, Hunter contacted the Haywoods and "respectfully requested the influence of some members of our old family" in helping him get the appointment. Marshall DeLancey Haywood visited the state superintendent of public instruction on Hunter's behalf, while Frank P. Haywood dispatched a letter of recommendation to the State Board of Examiners. The latter believed that Hunter was thoroughly qualified for the position and had the "ability equal to meet the demands of *his* people and to serve them unusually well." Hunter also asked for the assistance of state treasurer Benjamin R. Lacy in the belief that it would clinch the position for him. Lacy wrote Hunter, "It will give me a great deal of pleasure to do anything I can to help you . . . ," and he promised to take the matter up with the superintendent of public instruction.[24]

Hunter was so sure he would be appointed to the Board of Examiners that he failed to take the necessary steps to protect his job at the Berry O'Kelly School. He dropped hints that he would leave the school because he had many assurances of better positions elsewhere. He was badly disappointed when the State Board of Education in July 1917 rejected his nomination. He wrote to Giles, "I was awfully grieved when you all turned me down for it was the first time I had ever been turned down by white people." However, he was consoled with the knowledge that the "stroke did not fall from the hands of those who know me well and with whom I was raised." Two months later he received a notification of his release as principal of the Berry O'Kelly Training School. Hunter's predicament was partially self-inflicted, because in 1917 he began to engage in certain activities that were not characteristic of safe educators and leading black men. He started editing a newspaper that soon gained the reputation of being a radical organ, and the wartime situation provided him with opportunities to explore other options for employment. In fact, Hunter was actually participating in some of these endeavors before he was eliminated from the ranks of the black educators in North Carolina.[25]

On the evening of 2 April 1917, the day that Woodrow Wilson delivered his war message to Congress, Governor Thomas W. Bickett assured the nation of the loyalty of the black population of North Carolina. Several months later the loyalty of Hunter was questioned and the *Independent* (Raleigh), which he edited, was branded as a seditious publication. On 14 July 1917 the *Independent* published an open letter to Woodrow Wilson from professor D. J. Jordan, the head of the Department of History and Pedagogy at the Agricultural and Technical College in Greensboro. The letter was written in response to the race riot in East St. Louis, Illinois, and it was a scathing attack on the racial policies of the president, who was branded as an enemy of blacks. Jordan argued that Wilson's insensitivity to the rights of blacks as human beings had fostered mob rule across the land and encouraged such incidents as that at East St. Louis. The president was also reminded that he had made many statements on behalf of Belgians, Mexicans, Chinese, and Irishmen, and demanded that the world be made safe for democracy, but he had not "uttered even in whisper one word in behalf of twelve millions of your own fellow citizens . . . whose welfare you have chosen to conserve." Jordan hinted that the president could no longer take for granted the loyalty of black Americans, because millions were asking, "Is this the kind of Democracy I am asked to give my fortune and my life to make safe in the world?" The Jordan letter was an instant sensation and the response to it clearly proved that free speech was not tolerated in North Carolina when it tended to run against the grain of prevailing opinion. Instead of trying to refute Jordan's letter on a factual basis, which would have been difficult, whites simply condemned it as being "foolish, yet treasonable, dangerous and full of dynamite." An editorial in the *Raleigh Times* hinted that Jordan was crazy because black educators knew better than to make such statements. They were supposed to inculcate ideas of racial harmony and peace and help others of their race to "see the light." As if doubting its own words, the editorial also stated that, more than likely, Jordan was "yielding to an impulse strong in the educated class" of his race. Whatever, the *Times* thought that his letter was sure to be detrimental to all black North Carolinians at a time when the state was "exceptionally free from race oppression, enmity, and malice."[26]

Jordan's letter was an embarrassment to Governor Bickett who, many

## A Dreamer and a Schemer

believed, held the most liberal views on race relations of any chief executive in the history of the state. According to the *Greensboro Daily News*, Bickett was mad, and he feared that the letter would incite blacks throughout the state. Most whites agreed, and they thought that Jordan should not go unpunished for his inflammatory remarks. A copy of his letter was sent to the United States attorney general for possible action, and the *Raleigh Daily News* thought that Jordan should "hear something firm but kind" from the State of North Carolina. He needed a disciplining that he would never forget in order to teach him to "rule his tongue and steady his pen." The *Greensboro Daily News* suggested that President Dudley of the Agricultural and Technical College publicly repudiate the Jordan letter; otherwise he would have a hard time trying to get an appropriation from the state for his school.[27]

Jordan's head was spared when the leading black men of North Carolina asked whites to let them handle the matter. They promised to discipline Jordan, denounce his views, and demand his resignation. The leading men of Greensboro delivered a copy of Jordan's manuscript to a committee of their white friends for content and rhetorical analysis to determine if it was wantonly insulting to the president. The committee concluded that taken as a whole it was not. The leading blacks also wrote letters and sent telegrams to the governor apologizing for Jordan's remarks, and one claimed that nine-tenths of his race in the state disapproved of the letter. Jordan confessed to Hunter that maybe his letter was rather strong and direct, but the provocation was certainly much greater. Blacks had tried diplomacy for fifty years, and the only thing they had to show for it was a steady decline in their influence in government. "Perhaps it is time now for some plain words that we may sooner know where we are." Another thing that saved Jordan from harsher action was that whites could not severely punish him without attacking Hunter. Nevertheless, Hunter did not escape censure. The *Greensboro Daily News* regretted the fact that Jordan could not be punished by himself for sedition because the "Negro paper in Raleigh ran the article in great style." The *Raleigh Times* agreed, and its editor wrote that "rarely have we seen so much folly packed in a space equal to that used by the *Raleigh Independent* in giving the letter publicity." Hunter tried to get off the hook by explaining that he had been out of town and was not aware of Jordan's letter until he returned. He also sent a letter to Governor Bickett offering reassurances that he had always tried to promote a better understanding between the races. Indeed, he wrote, "My whole manhood life has

## A Dreamer and a Schemer

been devoted to labors in promotion of sensible views and wise action on the part of my race both politically and otherwise."[28]

"There is not a traitor among us," wrote Hunter to Congressman James H. Pou in August 1917. However, Hunter believed that blacks did have some doubts as to what was expected of them during the wartime crisis. They were patriotic and wanted to do the "right and manly thing," and above all they did not want to be an embarrassment to the government. Yet blacks themselves were embarrassed and insulted by the continued assaults upon their rights as human beings and citizens. Hunter hoped all Americans would discard every divisive issue during the national emergency, including the race problem, and work together for victory. But he told the congressman, "This does not mean that we are to change our honest conviction upon any question upon which we have heretofore been at variance."[29]

The Jordan letter exploded three days before the final selection of the black members for the Board of Examiners and Institute Conductors, and this may have been a reason why Hunter was not appointed. He later began to receive increased pressure from his creditors, who applied economic sanctions against him by calling in their debts. At length his indebtedness was brought to the attention of Edgar W. Knight, the superintendent of public instruction for Wake County. Knight informed Hunter that his position as an educator demanded that he satisfy his financial obligations. Hunter claimed that he could not pay his debts because of low pay and family emergencies. His entire salary for the year of 1916 was $350, which was barely enough to live on. He informed Knight that he had continued in educational work at the greatest sacrifice to himself and his family, and, "No one will ever know the nature and extent of the sacrifices I have made." As an example Hunter alleged that he had recently received an offer with a lucrative salary to go to Connecticut and supervise the placing of black laborers from the South. He stated that he declined this opportunity out of deference to prevailing opinions concerning migration; however, he was holding an order for 1,000 men and 300 women for work at Hartford. He confided to Knight that "in this there is much money for me, but so far I have held off." Hunter was less than truthful, for since the spring of 1917 he had been assisting the National League on Urban Conditions among Negroes in placing black male students on tobacco plantations in Connecticut during their summer vacations. He also tried to expand his relationship with the league to include the placement of adult workers from the South in northern industry. John C. Dancy, Jr., an official of the league, promised to

# A Dreamer and a Schemer

assist Hunter by finding work for any migrant that he could send up to New York.[30]

Again changing his mind about the South being the best place for blacks, Hunter stated publicly that their increased movement to the North was motivated by a desire to escape oppression. This idea was challenged by Judge Gilbert T. Stephenson of Winston-Salem, who claimed that he did not know of a single black who left that city because of unfair treatment. In words applicable to many of the leading blacks, he also maintained that many of those who alleged oppression were not speaking on behalf of migrants, but of the things that tempted them to leave the South. Lacking any intention to leave themselves, they were only trying to force whites "to do better by the Negro." Stephenson later advised Hunter that his *Independent* (Raleigh) should concentrate on the things that whites had done for blacks rather than dwelling on those things that had not been accomplished. The *Raleigh News and Observer* also called upon the leading blacks who were "largely responsible for the attitude of their fellows" to face the necessity of a strict performance of their duty to their race and state. The paper insisted that all means of "peaceable propaganda" be used to instill in blacks the truth that the "best friend of the North Carolina Negro is the North Carolina white and the best job for the North Carolina Negro is on North Carolina farms and in North Carolina industry."[31]

Hunter did not use the pages of his newspaper to reply to Stephenson, but in a letter to the editor of the *Raleigh News and Observer* he explained that patriotism was the only reason why people encouraged blacks to migrate North, because workers were needed in that region to fill jobs created by the wartime expansion of industry. However, the motives of migrants were different and they left with the hopes of higher wages, better educational opportunities, and equal protection under the laws. Furthermore, Hunter argued that many blacks actually feared that the "South has in store for them a heritage of hardships as they have not yet faced," and they saw the employment opportunities in the North as a means of escape. "We who are among the race and of it know these things to be true and I for one think that it is better to face the facts squarely and apply the corrective than to beat around upon false pretenses," he wrote. But he contended that blacks would stay in North Carolina if their opportunities were improved, and if they received higher wages. Although not opposed to migration, Hunter announced that he would not encourage it, and had he been inclined to do so, he could have made a lot of money as a labor agent.[32]

## A Dreamer and a Schemer

Hunter informed whites that the leading blacks were doing their duty in controlling the thoughts of their race through reasonable arguments. This was indeed the mission of the *Independent* of Raleigh, which had been organized by "Wake County Negroes, all of whom except himself were persons of great influence and large financial means." They decided that the paper would serve as a means of teaching and encouraging blacks to develop themselves in North Carolina, and Hunter challenged the state to use its resources in helping the leading blacks in this important work. It could begin by extending to blacks in the countryside the benefits of farm and home demonstration agents, and improving the conditions of rural schools, which Hunter claimed were "mere travesties." Hunter was released from Wake County schools within three weeks of the publication of this article. He had obviously irritated too many whites. However, some blacks were glad that Hunter was serving as an effective spokesman for his race. Charles H. Moore congratulated him on his fine article in the *News and Observer*, and he too believed that race relations could stand a major overhaul. He wrote in reference to the war that "the terrible conflict would not end until more than one injustice is overthrown in the interest of Democracy and the world was made safe for all the colored people."[33]

Hunter neglected to mention in his article that he was using the *Independent* and his position as its editor to drum up support for the National Association for the Advancement of Colored People (NAACP). However, he wrote to James Weldon Johnson, the organization's executive secretary, "I am stirring the branches in this State and hope to see them actively at work at no distant day." Hunter was actually hoping to see himself at work because he was badly in need of employment. In 1917 he was elected as a delegate to the midwinter conference of the NAACP, which was held in New York, and he saw this as an opportunity for personal gain. Several northern firms were advertising for laborers in the *Independent*, and Hunter knew that blacks in increasing numbers were leaving the state seeking employment. These factors prompted him to retry his hand as a labor agent. He informed the Butterworth-Judson Company of Newark, New Jersey, and James Weldon Johnson that he knew of a large number of good, reliable, and intelligent black men who were ready to migrate north. However, these men, who had never been away from home, desired accurate information from someone they trusted on transportation, employment, wages, and living conditions in the North. He alleged that these potential migrants wanted him to investigate the situation personally and report back to them.

## A Dreamer and a Schemer

He and his son-in-law, the Reverend James K. Satterwhite, were planning to come to New York for the NAACP conference, and they would gladly perform this service if the Butterworth-Judson Company paid their expenses. In return he promised the company "the pick of good workers from these parts." Hunter was willing to circumvent the laws of North Carolina that restricted the soliciting of laborers for employment outside the state, and he reasoned that because many blacks were voluntarily leaving, it was his duty to assist them as best he could. The migrants would leave the state as individuals and then he would mobilize them into companies of workers at Portsmouth or Richmond, Virginia, for subsequent movement north.[34]

When Hunter's latest venture into the labor business fell through, he attempted to recapture some of his status as a leading man and take advantage of wartime opportunities in North Carolina. In a speech delivered at the Johnston County Negro Fair in November 1917, Hunter attempted to convince blacks that they had a personal stake in an Allied victory. To him, the conflict in Europe as well as "the blood-lust of brutish mobocracy on this side of the water" were symbols of a decadent civilization, but people everywhere were engaged in a great world movement to purge humanity of evil and regenerate society. This was the Allies' cause, and their victory would be a victory for all mankind. The final settlement of the war would "adjust accumulated grievances of centuries, lift the heavy hand of oppression from the masses, depose aristocracy, and free the common people." It would also bring freedom and justice to the black race everywhere. Hunter acknowledged that American blacks were oppressed and hopeless, and some, like the ancient Israelites in Babylonian captivity, were ready to "hang their harps on willows and cry out, 'How can we sing our Lord's song in a strange land?'" Yet he advised these people to forget about their domestic problems for the moment, and they would be solved in time. All over the world "men are moving for freedom," and Hunter urged blacks as potential beneficiaries to join this movement and respond to their "call for world service."[35]

The black author and journalist S. G. Walker of Burlington praised Hunter's address, agreeing that an Allied victory would provide American blacks with an opportunity to place their "claims and causes upon the world's conscience which shall have been purged, rectified, and refined." Walker recommended to Governor Bickett that Hunter's speech be published by the state and disseminated to every black citizen. The governor's office rejected this suggestion on the grounds that the state did not have the

## A Dreamer and a Schemer

money for such a project. However, Santford Martin, Bickett's private secretary, advised that the speech be sent to the Committee on Public Information for publication by the federal government.[36]

In November 1917 Hunter contacted Henry A. Page, the food administrator for North Carolina, and offered to assist him in any possible way. He informed Page that the *Independent* was the major black newspaper in the state, and it could be used effectively to impress upon blacks the necessity for increased food production. According to Hunter the only things needed to get results from the black community were direction, organization, and "a little urging." The Food Administration accepted his services and placed the *Independent* on the agency's approved list of publications targeted for press releases. John Paul Lucas, the administration's executive secretary, thought that the *Independent* would be of inestimable value to his work and that Hunter personally could render the country and humanity a "marked service" during the national emergency. Within a week's time, Hunter developed a plan for increasing food production and mobilizing the black community behind the war effort.[37]

He proposed the organization of blacks throughout the state into community leagues with the object of impressing upon citizens the necessity of planting every uncultivated acre in food crops. All black preachers and educators would be used as propagandists to indoctrinate others on the importance of increasing yields and following good conservation practices. Hunter forwarded his plan to Page and informed him that blacks were not taking a major interest in the war effort. They were indifferent because "their leaders fear that it might be thought indecorous in them to butt in," and consequently a lot of blacks tended to regard the war as "a matter for white people in which we have but little interests." Hunter argued that the adoption of his plan would change this attitude. The opportunist in him surfaced when he suggested to Page that a "competent, active, energetic" person be appointed to supervise and coordinate his proposed program.[38]

Hunter undoubtedly thought he would receive this appointment because of his experience as an editor and educator. He confided to Lucas that he had always recommended that blacks engage in agriculture, conserve food, and increase food production. Furthermore, he claimed that he had advocated these measures "in the face of criticisms that I was catering to a prejudice against the literary training of my race." The Food Administration did not establish a supervisor's position to oversee work among blacks, but it did give Hunter an allowance to cover the expenses of his speaking engagements. He traveled across the state and spoke to audiences "at homes, schools, churches and farms" on the need for increased food production and conservation, and helped organize school farms, conservation leagues, victory gardens, and canning clubs. He also rallied support for the Thrift Campaign by urging blacks to purchase bonds and savings stamps. According to Hunter's reports, his efforts were effective, and blacks were zealously responding to his appeals. However, he was disturbed by the number of idle black youth who, he thought, were wasting time roaming about without direction and were sure to wind up in crime or poverty. He recommended that some effort be made to enlist these persons in the war effort by mobilizing them into a reserve army of workers in order to increase the productive power of the nation.[39]

Hoping for official recognition from the federal government for his work with the Food Administration, Hunter proceeded to bypass the state agency and report directly to Washington. In a letter to A. U. Craig of the Federal Food Administration, he disclosed his plans for increasing food production in North Carolina. While acknowledging that Page and Lucas were "men of exceptional ability and fine spirit," he suggested that Craig use his influence to force a full implementation of his plans. Hunter specifically desired an appointment as a special supervisor of the administration's work among blacks. He told Craig that whites did not know how to reach and influence sentiment among blacks and, "in the face of what they deem the larger affairs of their own race, they have not the time to devote to us." As a consequence, blacks were neglected in many very important concerns, and especially in the war effort they "do not measure up to our capacity for good." Hunter later reiterated this same idea to Congressman Rufus L. Doughton.[40]

In May 1918 the Food Administration for North Carolina terminated Hunter's services. It claimed a lack of funds to support his activities, and informed him that his duties had been turned over to volunteer workers from black churches and secret societies. Hunter probably believed with some justification that he had been unfairly thrown out of a system that he had helped create. He was surprised and disappointed at his dismissal and he responded by attempting to exploit the race issue to his advantage. Several months earlier he had praised blacks for their enthusiastic and patriotic support of the war, but these characteristics seemed to disappear along with his position. He wrote Lucas that blacks were loyal and true; however, during his travels throughout the state he had actually found a declining morale and "an insidious spirit of isolation-aloofness-creeping over them. The feeling is growing that this is a white man's war in which the Negro has no direct interest."[41]

Hunter claimed that his quasi-official status with the Food Administration had helped bolster the sagging morale of blacks, and that the termination of his position had deprived his race of what little recognition it had. Hence blacks could not be expected to do their best during the emergency. He informed Lucas that he could not do volunteer work, and he had already made a great sacrifice by working with the Food Administration when he could have made much more money as a labor agent. Now he intended to do that because he had many unfilled orders for workers in Connecticut and New Jersey. He asked Lucas, "What am I to do? Sit and starve in the presence of a full plate? The idea to me seems suicidal." Lucas was surprised at Hunter's statements about the declining morale of blacks, and he told him that they were contrary to information he had received from other leading men and his own tenants. Hunter attempted to get out of this by alleging that any statements refuting his assessment of the morale of blacks emanated from his old political enemies. Moreover, he and many of his black friends believed that "petty political bossism" was seeking to capitalize on the wartime situation and to stir up trouble between the races, in the same way that it had "entered and disrupted our churches, our Sunday schools, our benevolent organizations and even our business enterprises."[42]

Hunter saw an additional opportunity for employment when the United States Employment Service for North Carolina commenced operations in the state. He congratulated George S. Ramsey upon his appointment as labor director and gave him his personal evaluation of the labor situation. Hunter informed Ramsey that thousands of blacks were leaving North Carolina for the industrial centers of the North where their labor was in great demand. Not only this, but his travels throughout the state had convinced him that there was "a woeful amount of downright idleness among us" that should be prevented. With a little systematic study and some wise direction, Hunter was convinced that blacks could be persuaded to remain at home, and the energies of "all ages and sexes" could be mobilized into an efficient and productive labor force. Again he believed he was just the person to perform this task. Ramsey was very interested in Hunter's remarks on the labor situation, and he invited Hunter for a consultation on the matter.[43]

When rumors began to circulate alleging that blacks from outside the state would be brought in to supervise and coordinate the homefront, Hunter protested to Senator Furnifold M. Simmons and Congressman Rufus L. Doughton. He asserted that black North Carolinians would certainly resent the importation of others to do work that they were fully capable of doing for themselves. The state had blacks of character, ability, and intelligence who were the equals of those found anywhere in America. Further, Hunter claimed that no state could boast of a prouder record of his race's support of the war than North Carolina. He reminded the congressman that "The Negroes of our State have always been docile, tractable, receptive," and they had not sought advancement through preferential treatment. He thought that as a reward for this good behavior, they should be given any available government position assigned to their race in North Carolina.[44]

Hunter informed Doughton and Simmons of the work that he had done with the Food Administration and of his familiarity with labor and migration problems. He also claimed that he had personally prevented hundreds of blacks from leaving North Carolina by withholding information from potential migrants. "I could have made good money by recruiting these laborers," Hunter wrote, but he contended that he had not done so because of his belief in the opportunities for blacks in North Carolina. Doughton and Simmons, agreeing with Hunter, praised the patriotism and the effort that his race was making in support of the war and promised to do whatever they could to block the appointment of outside blacks to any position in North Carolina. Hunter was encouraged by these remarks, and he informed Doughton that he was ready and willing to throw "my personality and the weight of the *Raleigh Independent* with its 5,000 readers into the cause if a properly organized work can be started among our people." He also called a meeting of patriotic citizens of Raleigh, who drafted a petition to members of Congress from North Carolina. The petition contained Hunter's ideas as to what was absolutely essential for mobilizing the support of his race for the duration of the war.[45]

The petitioners agreed that blacks had done their best to support the war on a purely voluntary basis and without official recognition. However, the work required a systematic and sustained effort that could be accomplished only by a regularly employed force. Recognizing this fact, the federal government was in the process of sending "men of the race from other States to work among the Negroes of North Carolina." The petition ended with the usual refrain that friendly race relations had always existed in their state and called for the aid and sympathy of "North Carolina white people who had never turned a deaf ear to the appeal of North Carolina Negroes."[46]

# A Dreamer and a Schemer

The office of Furnifold M. Simmons announced that the petition was one of the "strongest letters of the sort that has reached its files," and that it was indeed a strong protest against the importation of blacks into the state to the neglect of local talent. North Carolina Congressman Edward W. Pou thought that the petition was valid, and he promised Hunter that he would be glad to support it in any possible way. Pou later made an address in Congress to dispel any ideas that North Carolina's black citizens were disloyal. He praised the fact that blacks had shown their patriotism by subscribing to liberty bonds, supporting the Red Cross, and cheerfully responding to the draft. According to Pou, "blacks had their faults but disloyalty was not one of them," as southern white people knew. They had seen blacks tested during the Civil War when, for four long years, helpless white women and children were left at the mercy of blacks. Pou sent Hunter a copy of the *Congressional Record* containing his speech and informed him that he was forwarding the petition to Herbert Hoover of the National Food Administration. "I am glad to do this and cherish the hope that the recommendation will be adopted."[47]

Hoover's office later notified Pou that it indeed planned to appoint a black in every state who would have charge of "Negro activities." Ernest T. Atwell, the Food Administration's black field agent, would visit North Carolina and, with the approval of Page, select a suitable black for this work. Learning of this, Hunter wrote his son-in-law, James K. Satterwhite, that their actions in petitioning their congressmen had borne fruit, and he instructed him to organize their NAACP men and make sure that they got to Atwell as soon as he arrived in Raleigh. Hunter urged Satterwhite not to "let others scoop the fruits of our victory," because "I really think I am entitled to the appointment even though I may decline it." Hunter wrote these words in June 1918, but by this time he had migrated from North Carolina. He had been without regular employment for almost a year, and his pay for editing the *Independent* (Raleigh) was not sufficient to cover his living expenses. Heavily in debt, he would have truly suffered had it not been "for the kindness of Mr. Drake of the Merchants National Bank." At other times, he was forced to borrow money often at interest rates as high as 300 percent in order to keep from starving. In May 1918 he wrote to N. C. Newbold, "I shall leave Raleigh to spend the remainder of my life elsewhere. There seems no hope here."[48]

Hunter applied for a job as a supervisor of black industrial workers in New York in the belief that such a position would give him an opportunity to "do great good for my people and my country." He thought the war

## A Dreamer and a Schemer

provided blacks with a chance to entrench themselves firmly in the industrial system of the nation, and that he could help give them the encouragement and direction that was necessary to accomplish this goal. He wrote to his friend, the attorney Edward A. Johnson, who had earlier migrated from Raleigh to New York City, that a position in the North would also give him a chance to "bring out some things that cannot be brought out down here, but which the good of all demands should be brought out." Hunter did not go to New York. On 14 June 1918 he left Raleigh for Portsmouth, Virginia, where his nephew Ed was pastor of the Emanuel Methodist Church. Less than a week after his departure, Governor Bickett convened a conference that was attended by seventeen leading blacks and five white citizens. This group was later reconstituted as the Committee on Negro Economics for North Carolina and it worked under the supervision of the Division of Negro Economics of the United States Department of Labor. Simon G. Atkins, the president of Slater Normal School of Winston-Salem, served as chairman of the committee, and Aaron M. Moore was appointed as supervisor of Negro economics and special agent of the United States Employment Service. The goals and activities of the committee were mainly based on Hunter's original plans for mobilizing the homefront and they were also used as a model for similar programs in other states.[49]

# CHAPTER

# 9

## A Season of Soul Rest

Once in Virginia, Hunter found employment in the Norfolk Navy Yard, and although approximately sixty-seven years old, he "took up the pick and shovel and went into the ditch." He also wasted no time in letting his supervisor know that he and the secretary of the navy personally knew each other, and that Josephus Daniels had always taken great interest in his welfare. Within a week he was promoted to gang foreman and he had hopes of an office job. Happy that he finally had a chance to serve the nation, Hunter frequently mentioned with pride that he had "joined forces in the great battle against the Huns." He wrote back home to John Paul Lucas of the Food Adminstration, "It seems that I could find no way of using myself in North Carolina so I came here. . . . I am doing my bit and proud of the opportunity."[1]

"I have joined the Navy," Hunter wrote to Edward E. Britton, who was Josephus Daniels's private secretary. After relating his recent experiences in the Navy Yard, he then reported that everyone in the Norfolk area knew Daniels and considered him as "the one great figure in the present crisis next to President Wilson," a fact in which black North Carolinians took immense pride. These flattering remarks were followed by a request for Britton to use his influence in looking out for him. He also wrote to Daniels, "I am proud of being under you and shall do my best." Naturally he asked Daniels to speak a word on his behalf to the authorities at the Navy Yard and help him get an office position. Hunter asked his friend and former student W. E. L. Sanford to pass his letter on to Daniels, "who knows me well and is one of my best white friends." Daniels answered Hunter's letter, and he was glad to know of his employment in the Navy Yard. "It shows a fine spirit," he wrote, and he claimed that it would give him "great pleasure in complying" with Hunter's request. Hunter was appreciative of Daniels's interest in him, and he thought that it made him the leading black in the Navy Yard. He claimed, "It gave me an influence which I have sought to use for the best interest of the government and our people." Everyone in the Navy Yard eventually learned that the secretary of the navy was Hunter's patron and protector, and although he never got a desk job, he wrote that while Daniels was in office, "No one thought to disturb me."[2]

Hunter fared well in Virginia, where for the first time in his life he enjoyed some measure of economic security. His weekly pay equaled the monthly salary of a black school principal in North Carolina. He boasted of this in a letter to his former superintendent, D. F. Giles. "You see I am doing just a little better than teaching school at Method," he wrote, and told Giles he was getting a decent salary, living like a gentleman, and had prospects for the future. In spite of this, Hunter did not particularly relish his job as a gang foreman, and he confided to Professor Zebulon Judd of the Alabama Polytechnic Institute that he would have preferred to have remained in the classroom where he could "sow the seed and see it grow." However, he was getting old, and "advancing years admonish me that I must make the most of these afternoon days of my long life and save something for the time when I am no longer active." He claimed that he was free, healthy, and happy in Virginia, and that he was having the best time of his life. He ate and slept better, enjoyed cheerful company and a high degree of spiritual life, but above all, "I am enjoying a season of real soul rest. My mind is at ease. I am no longer taunted by conditions hard to endure and for which I could find no remedy."[3]

Hunter was also pleased because he had gained some recognition as a patriotic leader in the Tidewater area of Virginia, and he was very active in the thrift campaigns in the black community. During one speech at the Navy Yard, he attempted to convince black workers that they had another reason to purchase war bonds besides patriotism. "It may seem a little sentimental for which I hope you will pardon me," he said, but he recalled that he and Josephus Daniels had worked together for the uplift of blacks in North Carolina. Daniels was a true friend of blacks and a great American. "He had never faltered or failed. He is safe. He is sound." Hunter urged the crowd to follow where Daniels led them. Blacks could express their appreciation for his services to their race by their response to the bond drive. Hunter must have been very convincing, for he was pleased to report to Daniels that of

# A Season of Soul Rest

the 2,950 black workers at the Navy Yard, 2,625 took one or more bonds, and subscribed a total of $180,000. Thanking Hunter for his friendship and recent tribute, Daniels wrote that "such words of commendation of the work I have been trying to do in the Navy Department are gratifying at any time, but they are doubly so in these days of stress." He also praised Hunter. The splendid showing of blacks in response to the loan campaign reflected great credit upon those who were instrumental in organizing the drive.[4]

On 2 November 1918 Hunter received a letter from the secretary of the Southern Sociological Congress apprising him of the fact that the war was nearing a conclusion, and that the period immediately thereafter would be the most critical one in history. He explained that the congress would have to act swiftly while public opinion was still amenable to reform. There had to be more justice, fuller democracy, and a genuine effort in America "to bring the ideal of our prayers for brotherhood down out of the Heavens and make it a living national reality." He invited Hunter to join other black and white leaders in the various state reconstruction conferences that would work toward these goals. This was all that Hunter needed to convince him that he had a leading role to play in the process of reconstruction. When the war ended and he learned that Daniels planned a trip to Europe, he offered his services and asked to be included in his official party. He wrote Daniels, "I am intensely interested in all that concerns you and to witness honors to be paid to you by other Nations would afford me the greatest delight." But there were other reasons why Hunter wanted to go along with Daniels. He claimed that he and other prominent blacks believed that "such a recognition would greatly increase my influence for good among my own people during the reconstruction upon which we are now entering at home and abroad." Daniels graciously thanked Hunter for his sentiments of friendship, but he told him that he would not need his services because his trip to Europe concerned naval contracts, and he was taking only experts in that area.[5]

Hunter's friend and correspondent Daniel W. Chase of Washington, D.C., admitted that Hunter would have a great task ahead of him during the period of reconstruction. But he wondered what business did American blacks have in Europe, and why were they preparing a memorial to the Peace Conference asking for the rights of black people throughout the world? He asked Hunter, "Aren't there things here among ourselves that need adjusting?" Hunter needed to look no further than the Tarheel State for an answer. During the last year of the war, lynchings at Rolesville and

Lewiston claimed the lives of two blacks, and less than a week after the signing of the Armistice, several persons were killed in a race riot in Winston-Salem. The general deterioration of race relations had upset the black community, who feared it had been excluded from the world crusade for democracy.[6]

During the Emancipation Day activities in Raleigh in 1919, Hunter's old NAACP group gained the upper hand over the more conservative element. It published a militant set of resolutions that decried the fact that blacks had sacrificed their lives and fortunes in the late war to make the world safe for democracy, which was still denied them at home. The resolutions also protested all forms of discrimination and everything else that interfered with the development, happiness, and progress of blacks. They condemned lynchings as relics of barbarism, and agreed that "These wild orgies can scarcely be matched by the wildest cannibals in the thickest jungles farthest removed from the light of civilization." If they did not stop, whites faced the prospect of continued agitation against mob violence. The patience of the black community was being severely tested, and blacks were seriously questioning the whites' ability to provide justice. In what was symptomatic of a new sense of race pride, the crowd was urged to boycott all kinds of Jim Crow facilities, and parents were instructed to teach their children that to be black was no disgrace. The resolutions were enthusiastically adopted by an audience of approximately 3,000.[7]

Whites were shocked and surprised at the Emancipation Day activities. The *News and Observer* bemoaned the fact that blacks had stressed their grievances instead of their blessings, and had voiced no appreciation for their white friends. But then, the paper reported that such could only be expected from the more educated blacks, who "chafed under the forced abridgement of their privileges." The editor warned blacks that they must cooperate with whites in a spirit of fairness, and that "fruitless resolutions" would only drive away "the intelligent and conscientious Southern white men who were the best friends of blacks in the world." The editor of the *Winston-Salem Journal* termed the resolutions an "unfortunate blunder," which discredited the black leadership of Raleigh and indicated a dangerous attitude. He wondered where were the more sensible and patriotic black leaders who did not demand political and social equality. An answer came from the editor of the *New York Age*, who advised him to open his eyes and he would see a "New Negro" with whom whites would have to deal in settling the race problem in North Carolina.[8]

# A Season of Soul Rest

The editor of the *Age* maintained that those blacks who complained of injustices and demanded their rights were the same ones who owned property, educated their children, and wholeheartedly supported the recent war effort. In a counterquestion, he asked, "If these do not constitute the better element, the more sensible and patriotic colored people of North Carolina, we should like to know who does?" He asserted that the black leaders who counseled patience and contentment with existing conditions had lost their status within the black community and whites had better recognize this fact. Furthermore, the hostile response that whites gave to the Raleigh resolutions was just another example of the fallacious claim that they understood blacks. The editor correctly noted that whites knew blacks only from the outside by their speech, whims, humor, and habits. They knew nothing of the "agony of soul that the race goes through, nothing of its hopes and aspirations."[9]

In the spring of 1919 the same group that published the Raleigh resolutions gave whites another shock when the Twentieth Century Voter's Club, as a protest against the insensitivity of the incumbent administration, offered a slate of black candidates for public offices in Raleigh. This move was designed also to show the strength of black voters and test public sentiment regarding their running for office. Because several hundred blacks were eligible to vote in Raleigh, the ticket naturally caused whites some alarm. In the midst of the campaign, Hunter alleged that parties of "high influence" wanted him to come to Raleigh for important political consultation. However, he declined because he wanted them to understand that "they could have kept me there had they been willing to do the right thing by me. I am somewhat independent of them now and will do as I please." Nevertheless, he did not like the idea of displacing the city administration, because it was composed of some of the best white men; and he probably realized, as events later proved, that the black ticket was doomed to failure.[10]

Hunter advised his son-in-law that blacks were living in grave times, and faced one of the most critical periods in their existence in America. Therefore, he thought it behooved them to "think deeply and profoundly" before assuming any attitude respecting race relations. He insisted that some blacks were impulsive, emotional, and "deficient in the logical region," and he hoped they would do nothing that would provoke a hostile reaction from whites. He claimed that he had reason to believe that some whites were "anxiously waiting an opportunity for our people to do something foolish so that they may issue forth in flaming edicts of condemnation." Judging from the governor's rhetoric, Hunter knew what he was talking about. At a barbecue staged in honor of returning black veterans in the spring of 1919, Governor Bickett warned them to behave themselves while in North Carolina. Otherwise, there would be serious consequences, and to make his point he reminded them of the fate of the "Red Man," who would not accommodate himself to white law.[11]

In 1919 Hunter's philosophy of race relations wavered between religious mysticism and realism. While the Great War was in progress, he viewed it as a holy struggle that would promote new men, new ideas, and a new world leadership that would recognize the universality of eternal principles of justice. People would no longer have to apologize for enforcing the precepts of Christianity, and the "Fatherhood of God and the brotherhood of man would become ruling principles," and not a mere bit of religious rhetoric. In the immediate aftermath of the war, Hunter thought that society was still in a state of transition whereby "old issues, dogmas, obsolete themes, sentiments and traditions that have grown heavy with centuries of fine indulgence" were gradually being displaced by liberal ideas and Christian ideals. But he believed that the process of regeneration would be slow, and he hoped that his people would not be discouraged by a lack of immediate results. He saw institutional racism as still the major problem in the United States, particularly in the South where prejudice, bolstered by the traditions and education of generations, had become a part of the very fibre and being of whites. This type of racism was second nature to whites. "Even though their philosophy may be faulty, their treatment of us may be harsh, and at times inhuman," the fact remains that these are the natural consequences of the system out of which they have grown, and no sensible black would expect them to renounce the teachings of centuries and remodel their whole life and civilization within a single generation. Hunter's understanding of the nature of whites made him unwilling to "anathematize" their entire race because it did not suddenly transform itself and start to think and act as he thought in all matters pertaining to race relations.[12]

Yet Hunter was able to sustain his optimism that this would happen by taking a millennial approach to the idea that relations between the races would eventually be settled on a basis of justice. In March 1919 he wrote to Daniel W. Chase that he was still trying to make a humble effort in behalf of "a higher civilization, a better, purer and sweeter National life, greater opportunity, and the coming of His Kingdom among us." He thought that

## A Season of Soul Rest

only the latter would destroy the conditions and circumstances that were causing blacks so much suffering, sorrow, oppression, and misery. Chase agreed that this might indeed be true, but he asked Hunter, "Do we anticipate it? Will it come? Does it mean that in this vile world of sin, we mortals can look for a new day—I mean here . . . ?" Hunter gave no answer, but he did challenge all Christians of America to kneel before Jehovah in contrition of heart, and in humble faith to pray, "Thy Kingdom Come."[13]

Hunter's hopes that a spiritual regeneration of America was somehow in the making were countered by the Reverend C. A. Ashby, rector of the Church of the Good Shepherd of Raleigh. In an address on "The Race Question in the United States," delivered before the Ministerial Association in Raleigh, Ashby maintained that the continued presence of blacks and whites in the same country was dangerous, and that race instinct and antipathy demanded segregation. He also noted that the spirit of friendship that had existed between the older generations was fading away, and the younger element of both races regarded each other with mutual aversion and distrust. Ashby also thought that resolutions like the ones passed at the Emancipation Day celebration were dangerous and prejudiced against whites, and they paralleled the remarks frequently made by W. E. B. DuBois, that the white South "preaches Christ crucified in prayer meetings and crucifies niggers in unrelenting daily life."[14]

Learning of Ashby's speech through the pages of the *Raleigh News and Observer*, Hunter wrote him that he was very much interested in what he had to say because it came from a learned white minister of the gospel, who was one of his own communion. He was glad to see that intelligent white Christians were discussing the race problem, and he was particularly concerned with their viewpoints as long as they were open-minded and approached the subject in the light of Christian ethics and a desire to arrive at a true and just solution. Hunter insisted that through prolonged thought and continuous investigation "the light will one day burst forth as the glory of the morning and we shall all see clearly the light in God's eye." Then God could work his will through people and all would act accordingly. Until this happened, Hunter claimed that he would not be discouraged by the solutions that whites offered to the race problem, but he would not agree with them. He only hoped that whites would reciprocate and be equally tolerant of his viewpoints. They should also try to place themselves in his situation, and then they would understand why blacks saw the race problem in a different light and arrived at different solutions.[15]

# A Season of Soul Rest

In a lengthy discourse, Hunter laid out for the good Reverend a defense of the Raleigh resolutions, which was one of his most candid and succinct statements on race relations. His position in 1919 shows that either he had suddenly matured in his thinking or he had been shamming in his previous statements in praise of the harmonious race relations in his native state. It is also likely that his new economic freedom and the fact that he was located outside the state of North Carolina enabled him to speak out forthrightly on racial issues. Hunter wanted Ashby to give serious thought to his views, and he hoped to express himself in terms that were clearly understandable. Hunter was still certain that whites were not instinctively averse to blacks because of their color, and he was sure that whites knew they were not. The two races lived together in every civilized country in the world, but only in the United States were blacks "humiliated, spurned, penalized, proscribed, ostracized, oppressed and sought out for the bitter malevolence of the white race." Hunter thought that the recent World War had produced a heightened awareness of race prejudice in America, particularly among blacks who had served abroad. Those who went to England and France were deeply impressed by the lack of race prejudice, "excepting the virus of racial discrimination sought to be injected by the men from America." Even in Germany citizens of both races were treated equally, and during the war enemy propaganda had taunted black Americans for giving their lives for a country that mistreated them.[16]

Hunter's personal experiences in slavery and freedom further convinced him that race prejudice was not based on color. During slavery white and black children were nourished from the same breast, and they played, ate, slept, fought, and were even spanked together. Neither his white child playmates nor their parents labored under any obsession of race consciousness. He claimed that since emancipation he could, in the presence of a white child entrusted to his care, ride in the finest cars, eat at the best tables, and be entertained in the most exclusive hotels and not be barred on account of color. He had also traveled alone in other sections of the country and had been received and treated as any other gentleman by some of the best white people in America "who did not seem to take account of my color or race." Hunter explained that his case was not unique, and "even now in these days of stress and strain and hysteria," blacks lived in the homes of whites as domestics. He could also agree with the late Booker T. Washington that every self-respecting black in the South could boast of at least one loyal white friend. Consequently, he estimated that there were approximately nine million blacks and an equal number of whites who lived together primarily in the South on the most amicable of terms. If this was so, why were blacks complaining, and what was their problem? He answered that they hoped and prayed that these friendly sentiments between the races would move beyond the realm of personal relationships and find universal application. He then unfolded the nature of black dissatisfaction and the black problem as seen by himself and others of his race.[17]

To begin with, blacks were seriously concerned over the systematic violation of their civil rights and they were daily humiliated and offended by segregation laws and Jim Crow practices. He was also sure that no well-informed person would admit that blacks received justice in the courts. To him, the black man entered the court room with everything against him, particularly in cases involving disputes with whites. "His evidence is desecrated, his case is prejudiced and unless supported by some influential white person, he is doomed from the beginning." Furthermore, Hunter claimed that neither the law nor society offered black women any protection from the insults and outrages of white offenders, and this could be seen in several recent occurrences in Wake County. One involved a young black woman who while defending her home from a group of whites shot and killed a man. Even though the victim in a dying declaration absolved the woman from any guilt, she was tried and convicted for involuntary manslaughter and forced to serve three years on the county roads. In another instance, a white man broke into the home of a black woman and committed criminal assault upon her in the presence of her children. The offender was permitted to plead guilty to simple assault and let off with a $25 fine.[18]

Hunter insisted that whites had rejected the ideals of human rights and that they consistently violated the organic laws of the land by denying blacks equal rights, privileges, and immunities; due process; and legal protection. On the other hand, blacks were forced to assume all the obligations of citizenship, obey all laws, pay all taxes, and even die in defense of a country in which they had no voice, no vote, and no consent. He alleged that the 300,000 black soldiers who had served in the recent war all believed that they had in some way contributed to the fount of democracy. He wondered if these men would be disappointed by "another setback," and if "Democracy for the world included the Negro." If not, Hunter asked, "Is this the white man's concept of just government?"[19]

During the course of his argument, Hunter reversed his earlier positions on suffrage and Reconstruction. Now he called for an unrestricted enfranchisement of blacks. He acknowledged that there were those who believed that this would endanger good government and would surely point to the Reconstruction era as an example. But, said Hunter, "I am not ready to stigmatize and condemn as ignorant and corrupt the Negro voters of those days." Indeed, he claimed that they voted intelligently, logically, and in their self-interest, and the ballot was their one possession that was untainted and incorruptible. He still agreed that there was corruption during Reconstruction, but in 1919 he saw it as the work of "bold, bad white men," who used blacks for their own corrupt purposes. Hunter maintained that even the fear of a repeat of the conditions of Reconstruction was not enough to justify the violent suppression of the black vote and a denial of this fundamental right of citizenship.[20]

Hunter concluded by exposing the crux of the race problem as he saw it. It was not race and color, nor the fear of political and social equality. The real trouble was the fact that blacks were once slaves and whites their masters, and the whole idea of any equality between these two groups was the race problem. In a final word of advice to the Reverend Mr. Ashby, Hunter told him that the race problem would not disappear until whites became willing to submit to God's way. Once again, Hunter had placed whites in a precarious position. They had either to accord justice to blacks, or to admit to the world that they rejected the basic tenets of their religion and government. There is every indication that the majority of white North Carolinians chose the latter course, and like their contemporaries elsewhere in the South, they could not even imagine living in a society in which blacks had any degree of political or social equality.[21]

Indications of this attitude can be seen in the popularity and resurgence of the Ku Klux Klan in North Carolina after the war. During the spring of 1919 newspapers thoughout the state carried half-page advertisements of the Loyal Order of the Klansmen, announcing its intention to establish a large planned community in Richmond County. This facility, known as the Great Range, was to be a vast residential, educational, cultural, medical, and industrial complex, and from this base of operations, the Klan proposed to undermine the government of North Carolina, and eventually that of the United States. Though probably part of a scheme to swindle money out of ignorant or unsuspecting whites, the publicity given to this project alarmed many blacks. To allay their fear Governor Bickett spoke out against the "silly and sinful" Klan, and he condemned the Loyal Order for making a

# A Season of Soul Rest

wicked appeal to race prejudice and advocating a return to the "lawlesness and terror stricken days of Reconstruction." He also branded those who appealed to suspicion and hatred as enemies of both races, and he called for better race relations.[22]

Even the racial violence that erupted in the North during the "Red Summer of 1919" had repercussions in the Tarheel State. Hunter was vacationing in Washington, D.C., when a riot broke out, and he wrote to a friend, "I was in the middle of this disturbance and it was simply awful." However, his friend John E. Hamlin of Raleigh was glad that blacks had finally demonstrated to whites their ability to protect themselves and their homes. Hamlin was also pleased because he had not seen many newspaper editorials condemning blacks for their stand in the riots, and he wrote Hunter that many papers, including the *News and Observer*, had actually sympathized with them. Hamlin had misinterpreted the intentions of the North Carolina press, which used the northern riots to justify its claims that the South was the best place for blacks, that northerners were really hypocrites when they denounced lynch law and racial injustices in the South, and that white supremacy, segregation, and disfranchisement were necessary to control blacks. Responding to this sentiment an editorial in the *News and Observer* noted that it was rather pleasant to sit back and offer some advice to the North on how they should treat blacks.[23]

The *News and Observer* contended that the increased black population in the North had brought that region face to face with the black problem, and it could no longer afford to deal in theories but had to face facts. The violent outbreaks were not deliberately prearranged but occurred as a result of an all-pervasive and ever present race prejudice that was instinctive in nature. Furthermore, no sensible person knew what to do about the race problem simply because no one had ever figured out a way to eliminate race instincts. Northerners had to understand that inflamed race instincts could result in violent confrontations at any time, and they had to adopt southern methods of controlling these instincts to the point where laws and not mobs meted out justice to blacks. Northerners were also chided for having "long-range theoretical sympathy for blacks but mighty little short-range friendliness." The *News and Observer* claimed that southern whites and blacks were friends and neighbors who knew each other. But in the North, blacks were strangers and because of this their race was condemned as a mass for that which an "odd one does."[24]

When a group of Chicago blacks thought of availing themselves of the

## A Season of Soul Rest

good race relations in North Carolina, Governor Bickett told them just what they could expect if they came to the state. According to him, North Carolina was the best place in the world for a decent black man to make a living, and whites "by inheritance had a sympathetic understanding of his virtues and his limitations." The state was doing all it could to promote friendly feelings between the races, and to secure for blacks equal privileges in industry, education, and religion. However, the "liberal and progressive" Bickett warned that socially the races were kept separate and apart. Any person who attempted to break the social barriers was held in utter contempt by the best people of both races. It was also necessary for the protection, progress, and happiness of both races for the government to be run by white people, and the governor asserted that "it was the unalterable determination of the whites to keep in their own hands the reins of government."[25]

Bickett thought the state could use about 25,000 black workers, but if during their stay in Chicago they had become "tainted or intoxicated with dreams of social equality or political domination, it would be well for them to remain where they are." Such things were forever impossible in the South. The editor of the *News and Observer* thought the governor had issued some sound advice. He alleged that Chicago blacks were diseased and North Carolina did not need any of them until they were able to produce a "clean bill of health," morally and physically. This was indeed true of blacks from the Second Ward of Chicago, which he claimed was probably the "most abandoned Sodom in existence." There, blacks played in politics and wallowed in vice and crime and they were sure to contaminate any section that was foolish enough to accept them.[26]

Some whites in North Carolina had reason to believe that their fellow black citizens had already been contaminated, and that the state had produced a crop of "New Negroes." For example, during the closing exercises at Saint Augustine College, students read militant essays that reflected an air of impatience and dissatisfaction with the conservatism of their elders and the state of race relations in general. The students insisted that blacks were fully prepared and ready to assume their rights as citizens, and should not have to wait any longer to exercise privileges that were already theirs. They called for economic and political equality, suffrage for women, and inclusion in any program for social justice. The students urged others of their race to agitate for these issues and warned lawmakers that if they persisted in refusing to grant blacks their rights there would indeed be a great social upheaval. The aspirations of these youths were promptly stifled and their arguments countered by James Y. Joyner, the former state superintendent of public instruction, who delivered the graduation address. He insinuated that society in North Carolina as it existed was constructed according to God's plan, and that "certain race differences and instinctive race prejudices" demanded segregation. Furthermore, blacks were not ready for equality, and any attempt to obtain it prematurely through revolution, force, blood, or legislation would be a tragedy for any individual or race and a "violation of God's eternal laws as fixed as the stars."[27]

Meanwhile, other speakers offered graduating classes similar advice. At Shaw University, the Reverend J. C. Massee reminded students that it would take a long time to readjust race relations to a plane of equality, and this was especially true when one race had been "the master and owning class and the other had been the owned and servicing class." He advised the graduates that the best thing they could do would be to acquire a good name and cultivate the friendship of the best people of both races. Robert R. Moton, the president of Tuskegee Institute, had been called to North Carolina by Governor Bickett to help calm blacks and improve race relations and, while in the state, he delivered the closing address at the Berry O'Kelly Training School. In his remarks Moton proceeded to tell blacks how well-off they were in comparison to French peasants, and he thought their condition would be even better if they obeyed all laws, state, local, and natural. Though blacks were more suspicious of whites than ever before, he advised them to "get away from this unrest and escape the consequences of the last reconstruction period."[28]

The veiled threats issued by the graduation speakers of 1919 were part of an attempt by whites to nip in the bud any ideas that blacks had about using radical protest to effect social change. Whites also threatened the black community with violence. Bickett stated in no uncertain terms that any attempt by blacks to use radical means of any kind would "lock the wheels of their progress" for fifty years, and it would be a tragedy for their race. He warned, "Appeal to fear and you will reap a riot. Resort to force and you will stir up the Ku Klux Klan. Make a drive for political domination and the Red Shirts will again take to the saddle." The *Raleigh News and Observer* chimed in by admonishing blacks that they were courting disaster, and if they tried to get redress for their wrongs through radical means such as the use of force or direct action, it would be "worse than running into a stone wall."[29]

## A Season of Soul Rest

In their effort to curtail any incipient radicalism or militancy within the black community, whites again decided that they would have to exercise even greater control over the minds of blacks in order to keep them in harmony with their civilization and society. They also sought reassurances that the leading blacks were fulfilling their responsibility of suppressing radical ideas among their race. In the fall of 1919 the *News and Observer* reported that although the leading men recognized that it was a critical time in the history of their race, they were doing their duty and were trying to save their people from the unwise teachings of thoughtless firebrands. They had asked the black community to remember the spirit of J. C. Price and Booker T. Washington, and to strive for racial love, peace, and harmony without agitation or radicalism. These blacks also unwittingly revealed their interest in maintaining the goodwill of whites. Primarily educators, they told their race to remember that its educational progress was in the hands of the best white people, who held and could foreclose mortgages on Shaw University and Saint Augustine and Kittrell colleges while others supported these institutions with generous gifts.[30]

The thoughtless firebrands who were causing so much alarm in North Carolina were for the most part nameless and faceless figures. When one could be fingered, it was usually W. E. B. DuBois who was portrayed as the archetype of radicalism. To many whites he was a "raving madman" who preached revolution and revolt in retaliation against injustices to his race, and they were certain that he was bent upon "moving heaven and earth" to destroy all of the good work of Booker T. Washington while displacing conservative blacks from positions of power and prestige. DuBois was also closely associated with the NAACP, an organization that many white North Carolinians believed contained the "most dangerous class of agitators" ever brought together in the nation, with a goal of destroying friendly race relations in the South. The *Charlotte Observer* urged the leading blacks to protect their people from "contamination with such doctrine as is being preached by this miscalled organization for the advancement of the Negro." The president of Bennett College, a black women's school in Greensboro, agreed, and he announced that he had banned the *Crisis* from his campus because he disapproved of the journal and considered its doctrine "objectionable."[31]

In an attempt to pacify blacks and to make sure that their educational process was producing contented youth, Dr. Eugene C. Brooks, the state superintendent of public instruction, asked the executive committee of the

# A Season of Soul Rest

North Carolina State Teachers' Association and other "representative" blacks to meet with him and develop a mutually beneficial platform for race relations. Under the guiding hand of Brooks and N. C. Newbold, the state agent for Negro rural schools, the leading men held a conference in Raleigh in September 1919. At the outset Brooks reiterated the threat that blacks had better get in line because many whites who had championed their education in the past "were growing suspicious of the Negro's aims and purposes." Racial unrest and rumors of the inevitability of racial strife had even presented difficulties for the Department of Public Instruction, and Brooks contended that it would be unable to carry out plans for the education of blacks unless the leaders of both races could agree upon a safe program for race relations. Furthermore, he maintained that black educators had to make the "social background" of their schools safe for the education of their children. [32]

The leading blacks agreed that the times did indeed demand adherence to their "wisest and safest" leaders. Those who advocated social equality or the use of violence to achieve social justice should be "cast to the rear." The blueprint for race relations adopted at the conference was designed to pacify blacks and make them happier in their own communities by promising them better educational, health, and recreational facilities, and greater access to public utilities. It also called for increased employment opportunities and "better" justice in courts of law. To allay suspicions that blacks were trying to assert themselves, it was agreed that Brooks would publicly announce the work of the conference. In so doing, he urged all school officials of both races to strive at all times to make right and justice prevail in North Carolina. The *Raleigh News and Observer* praised the black educators for having developed a program of "safety and sanity for the colored people" that was sure to improve relations. This safe and sane program later became the core of the various movements for racial justice in North Carolina. Responding to their Christian duty, a few whites joined such organizations as the Commission of Inter-racial Justice, the Christian Leader's Conference on Inter-racial Cooperation, and the Women's Committee on Interracial Conferences. Composed primarily of ministers and professionals, these groups focused on improving the quality of life in the black community while denying its members civil and political equality. They did a lot of talking about the "Negro Problem" and, like Hunter, they could defer its solution until the realization of God's kingdom on earth. [33]

When Hunter learned of the conference of the leading men, he could not resist the opportunity to comment on its activities, and get a little personal recognition in the process. In letters to Brooks, Newbold, and the editor of the *Raleigh News and Observer*, he lauded the work of the conference and offered his assistance in carrying out its objectives. He wrote that his "manhood life had been spent in efforts to allay strife and bitter antagonisms whenever they have come to the surface and to promote that peace without which both races must suffer." This plus his forty-two years of teaching in North Carolina led Hunter to believe that he was entitled to a voice in the conference. He hoped that whites would not interpret the educators' program as an attempt at social equality, because sensible blacks would never entertain thoughts of such "utter absurdity." Neither would they advocate the use of force in appealing for justice. Whites should realize that under the laws of the land all citizens, including blacks, were justified in using force to protect themselves and to prevent others from committing unlawful acts. Blacks wanted the friendship of whites, but they also wanted justice. He wondered if "The great and powerful white race which is rich in achievement, splendid in its civilization, powerful in its resources for self-protection, and under the benign influence of Christianity" would do itself justice by denying to blacks those things "which we so meekly ask."[34]

Brooks thanked Hunter for his letter and promised that he would strive to bring about better relations between the races, and to see to it that right and justice prevailed in every phase of society. He was also glad to know that responsible black representatives like Hunter approved of what he was trying to do and were offering him their cooperation and support. Hunter was certain that the best whites and blacks could live in peace and harmony, and together they could "transform the Sunny Southland into the Eden of the Great Republic." Yet despite his best efforts, he was never included in any of the interracial organizations designed to improve race relations in North Carolina. Blacks who were affiliated with these groups, generally heads of institutions of higher learning or businessmen, were persons who were conservative and consistent in their racial attitudes, characteristics Hunter did not possess. Additionally, his penchant for politics would not commend him for membership in these bodies.[35]

Though outside North Carolina, Hunter remained involved in its internal politics, and he was thought to have had some influence over black voters. In 1919 Robert Newton Page asked him to support his candidacy for the Democratic nomination for governor. Hunter, who knew Page's family well, claimed friendship with Walter Hines Page and had worked for Henry Page, who headed the Food Administration in North Carolina during the war. Both of these men were brothers of the gubernatorial aspirant. In a note of sarcasm, Hunter wrote Page, "I am not sure but what you are mistaken as to my race and identity as I am a Negro." He also insisted that he had no party allegiance, and had for many years contented himself by casting a personal vote for men of superior merit. He had voted for the Democrats Aycock and Bickett, and one of the best men in the world, state treasurer Benjamin R. Lacy. Regretting the fact that as a citizen who loved his state, and who was interested in the welfare and happiness of all its people, Hunter stated that he could not give public expression to political views and actively campaign on Page's behalf for fear of "setting into motion a current of adverse influences." Hunter's coldness to Page's request no doubt dated back to his squabbles with Henry Page while working with the Food Administration. Nevertheless, he did promise to commend Page to his "many warm and personal friends who belonged to the Democratic party."[36]

Hunter also had a few words to say about the lily-white Republicans of North Carolina, who at their convention in 1920 nominated John J. Parker for governor. During the course of this gathering, Parker insisted that the Republican party had accepted the suffrage amendment of 1900 in the spirit in which it was passed. "The Negro is no longer a political factor," he declared. "He does not desire the ballot, and the Republican party of North Carolina does not desire him to participate in the political life of the State." Parker's statement was later endorsed by John Motley Morehead, the Republican national committeeman from North Carolina. There may have been some truth to Parker's statement that blacks did not want the ballot. In January 1920 it was estimated that there were at least 50,000 blacks in the state who were qualified to vote, but only 30 or 40 percent voted regularly in any election of importance. The remainder were very indifferent and unwilling to exercise the right and privilege of the ballot.[37]

Regardless of this, Hunter and his comrades resented the lily-whites and challenged Parker's authority to speak for their race. Hunter's friend, the attorney George C. Scurlock, though not surprised at Parker's oration, was shocked by the endorsement of Morehead whom he considered "as being true blue." Scurlock lamented that "it seems that now, he too has gone over to the lily whites." In 1920 blacks once again summoned the old Negro Republican Executive Committee into action, and a convention was called for the purpose of denouncing the lily-white movement and asserting the blacks' right to full recognition in the political parties of the state and the nation. Proof of the Janus-faced character of the leading blacks was that many of the same men who had met with Brooks and Newbold to develop a safe program for race relations, which made no mention of political rights, showed up at this convention. After selecting the usual contesting delegation to the Republican National Convention, the delegates issued a declaration of principles that demanded equal rights for all citizens, the abolition of the Jim Crow spirit from all American institutions, equal pay for equal work, the right to select leaders of their choice who would be responsible to their race, a federal antilynch law, and absolute 100 percent Americanism. For the moment these blacks had decided to stand squarely on the national agenda of the NAACP. In reporting the activities of the convention, the *Greensboro Daily News* noted, "John J. Parker got a good drubbing for his Greensboro speech, and if there is anything in today's convention that looks like one vote for Parker, nobody sees it."[38]

Hunter strongly approved of the convention for having delivered "a stinging rebuke to the coterie of self seeking barnacles" in charge of the Republican party machinery in North Carolina. He also agreed that no self-respecting black could ever be expected to support the "miserable measly-minded crew that has wantonly and gratuitously repudiated us after our years of fervent zeal, unwavering support, and terrible sacrifices for them and the party." But he wished that the convention had made some plans to force the attention of the national Republicans on the political situation in North Carolina, as it was time for a showdown. If the national convention sustained the lily-white faction of the Republican party in North Carolina, then it was time for blacks to break their allegiance to the Grand Old Party. Regarding the Republican party in the state, Hunter thought, "Between them and the Democratic party it is a case of spoilt fish in which we have no choice." But at least the Democrats had never deceived blacks, hence they were not guilty of the "greatest, blackest and most damnable sin of ingratitude."[39]

North Carolina lily-whites in 1920 also endorsed Jeter C. Pritchard as a favorite-son candidate for president and instructed their delegates to vote for him at least on the first ballot at the national convention. Because Pritchard was anathema to blacks in North Carolina, they were delighted to learn of General Leonard Wood's decision to enter the state presidential-preference primary. In April 1920 Hunter wrote to Senator George H. Moses, Wood's campaign manager, that the lily-whites of the state had turned their guns on blacks and were more open and flagrant in their oppression and hatred of his race than the Democrats. After outlining for Moses a history of lily-whitism in North Carolina, he appraised the political situation. He saw the nomination of Pritchard as a "brazen transparent subterfuge" to enable white bosses to control the state delegation, so that they could at an opportune moment switch to some fortunate bandwagon.[40] By this they hoped to gain some influence with the next administration in the parceling out of patronage positions in the state. He confided to Moses that black North Carolinians wanted to vote for some bona-fide candidate who represented Republican principles, and for that reason they would almost unanimously support General Wood. He insisted that although residing outside the state, he still had some influence and could "keep a line on things at home."[41]

Meanwhile, in the Tarheel State, Greensboro became the seat of anti-Parker resistance, and Hunter's friend Charles H. Moore was one of the movement's leaders. In an era that was concerned with 100 percent Americanism, he and others tried to prove that lily-whitism was contrary to this idea. On 11 April 1920 an anonymous address, "To the Negro Ex-Soldiers and Other Voters of North Carolina," appeared in the *Greensboro Daily News*. Designed to appeal to those who had reached voting age since the passage of the disfranchisement amendment, it was also an attempt to wean blacks away from the Republican party. It noted that the historic commitment of blacks to the party had been due to the fact that Republicans had granted them freedom, but for many years the Democrats had warned that the average white Republican was "at heart no better friend to the Negro" than they were. However, most blacks refused to believe this and had continued to vote a straight Republican ticket. Democrats viewed this as a crime against the state for which blacks were eventually disfranchised. The author contended that the worst feature of the disfranchisement movement was the fact that some white Republicans supported and voted for the measure. Furthermore, John J. Parker and lily-whites were still praising the amendment despite the fact that a Democratic-controlled Supreme Court had in 1915 declared grandfather clauses unconstitutional. This was clearly un-American and Parker and his lily-white friends were enemies of the Republic. Consequently, the address argued that it was the duty of every black veteran who had ever taken an oath to defend the Constitution against all enemies to continue to do so by casting his vote in opposition to Parker.[42]

At the Republican National Convention in 1920 the black contesting delegation from North Carolina was not seated, but during the preconvention proceedings Charles H. Moore was given an opportunity to present the case against lily-whitism. An immediate result of his testimony was that the convention later adopted a resolution, offered by Senator Charles B. Warren of Michigan, outlawing the lily-white practice of calling meetings and conventions in places where custom and law denied blacks entry. This resolution was subsequently ignored in North Carolina. The convention bypassed Leonard Wood in favor of Warren G. Harding and Calvin Coolidge. Moore reported that this ticket was a sure winner even though he knew Harding only by reputation. He was personally acquainted with Coolidge, a fellow graduate of Amherst College, who, he was sure, had been schooled in principles of "righteousness and justice." As far as the vice-presidential nominee was concerned, blacks need not "feel shaky" about their civil and social rights under the Constitution.[43]

Black North Carolinians wanted similar assurances from Harding, and Bishop George W. Clinton of Charlotte was authorized by the General Council of the African Methodist Episcopal Zion church to write him an open letter. In this communication Clinton alleged that blacks, thinking as never before, were weighing with utmost care the rhetoric of politicians. They were no longer going to vote blindly, and intended to cast their ballots where past performance and consistent utterings of candidates led them to believe they were voting in the interest of their own race. Clinton appealed to Harding, as the standardbearer of the Republican party, to assume the leadership in striking down racial injustices, and said that if this happened, 90 percent of all black voters would give him their full support.[44]

As the campaign progressed in North Carolina, blacks began to feel a little shaky. Democrats had actively encouraged blacks in their battle against lily-white Republicans, but they still made no effort to invite them into their own party. Nevertheless, it was reported that 90 percent of the black voters in the state would support the Democratic nominee for governor. In 1920 the Democrats nominated for governor Cameron Morrison, one of the leaders of the Red Shirts during the white-supremacy campaign, and who, according to Furnifold M. Simmons, deserved as much credit for the movement as anyone. In June 1920 the veteran black politician W. Lee

# A Season of Soul Rest

Persons wrote Hunter that Morrison and his campaign were advocating a return to "Red Shirt methods," and if this happened, it would create disturbances and restlessness unknown to blacks for twenty years. He asked Hunter to use his "mighty pen" and write strong letters to the *Raleigh News and Observer* and the *Greensboro Daily News* extolling the peace and tranquillity between the races under all the governors from Aycock to Bickett. He also wanted him to write to his friends in other parts of the state and solicit their support for a sustained propaganda campaign for good race relations that would be conducted until the primary elections were over.[45]

Hunter failed to receive Persons's letter in time to do this because he was vacationing in New York, Boston, and Raleigh. Of his travels in the North, he wrote, "I have been living in another world, breathing a purer sweeter atmosphere, drawing inspiration from lofty ideals, treading broader plains and catching glimpses of a coming beautiful tomorrow." Hunter's brief trip to the North provided him with an opportunity to expand further his views on race relations in America. While in Massachusetts he became acquainted with Wendell Phillips Wright, an intelligent black resident of Salem, and the two entered into a prolonged and rather advanced dialogue concerning the race problem. Wright was impressed by Hunter's catholic and tolerant attitudes and his ability to discuss the race issue in an objective manner. He thought that most blacks were unable to do this, and with a few exceptions were inhospitable to opposing viewpoints. He was pleased that Hunter and he both had the capacity to view the race problem objectively and discuss it in the same way as sincere white intellectuals. Wright insisted that objectivity in interracial dialogues was of paramount importance if both sides of the race question were to be examined in any meaningful way. Otherwise, whites would speak to blacks in sympathetic rather than scientific terms. He wrote Hunter, "I and you talk to white men about black men, talk in an undetached way. Talk like a white man."[46]

Wright considered Hunter's viewpoints far in advance of those of any other black whom he had met, but he could not always agree with them. He believed that Hunter had to realize that any discussion of the race question had to begin with addressing its ethnic and ethical aspects. In Wright's opinion, American blacks were structurally, mentally, and ethnically different from white people, and he could not agree with the oft-repeated contention of Professor Charles Eliot Norton that blacks were only "painted white men." Of all the differences, Wright thought that color was the most important, because it was the basis of prejudice against their race. Wright rejected

# A Season of Soul Rest

Hunter's contention that whites were not averse to blacks on account of their race but because of the fact that they had been slaves, and that the basis of prejudice lay in class rather than caste antagonism. He informed Hunter that caste in color and prejudice against blacks had existed in the civilized world well before the birth of Christ. As proof he cited the fact that graphic representations of life in ancient times always depicted blacks in servile roles. When the woman in the Song of Solomon said, "I am black but comely," she was in fact apologizing for her color; and in Shakespeare's works one could find the color caste tradition. The Prince of Morocco in *The Merchant of Venice* also apologized for his color. Indeed, Wright contended that from the history of literature he could "pull up quotations to prove the primacy of the black man's inequality."[47]

Wright also thought that Hunter overstated the role of ethics and justice as solutions to the race problem. To Wright, justice was at best superficial; it could never be exact or arbitrary, but only appropriate to the occasion. He maintained that political expediency would get better and faster results in solving the race problem than appeals to justice. For almost a century, blacks had been under the guardianship of the reformer and philanthropist, but in 1920 they were under the trusteeship of the statesman. Therefore blacks should always make their demands to whites within the framework of polity and expediency. Striking at the heart of Hunter's creed, Wright discounted the effectiveness of personal sentimental relationships as a means for improving race relations, because they were at best reactive and transitory. Neither did he think that blacks through self-help could make it alone in America. He wrote Hunter, "We cannot say hands off we can make our way," because the race had been severely crippled by two centuries of slavery. The best weapons for blacks to use in their search for an adjustment of the race problem in America were time, patience, disguised toleration, wise diplomacy, political expediency, and concessions in the nonessential areas. He further cautioned Hunter against placing too much faith in the idea that the race problem in the South would eventually be solved on the basis of Christian ethics by reminding him that there were slaveholders who were as sincere Christians as William Lloyd Garrison, Charles Sumner, and Wendell Phillips, "yet the South of old never attained the moral solemnity of the North." Hunter, forced to concede this point, also agreed that the attitudes of whites toward blacks and their treatment of his race were unjust, unchristian, and inhuman, and would indeed "set aside the blessed tenets of our religion." However, Hunter never admitted that whites were prejudiced against blacks on account of their color. By doing so he would have eliminated all of his hopes that prejudice and its vicious effects would in time disappear from American life.[48]

Hunter published an account of this New England visit in the *Raleigh News and Observer*. He wrote that he found northerners of all classes, colors, and political parties eager to learn about the race problem in the South. Many regarded southern whites as a "set of heartless brutes always ready to wreak vengeance upon Negroes for the most trivial offenses and often for no offense at all." These opinions were based upon reports and other published accounts that focused on lynchings, burnings at the stake, shootings, hangings, torture, and other sorts of barbarities inflicted on blacks. He claimed that northerners wanted enlightenment on the race problem, and "I stated the facts of my personal experiences and pointed the way to better things." But he could not "excuse palliate or extenuate" the wave of crime against blacks that was sweeping the South, and neither did he attempt to justify the gross wrongs, the rank injustices, and the hampering conditions that legal restrictions placed upon his race. He claimed that he did tell Northerners that the better class of whites did not hate the Negro because he was a Negro, and that the prejudices against his race were confined to the lowest class.[49]

Hunter later revealed that the purpose of this article was to inform white North Carolinians how they were perceived in other parts of the country and that the outside world was taking note of and condemning their treatment of blacks. He also planned to make a return trip to Massachusetts in 1921, to deliver a series of lectures on the true condition of blacks in the South, and white attitudes toward them. He was sure that his talks would arouse public opinion and elevate the nation's conscience. By now Hunter clearly realized the importance of public opinion as a force for social change, and he believed that the time was at hand for blacks to use it to their advantage. "Laws are nothing," he wrote. "Presidential pronunciamentos are futile, even the preaching of the Gospel is of good only as it tends to an advancement of the public conscience." He thought that Boston and its surrounding environs, the former cradle of abolitionism, were ideal places to initiate his crusade because they were "holy ground where the spirit of liberty and law was alive. They form a forum from which I can make myself heard."[50]

After leaving the North, Hunter vacationed in his hometown of Raleigh. Arriving at the time when the primary elections of 1920 were in full swing, he found the Democrats chanting the same old song of "Nigger, Nigger,

Nigger." To him, it sounded "like eeries, discarded canticles from some far off ghost land . . . a voice from ancient tombs . . . ," which was relied upon to "conjure intelligent, Christian white people." The adoption of the Nineteenth Amendment in 1920 added another dimension to the already bitter political contest of that year. Both parties were confused because they did not know how the constitutional amendment of 1900 would affect women voters. Republicans generally believed that women, not governed by the provisions of the disfranchisement amendment, should be placed on the election books without question. Democrats were split on the issue. Some wanted to apply the literacy test to all women, while others thought that black women should not be registered to vote under any circumstance. Cameron Morrison appealed to white women to join with their male counterparts to "see to it that Negro women no more vote in North Carolina than Negro men." Other white men urged their women to subordinate sexual identity to that of race. For example, James H. Mewborn wrote Gertrude Weil that he feared all the good work of the Democrats would be ended with the passage of the abolitionist-inspired Nineteenth Amendment. If Miss Weil thought anything of herself and her sex, he advised her never to endorse women's suffrage. Mewborn asked, "How would you feel should two negro women take you by the arm and carry you to the voting place bawling out, give way we have a white lady that we are going to vote?" The very thought of such a spectacle made "cold chills" run through him.[51]

Black women who attempted to register were forced to take extremely difficult literacy tests, and in some cases they were told outright that they would not be registered. For instance, a black woman in New Bern was required to read and write the entire constitution of the state. After reading the document, she started to write and then was told that "if she were the President of Yale and colored she could not register." White officials at Charlotte refused to register Mrs. George W. Clinton, the wife of a bishop of the African Methodist Episcopal Zion church and a woman of "culture, intelligence and social standing." This caused many blacks to fear that women of lesser stature thoughout the state would meet with a similar fate. Whites were aided in their attempt to prevent black women from registering by Hunter's friend, James B. Dudley, the president of the Agricultural and Technical College. In October 1920 every major newspaper in the state published a letter by Dudley counseling the women of his race to refrain from registering and voting.[52]

## A Season of Soul Rest

Dudley advised black women that all lawful things were not always expedient and that by exercising their right to vote they would only increase race hatred, prejudice, and political strife. They would also impede the progress of the state and postpone the day of political freedom and independence for blacks. Dudley insisted that black women were only imitating their white sisters, and he did not think that "the white women who are going to become politicians and partisans are setting the best examples." Black women should never condescend to the low level of political equality with men. They would be better off using the latent power of their sex to teach men how to vote. In Dudley's opinion, black males had made an "awful botch" of politics, and after fifty years they were still but the bone of political contention for hungry politicians. Dudley's letter was enthusiastically endorsed by Democrats and lily-white Republicans. The *Greensboro Daily News* commended his advice to blacks as "safe and sound," and warned that if they should attempt to exercise the balance of power in the upcoming election they would get a "reproduction of the conditions of 1898. The Red Shirt has been laid away for more than twenty years but it would require just one hint of Negro domination to bring it out again." A few speculated that Dudley might have been coerced into writing the letter by Democrats who controlled his institution. However, most blacks refused to accept this excuse, and it was reported that black women in the state, especially those in Greensboro, were so incensed by Dudley's "cowardly attitude" that they were determined to register and qualify to vote.[53]

In the election of 1920 the Democrats of North Carolina easily handed Cameron Morrison a belated reward for his role in the white-supremacy campaign of two decades earlier. Although blacks believed that the racist campaign had stirred up prejudice and widened the gap between the races for the sole purpose of political aggrandizement, they could find some consolation in the defeat of the lily-white Republican candidate for governor. John J. Parker was brought to the attention of the nation by black North Carolinians in 1920, and his remarks during the campaign of that year were not forgotten. They came back to haunt him ten years later during his bid for a seat on the United States Supreme Court. The successful fight to prevent Parker's elevation to the bench in 1930 was led by the NAACP, but the movement originated in an inquiry made by that organization into his campaign for governor of North Carolina in 1920. The defeat of Parker was considered by the NAACP as the "major political demonstration by the

Negro since the Civil War," and black North Carolinians would in good faith claim some credit for this achievement. They preserved a record of Parker's racist rhetoric, which they brought forth at the proper moment.[54]

Referring to Harding's election, Hunter wrote, "Oh My; What a change and how tremendous." He seemed convinced that a return of the national administration to Republican control offered renewed hope for black Americans. But some of his associates were not too sure of the Republican's good intentions. From Washington, George C. Scurlock wrote that he saw nothing in the results of the election that was particularly hopeful for blacks. He believed that the Grand Old Party would try to erect a strong organization in the South based on white voters, and that for the sake of expediency, "a sop may be thrown to the colored brother of the North." He told Hunter that this would not be enough to satisfy blacks, who wanted an acknowledgment of their rights and wanted the national government to force the South to respect those rights. Until this happened, Scurlock thought that blacks had to continue to voice their demands through intelligent agitation. A fomer student of Hunter's also advised him against being overly optimistic, because blacks were still living in the "darkest days of their lives and they had to do something real soon particularly in North Carolina; otherwise they were going to be down and out." Hunter agreed that the time was ripe for vigorous, constructive action, and he recommended that during the next Emancipation Day celebration, instead of the usual orations "couched in high sounding phrases," blacks should deliver a strong, dignfied address to the American people stating their side of the race problem.[55]

Someone must have followed Hunter's advice, for the 1921 celebration of the Emancipation Proclamation in Raleigh reflected a revitalized race consciousness. The singing of the "Negro National Anthem," a recitation from the writings of Wendell Phillips, a tribute to Toussaint l'Ouverture, and a reading from W. E. B. DuBois's *Darkwater*, which had previously been condemned by whites in the state as having a "lamentable effect" on race relations, set the tone for the occasion. They also showed that many of the leading blacks had severed their connection with the Tuskegee line, and were looking northward for guidance in their struggle for equality.[56]

The secretary of the International YMCA, Channing Tobias of New York, delivered the annual oration, and he told the crowd that many people had mistaken the quiet patience with which blacks had accepted their place in society for a sign of weakness. But the black spirit was not submissive; it

# A Season of Soul Rest

was merely voiceless. When blacks became articulate, they wanted the same things as all other American citizens. Speaking on behalf of the masses of blacks, Tobias chastised those interracial movements led by the "so called friends of the Negro" for falling short of equal justice, because they did not embrace political equality. Just as guilty in this regard were the "time serving stall fed Negroes" who professed the same spirit. He also urged black North Carolinians to accept a new program of reform that included the selection of their own leaders, full support of the NAACP, and cooperation with all persons and movements that worked in their interest. Following Tobias's speech, the audience unanimously adopted resolutions calling on black men and women to organize and use their ballots as the indispensable means for securing freedom. It was also resolved that the races come together and teach and practice the Second Commandment, "Love thy neighbor as thyself." Until this became a reality in this world, blacks agreed to use their collective resources to support the prosecution of equal rights cases in the courts, and the efforts of the NAACP to force Congress to move against states that still deprived blacks of suffrage.[57]

The twin themes of race pride and self-help were also dominant notes at other Emancipation Day celebrations during the early 1920s. Blacks continued to support their own businesses everywhere in the realization that the salvation of their race depended to a large extent on its economic development. They also agreed to support every organization that helped prevent the exploitation of blacks and wage earners everywhere. More importantly, blacks publicly announced their refusal to believe themselves "unequal in any human way to any human being or any human task." Reflecting on this, Hunter wrote in March of 1921 that the black man had gained a heightened awareness of the injustices against him. Everywhere he encountered "bars and bans, proscriptions and circumscriptions. He is penalized, ostracized, and stigmatized. He is made an outcast of our civilization." Hunter proclaimed that the wounds of his race were fast becoming festering sores. Many blacks were becoming desperate, and they were going to take extreme measures to defend themselves, even if it meant an alliance with radicals. He thought that the condition of his race was indeed fertile soil for the propagation of socialism, anarchism, and even atheism.[58]

Hunter also argued that the good white men of the South would have to accept some of the responsibility if blacks in that section took radical means to lighten their oppression. Again, he admitted that the best white men often had good intentions, but they had failed to prevent mob violence and other outrages against his race. They were still disorganized, they did not speak out, and they were under the influence of "no directing genius." Therefore he claimed that they "must bear the blame and share the shame of encouraging by their silence this disgraceful evil." Hunter vented these thoughts in a letter to the editor of the Norfolk, Virginia, *Pilot*, and asked that it be printed because it contained ideas that wise southerners had to look straight in the face. The editor of the *Pilot*, Louis Jaffee, declined to print the letter on the flimsy grounds that it was too lengthy.[59]

When Hunter wrote his letter to the *Pilot* he was trying to mobilize the best white men in an effort to save the jobs of black workers at the Navy Yard. In January 1921 there was a general reduction in the labor force, and he feared that his job would be terminated at any moment. The reduction was necessitated by the nation's demobilization, but Hunter also felt that black employees deserved some preferential consideration from the incoming administration as a reward for supporting the Republicans in the recent election. Blacks had received very little in the way of party patronage and "nothing in an official way from the Navy Department." Republicans could at least show their gratitude to black voters by letting them keep their jobs.[60]

Hunter was also aware of the fact that a mass discharge of black workers would have severe repercussions throughout their community because the success of churches, schools, lodges, and business enterprises was dependent upon income derived from employment at the Navy Yard. His own self-interest prompted Hunter to appeal to the incoming administration to retain as many black workers as possible. He asked his friend Edward A. Johnson of New York to contact Theodore Roosevelt, Jr., the Republican designee for the office of assistant secretary of the navy. Hunter confided to Johnson that if Roosevelt could use his influence in "continuing me in my present position I can in return, so use myself as to help my people." Hunter also wrote Roosevelt, "My people would regard it as discouragement were I displaced, hence their appeal to you. If it is thought well to continue my services, I am willing to remain a little longer."[61]

On the very day that Hunter penned his letter to Roosevelt, he received a demotion from the position of leading man to that of a common laborer, along with a corresponding decrease in pay. He refused to accept this and forthrightly applied for and received a discharge. Hunter, the adviser to his race on the need for efficiency in work performance, was upset when the industrial manager of the Navy Yard stated that relative efficiency was the sole determinant in making selections for the reduction of supervisory personnel. Hunter could not accept the fact that he had been deemed less than efficient, and during the spring of 1921 he took on the United States Navy Department in a fight to get reinstated in his job. He contacted a number of the leading black men in North Carolina and Virginia, told them that he was a victim of race prejudice, and asked that they come to his aid by writing letters in his behalf to Roosevelt. The letters of the leading men attested to his good character, citizenship, patriotism, and reputation as a safe and responsible leader in the movement for better race relations. Many of the leading men also stated that the unjust and discriminatory treatment of Hunter by Navy Yard officials had an adverse effect upon the black community. Among the supporters of Hunter were James B. Dudley and John H. Love of North Carolina, Plummer B. Young, the editor and publisher of the *Norfolk Journal and Guide*, and a number of black ministers who signed a petition circulated by nephew Ed. Roosevelt promised these men that he would do his best to see to it that Hunter got a fair hearing.[62]

In the meantime Hunter, steadily working in his own behalf, injected the issue of partisan politics to strengthen his case. He confided to a friend that his close association with Josephus Daniels was probably the real reason for his demotion. "I knew it would come just as soon as Mr. Daniels' term expired. I was prepared for it." According to Hunter, on the very day that Daniels relinquished his post as secretary of the navy, "a few little, measley minded whites got together and urged that I be demoted from Leadingman to common laborer." He wrote to Daniels that it seemed that certain ones were only waiting for the expiration of his term of office in order to "strike at me."[63]

On the day after Harding's inauguration, Hunter dispatched a telegram to Daniels welcoming him back to North Carolina on behalf of the citizens of both races from Cherokee to Currituck. Assuming the role of a national spokesman, he thanked the former secretary of the navy for his great wartime service to the nation. "Your name and your superb leadership will shine out with increasing lustre in the coming years. A grateful country salutes you as a child of this great Republic." Hunter followed up his telegram with a letter thanking Daniels for the personal and official interest that he had given him. Hunter explained that during his years at the Navy Yard, he had always tried to render the government his best service and to stimulate in the other black men a spirit of fidelity and efficiency. Above all, he was pleased to report that he had succeeded in living up to Daniels's

## A Season of Soul Rest

expectations by achieving a stainless record. Daniels thanked Hunter for his warm and generous telegram, and he told him, "You can never know how much I value your friendship.[64]

Hunter was so pleased with these words that he later quoted them as evidence of Daniels's good intentions toward blacks. He wrote to Simon G. Atkins that Daniels was a warm friend of blacks, who "possessed great power over the life and thought of the State. . . . We must get close to men of this stamp and draw from them the help they can give." Atkins thoroughly agreed because he too believed that blacks could never succeed in solving their problems without the help and cooperation of men like Daniels. As to his job at the Navy Yard, Hunter told Atkins that he had no idea that "Lily whites will allow me to remain in the enjoyment of my present distinction." Nevertheless, Hunter still hoped that he could reclaim his position. In correspondence with Theodore Roosevelt, Jr., he explained that although he owed his position to the personal endorsement of Daniels, he was and had always been a loyal supporter of the Republican party. However, he was beginning to have some doubts of that party's good intentions toward blacks. Reliable information had led him to believe that some prejudiced "little mean souls" at the Navy Yard were seeking by the process of elimination to displace all blacks from positions above that of a common laborer. Therefore Hunter alleged that he and many of his friends feared that his demotion was only indicative of the policy of the new administration toward its black supporters.[65]

Hunter contended that the loss of an insignificant job would not hurt him because "it so happens that I am always in demand." But he would feel the impact of any adverse policy of the Harding administration toward his race. Moreover, he told Roosevelt that he wanted personal satisfaction for suffering a "grave and inexcusable injustice." He appealed to Roosevelt with the full assurances that he had "inherited from his illustrious" father a spirit of friendship for the black race and a devotion to the principle of a square deal for all. Hunter next presented his case to Will H. Hays, the chairman of the Republican National Executive Committee, and postmaster general of the United States. He reported that all of the black workers in the Navy Yard were loyal Republicans and patriotic citizens, but since the advent of the Harding adminstration, a concerted effort had been made to remove all blacks from high ratings. He wanted Hays to know that blacks deserved better treatment and that he was registering a protest against the discrimina-

# A Season of Soul Rest

tory policies at the Navy Yard. He also thought that his race should be given some protection, and he told Hays, "We are not represented in high official stations and I think it unreasonable and oppressive that we should be barred from such places as we have attained by reasons of merit alone." Hunter sent a copy of his letter to Hays to the Headquarters for Race Legislation, a Washington-based organization that lobbied for legislation to protect blacks in the full enjoyment of life, property, liberty, and suffrage. He asked this group for help in his fight on behalf of the black workers at the Navy Yard. Although Hunter's request did not fall within the purview of its primary purposes, the Headquarters promised to do what it could to assist.[66]

Will H. Hays promised Hunter that the Republican party would carefully consider his complaint and that he would get satisfaction. However, by the middle of April 1921 Hunter was growing impatient. Those who had written letters on his behalf had received replies, but he had heard nothing officially from either Theodore Roosevelt, Jr., or the Navy Department. He asked Edward W. Pou, the Democratic congressman from his home district in North Carolina, to investigate the status of his case. Pou promised to see Roosevelt and ask him to correct any injustices. Finally, Hunter wrote his last letter to Roosevelt asking why he did not have the decency to reply to his correspondence. Hunter admitted that he was a humble American citizen and the government could, through its officers, "wrong, mistreat, and rob me and then close every door of redress. It may even deign a reply to my request. Yet it cannot still the voice of protest until the wrong is righted—or death." Hunter told Roosevelt that he would not accept the excuse that his demotion was necessitated by any reduction in personnel, nor would he accept a discharge as a common laborer. He stated that the demotion was because "I was a Negro, that is all," and if Roosevelt had paid any attention to his case, he would have clearly seen the injustice of the matter.[67]

Roosevelt still did not answer. Instead, Edwin Denby, the secretary of the navy, informed Hunter that an investigation of his case revealed no instance of racial discrimination or unfair treatment. He was demoted solely because his services were less efficient than those of the employees retained. Furthermore, because Hunter had voluntarily applied for a discharge, the United States Navy Department considered his case closed. Hunter probably expected the matter would end this way, for he had no intention of returning to the Navy Yard even if reinstated in his job. While his case was pending, he contacted N. C. Newbold about the possibility of a teaching position in North Carolina, and also asked Josephus Daniels to intervene on his behalf with the superintendent of public instruction. On a visit to Raleigh in April 1921, Hunter had a long conference with Daniels, who seemed glad to see him. In fact, Hunter claimed that all the white people in Raleigh were glad to see him, and they "gave me an especial welcome."[68]

CHAPTER

# 10

## A Matter of Principle

Once back in North Carolina, Hunter immediately resumed his fight with lily-white Republicans. In April 1921 he wrote a letter to President Harding recommending the appointment of Henry Groves Connor, a Democrat, to the vacancy on the Circuit Court of Appeals caused by the death of Jeter C. Pritchard. He wrote Harding that though a black Republican who had always voted his party's ticket, he believed that in the appointment of judges the paramount considerations should be eminence, fitness, and a high sense of justice. Hunter felt that Connor possessed these qualities and thought his appointment would greatly enhance the respect and confidence of the judiciary in the eyes of all people. In endorsing Connor he maintained that he had the concurrence of the masses of blacks in North Carolina. Hunter's concern with strengthening the judiciary, along with his hostility to lily-whites, also led to his involvement in the sensational battle to prevent the confirmation of Frank A. Linney as United States district attorney for the Western District of North Carolina.[1]

Linney had been the Republican candidate for governor in 1916 and during his campaign he had publicly endorsed Clarence Poe's scheme for rural apartheid. In the political campaign of 1920 an open letter addressed to the white women voters and bearing Linney's signature as chairman of the Republican party of North Carolina appeared throughout the state. The letter endorsed disfranchisement and called for a coalition of lily-whites and Democrats to secure the total elimination of blacks from politics. It also suggested that the women appeal to the chairman of the Democratic Executive Committee for help in securing these goals, because it was obvious that no black could vote unless a Democratic registrar permitted him to do so.

## A Matter of Principle

Linney informed these women that they should not be ashamed of voting the Republican ticket, and he pledged that if "we carry the election you will have a strictly white government."[2]

When Harding nominated Linney for district attorney in 1921, black North Carolinians lodged an immediate protest with the president and with the attorney general of the United States, Harry M. Daugherty. They also sent a letter of opposition to the Senate Judiciary Committee along with a copy of the open letter to white women voters. The committee, agreeing that Linney had written the "wrong sort of letter," subsequently rejected his nomination. Senator Lee S. Overman of North Carolina was a member of the Judiciary Committee, and he asked that it not transmit its findings to the Senate until Linney had received a hearing. Accordingly, a subcommittee consisting of Senators Richard P. Ernst, Albert B. Cummings, and Overman was appointed to conduct the hearing.[3]

Publicly, and to blacks, Overman explained that he requested the hearing for Linney because he thought that it would be unfair to condemn any man without giving him a chance to tell his side of the story. However, privately Overman boasted to attorney Samuel J. Ervin and other whites that he had saved Linney from humiliation and defeat and that he would be glad to support him because he was "very anxious to secure his confirmation." Strangely enough, other Democrats from across the state came to the rescue of their former political enemy, Linney, and they forwarded letters of recommendation on his behalf to Overman. The letters reminded Overman that the time had definitely come to take a firm stand for white supremacy, and that Linney, although a Republican, was right about "the nigger matter," and on the same side of the issue as the Democrats. They could not stand to see him defeated because he had the courage to express sentiments "appropriate to a Southern white man and gentleman."[4]

The Linney case now ceased to be a squabble between lily-white and black Republicans and, reduced to its simplest terms, the issue was blacks versus whites. Dr. A. M. Rivera, the president of the Greensboro branch of the NAACP, asked the organization's national headquarters to join in the protest against Linney. The national headquarters contacted prominent Republicans, and also through its twenty-four branches in Ohio brought pressure on Attorney General Daugherty. Walter White, the assistant secretary of the NAACP, who was in Washington at the time of the Linney controversy, solicited the aid of Senators Hiram Johnson and William E. Borah, who diligently worked to prevent Linney's confirmation. White North

# A Matter of Principle

Carolinians were convinced that the Linney matter concerned not only the Republican party but the entire South. The overriding question was whether blacks or decent white Republicans should control the offices of the federal government in the South, and Linney's failure to receive confirmation was only part of a design to turn over the reins of political power to blacks. The *Greensboro Daily News* sounded the keynote for the ensuing contest by announcing that the Linney matter was one of life or death, and the only way that blacks would ever assert political power in America, it declared, was by first killing off the whites.[5]

Hunter entered the contest by announcing at the outset that the issue was not one of black domination, but of principle. He agreed with the editor of the *Greensboro Daily News* concerning the impossibility of blacks ever holding political power, and he told the editor that the thoughts of such an idea were "grotesquely absurd." Blacks were conscious of their weakness and of the fact that they were not represented in any branch of government anywhere in the nation. They were not "whining about that." All they wanted was for the Constitution and laws, which were made and interpreted by white men, to be applied equally to all citizens. As to Linney, Hunter stated that blacks opposed his confirmation because he had openly and flagrantly proposed in his letter to enter into a conspiracy to violate the Constitution and the law. Such a man was therefore unfit for office. He also advised the *Greensboro Daily News* that instead of "throwing up its hands in holy horror and solemnly asseverate that the action of the Judiciary Committee was a disguise to turn over the state of affairs to blacks," it should thank God that there were Christian men on that committee who had conscientious convictions.[6]

Whites warned blacks that their protest against Linney would only bear evil fruit. Before disfranchisement the whole effort of the white race had one aim, and that was to keep blacks out of politics. But since then the two races had developed a modus vivendi and whites gave blacks a chance to acquire property and educate their children. The Red Shirts and the Ku Klux Klan had abandoned the scene, and blacks had secured an opportunity to live in peace and security. Thus the policy of excluding blacks from political power was in reality a humanitarian gesture because it kept them from getting killed. For the moment blacks paid no attention to the admonitions of whites and they continued their protest against Linney. David C. Suggs, the president of Livingstone College, directed the movement, and it was supported by the African Methodist Episcopal Zion church. Hunter played a commanding role in marshaling support and developing strategy. Blacks asked for permission to present their case before the Senate Judiciary Committee during the Linney hearing, and Overman notified Suggs that the signers of the original protest and any other black men in the country could come to Washington, and the Senate subcommittee would be glad to hear them. He also told Suggs that Linney claimed he did not write the open letter, and that it was composed while he was sick and someone else had signed his name to it. In requesting an appearance before the Senate, black North Carolinians had put the national Republican party and the Harding administration in a dilemma. They could either reject Linney, the chairman of the strongest Republican organization in the South, and antagonize their southern supporters or through his confirmation admit that the party sanctioned a dual policy for blacks. The latter course was sure to alienate all blacks as well as those white Republicans in states outside the South having large black constituencies.[7]

Hunter preferred not to deal with Overman, and he and Attorney Wade H. Ancrum of Raleigh lodged a protest on behalf of all black citizens of the state with Senator William E. Borah, who earlier had voted against Linney's confirmation. They complained that Linney, as chairman of the Republican party of North Carolina, used that position to promote a lily-white policy that effectively suppressed the entire black Republican vote in the state. In so doing he had openly and avowedly violated the Fourteenth and Fifteenth amendments and all the laws passed by Congress to enforce them. Hence it was illogical for anyone to assume that a man who thought and acted like Linney could ever honestly take an oath of office or prosecute cases arising from violations of these amendments.[8]

Edward E. Britton, the Washington correspondent of the *Raleigh News and Observer*, wired the Raleigh office of the paper and asked that someone contact Hunter and get a copy of the letter and tell him "that Borah said that it was alright to let it be published." Hunter's letter was later publicized by the *News and Observer* as proof that blacks were "hot in the collar" and had no intention of backing down in their fight against Linney's confirmation. Also published was a personal letter from Hunter, which was probably designed to allay racial animosity, defuse any arguments over black domination, and attract conservative blacks to the cause. According to Hunter "no sensible Negro was seeking Negro rule" and whites should and would rule because of their superior ability. He admitted that though he was not a politician, he was a black Republican who had always supported the party's ticket "when there was any such ticket to be voted for." However, he had not hesitated to vote for Democrats, and for this he had often been "pilloried by white Republicans who are now trying to distance the Democrats in their opposition to Negro suffrage and attempts to suppress the Negro vote." Because of this, he and other blacks would much prefer to see all federal offices in the state remain in the hands of Democrats than to pass them on to the likes of Linney.[9]

Hunter received praise and encouragement for this protest against Linney from various segments of the black community. His nephew Ed wished him success, believing that men who "blow hot and cold on the fundamental principles of government" should be brought to light and exposed. Harrison H. Taylor, Hunter's old colleague on the Negro Republican Executive Committee, congratulated him for his efforts in exposing the "meanness of the Linney and Morehead machine towards us as a race in the South." He urged Hunter to "hit em again and hit em hard" and to include in his next bill of indictment the fact that blacks were excluded from serving on federal juries in the state. Significantly, the top management of the North Carolina Mutual Insurance Company encouraged and supported Hunter. Charles C. Spaulding, the organization's secretary-treasurer, praised him as a splendid writer, and told him that he voiced the sentiments of thousands of blacks in North Carolina, who would say the same thing if they had the opportunity or know-how. "Our white friends do not understand us," wrote Spaulding, and he believed that if they knew more about the "real conditions and along which lines we are thinking," blacks would receive better treatment. He urged Hunter to continue to speak out with his pen. Spaulding also told Hunter that his letter to him was personal in nature and not for publication. John M. Avery, the insurance company's vice-president, also commended Hunter for his services to the race in the Linney fight and offered his heartiest support. Avery later gave Hunter valuable financial assistance.[10]

Walter White of the NAACP promised Hunter that he could rest assured that the organization would use every possible means to prevent the confirmation of Linney because it realized the tremendous importance of such a result. James Weldon Johnson, secretary of the NAACP, would be present at the Linney hearing to assist the North Carolina black delegation. Johnson later notified Hunter that he could not attend the hearings because Walter White had to go to Oklahoma to investigate the Tulsa riots, and he was left alone to manage the national office. However, he asked several other men of political prominence to attend the proceedings. On 2 June 1921 Hunter received a telegram from Senator Knute Nelson, the chairman of the Senate Judiciary Committee, notifying him that the Linney hearings were scheduled for 8 June and that everyone would have an opportunity to make statements. When Hunter arrived in Washington he learned that the "Linney gang" intended to justify their position by attacking the entire history of black suffrage. Lily-whites would also try to prove that black voters were responsible for all of the evils of the Reconstruction period following the Civil War. Hunter believed that he was one of the few people familiar with all of the facts relating to the history of blacks as voters and thus he was in the best position to offer a counterargument. He prepared a circular on the history of the political participation of blacks in North Carolina, which he presented at the hearing. He also made sure that a copy of the circular was placed in the hands of every Republican senator, and he held conferences with a number of these gentlemen, who were amazed at the contents of this document. Hunter also delivered his circular to various newspapers in Washington.[11]

The Linney hearing was continued until 24 June, and Hunter returned to Raleigh to resume his journalistic crusade against Linney. By this time he was somewhat of a national hero. From New York a correspondent wrote that she had followed the Linney case and hoped that Hunter would "put it over on him good and proper," because she knew that Linney was a "Negro hater." Another black, from Jacksonville, Florida, thought that Linney was undoubtedly a lily-white Republican, and as such would seek to get blacks out of politics by any means, "fair or foul." A letter from Washington, D.C., encouraged Hunter to continue the struggle because things did not look very good for the Harding administration. Dr. W. M. Reid from Portsmouth, Virginia, assured Hunter that he was with him "heart and soul" in the Linney contest, and he sent a contribution to help in the fight. Hunter was in need of money, and he had earlier written that North Carolina blacks had gone to great personal expense in their fight against Linney. Transportation and printing costs were great, and he thought that Tarheel blacks should not have to bear this by themselves because the Linney matter was one both to determine the status of blacks in the Republican party and to explicate the higher principle of constitutional law. J. M. Avery of the North Carolina Mutual Insurance Company came to Hunter's rescue, for he thought that Hunter's role was so important that Hunter had to return to Washington. Avery promised that if the Raleigh branch of the NAACP did not take care of Hunter's expenses, he would make arrangements to cover them.[12]

## A Matter of Principle

North Carolina blacks decided to dispatch an even larger delegation to Washington when the hearings resumed, and it was reported that private individuals, societies, and churches had contributed monies to meet its expenses. Clearly confident of success, Suggs wrote Hunter that compromise was unacceptable, and the only outcome could be triumph or defeat. Meanwhile, the Linney forces, led by John Motley Morehead, Charles Reynolds, Zeb Vance Walser, Isaac Meekins, and John J. Parker, were rallying support throughout North Carolina by obtaining resolutions supporting lily-whitism as the only way to build a strong state Republican party. They too decided to send a large delegation to Washington. On 24 June 1921 a large crowd representing both factions, along with a number of congressmen and members of the press, assembled in the Senate Judiciary Committee room. However, they were not privy to the hearing because it was held in executive session to which selected members of both sides were invited. Professor D. C. Suggs, Dr. J. H. Johnson, and Professor William H. Hannum, all of Salisbury, along with Dr. H. W. Bruce of Asheville, Hunter, and Henry Lincoln Johnson, a black Republican National committeeman from Georgia, represented blacks.[13]

Blacks were given the first opportunity to present their case. Professor Suggs claimed that no blacks at the hearing were office-seekers. Rather, they were professionals, businessmen, or farmers who were interested in guaranteeing political and civil rights for themselves and their posterity. They were Republicans nationally, but lately they had supported Democrats in state elections because they were the best men as far as blacks were concerned. He then presented a petition of protest alleging that Linney was derelict in his duties as chairman of the Republican party of North Carolina, a state with approximately 150,000 blacks who could vote. By ignoring this element, Suggs argued that Linney had possibly prevented a Republican majority in the state in the 1920 election. Suggs then recounted the contents of the Linney letter to the white women voters. Blacks also used the hearing as a forum to strike out against John J. Parker and John Motley Morehead by recalling that these two leading Republicans had endorsed disfranchisement during the most recent elections.[14]

Isaac Meekins, then the general counsel for the Alien Property Custodian, presented Linney's defense. According to Meekins, Linney did not author the infamous letter, and it was in fact a composite document written by two other men and himself. He defended Linney's attitude and the lily-white movement as the only safe and realistic means of purifying and

## A Matter of Principle

strengthening the Republican party in North Carolina. He also argued that whites would not join or remain in a party if they had to contend with blacks. Furthermore, he asserted that if Linney's confirmation were rejected, the lily-whites would not nominate another person, and if Harding wanted to recognize the black Republicans of North Carolina, he could then do so by appointing a black United States district attorney.[15]

In his testimony Linney also denied penning the letter, and claimed that he was unaware of its existence for several days. He was absent from Republican headquarters because of illness, and had authorized Alfred Eugene Holton, a former party chairman, to sign his name to any document he desired to issue. He did not repudiate the letter when he heard of it, because he felt its intent was to eliminate the black issue from political contests rather the black as a voter. Under cross-examination by Senators Ernst and Cummings, Linney was forced to denounce the Red Shirt and white-supremacy campaigns of 1898 as movements motivated by extreme race prejudice and which terrorized, killed, and made the condition of blacks so intolerable that a "great number of the intelligent, influential, and honorable Negroes were forced to leave the state." He also acknowledged that he had actually opposed the disfranchisement amendment in 1900, and that he and his father, former Congressman Romulus Z. Linney, had both favored a force bill to protect voting rights. Linney further conceded that he was in favor of blacks having a political status in North Carolina, and that the literary qualification for voting should be applied equally to both races. He promised that if confirmed he would honestly and impartially enforce the law and would prosecute any white registrar who failed to register blacks. Regardless of his sudden conversion to the principles of political equality, Linney's chances for confirmation were rather slim in view of his past record to the contrary.[16]

At this point, the case took a strange turn. To the amazement of many present Henry Lincoln Johnson, the leader of the black and tan faction in Georgia politics, testified that he, Linney, and Meekins were all good friends. He announced that blacks misunderstood Linney, agreed to withdraw their petition of protest, and would interpose no further objections to his confirmation. Praising Linney for his frank and courageous testimony, Johnson tried to dismiss the whole affair as just a misunderstanding between friends. According to a reporter of the *Raleigh News and Observer*, when this news reached the crowd of blacks outside the hearing room, they "looked glum and appeared dazed, for they had spent piles of money to make two trips to Washington only to learn that Linney was alright and would be confirmed." Senator Borah was also shocked to know that blacks had withdrawn their protest, and he commented, "Those North Carolina Negroes who are following Henry Lincoln Johnson deserve to be disfranchised."[17]

Obviously something other than Linney's testimony happened to make the protest leaders reverse their commitment to total victory. There is evidence that the movement did not have as broad a base of support as its leaders claimed. As usual there were some blacks on the other side of the fence. For example, a black educator, Charles M. Eppes, informed Overman that he was sure the masses of blacks were not against Linney, and that his defeat would only hurt them. They had had enough politics, and wanted only protection, economic and educational freedom, and the elimination of peonage. Eppes was also sure that James B. Dudley, the president of the Agricultural and Technical College, Simon G. Atkins, the president of Winston-Salem College, and Aaron M. Moore of the North Carolina Mutual Insurance Company endorsed this attitude. It is also quite likely that some blacks, particularly educators, were intimidated by their white employers. Representative of this is the fact that during the heat of the Linney controversy, Nathan C. Newbold, the state agent for rural schools, in an address to the black State Teachers' Association frankly declared that there were "two red flags for blacks"—politics and social equality—and advised blacks to be "very cautious in things political." It was also reported that during the hearings Isaac Meekins had warned Henry Lincoln Johnson that North Carolina whites had had enough of the race issue and were firmly committed to white supremacy. Said Meekins, ". . . we had to take out our rifles to your race after the war between the states. . . . We don't want anything like that again."[18]

Another explanation lies in the fact that Linney's confirmation stood a good chance of being rejected by the Senate, and this would have been an embarrassment for President Harding. Consequently, there were some trade-offs as blacks used the Linney matter to get political concessions. The Harding administration promised to create a new Internal Revenue District in New York, which would be headed by a black. It was also hinted that Harding would appoint a black to be registrar of the treasury, and that North Carolina blacks would receive two important appointments, possibly consularships. However, the only black nominated for anything was Henry Lincoln Johnson, who was recommended by Harding to be recorder of

## A Matter of Principle

deeds for the District of Columbia within a week of the Linney hearing. His nomination was later rejected because whites were against a black holding a position of authority over white women, and also because of "his own bad record."[19]

Hunter, Suggs, and many other blacks interpreted Linney's humiliation, his public renunciation of lily-whitism, and his pledge to prosecute all violations of the Constitution as a major victory. Suggs explained to Senator Borah that blacks felt that Linney had conceded every point raised in their protest. They did not withdraw it, but considered the matter "satisfactorily resolved." Hunter's comrade, Wade H. Ancrum, felt that blacks had made the best possible deal, and in this they were supported by the best thinking men. "To have demanded that Harding withdraw Linney's name, would have been too much for blacks to ask."[20]

North Carolina blacks did receive some other benefits from the Linney affair. They gained valuable experience in learning how to mobilize the support of the national black community. By striking an alliance with white liberals from other parts of the country, they also learned how to use politics as a medium for focusing attention on race relations. They had additional opportunity to pursue their twenty-year-old commitment to the idea that the Republican party in North Carolina would not succeed as a lily-white organization. Although Linney got his appointment, he and the lily-whites were probably the greatest losers. Overman voted against his confirmation, and demanded that Linney's testimony be made public so the people of North Carolina could see where he stood. The *Raleigh News and Observer* accused him of bowing to the wishes of blacks in North Carolina by denying the great ideals of white supremacy, and it cited his testimony before the Senate Judiciary Committee as positive proof that the Republican party of North Carolina was still the black party.[21]

Hunter did not believe this, and it was clearly evident to him that the Republican party had finally accepted the principle of "lily whites" and "lily blacks" in the South. The recent political campaign and the Linney matter had shown that there were no real differences separating Democrats from Republicans on the issue of race. The Grand Old Party had abandoned its commitment to human and constitutional rights for blacks, and this was the one thing that had historically distinguished it from the Democrats. He believed that 1921 marked the year when the Republican party renounced the great principles upon which it was founded, and consequently it ceased to be a viable political force in the South. Furthermore, he felt that a

# A Matter of Principle

national party could not and did not deserve to exist with separate policies for northern and southern blacks, and without a national creed, common principles, and a common faith. Even though black Republicans in the South were suppressed and flatly told that they were not wanted, Hunter did not advocate that they leave the party, simply because they had nowhere else to go. But he did advise them not to be fools in political matters, to think for themselves, to keep the faith, and also to remember that Republicans would win no more elections in North Carolina.[22]

Hunter had mixed emotions over his role in the Linney matter. He was undoubtedly proud of the accolades he received, yet he was somewhat remorseful because the incident had contributed to a deterioration of race relations. He wrote that everywhere one could see evidence of race hatred, but he continued to believe that somewhere in North Carolina, there had to be an inconspicuous group of white men of the "Aycock tradition" who disapproved of this and held favorable attitudes toward blacks. The problem of the hour was how to seek out and unite this group with the better element of his race. He thought that if blacks could only find the "good side of whites and if they will find our good side then the era of estrangement and bitterness will pass." He continued to insist that even though slavery had been dead for over a half century, there existed a spirit of love and cordiality between the few former slaves and their onetime masters, and he came up with the idea of another reunion so that whites and blacks could touch each other on their better side. "We all have a good side and a bad side," he wrote. "Just how we will think, feel and treat each other, depends on the side affected by approach."[23]

Hunter dispatched a circular outlining his proposals for the exslave reunion to some of the most prominent whites in the state. Attached were copies of an earlier letter to the editor of the *Raleigh News and Observer*. In this he had asserted that the activities of the Ku Klux Klan and other instances of racial violence did not represent the true state of race relations in North Carolina, nor did they express the sentiments of the best class of whites. Though his tactic may have been to gauge the racial sentiments of these men, he had actually forced them into agreement because few cared to admit that they were not of the best class of whites. Of those who responded, not one disapproved of the reunion, and a majority agreed with his assessment of race relations. By far the most objective response came from Judge Henry Groves Connor, who saw race relations as the one problem that would deeply and permanently affect the happiness and welfare of both races. Although he welcomed any effort that would help strengthen and maintain better relations between blacks and whites, Connor insisted that the race problem could not be solved until people began to cultivate and translate into their daily lives "the confidence, respect for, and recognition of" human rights. For reasons unexplained the reunion did not occur, and Hunter announced that his proposal was only a "suggestion and not a final action." But he was pleased with the favorable responses received from many of the state's most prominent white citizens, who conveyed "the true and genuine expression of the true and genuine North Carolinian."[24]

At the same time that Hunter was proposing his reunion, N. C. Newbold invited selected leading blacks to an interracial conference on the race problem. As it turned out, this was hardly a harmonious gathering. Newbold asked blacks to join with state officials and Cameron Morrison in a campaign to promote goodwill, and to dispel the negative image that the governor had projected to their community during his recent campaign. Newbold admitted that many things said during that time were not encouraging to blacks, and for those statements the governor bore the stigma, but he was sure that Morrison was not as bitter toward blacks as he was pictured to be. As proof of this he claimed that Morrison and the white people of the state had decided to give blacks a fair deal, particularly in education. This statement was immediately challenged by the black educators, who wanted to know why this fair deal did not include an equitable division of educational funds on a per-capita student basis. They frankly told Newbold that because of this inequity their students' progress was unfavorable in comparison with whites, and this fact was used to substantiate allegations of the innate inferiority of black children. A reporter at the conference commented that these charges confused Newbold, and he conceded the points raised by blacks without any explanation.[25]

Morrison later addressed the black schoolteachers at their annual assembly, and he told them that "no man ever loved the black man more than I have loved him." Furthermore, he stated that any white man who did not love the black man should be driven from the state. He surmised that many blacks feared him because of his role in the white-supremacy campaign of 1898, but he wanted them to know that at that time he was forced to give them "a merited chastisement when they established a government that would have destroyed both races." Afterward, blacks had not caused much trouble, and the governor wanted the educators to know that whites appreci-

# A Matter of Principle

ated the fact that they had been "behaving themselves better than ever before." If the members of the audience thought that their good behavior would be rewarded by improved educational opportunities, such ideas were immediately squashed. Morrison let them know that they were receiving "as much education as you are ready for. You cannot use the highly organized system that is provided for whites." When blacks were ready for more education, the governor assured them that whites would be prepared to give it.[26]

Morrison also appeared at the black fair of 1921, and the crowd warmly cheered as the governor was introduced. In his remarks he again praised them for their good behavior and contributions to the state as laborers, ignoring the achievements and contributions of black businessmen, professionals, and intellectuals. His insensitivity toward blacks also came through when he praised them for their patriotism and splendid record during the World War, and their blind submission to authority. He had never heard of "a black who would not go under the leadership of the white to death if needed," and he had never heard of a Bolshevist "Nigger" in his life. The governor also boldly asserted that North Carolina was doing more for blacks than any other state in the Union, and "history did not reveal a single instance where the two races ever lived together in the same concord and harmony that we have here." Morrison must have known that his remarks were inconsistent with the reality of race relations, or he too was caught up in the myth that North Carolina was the best place in the world for blacks. Though no black questioned the veracity of the governor's remarks on the spot, several months later the leading men of Raleigh reaffirmed their commitment to shouldering the "black man's" burden. They would have to do everything in their power to educate whites on the "Negro Problem" so that they could understand the aspirations and ideals of the black community.[27]

President Harding gave Hunter an opportunity to continue his efforts in this direction. In the fall of 1921 Harding proposed a program for race relations in the United States that included equal economic and educational opportunities for blacks, and suffrage for those "fit to vote." He also explicitly stated that blacks had to forget about social equality because it was neither desirable nor possible, and any attempts toward it would not be tolerated. Hunter, who thoroughly approved of the president's views, asked his private secretary to convey this to Harding. Hunter wrote that the whole country echoed the president's courageous, logical, noble, and statesman-like attitude, including thousands of white southerners who had no sympathy with the lily-white movement. "I desire that he shall know this. I am a Negro. I was reared in slavery. I know them."[28]

Hunter's evaluation of the impact of Harding's proposal was somewhat inaccurate, and it later provoked indignation and censure throughout the South. The *News and Observer* hinted that the president's program for race relations was prompted by North Carolina blacks. Harding's proposal did come on the heels of an article written by Charles H. Moore in the *Independent* (Raleigh) that denounced the president for his lack of consideration for blacks and for the fact that they were not receiving the political recognition due them in light of his campaign promises. The *News and Observer* also noted that Harding's ideas did not square with the actions of a large number of Republicans who were guilty of treating with blacks on terms of social equality. To make matters worse, James Weldon Johnson of the NAACP theorized that although the president had disavowed "social equality," his proposal would lead to that end and this was exactly what blacks wanted. Responding to this, the *News and Observer* warned blacks not to get their hopes up, because social equality would never happen: "The white man will stand guard at the threshold of his social life," and if blacks tried to intrude, they would only provoke a repeat of the "terrible days of Reconstruction."[29]

Hunter took the responsibility of trying to interpret Harding's statement and its meaning to the black community in a letter to the *News and Observer*. He believed that the president never intended his remarks to be construed as favoring social equality. To Hunter, the whole idea of social equality was "a mere bug-bear—a bogy, something that was held up as a conjuration with which to awe timid and witless white people." He knew the best white people were so firmly secured in their social status that they were not bothered about any social equality with blacks or any other class. This was the reason why black North Carolinians had always appealed to the Christian consciousness of the best whites. Furthermore, intelligent blacks did not desire social equality either. They wanted equal economic, political, and educational opportunities, protection under the laws, peace, and the sympathetic cooperation between the races. Most of all, blacks wanted to see the spirit of Jesus Christ prevail and permeate the life of their state and, when this happened, he was sure there would be "no race problem, no Negro domination, no white supremacy, no race bitterness." Hunter maintained that there was no need for whites to be upset because blacks were not going to ask for anything new. The things they desired in 1921 were the same things they had asked for in their convention of 1865, and the sentiments voiced by that body were still the dominant notes in the hearts of blacks.[30]

Dr. Willis G. Crawford of Goldsboro read Hunter's article in the *News and Observer* and thought it was "decidedly the best thing" he had ever seen on the subject and that it did indeed speak for the great majority of blacks. Crawford thought he was qualified to know what blacks were thinking by virtue of "having had my 'black mammay' in the years ago," and from thirty years of medical practice among their race. During this time he had never heard blacks even hint about social equality, and he thought they were as averse to the idea as they were to associating with "Po white trash" in antebellum days. He also believed that the demands of blacks as stated by Hunter were just, and that whites should grant them from a Christian standpoint. Hunter thanked him for his kind words of encouragement, and wrote that his one great passion concerning earthly things was to see peaceful relations between the races in America. "I have given my life to this end and shall devote the remaining years allotted me to the same lofty purpose."[31]

The results of a survey conducted several years later by the editor of the *Independent* of Elizabeth City tended to prove that both Hunter and Crawford were justified in their beliefs concerning social equality, at least as far as the black educators were concerned. The paper contacted 300 black schoolteachers and asked them to tell, anonymously, of their wants and desires. The results led to the conclusion that blacks were eager to live among themselves, to create a separate culture, society, and institutions, and to forever "respectfully recognize the barrier of color." Of course, black teachers were supposed to think this way. This may explain Hunter's new conservatism because he was trying to reestablish himself as an educator.[32]

When Hunter returned to North Carolina in 1921, he sought work in Raleigh and Wake County, and also submitted applications for employment throughout the state. Without a college degree, he was unable to receive the necessary certification for teaching in urban schools. Throughout most of his life he had urged blacks to improve their educational status, but again he did not follow his own advice. His egotism precluded the possibility of admitting an educational deficiency, and it also seems that he thought the personal intervention of his white patrons was sufficient to guarantee him employment. But he did not succeed. Denied employment in his native city and county, the last decade of his life found him teaching in various rural schools.

In 1921 Hunter got a job in Chatham County, and to pave the way for his arrival, he probably asked Henry M. London, the librarian of the North Carolina Historical Commission, to write a letter attesting to his character and qualifications. Hunter was recommended as a very respectable and worthy "colored" man, well trained and experienced as a teacher. London also wrote that Hunter had always adopted the policy of securing the friendly interest and support of white people and endeavored to teach blacks that they were their true friends. Because of this, London was certain that Hunter had earned the esteem of the best class of whites and blacks.[33]

Assigned to the Haywood School, Hunter immediately set out to improve not only this facility, but the black community in general. He solicited funds for his school work from his many friends in other parts of the state, and he also began to publish a school paper, the *Haywood Register*. The paper featured articles of general interest to the community along with sketches of black historical personalities. Within a short time he had gained the support and praise of some of the most influential whites in Chatham County. Colin G. Shaw, the editor and owner of the *Chatham Record* of Pittsboro and the *Siler City Weekly Herald*, considered Hunter a progressive educator and "one of the best colored men that the State has ever produced." Hunter's paper also received recognition from those interested in its historical contents. The North Carolina Library Commission subscribed to the publication, and James E. Sanford of Method thought that its historical sketches helped to educate blacks, "who certainly know less about the heroes of their race than any other people on earth." Charles S. Johnson, the editor of *Opportunity*, the official magazine of the National Urban League, was so impressed with the quality of Hunter's sketches that he suggested they be made available to the general public in permanent form.[34]

Once safely entrenched in Chatham County, and to the satisfaction of the best white men, Hunter slipped back into the role of a "safe and sound" educator. This attitude came through in his address at the 1923 Emancipation Day activities in Pittsboro. He mentioned nothing about political or civil rights for his race, but instead proclaimed that North Carolina blacks were the most prosperous of any in the nation. This spoke well for the white citizens of the state, without whom such progress could not have been possible. Admittedly, after sixty years of freedom, "The Negro Problem still throws its dark shadows over the land," but it could not be solved by political parties, legislative acts, or even constitutional guarantees. The solution lay in Divine Providence. He predicted that the next great proclamation of black emancipation would come from the South, and that God was preparing "some great big Southern heart and mind to lead us out of the bogs of doubt, and fear, and misunderstanding into the joyful sunlight of a new and happy day."[35]

In contrast to Hunter's conservatism, the black community in his hometown of Raleigh staged a rather militant Emancipation Day celebration. Reverend D. Ormonde Walker, the pastor of Saint Paul's African Methodist Episcopal Church, delivered the annual oration, and he told the crowd that it was time for blacks to stop shamming with whites and deal with them honestly and openly. He then proceeded to condemn the Ku Klux Klan, American imperialism in Haiti, and the "Back to Africa Movement" of Marcus Garvey. The tone was set for the main resolutions when Walker cast doubts about Lincoln's humanitarian motives in freeing the slaves. He also claimed that blacks had been lied to, exploited, and misled by Republican carpetbaggers and scalawags during Reconstruction. Two thousand blacks cheered and unanimously adopted a resolution that declared their debt to the Republican party "paid in full," and announced an end to their allegiance to that organization. They agreed that the Grand Old Party, once full of great principles, had degenerated to "the skeleton from which the soul of a once great party had departed."[36]

During the course of Walker's remarks, he intimated that in the future whites would have to readjust their attitudes toward blacks and realize that they were dealing no longer with former slaves but with their children. This seemed to reflect the current sentiment that the race had divided itself into old and new blacks, with the latter having superior characteristics. Hunter rejected this concept, and he believed that slavery produced many men and women who were "uncrowned Kings and Queens." They were naturally endowed with good hearts and souls, traits that Hunter thought were indicative of a higher culture. He insisted that had their opportunities corresponded with their natural abilities, "their names would have been written high, and in characters large, upon the scroll of the world's highest and best."[37]

One of Hunter's "uncrowned Queens" of the Old South was the black mammy. He was delighted when Representative Charles M. Stedman of North Carolina spoke in behalf of a bill pending in Congress in 1923 that

# A Matter of Principle

would have granted permission to the Jefferson Davis Chapter of the United Daughters of the Confederacy to erect a monument in the nation's capital in memory of the "faithful colored mammies of the South." He recalled the great civilization of the antebellum South, which produced statesmen, orators, and scholars at a time when men were brave and women gentle and true. To him, the central figure in this civilization was the loyal and loving mammy who nurtured her white charges, watched them grow, and frequently assisted in the last rites of their burial. Mammies, loved, respected, and content, had desired no change in their condition. Hunter wrote Stedman that this tribute was beautiful, ornate, and appropriate. He knew that it would be hard and even mysterious for those who had never been slaves to imagine the mammy in her true role, and he thought that Stedman's remarks would do much to dispel the belief that "mammy is a cherished sentimentality-myth—never having had embodiment, a real life genuine spirit actuality." People should know that mammy was not only an exalted personality, but an institution of the Old South. She was a precious memory, and Hunter hoped a monument would be erected, showing her "typical figure bearing benediction as of old." He also published his own tribute to mammy in the *Haywood Register* because he wanted the youth of both races to know of the real heart of the Old South, which he thought was beautiful in many respects. "Its 'Uncle Toms' and little 'Evas' were not rarities but ruling spirits of the whole household," he wrote to Frank P. Haywood, a descendant of the family that had once owned him.[38]

Hunter and many others of his generation believed that they had established the basis for an amicable adjustment of race relations during their convention of 1865, and that they had been in the vanguard of the struggle for equal rights ever since. Younger blacks were only building upon the aspirations, hopes, and prayers of their forefathers, who, as soon as they were freed, began to develop institutions and to educate their children so that they could better carry on the fight. To Hunter, the "new Negro" wanted only what his parents had wanted and fought for, except that many of the younger generation of both races had alienated whites and blacks by foolishly demanding social equality. Furthermore, Hunter believed that it was the elders of the race who throughout the years had maintained the closest contact with the best class of whites and kept alive the residue of friendly feelings that survived the institution of slavery. This was extremely important, for he sincerely believed that the old-timers of both races best understood each other, and would in the end solve the race problem.[39]

Although Hunter thought that the older generation of blacks would cor-

## A Matter of Principle

rectly chart the course for race relations, at times he, along with the "new Negroes," disagreed with their methods. Many old blacks for a variety of reasons overplayed the accommodationist role and overstressed the idea that North Carolina was the best place in the nation for blacks. Among these was Hunter's friend, James B. Dudley, the president of the Agricultural and Technical College in Greensboro. In the spring and early summer of 1923, Dudley sent speakers from his institution throughout the state to caution blacks against migrating to the North, and to remind them that their place was in North Carolina. He also announced in a statement to the Associated Press that the state was losing only a few of its "best Negroes," and most were happy because they enjoyed justice in the courts and good schools. They had also realized that it was best for them to remain at home and work out their destiny among friends, rather than seek a solution among strangers in the North where race prejudice was far more deadly than anywhere in the South.[40]

Dudley's unrealistic statement appalled even Hunter. In a letter to the editor of the *Greensboro Daily News*, he admitted that he rarely had occasion to disagree with Professor Dudley, whose "earnest desire to promote better race relations had led him into glaring inaccuracies which should not go unchallenged." Hunter wrote that blacks like all other people migrate to where they can realize their potential with the greatest degree of happiness and freedom. Furthermore, as one who had traveled and lived in the North, he had never encountered the race prejudice that troubled blacks in the South, and he thought that anyone conversant with the administration of justice in North Carolina could never accept Dudley's contention. Hunter cautioned blacks of the very thing of which he had been so often guilty: in their zeal to propitiate the kindly feelings of whites, they should not let their rhetoric run counter to facts. A. Myron Cochran, the pastor of Hunter's church in Raleigh, and Charles H. Moore both congratulated him on his excellent and comprehensive analysis of Dudley's appeal to the "white gallery of the Old North State." Moore wrote Hunter that his statement met with the approval of the black community in his hometown of Greensboro, and he also believed that his article proved that there were some members of his race still alive who constituted a connecting link between the old and the new black. Though they might be old chronologically, such men were young, progressive, and uncompromising in spirit, and had never and would not "bow their knees to the hydra-headed monster, The Baal of Southern prejudices."[41]

Hunter escaped censure for his reply to Dudley, and in 1923 he was appointed principal of the new school for blacks at Pittsboro, with full authority for running the institution, including the selection of teachers. In announcing this appointment, the *Chatham Record* noted that Pittsboro was indeed fortunate to have in its midst a man like Hunter, "who bore flattering testimonials from many of the most prominent citizens of the state, white and colored." The assistant editor of the paper wrote that he had known Hunter for years and could personally vouch for the fact that he was "an honorable Negro," full of ambition and a leader among his race for greater achievements and a higher moral standard of living. Hunter announced that he would put forth every effort to make the new school a distinct asset to the community of Pittsboro. He also recommended that the school be named after George Moses Horton, the distinguished slave poet of North Carolina, who, Hunter thought, was one of the most remarkable men ever produced by Chatham County. In his opinion such a distinction would help perpetuate the memory of slavery and the Old South and stimulate in black youth a desire to study the notable characters of their own race while giving them a sense of self-respect and race pride.[42]

But it appeared in 1924 that many of the "new Negroes" were neither proud of nor interested in the history of their progenitors as slaves, and in some instances they were attempting to erase it from the collective memory of their race. By the beginning of 1924 there was even an effort on the part of some younger blacks to do away with Emancipation Day celebrations. They thought that such occasions only served to remind whites that blacks were not far enough removed from slavery, nor sufficiently along in their training period as free citizens, to justify a full participation in affairs of state and national importance. Besides, most of the former slaves were dead, and those who were still alive had not benefited substantially from the rhetoric of annual orations and the parades and barbecues held on Emancipation Day. The younger generation contended that they had enough disabilities without being further hindered by the annual reminders of their slave ancestry.[43]

Hunter lasted a term at the Horton School, and by 1924 he was ready to move on. He was upset by the lack of a progressive spirit among the black residents of the town. Colin G. Shaw was sorry to see Hunter leave, but he explained, "The Negroes in Chatham County can be excused for their apathy towards better conditions, because they follow precepts and examples set before them by the superior race." Shaw only wished there were

# A Matter of Principle

more people of both races who, like Hunter, were willing to improve the conditions of their county and state. Hunter, who wanted to return to Raleigh, should have known that his chances were rather slim, because he had recently antagonized some very influential residents of the city. In 1923 he was still agitating for a new school for blacks in the section of Raleigh north of New Bern Avenue and east of Hargett Street. There was no facility for blacks in this area and children had to walk long distances to attend schools in the western section of the township. At the time Hunter renewed his proposal, a campaign was under way in Raleigh to pass a $1 million school bond issue. As in the past, he and others were led to believe that if the bond issue passed, they would get a school in the desired area. Consequently, they lobbied, campaigned, and voted for the measure.[44]

Whites again reneged on their promise when the bond issue passed, and they appropriated the entire amount for their own schools. Hunter protested this in a letter to Clarence Poe, who was a member of the Raleigh Township School Committee. He charged the committee with being insensitive to the needs of black children by denying them access to neighborhood schools. Hunter could not see how whites could justify themselves in "scooping in the entire million dollars," and in his opinion it was unjust, oppressive, and a gross wrong. Blacks were taxpayers and their property was yearly increasing, yet it seemed to Hunter as if the School Committee had adopted a policy of appropriating funds for the education of his race "in inverse ratio to the increase in Negro taxable values." Poe replied that the School Committee had lived up to its commitment. During the campaign blacks had been promised an additional school, which had already been built, and nothing was ever promised in the way of a school in the northeast section of Raleigh. In 1924 Hunter had the nerve to ask Poe to help him get a position in the Raleigh school system. Strangely enough, Poe obliged him, but the superintendent rejected his application because he did not have the proper certification.[45]

Hunter wanted to get back to Raleigh because it was close to the scene of events of major importance, and this was especially true in the summer of 1924, when he was once again infected with political fever. In evaluating the political situation in the state, he found the Democratic party in disrepute and vulnerable because of factional disputes and scandals. The lieutenant governor was under indictment for embezzling funds from his bank, and the former chairman of the State Democratic Executive Committee had to resign his office for a similar offense. The party whip also had left his office in disgrace after having been caught by the Raleigh police with his pants off in the bedroom of a black woman. Although some Democrats were willing literally to sleep with blacks, they still would not countenance any official political affiliation with them. Hunter nevertheless thought they were less obnoxious and antagonistic in their attitudes and actions toward blacks than were the Republicans who had rejected 100,000 blacks who could vote under "the unconstitutional constitutional amendment." To make matters worse, the lily-whites at their convention in 1924 nominated Isaac M. Meekins as their candidate for governor.[46]

Hunter and his friends never forgave Meekins for his strong defense of Linney and they planned to use this against him. In April 1924 Hunter asked Senator Overman for a copy of the confidential Linney hearings before the Senate Judiciary Committee. Overman was glad to provide Hunter with this information, because he probably knew that it would be used in ways that would benefit Democrats. Blacks did intend to discredit Meekins nationwide by now showing that he was the author of the Linney letter, and showing that his testimony before the Senate proved he was openly hostile to black Republicans. They also planned to use their influence to deprive lily-whites of any campaign funds from the Republican National Committee. Charles H. Moore informed Hunter that he had written friends who were close to William M. Butler, the chairman of the Republican National Committee, telling them not to pay any attention to the "high talk of Ike Meekins and his gang" about the favorable chances for a victory in the state. Moore thought the Republicans had as much chance of carrying North Carolina as a "snowball in torment," and that the National Committee should not waste its money in the state.[47]

Hunter's enthusiasm for state politics waned when he realized that in 1924 blacks in North Carolina were voters without a party, and this made them totally indifferent to the campaign. He eventually thought his political influence could best be used in the North among the thousands of black migrants from the South. These people, representing a large bloc of potential Republican voters, were also indifferent because of their effective isolation from the political process in the North. Hunter designed an ingenious plan for voter registration and education, which he presented to the chairman of the Republican National Committee. He hinted that the Democrats were scheming to capture the black vote in many of the northern and western states, and he urged the Republicans to do their utmost to counter this move.[48]

# A Matter of Principle

Hunter suggested that Republicans concentrate their efforts on recent migrants from the South. They should be personally contacted, instructed, registered, and monitored to make sure they voted the Republican ticket on election day. Hunter wanted to supervise this work in the North, and he offered his services to the Republican National Committee. He insisted that many blacks in the North knew him personally or by reputation, and because of this he would be very effective in New York, Boston, and New Jersey. Hunter succeeded in getting a number of blacks to endorse his proposal, and their letters of recommendation referred to him as a prominent black educator, a loyal and efficient Republican, and one of the few blacks who had been able to instill in his people the truth necessary to convince them of the value of Republican principles. He had also gained the dubious distinction of being one of the most "prominent race men" in North Carolina who had always taken the lead in matters of race uplift. Hunter even had the nerve to ask Gilliam T. Grissom, the collector of internal revenue for the Fourth North Carolina District, and one of the alleged authors of the infamous Linney letter, if he could use his name as a character reference. The chairman of the Republican National Committee was impressed with Hunter's plan, and he forwarded it to Colonel Roscoe C. Simmons, the director of the committee's Colored Bureau for action. Although Simmons wrote Hunter that he would like to have his services, nothing further came of the proposal. Hunter probably felt about the results as did his daughter, Eva, who wrote that she became doubtful of his chances of success upon learning that he "would have to reach the powers to be through a negro."[49]

Hunter was more than likely sincere in his desire for political work in the North, but he was also attempting to create an opportunity for financial gain because he clearly thought the Republican National Committee would pay for his services. He needed money and also wanted to get back to the North to resume his lectures on the race problem. He tried unsuccessfully to obtain free transportation by way of a railroad pass from the Southern Railroad. William H. Miller, the vice-president of the Southern, wanted to honor Hunter's request because of their long friendship and the respect he had obtained among the black and white citizens of Raleigh; however, he informed Hunter that he was forbidden by law from doing so.[50]

Thus Hunter was forced to remain in North Carolina and watch from the sidelines what he considered a rather lackluster campaign. According to him, the Democrats imported Senators Cole Blease and Pat Harrison in an attempt to inject some of the old-time pep and enthusiasm into the apathetic ranks of their party. A prominent Democrat later told him that the arguments of Blease and Harrison consisted of the same old racist stuff whites had been hearing for a half century and there was no excuse in bringing up such issues because they were not in any danger. In the general election, the Democrat Angus W. McLean defeated Meekins in the gubernatorial race, and Hunter was relieved to know that the governorship was again in the hands of one of the best white men. He had known the McLean family during his stay in Shoe Heel in the 1870s, and he was convinced that the governor-elect had inherited "high character and a sturdy purpose" from his noble ancestors. Congratulating McLean on his victory, Hunter informed him that he, although a black Republican, had supported his candidacy, and Hunter assured the incoming governor that blacks would give him the same support and affection that they gave to Aycock and Bickett.[51]

Hunter also congratulated Heriot Clarkson, who had just won a seat on the state Supreme Court. He wrote to Clarkson, "I also have to congratulate myself upon the opportunity it afforded me for breaking party bonds and paying my personal tribute by my vote to the high character of a North Carolina gentleman." He believed that this statement reflected the sentiments of thousands of sensible blacks in all parts of the state. As usual, Hunter was certain that the black masses joined with him in reelecting his old friend Benjamin R. Lacy as treasurer of North Carolina. In congratulating Lacy, Hunter took the occasion to recall their long friendship, which had always been characterized by trust, mutual confidence, and a similarity of interests. If a relationship of this type could exist on a personal basis, he asked, then why not between the races? He wrote to Lacy that if only the better and more sensible people of both races could realize they shared similar views and interests, "North Carolina will be the greatest, grandest, dearest spot on earth to us all."[52]

Prior to the election, a friend wrote Hunter from Washington, and urged him to vote for Coolidge, "a man from New England, a real man." Blacks would have nothing to fear from Coolidge, and his election would signal a positive change in the attitude of the Republican party toward lily-whitism. On the other hand, quite a few North Carolinians, many of whom were Democrats, hoped that the Republican party would become an all-white national organization. These people detected signs indicating that the Democratic party was becoming radicalized. They were particularly disturbed by the appearance of a liberal element, headed by Governor Alfred

# A Matter of Principle

E. Smith of New York, and the presence within the party of an increasing number of Catholics and Jews, only a few of whom were considered to be "real Americans." For example, the wealthy, influential Charles S. Bryan found many substantial men from Greensboro to New Bern who, because of their business interests, hoped that Coolidge would win the election, even though they dared not support him because of "the damned Negro." He thought that if the Republican party nationwide purged itself of all blacks, it would become the party of true conservatism and attract southerners who were "100% American." Following the election, he wrote that he intended to go to Washington and suggest to Coolidge that the Republican party "openly drop the Negro."[53]

The death of Henry Groves Connor, the United States judge from the Eastern District of North Carolina, gave Coolidge an opportunity to reveal his attitude toward the lily-whites of the state. Isaac M. Meekins wanted to replace Connor on the bench, and Hunter was determined that as a matter of principle this would not happen without a fight. He had also been told by many of the leading men in many sections of the state that if the president nominated Meekins it would invite a response similar to that encountered by Linney. They would protest this move by exposing Meekins's violent opposition to suffrage for blacks, and thereby place the president in an embarrassing situation. Charles H. Moore advised Hunter that any attempt on the part of blacks to block the nomination of Meekins would be an exercise in futility, for he was sure to have the backing of the Republican machinery of North Carolina, and Coolidge in "nine cases out of ten, if not ten" would be inclined to follow the recommendations of the state organization.[54]

This bit of advice failed to discourage Hunter, and he carried his protest straight to the White House and the Department of Justice. In letters to Coolidge and the attorney general, which were also published in the *Raleigh News and Observer*, he claimed that there were many eminent jurists in North Carolina who had a fine sense of legal ethics and would uphold the dignity of the court. Meekins was not one of them, and he hoped the president would forget about him and select a man who had the confidence, respect, and esteem of both races. Hunter insisted that Meekins was temperamentally unfit for any judicial office. Blacks could neither expect justice from him nor escape the influence of his prejudice in any court, especially when issues involved the enforcement of the Fourteenth and Fifteenth amendments. Meekins was also professionally unqualified for the bench. Having advocated the disfranchisment amendment containing a grandfather clause that was later declared unconstitutional by the Supreme Court of the United States, he showed an "utter and glaring ignorance which should summarily dispose" of his aspirations for a judgeship. Naturally Meekins was indicted for having admitted authoring the Linney letter, and Hunter wrote that the sinister intent of this document was so apparent and "disgustingly disgraceful" that the Democrats would not even touch it. If Coolidge ever received Hunter's lone protest, he ignored it and appointed Meekins to the vacancy.[55]

CHAPTER

# 11

## Unwept, Unhonored, and Unsung

In 1925 Hunter was hired as principal of a school in Wilson's Mills, a rural community in Johnston County. Within a year he had succeeded in getting a new school, and at the same time proved himself so objectionable that the black community recommended he be fired. Indeed, blacks claimed that they would not accept him as their principal under any circumstance. Hunter knew when he took the position that he would probably encounter some opposition because he could not please everyone. He reported that the school was in a sorry condition; students could not read, and many had been advanced to grades above their level of competency. He also sensed that there was an "undercurrent of nasty thoughts and nasty life" running through the school. Its pupils were "intractable, disorderly, heady, stubborn, rowdy, and disrespectful." To him, they were as "near a reversion to the original type" as he had ever seen. He believed that these conditions had not surfaced overnight but, rather, that they had been allowed to exist over time, and often with the encouragement of parents, some of whom were members of the School Committee. He thought that it was his duty to change these conditions; otherwise the school, instead of being a source of health, strength, and benefit to the community, would surely become "a menace, a breeder of vice and lawlessness, a source of moral corruption." To Hunter, black teachers had no higher mission than to check the spirit of insubordination and defiance among their students, and replace it with a sense of obedience to authority.[1]

When Hunter took the position at Wilson's Mills, he hoped that he would have the full support of the community's intelligent white businessmen who comprised the district's School Committee. He did not anticipate having to work with a subcommittee of blacks who had a great deal to say about the management of his school. His problem lay in the fact that he could never accept the idea of having his work supervised by blacks who, he surmised, were his intellectual inferiors. He thought the black School Committee contributed nothing toward the improvement of his school, because its members were ignorant of school law, courses of study, and the overall plans of the county superintendent. They continually harassed and lorded their positions over teachers and principals and kept them in a constant state of fear. Submitting his appraisal to Henry B. Marrow, the superintendent of public instruction for Johnston County, Hunter recommended the dissolution of the black subcommittee, whose members were "a hindrance and not a help. They are an incubus." He made these remarks after the black subcommittee had accused him of a general neglect of his duties as a teacher and of not paying enough attention to the educational advancement of their children. This charge deeply wounded his pride, and he believed that blacks had deliberately damaged his professional and personal reputation, especially in the eyes of whites. But then, he thought, "Negroes have no idea of the sacredness of character." Hunter tried to strengthen his position by bringing up the race issue. He confided to Marrow that some of the blacks of the community did not like to hear him speak well of whites, and they did not like to hear whites speak kindly of him. None of his strategy worked and, in the end, he was informed that it would be best to let the people of Wilson's Mills have a principal with whom they were willing to cooperate.[2]

Marrow later wrote that he found Hunter to be the best-educated black that had ever been employed in Johnston County, and that his only problem was he was too far advanced for the community. This was probably true, because Hunter, an urbane, egotistical elitist, was like a fish out of water in a rural environment. In fact Professor Marcus C. S. Noble of the School of Education at the University of North Carolina, had asked him, "How in the world does it happen that you are down at Wilson's Mills?" Although Marrow offered Hunter employment at another school in Johnston County, he advised Hunter that his talents could be best utilized in an urban setting.[3]

Hunter agreed, and he secured the influence of Benjamin R. Lacy to help him get a job in Raleigh. Lacy wrote to Hubbard F. Srygley, the Raleigh superintendent of schools, that he had known Hunter for a great many years and considered him an experienced educator of good character. In Lacy's opinion, Hunter "had done more than any Negro in North Carolina to allay all friction between the races," and he was sure that his employment in Raleigh would "give a good deal of pleasure to his white friends." Srygley was obviously not concerned with pleasing Hunter or his white friends. Hunter did not get a job, and this decision was probably influenced by the fact that he was once again involved in a controversy concerning a new school for blacks in Raleigh. In 1926 blacks had supported still another bond issue with the assurances that they would be granted an additional school. After the issue passed, whites agreed to build the school, but not in the location desired by blacks. The school would be erected on a barren strip of land adjacent to the city dump and a rock quarry filled with stagnant water.[4]

This decision was totally unacceptable to blacks, who saw it as part of a continuing scheme to humiliate and degrade their race. N. C. Newbold, the director of the Divison of Negro Education in the Department of Public Instruction, advised Hunter that the issue was a delicate one, which blacks should approach with a great deal of goodwill and patience. This time Raleigh's black citizens refused to follow Newbold's advice. For twenty years they had been agitating for a school in the northeast section, and had been patient, unobtrusive, and tried to adjust themselves to existing conditions, in the hopes that such an attitude would commend them to the white community. But this had not happened, as evidenced by the recent actions of the School Committee of Raleigh Township. Therefore it was time for blacks to register a solemn protest, and once again appeal to the conscience of the community's white Christians. Blacks could do nothing else because they had no voice and no vote in the selection of school committeemen and in the levying and expending of taxes. They could only hope that the School Committee would apply the acid test of the Golden Rule to the question of whether or not they would locate a building for white children on a site with the same features as the one selected for the black school.[5]

While the school controversy was in progress, Hunter received a job as teacher in the Manchester School in Cumberland County. Anne Chesnutt, the supervisor of colored schools, believed the county was very fortunate in having been able to acquire the services of Hunter, but she probably had second thoughts later. Within a month after accepting the position, Hunter had stirred up a hornet's nest. This time the issue was money. When Hunter took the job, he asked for a contract but was told that contracts were not awarded by the superintendent of schools. He later managed to obtain one that omitted his salary, but he signed it anyway under the assumption that he would be paid according to the state schedule. However, when he received his first pay, he found it was $55, which was $22 less than the minimum amount per month specified by the state. This meant chaos for Hunter, who was consistently in financial trouble. Hunter wrote to N. C. Newbold that it was "a burning shame and an outrage that we Negro teachers have been treated so unjustly. I have been robbed of $22.00 per month." As a victim of discrimination he decided to conduct a personal investigation of the Cumberland County schools. He found out that although the county received monies from the State Equalization Fund, it had not adopted the state salary schedule for teachers, that the superintendent of schools, B. F. McBryde, paid teachers less than the amount specified in his budget to the county commissioners, and that he had budgeted for four teachers for the Manchester School, but hired only three. Additionally, Hunter alleged that black schools were not allocated any funds for incidental expenses, and their physical facilities were disgraceful. At the Manchester School, there was not a single desk, nor were there seats enough for students. The few seats that were available were dilapidated ones that had been discarded by white schools.[6]

Hunter presented his findings to the director of Negro education in the office of the state superintendent of public instruction. He also contacted an attorney and contemplated bringing suit against the Cumberland County School Board to force it to adopt the state salary schedule. He wrote, "If I can do nothing else I can expose the gross injustice inflicted upon me and upon the Negro teachers of the county." He was aware that his case would have the effects of a class-action suit, and that all black teachers would benefit by a favorable decision. But this was clearly not his intent. In a bit of selfish reasoning, he thought that because no other black teachers were presenting any claims, and if Cumberland County really wanted to save money, it could pay him according to the salary schedule and forget about the other educators of his race.[7]

The director of finance in the office of the superintendent of public instruction investigated Hunter's complaint and determined that his charges were either without basis or fell within the prerogative of local school boards. Arch T. Allen, the superintendent of public instruction, wrote Hunter that he deeply regretted the fact that Cumberland County did not pay its black teachers according to the state salary schedule, but this too was a matter of local control. However, under a recent equalization law, Cumberland County would in the future receive a proportionate reduction in the monies from the State Equalization Fund if it did not pay blacks according to the state schedule.[8]

Hunter took time out from his fight with the Cumberland County schools to do a little "politicking" in Raleigh. In February 1927 he assured Samuel A. Ashe that blacks were no longer a political factor, and that they were devoting their time to moral, educational, business, and religious activities. Yet within a matter of weeks, he was involved in municipal politics in his hometown. Other blacks were still politically active, and since 1925 those in Raleigh had decided to increase their voting strength with each election, and become a "force and factor." In 1927 they conducted a massive voter-registration drive, and Hunter and a majority of the leading blacks supported the incumbent city administration. Hunter also offered to assist personally in the campaigns of Ed G. Birdsong, the commissioner of public safety, and Wiley G. Barnes, a judge of the city court. Hunter was on the opposite side of his friend Josephus Daniels, who wanted to oust the incumbents. Daniels injected the race issue into the contest, accusing the city administration of being in collusion with blacks. According to Hunter, Daniels used his *News and Observer* to make "a most bitter appeal to the passions and prejudices of whites, invoking the archaic war cries of a half century ago. . . . It was Nigger, Nigger, Nigger." The paper also warned of an impending era of black political domination, the end of white supremacy, and a return to the terrible days of Reconstruction and "Russellism."[9]

The incumbent administration was returned to office by a substantial margin as whites rejected Daniels's racist appeals. Hunter was pleased, and he saw in the results of the election indications that intelligent whites could no longer be aroused by the racists' "war-hoops." But he was also disturbed and dismayed over Daniels's role in the election. In a letter to the editor of the *Norfolk Journal and Guide*, while openly acknowledging his friendship for Daniels, he wrote that he could not understand why the "honorable Josephus Daniels would have lent himself and the influence of his great paper to a cause that was obviously detrimental to the public good and so destructive of the amicable relations between the races."[10]

Hunter lasted one school term in Cumberland County, and the school authorities were probably relieved to see him get out of town. By now his age was another factor against him in his efforts to gain employment. He was well past his seventy-fifth year. Many of his old contacts had died, and the younger generation of both races did not know him personally or by reputation. In 1927 he applied for a job in Siler City, and was turned down on the grounds that the children were very hard to manage, and had little regard for old people. Hunter rejected this explanation, and he informed Tod R. Edwards, a member of the local School Committee, that the problem was not with the children but the community. If the School Committee and the parents could not manage their children, "I think the school needs a man just about my age," wrote Hunter to Edwards. He also suggested that an educational institution with such an intractable group of students was a "pest, a disease, a breeder of lawlessness, a promoter of evil, a destroyer of the young, and not a helpful influence," and that the best thing the community could do would be to set fire to the school and send all the children to the reformatory. Despite these caustic remarks, Edwards offered to assist him in finding employment in another location. Hunter refused, remarking, "It may well be that I am not too old to make a job for myself and that will be better." He found employment as principal of the Laurel Hill School in Lumber Bridge in Robeson County. Hunter was obviously effective, because he was told by the superintendent that he had laid the foundations for "some good work" and would be employed for a second term.[11]

During the remainder of his life, Hunter also spent considerable time trying to put together a history of his race in North Carolina. For years he had been collecting material on this subject, and he thought it was time to make it available to the general public. White scholars in the state knew Hunter possessed a wealth of information on black history, and on occasions had asked for material for their own purposes. They also were aware of the fact that Hunter was either an eyewitness of or a participant in many of the major events that affected his race, and as such he was a valuable source of knowledge. For example, in 1922 N. C. Newbold asked Hunter to provide him information and assistance in his study on the "Historical Beginnings of Negro Education in North Carolina." A similar request came in 1925 from Professor Marcus C. S. Noble of the University of North Carolina. Requesting materials relating to education during Reconstrucion, Noble also wanted Hunter's personal impressions, which were "just as valuable from a historical point of view as anything documentary." Noble later wrote that Hunter provided him with valuable assistance in the form of some very interesting and useful information. Hunter informed his friends with pride of the services he had rendered to Noble, and he seemingly rejoiced over the idea of having something that whites wanted. A friend from New York wrote him that she was happy to know "you have them

Unwept, Unhonored, and Unsung

falling at your feet." Yet she wondered why whites did not ask Hunter to prepare studies himself, and thereby give him an opportunity to "sign his name to his brains" and receive full credit for preserving the history of his race.[12]

Whites did encourage and support Hunter in his historical activities, and this was especially true of Fred A. Olds and Samuel A. Ashe. Olds, the collector for the Hall of History of the North Carolina Historical Commission, thought that Hunter was a man of fairness and ability who was well informed about the history of his race. In 1925 he unsuccessfully tried to persuade Richard H. Edmonds, the editor of the *Manufacturer's Record*, to publish a series of articles by Hunter on the progress of the black race in North Carolina. Olds also asked him for ideas and materials for his own work. In 1926 he was interested in the black convention of 1865, which he thought had offered "some fine resolutions regarding the white home folks." When he found out that Hunter had the proceedings of that convention, Olds suggested that they be printed by the State Historical Commission and made available to libraries and educational institutions throughout the country. Olds also recommended that Hunter include in his publications references to the convention or that he publish its complete record.[13]

Hunter had been intermittently preaching for decades that the actions of blacks at their first convention had set the tone for race relations in the state. He was glad that some whites had finally discovered this and were beginning to agree with him. He was also pleased to see that southern whites were starting to give serious attention to the scientific study of blacks. In 1927 he thought they were the only whites in the nation who were doing this, because "The Northern white people are no longer interested in the Negro as a citizen."[14]

The interest shown by whites in his work strengthened Hunter's conviction that his historical studies could be used to serve the cause of better race relations. He intended to write a folk history of blacks in North Carolina, based upon the testimony of those with firsthand experience of slavery. For years he had collected material along this line from a number of sources, including former Governors Vance and Fowle and Dr. Kemp P. Battle. He had also travelled across the state conducting interviews with many blacks concerning their experiences as slaves. His evidence showed that slavery was an abominable institution that was revolting in many of its features. There were "oppressive masters, heartless overseers, crushing laws, and the merciless lash." He thought these factors caused many to believe that slavery was the sum total of all iniquities, and slaveholders had "no human instincts, no feeling of sympathy, no kindly promptings," and they were totally devoid of any spirit of Christianity.[15]

Yet Hunter contended that there was another side to slavery and his interviews further convinced him that the institution was not all bad. He was deeply touched by the absence of any spirit of bitterness, and with the fact that both races spoke of the kind feelings that existed between whites and blacks during the antebellum period. He thought this was the side most often omitted in writings about slavery, especially those done by abolitionists who could not see any good in the peculiar institution. "We have had enough of these views," he wrote to Olds; "let us now in the later years recall some of the happy contacts and resulting good." He maintained that a balanced history of slavery in North Carolina should stress the friendly interpersonal relationships and the tender attachments between the races. He asserted that blacks and whites did love each other. He asked, "How could the nurse help loving the child entrusted to her care or the mistress her faithful maid, or the children the loving dear old mammy?" He still could not see that these relationships were of a superior-subordinate nature and took place within an institution of enforced human bondage. Neither did he understand that the child who suckled at the breast of the black woman, and the children who loved old mammy, would one day claim them as property.[16]

To prove that slavery was not a totally brutalizing experience, Hunter cited the fact that it had produced "the most intelligent, the most highly civilized, the most progressive, the most prosperous, the most promising community of blacks to be found anywhere on the face of the earth." Slaves constantly imitated and observed their owners, and because of this, Hunter claimed that the best hope and the brightest promise for his race rested in American blacks, who had internalized the value systems, ideals, and institutions of whites. Above all, they had received from whites the Christian religion, which had been the "sheet anchor, the heart and soul" of the splendid devlopment of their race. With such ideas it was relatively easy for Hunter to conclude that "slavery was God's providence" for the redemption of the black race. Hunter in 1927 had resurrected the old proslavery argument of antebellum days![17]

In an attempt to make the past serve the needs of the present, Hunter in 1927 published an account of the black convention of 1865. He prefaced it with a lengthy statement on race relations in which he saw the cause of prejudice as the result of a mutual misunderstaning between the races, rather than any inherent antagonism. "This misunderstanding should be cleared up, the chasm should be bridged. . . . We are too far apart." The races had to understand that their destinies and interests intersected at many points, and that the things that tended to hinder or help the progess of blacks would have a reflexive influence on the white community. Hunter also tended to dismiss the idea, which was gaining some popularity in the 1920s, of blacks having a separate cultural identity. He claimed that blacks in any community absorbed and reflected the same interests, character, and culture of the whites among whom they lived. This was true both in the days of slavery and immediately after emancipation, and nowhere could it be better seen than in the attitudes set forth at the first state convention of blacks. On that historic occasion, blacks invited whites to join with them to perpetuate and strengthen the kind attachments formed in slavery and to assist them in becoming moral and useful citizens. Fred A. Olds thought Hunter's article was in "capital taste," and he hoped that it would be absorbed by the younger generations of both races and bring forth fruit. Like Hunter, Olds was convinced that race relations in North Carolina were better than in any other state.[18]

Dr. Charles A. Dunston, a prominent black dentist of Raleigh, was so impressed with Hunter's article that he wished it could be printed in every newspaper. He wanted the people of both races and their posterity to know that black men in 1865 realized the true basis of race relations and had the courage to express their convictions. Dunston had read the article to some of his friends, and none was aware of the convention. He believed that blacks would never know of the many things of importance to them until they had their own histories, and he thanked Hunter for his efforts to provide his race with a knowledge of its past. "If it were not for men like you," he wrote, "much that we as a race should know, would be lost. With your vast storehouse of knowledge you would be doing the race an everlasting good and certainly a great honor" to write its history.[19]

In the fall of 1927 Hunter published his "Review of Negro Life in North Carolina with My Recollections." This pamphlet contained only thirty-four pages and sold for twenty-five cents a copy. Hunter claimed that his publication was designed to stimulate interest in the history of blacks, promote the cause of friendly race relations, and generate revenues for a continuation of his historical work. He hoped eventually to publish a volume or a series of periodicals on the progress of the black race in North Carolina. He wanted to recapture the social and institutional history of his race because blacks needed to know their sources, antiquity, and achievements. Hunter asked all blacks to join with him in making his project a success, for "The greatest service we can render to the race in North Carolina would be to devote the remaining years of our lives to the research, investigation, and compilation of the facts of our race life."[20]

Hunter sent complimentary copies of his publication to a number of persons, including Ashe, Olds, and Governor McLean. He later wrote that the response was generally favorable, but mostly on the part of white people. The black community did not seem to be overly interested in his brand of history or his "Recollections." This disappointed him because he thought that although he could get whites to finance his work, he should have some evidence of support from the black community. He suggested that this could possibly be generated if Dunston would sponsor a public testimonial in his honor commemorating his half century of service as an educator. This proposal may have been intended as a promotional scheme for his pamphlet, but it also reflected Hunter's desire for a wider recognition of his talents and service. He asked Dunston, "Why wait until one is dead, until he is passed beyond the influence, the help, the inspiration of kind words, appreciating sentiments, flowers and eulogy, to make the manifestation." It would be infinitely better for people to show their appreciation for a person while he was still alive to stimulate him to greater deeds.[21]

When the testimonial did not materialize, Hunter decided to promote his pamphlet with the assistance of his white friends. He confided to Fred A. Olds that his chief support always came from the white people of the state, and "when rightly approached they are ready and willing to do their part." Samuel A. Ashe, who had encouraged him to publish his pamphlet, promised to use his influence to promote it because the vast majority of whites approved of what he was trying to do. It seems as if he and Ashe had a mutual admiration for each other. Ashe praised Hunter's work and provided him with advice and technical assistance. In turn, Hunter believed that Ashe was greatly loved by whites and blacks and was an honor to the state. Like himself, Ashe was also a "connecting link between the Old and New South." Ashe reviewed Hunter's pamphlet and recommended it in the *Raleigh Times*. Ashe hoped the general public would support the author's plan to publish a regular periodical on black life in North Carolina. He insisted that the periodical would help regenerate the good feelings that once existed between the two races, and that Hunter was "well qualified by virtue of his education, information, sentiments, and disposition to do it admirably."[22]

Hunter also asked Olds to endorse his publication in the Raleigh press, hoping that such would call attention to his work and attract the support of both races. Olds promised to do this, and he saw no reason why Hunter's pamphlet should not appeal to everyone. He liked his style and methodological approach, and thought that a study of black history based on oral testimony was just as important as one derived from printed sources. Olds also advised him to send his pamphlet to the literary editors of northern newspapers, because many people in the North were interested in his work and would be willing to help him. Hunter's publication eventually found its way into the hands of people in Florida, Maine, Maryland, Massachusetts, Pennsylvania, Texas, and Virginia. The State Library of North Carolina, the Library of the University of Pennsylvania, the American Library in Paris, and the American Antiquarian Society also obtained copies of his "Recollections." Occasionally a few whites from outside the state encouraged him in his work and commented on his pamphlet. From Baltimore, a former North Carolinian and descendant of a large slaveholding family, Bruce Cotten, wrote that he approved of Hunter's efforts to save from oblivion the lives and character of the many "noble and splendid Negroes who have lived, worked, and died in our Old North State." Henry E. Litchford, the chief executive of the Union Bank and Trust Company of Richmond, Virginia, was another former resident of the state who approved of Hunter's historical endeavors. He sent a small donation to further the cause along with the notation, "You must know Chas. that you are one of the many people in Raleigh for whom I entertain the highest regard. I am especially appreciable for what you have tried to do for your Race and Raleigh."[23]

But kind words, small donations, and even smaller revenues from the sale of Hunter's pamphlet were not enough to sustain the costs of additional publications. In 1929 he wrote to Carter G. Woodson, the director of the Association for the Study of Negro Life and History, and asked for financial assistance. He informed Woodson that he was the only black who possessed much of the data concerning the history of his race in North Carolina, and "unless I make use of it, it will be lost forever." This and other attempts to secure funding failed, but for the rest of his life he still hoped to write his history of blacks in North Carolina. In 1931, the year of his death, he wrote to E. E. Smith that the idea "has become my one obsession."[24]

One reason why black North Carolinians did not support Hunter's historical work was that it seems that some were not proud of their slave ancestry and were desperately trying to escape that part of their past. Hunter, who knew this, admitted that some blacks were not only ashamed of the history of their race as slaves, but were even ashamed of their parents who had been slaves. Not only this, but blacks were also relinquishing their enthusiasm for Emancipation Day celebrations. Hunter was disappointed at the diminished size of the crowd at the Raleigh celebration in 1927 and was disturbed when the reading of the Emancipation Proclamation was omitted from the program. He thought "it was like a play of Hamlet with Hamlet left out." When he asked the black school principals of the city why the proclamation was not read, he was told that the slave experience in North Carolina was a humiliating one, and that black children should not be taught or constantly reminded that their forefathers were slaves. Of this he wrote, "I was utterly disgusted, I am not proud of having been a slave, but I certainly am not ashamed of it."[25]

The reading of the Emancipation Proclamation was also omitted from the celebration in 1928, and instead, Professor William S. Turner, the dean of Shaw University, gave an interpretation of that document. He insisted that Lincoln was not motivated by any spirit of benevolence when he issued the proclamation, and that it was merely for the purposes of adding idealism to the Union cause and furthering the war effort. Turner also thought the proclamation was an unconstitutional edict issued in the expectation that it would create a black insurrection behind enemy lines. But the scheme backfired. There was no slave rebellion or terrorism by southern blacks, and they deserved a lot of credit for having the courage, morality, and decency to refuse freedom on Lincoln's terms. Slaves were eventually freed by the Thirteenth Amendment, and Turner hinted that even this did not do the job. It only relieved blacks from bondage, but they were far from free.[26]

Hunter was shocked by this novel interpretation of the Emancipation Proclamation. Although he regarded Turner as "one of the most valuable men of his race and usually a keen thinker," his argument was ill conceived, illogical, and filled with erroneous assumptions. According to Hunter, Lincoln did have the constitutional authority to issue the proclamation by virtue of his supreme powers as wartime commander in chief, and there had never been any court decisions questioning this matter. At the time of Lee's surrender, and certainly after the adoption of the Thirteenth Amendment, all slaves in the South were legally free. Hunter explained that the Thirteenth Amendment only amplified the Emancipation Proclamation by extending it to all of the states of the Union. If Raleigh's blacks accepted Turner's interpretation, it would place them in the category of "ungrateful beneficiaries of one of the grandest acts of moral heroism and Christian exultation that brighten the pages of the World's history." As for himself, he proclaimed, "I do love Abraham Lincoln. I revere the Proclamation of Emancipation." Turner dismissed any further argument by claiming that his interpretation was shared by Charles A. Beard, David S. Muzzey, and Carter G. Woodson, and if Hunter wished to pursue the matter further, it would be with these historians. Further, he thought that if the old timers wanted to assemble every New Year's Day to read the Emancipation Proclamation and eat barbecue dinners, it was their business. The younger generation of blacks in Raleigh insisted upon following their own methods in their search for political and social values.[27]

Turner's critique might have been an act of historical revisionism, but it was more than likely part of a continuing campaign by some blacks to complete the divorce proceedings between their race and the Republican party. To do this they had to discredit Lincoln, the omnipotent symbol of Republicanism, in order to wean blacks away from the Grand Old Party. To the masses, Honest Abe was a deity who was worshiped for having issued the fiat of freedom for their race. They had never questioned his motives or racial attitudes, and they truly believed that he was a great humanitarian who was filled with love for blacks. Every four years, many of those who could vote performed a sacrificial rite to Lincoln by offering up their votes to the national Republican party. However, when it began to sanction a lily-white policy, many of the leading blacks in North Carolina edged closer to the national Democratic party. At their Emancipation Day celebration in 1928, the blacks of Raleigh again proclaimed their break with the Republican party. Announcing their political independence they resolved that "The Negro has no future and can never have any as a political partisan."[28]

In the last presidential election of his lifetime, Hunter, like other black voters in North Carolina, was caught in the middle of a triangle composed of pro-Smith Democrats, anti-Smith Democrats, and Republicans. In July 1928 he presented his analysis of the political situation, along with his recommendation for a Republican victory in the state, to Hubert C. Work, the chairman of the Republican National Executive Committee. Hunter thought the Republicans had a good chance of winning the state's electoral vote because the Democrats were badly divided. He predicted that thousands of Democrats in North Carolina who resented the nomination of Alfred E. Smith would either vote for Herbert Hoover or refrain from casting their ballots for any presidential candidate. In such an event, the 100,000 blacks who could qualify to vote under the "unconstitutional constitutional amendment" could swing the election in North Carolina in favor of the Republicans if the party would only abandon its lily-white policy.[29]

Hunter alleged that blacks in North Carolina, although inclined to vote the Republican ticket, were for the moment neutral. Apathetic, they took little interest in politics because they had been ostracized and alienated by lily-whites. The few blacks who had regularly voted generally supported some Democrat for state office. However, he thought that if the Republican National Committee would appoint a black campaign manager "to conduct an energetic and intensive, but quiet canvass of black voters" in the state, the majority would at least support the party's national ticket. But "This is about as far as most would go." Hunter sent his letter to Work through his friend John R. Hawkins, a former North Carolinian, and chairman of the Colored Voters' Division of the Republican National Committee. Hawkins later informed him that the state chairman of the Republican party had an excellent organization in North Carolina, and he was confident of success.[30]

Hunter, disappointed, also edged toward the uncommitted camp. The campaign of 1928 was a particularly bitter affair in North Carolina, mainly fought over the issues of prohibition and religion. However, both parties vigorously exploited racial themes in a manner reminiscent of the campaigns of 1868 and 1898. Hunter was disturbed over the effect this would have on the course of race relations, and he was again vindicated in his contention that a lot of racial antagonism was generated by politicians. But at the same time he could also see that his recent praise of the friendly race relations in North Carolina was not based on facts. Hunter wrote a lengthy article, "What Shall the Negro Do?" to allay race friction and point out the "ridiculousness of the revival of the Negro issue." He frantically appealed to whites not to be taken in by "attempts to resurrect and rejuvenate the ancient bugaboo of Nigger." There was a time when the war cry of "Nigger" was an effective means of winning elections, and Democratic politicians needed no other argument to ensure victory. But Hunter wanted whites to remember that, along with success at the polls and the disfranchisement of his race, the cry of "Nigger" also produced "a crop of wild, reckless, violent spirits such at Tillman, Blease, Vardaman, Heflin, *et id omne genus*" and inflamed racial passions, prejudices, and antagonisms.[31]

With all of its injustices Hunter still believed the unconstitutional disfranchisement of blacks had helped emancipate his people by freeing them from partisan politics, which had taken so much of their time and energy. They then began to realize that true freedom rested in their moral, mental, and material advancement, and abandoned the political field. For nearly fifty years they had been passive and quiescent and seemed to have lost all interest in politics. Moreover, blacks had accepted the fact and thought it was best for whites to be in full control of all levels of government. The few blacks who were interested in politics were not concerned with office holding, but with important issues such as taxation, improved educational facilities, equal protection under the laws, and good government.[32]

Hunter alleged that since disfranchisement, race relations, although not ideal, had steadily improved, and the animosity that whites had for blacks was gradually giving way to a revitalized Christian conscience. Then too, a new generation of progressive whites had emerged, who were working in close cooperation with black leaders to improve the state's prosperity. Hunter explained that politicians, by invoking the cries of black domination, social equality, and white supremacy, were asking whites to reverse their liberal and progressive impulses, and "do homage to the weird whinings of the ghost of an obsolete and defunct past." To him, the white politician lagging behind the progressive element of his race was still under the impression that thinking, intelligent, and self-reliant whites could be scared and frightened by the "Nigger" scarecrow. These old-style politicians were actually "presuming upon the stupidity and insulting the intelligence" of whites, and Hunter noted that an increasing number of southern Democrats were "surfeited and disgusted with such stuff."[33]

Hunter sent his article to the *New York Herald Tribune*, the *New York World*, and the *Raleigh Times*. The New York papers refused to touch it, and Robert L. Gray, the editor of the *Times*, thought that it would be unwise to publish it in his paper. Though he fully agreed with Hunter's viewpoints, it was his firm opinion that the "danger of a revival of the Negro issue in this campaign is such that it is the part of wisdom to say the least possible about it until the necessity arrives."[34]

## Unwept, Unhonored, and Unsung

The necessity was there because Furnifold M. Simmons, the leader of the anti-Smith faction of the Democratic party, still thought that a campaign of hate was effective in winning elections. Advertised as the "General of the White Supremacy Campaigns of 1898 and 1900," Simmons recounted in speeches and radio broadcasts the evil influence of blacks in politics, and the role that he and Aycock played in their disfranchisement. He claimed that he did this for the benefit of the younger generation of whites who were not aware of the terrorism associated with black domination. He also flooded the state with vicious propaganda attacking Smith's religious beliefs and his alleged liberality to blacks. Politicians and preachers were brought into the state from other areas to join the fight against Smith, including a full-time lecturer of the Ku Klux Klan. Amos C. Duncan, the Grand Dragon of the North Carolina Klan, published letters urging Klansmen to give their full support to defeat Smith. Indeed, Simmons's campaign tactics were so bad that the editor of the *News and Observer* thought they would surely damage the Democratic party.[35]

Hunter believed that the Klan and others who were opposed to Smith attacked him for allegedly appointing 5,000 blacks to positions in New York, and for being the "High Priest" of social equality who encouraged the mingling of the races in cabarets, hotels, and nightclubs. They also claimed that it was Smith's avowed purpose to appoint a black to his cabinet if elected. Conversely, Smith Democrats pointed to Herbert Hoover as the "Arch Apostle" of social equality, and claimed that he had issued an order abolishing segregation in offices under his control. Because of this, white women and black men were forced to work at the same desks, sit at the same tables, use the same toilets, and "perconsequence mate in Holy wedlock."[36]

Willis G. Briggs, one of Hunter's white friends in Raleigh, wrote him that hate and prejudice never produced the real solution to any question, and that the literature circulated during the campaign was enough to "sicken and disgust decent people." But Hunter did not seem to think that it bothered the majority of blacks in North Carolina, who were neither concerned nor distressed over the turmoils of politicians and parties. Indeed, he claimed, "In the midst of the strife the Negro sits high upon the fence, with legs crossed, and smokes his cigarette in joyful complacency." However, as election day neared, blacks awoke from their political lethargy and became interested in the campaign. Yet they were somewhat confused over the issues, and in Hunter's words, "they are all at sea and were looking for leadership." Hunter could understand this situation because black leaders throughout the nation were giving their race conflicting advice. Bishops Reverdy C. Ranson and George G. Clement told blacks that their best hope rested in Alfred E. Smith. Hunter thought that some blacks would support Smith because of his liberal racial views, and also because the Democrats in St. Louis, Missouri, had nominated a black candidate for Congress. On the other hand, Kelly Miller and others advised blacks to support Hoover on the sole issue of prohibition. Republicans in Chicago had also nominated a black for Congress. Then there was W. E. B. DuBois, who urged blacks to vote for the Socialist candidate for president. To make matters worse, a number of leading men in various locales were telling backs to pursue independent courses in national politics and to support those state and local candidates who offered the best chances for good government.[37]

The Negro Republican Executive Committee of North Carolina was the only statewide political organization to which blacks could appeal for advice. From across the state they asked the committee to hold a convention for the purposes of discussing the issues and developing a policy statement for the guidance of voters. Hunter was still secretary of the Executive Committee, but he was reluctant to call a convention for fear that blacks would not adopt a "sensible course." He also probably knew that he would not be able to influence or control the thinking of any large gathering of blacks. A statewide meeting under the auspices of the Negro Republican Executive Committee would tend to indicate that the masses of blacks were still wedded to the Republican party. Pending any conference or convention, Hunter drafted an address to the black voters, which he thought charted a proper course and offered an impregnable position against any possible attack from whites who were becoming increasingly concerned over the attitude of black voters.[38]

Hunter reminded blacks that they had been peacefully submissive and unobtrusive long enough. It was inconceivable that they should remain indifferent and "supinely inert" in a great national upheaval that vitally involved their rights, and he tried to assure them that they would not get into any trouble by voting. They would only be exercising their right and performing their duties as citizens. Hunter reviewed the various issues of the campaign as they affected his race, but his argument was heavily weighted against Republicans, especially the lily-whites whom he accused of trying to set up an organization that was more proscriptive against blacks than the Democrats. Hunter alleged that northern Republicans had even been led to believe that blacks were "an incubus and the only drawback in breaking the Solid South," and they were hoping that dry Democrats would bolt their party and join in the formation of a "respectable party in the South made up of whites only."[39]

Hunter saw the campaign of 1928 as one full of abnormalities. Both political parties were in a period of crisis and transition, party lines everywhere were crumbling, and a new political alignment seemed inevitable. He predicted that when the election was over, there would be a readjustment and recasting of party policies. In the meantime, he advised blacks to refrain from any precipitate judgment or rash action, and to give careful consideration in casting their ballots. If they needed advice, Hunter urged them to "seek the counsel of the best white people" in their respective communities, who would gladly respond to their requests. "Never mind the political demagogue whose very existence depends upon race hatred. He is, let us hope, nearing his finality."[40]

Hunter probably hoped his conservative address would ease the way for the resurgence of black voters, who might be given some degree of official recognition by the Democratic party. Furnifold M. Simmons thought that this had already happened, and in October 1928 he accused Smith Democrats of having taken the unprecedented step of registering blacks and organizing them into Democratic clubs in Wake and Forsyth counties. Smith Democrats naturally denied this, retorting with the charge that Simmons was really a "black Republican" who had recently been invited to join that party by "a worthless, cunning and shrewd Negro." Even though Simmons thought that everyone in the state knew this was a lie, he was forced to make a public statement denying the charge.[41]

In the election of 1928 the Democrats were successful in electing their slate of state officers, but the Republican, Herbert Hoover, won a majority of the votes cast for president in North Carolina. Whites had not changed their party but had selectively divided their votes. Approximately three months after Hoover's inauguration, those whites who had claimed that he was the "Arch Apostle of social equality" had reason to believe they were right. When Mrs. Hoover entertained the wives of congressmen at a tea in the White House the party included Mrs. Oscar DePriest, the wife of the newly elected black representative from Illinois and the only member of his race in Congress.

Hunter's niece-in-law, Jennie Hunter, thought that if Mrs. Hoover was entertaining the wives of congressmen, the only decent thing for her to do was to invite Mrs. DePriest, and the only courteous thing for the latter to do was to accept the invitation. To Jennie, any interpretation to the contrary was "much ado about nothing." However, this simple act had repercussions in the Tarheel State and further increased racial tensions. The two major newspapers of Raleigh thought Mrs. Hoover's action and the president's silence regarding this incident were insults to the South that would only serve to stimulate the black appetite for social equality. The *Raleigh Times* read into the incident the danger that blacks in North Carolina would fall under the influence of Congressman DePriest and accept him as their national leader.[42]

The *News and Observer* was equally disturbed, and its editor dusted off and reprinted the speech that Aycock made to blacks at their fair in 1901. The editor alleged that Aycock was the "most respected white man among blacks in life and death," and that he had warned them against any attempts at social equality. In so doing, he had voiced the "best sentiment of the best men of both races. . . . Anything that tends to disturb the conditions he set forth is regrettable and dangerous." The paper asked everyone to reread Aycock's speech, because it was especially pertinent in 1929 when the wife of a black congressman was entertained at a White House tea in the midst of two score white women.[43]

The DePriest affair was further agitated when the *Carolina Times*, a black newspaper published in Durham, announced that Mrs. Hoover's actions met with the approval of the majority of blacks North and South. The paper used the occasion to correct some serious misunderstandings prevalent among whites. For one thing, whites believed there was a divergence of opinion among northern and southern blacks concerning issues vital to their race. This simply was not true, and there was no difference in the "soul burnings, desires, hopes, nor aims" of the black race. All blacks desired equal justice, opportunity, and citizenship. However, there was a difference in the way in which southern blacks expresssed their opposition and resentment toward injustices. Conditions in the South made public rhetoric less vocal and bitter, but underneath southern blacks were more virulent in their opposition than their northern brothers. The greatest misunderstanding of whites was their belief that the blacks in their midst were happy and content. Not so, said the *Carolina Times*. These blacks were really "creatures of the hypocritical smile, of feigned goodwill, of hatred hidden by fawning."[44]

This was disturbing news for whites and more so in view of the fact that it originated from Durham, the land of pacified and satisfied blacks. The editor of the *Raleigh Times* charged that the Durham article not only was an ill-conceived threat, but painted a sinister picture of race relations. Furthermore, it was indeed upsetting for whites to know that the southern black "bides his time while he whets his knife" and still harbors notions that the "wartime amendments may yet be put into effect in the South that has made their nullification a religion." Whites were alerted to the inherent dangers in such talk, but the editor of the *Raleigh Times* thought they could still be optimistic and hopeful that the masses of blacks were self-respecting, hardworking, and contented individuals who had accepted their place in the social order. The response of North Carolinians to the DePriest controversy was significant because it showed that despite the machinations of interracial conferences and committees, and the claims of the best men to the contrary, the racial attitudes of many whites had not progressed to any appreciable degree in the twentieth century. They still believed that race relations were best when blacks remained happily content in their separate and subordinate position in society.[45]

Surprisingly, Hunter made no public statement about the DePriest incident, possibly because he did not want to incur the disfavor of whites. He needed their support and cooperation if he were to succeed in the last major project of his life. In 1929 he was trying to resuscitate the Negro State Fair, which was on the verge of extinction. In 1926 and 1927 the event did not take place because whites deprived blacks of the use of the Raleigh fairgrounds. The state then withdrew its annual appropriation to the North Carolina Industrial Association on the grounds that it did not hold its fair. Hunter was also upset over what he thought was a declining interest in the fair on the part of the state's leading black men. In the summer of 1928 he met with a committee of blacks to discuss the situation, and it was agreed to continue the fair as a separate event for their race to be held on the state fairgrounds the week after the state fair for whites. It was also decided that the conduct of the black fair should be under the auspices of a board of directors who would be appointed by the governor on the recommendation of the general manager of the white state fair.[46]

Henry P. Cheatham, the president of the NCIA, and Judge Wiley G. Barnes then called on Governor McLean to enlist his support in reviving the black fair. They found the governor receptive to the idea and somewhat disturbed to learn that the NCIA had lost its appropriation. He told Cheatham and Barnes that the state had provided its citizens with a fair-

## Unwept, Unhonored, and Unsung

ground, and $200,000 had been set aside for buildings and maintenance; "The $500 heretofore given is very little and can afford you little relief." McLean promised to contact the Board of Directors of the state fair immediately, and work out a plan for financial support because blacks were entitled to any benefits the state could bestow.[47]

Hunter was delighted over the idea of a black fair managed by a board of directors appointed by whites and partially funded by the state. Along with his desire to see the black fair continue, he also saw a new chance for permanent employment in Raleigh. He wrote to Fred A. Olds that if the governor could get the appropriation restored, "it would present an opportunity to me for the speedy completion of my Historical Sketches provided I can secure election as Secretary of the Fair. It would be an all time job." He asked Olds's help in accomplishing this goal. Olds, associated with the first fair for whites in North Carolina, appreciated Hunter's work in providing a similar activity for blacks. He wrote him that he was sure that Governor McLean would "fix matters all right." The crafty old Hunter then engineered a plan to displace the management of the NCIA. He suggested to J. Melville Broughton, the senator from Wake County and chairman of the Senate Judiciary Committee, to look into the operations of the NCIA because it "needed a thorough shaking up and cleaning out." He alleged that for many years the organization had been corrupt and was nothing more than "an exploitation run as the private business of one man." It had so discredited itself that reputable blacks were no longer willing to give it their support. He maintained that he had tried unsuccessfully for the past two years to rescue the enterprise from the clutches of private individuals, and restore to it the high purposes for which it was originally founded. He suggested to the senator that the Board of Directors of the North Carolina State Fair take over the management and supervision of the black fair.[48]

In 1929 the NCIA decided not to hold its fair because whites once again denied blacks the use of the state fairgrounds. The following year Hunter successfully persuaded the organization to return to its original purposes and accept the challenge of using its own resources to stage a fair. The association unanimously elected him executive secretary with authority to proceed immediately with plans for the fair. Hunter claimed that he accepted the position with the distinct reservation that "if after consultation with a number of our white citizens the undertaking gave promise of success," he would continue. If not, he would tender his immediate resignation. He did not get the full-time position that he hoped for but had made a step in that direction. He successfully petitioned whites for the use of their fairgrounds, and the black fair was held in 1930 under his management.[49]

Hunter also tried to get the annual state appropriation to the NCIA reinstated. Although aware that the state funded the white fair in the amount of $200,000, blacks did not ask for a proportionate share of monies. Instead, Hunter petitioned the legislature requesting that the $500 annual appropriation be restored retroactively from the year 1925. Hunter's past successes in dealing with whites made him confident that they would approve the petition because it bore the imprint of his signature. He confided to Representative Rayford B. Whitley of Wake County that he had been before the General Assembly on four previous occasions asking for appropriations, and in each instance his request was granted. He was sure that Whitley and the other legislators, particularly those from Wake County, would give the petition their favorable consideration, for "our people ask but little" and "we do not get much."[50]

In somewhat stronger terms, Hunter asked John W. Hinsdale, the senator from Wake County, to lend his influence and assistance in restoring to the NCIA its annual appropriation. He wrote Hinsdale, "I want you white people who can help me and our people in this State to do so. . . . I was born and raised among you and am one of you. . . ." However, the whites who made up the General Assembly thought differently. Following an interview with state authorities, Hunter reported to the Executive Committee of the NCIA on 17 June 1931 that there was no prospect of an appropriation for the black fair. The NCIA then decided to hold its 1931 fair in conjunction with the Wake County Negro Fair, but this event did not materialize. Hunter became sick in the summer of 1931 and died on 4 September of that year. A month later the *News and Observer* reported that there would be no black fair. "Professor Hunter's death put a stop to the arrangements."[51]

Three months before his death, Hunter was still pleading for closer relations between the races, and persisting in his contention that this was an absolute prerequisite for the progresss of blacks. In a letter to Dr. Joseph L. Peacock upon his retirement as president of Shaw University, Hunter wrote, "I feel that we are slipping backward just in proportion as we lose contact with white people. Our life is growing wild, rowdy, reckless, savage." He gave no indication of just where or among whom he observed these retrogressive tendencies, but he did claim that he had met some success in

## Unwept, Unhonored, and Unsung

checking them, especially when he could attract the attention, interest, and active cooperation of whites.[52]

It was ironic that Hunter's obituary mentioned only that he was a prominent educational leader. It said nothing about his untiring efforts to promote racial justice and friendly race relations. But in death Hunter fulfilled the prophecy of his friend Charles H. Moore. In 1923 Moore wrote Hunter that nothing worthwhile in the way of friendly race relations could be permanently gained by trying to smother the truth to enhance one's selfish and personal interests at the sacrifice of a whole race's happiness and welfare. In words applicable to Hunter, Moore predicted that the man who attempts to do such a thing "will in the course of time pass away, unwept, unhonored and unsung even by those whose whims and prejudices he catered to serve."[53]

# Conclusion

Hunter's personal experiences in slavery, and his friendly relationships with a select group of former slave-holders after emancipation, skewed his thinking on race relations and led him to his obsessive conclusion that North Carolina's race problem would be solved by the white men of his generation. Nothing could have been further from the truth. Shortly after his death, a survey was made of the racial attitudes of county officials and their perceptions of the place of blacks in North Carolina. The people surveyed were middle-aged or elderly men located in various parts of the state. These were the leading whites who were closest to the masses of blacks, and their responses show that the majority had no idea of ever giving them equality or justice. All respondents agreed that blacks were racially inferior to whites, 54.1 percent believed that blacks should have no education or none beyond the seventh grade, 77.8 percent were opposed to black suffrage, and approximately one-eighth thought that blacks should not own land. Wiley B. Saunders, the compiler of the survey, concluded that the roots of prejudices against blacks "reaches back immeasurably into the past," and the respondents were in fact "victims of the race prejudices of their ancestors." He also noted that from an abstract or intellectual standpoint, whites agreed that in a Christian and democratic country blacks should have equality. But they also acknowledged that equality for blacks would destroy the structure of their own civilization and society. Thus, when faced with the dilemma of sacrificing their civilization or their principles, whites were perfectly willing to choose the latter course.[1]

Hunter suspected that whites were caught up in this situation, and he

# Conclusion

understood that their treatment of his race ran counter to Christian ethics and the principles of the American liberal and democratic traditions. Although not based on logic or the realities of his own experiences in North Carolina, he was convinced that the inherent goodness of whites would eventually force them to correct all racial injustices. In the meantime he helped prick their conscience by constantly reminding them, in terms that they could not reasonably deny, of the discontinuity between their professed beliefs and their actions. In so doing he helped establish a tradition of passive and respectful protest against race prejudice and discrimination.

Hunter was correct in his conviction that blacks could not afford to take an activist and militant stance against racial injustices, and that if they wanted to remain in the state they would have to accommodate themselves to the dominant white society. There was nothing wrong with being an accommodationist. It was not heroic, but it was a realistic approach to race relations, and a way for blacks to prosper in North Carolina. However, Hunter and the leading men who thought and acted like him can be and were eventually censured for their fanatical acceptance of their subordinate position, and for repeatedly extolling the virtues of the race that had forced them into that status. At times Hunter and the leading men overplayed the role of an accommodationist. Their advocacy of disfranchisement, their incessant denials of any desires for social equality, their denunciation of black politicians, and their frequent pronouncements on the undesirable features of the black community at large would have been better left unsaid. It is questionable whether these more than momentarily enhanced their status. They did nothing to improve the image of their race and only served to reinforce the basic prejudices of whites.

Even though Hunter's life was characterized by a coexistence of contradictory tendencies, he did help to improve the condition of his race. When the faint hope of equality faded with Reconstruction, his administrative and organizing skills were important factors in helping to develop the institutional life of the black community. His ability as a journalist and his access to the press enabled him occasionally to publicize in meaningful terms the goals and progress of his race, along with the disabilities it suffered at the hands of white society. This and his personal contacts with whites helped keep lines of communication open between the races. Hunter was right in advocating that blacks should use their own resources and work to improve themselves mentally, morally, and materially, but he was wrong in recom-

# Conclusion

mending that they voluntarily divorce themselves from politics. The evidence shows that the black community in North Carolina prospered and fared best when its political power was the greatest.

Hunter also played a part in sustaining the myth of superior race relations in North Carolina, and that the state was the best place for blacks. This was not true, and he occasionally admitted as much. The idea of leaving North Carolina was never far from his mind. But there is another way of looking at myths. The French syndicalist Georges Sorel noted that most myths contain a utopian element not based on the reality of past events. Rather, they express a vision of the future and prepare people for a struggle that would destroy the existing order. If Hunter and the others who nurtured the myth that race relations were better in North Carolina than anywhere else thought as did Sorel then their myth had validity.[2]

Three decades after Hunter's death, the movement to destroy the existing order erupted in North Carolina, but it was not as he had envisioned. The civil rights movement of the 1960s was not initiated by the elders who, Hunter thought, would properly chart the course of race relations, but by the youth, who realized that the methods of past generations of blacks to bring about racial justice had not worked. Rejecting the tactics of their forefathers as well as their desires for civil peace, these youths made a direct assault on the more overt and obnoxious manifestations of segregation and discrimination. With the possible exception of a few old-line accommodationists, the youth-inspired revolt enjoyed the popular support of almost the entire black community, and herein may lie the greatest legacy of Hunter and the other leading men. They were never really locked into total acceptance of their inferior civil and political status. They publicized their oppression, pleaded in vain for equality and justice, and kindled a resistance movement that psychologically prepared the masses to rally around the black revolution of the 1960s. The substantive changes that did occur in race relations were not the result of any magnanimity on the part of the good white men that Hunter had predicted. Change was instead brought about by outside forces. Although the commitment to the ideology of white supremacy was very much a part of the mentality of the leadership of North Carolina, the state, just as was the case during Reconstruction, was forced to accommodate itself to the superior power of the federal government and alter its pattern of race relations.

# Notes

## Preface

1. Hunter to Albert L. Cox and Brother, 29 December 1919; Hunter to Sherman Miles, 25 May 1925; Hunter to Jacob F. Chur, 27 May 1867, Hunter Papers.
2. *State Journal*, 10 April 1914; *Raleigh Times*, 27 December 1913, Hunter Scrapbook 1891–1911; Hunter to C. A. Ashby, 30 May 1919, Hunter Papers.
3. Drake and Cayton, *Black Metropolis*, pp. 390–91.
4. Logan, *The Negro in North Carolina*, p. viii; Woodward, *American Counterpoint*, pp. 239–40.
5. Woodward, "The Antislavery Myth," pp. 325–26; Geyl, *Use and Abuse of History*, pp. 56, 76; Olson, *Myth, Symbol, and Reality*, pp. 5, 30–31; Chafe, *Civilities and Civil Rights*, pp. 6–10.

## Chapter 1

1. There is conflicting information concerning Hunter's age. He either did not know exactly when he was born or he misrepresented his age at various times. In 1889 he gave his age as thirty-seven years old, in 1910 he stated that he was fifty-six years old, and his obituary in the *Raleigh News and Observer* on 5 September 1931 stated that he was born a slave "over 80 years ago." A 1978 pamphlet published by the North Carolina Museum of History gives the inclusive dates of Hunter's life as 1851–1931. Charles N. Hunter to H. W. Shaffer, 26 July 1889; "An Examination for Wake County Teachers," 12 November 1910; Hunter, "Story of a Check, Dated October 27, 1913"; *Raleigh Gazette*, 10

October 1891, Hunter Scrapbook 1902–27, Hunter Papers; Crow and Winters, *The Black Presence in North Carolina*, p. 5.

2. Hunter to Ernest Haywood, 10 November 1920; Hunter, "Story of a Check, Dated 27 October 1913"; *Raleigh Times*, 27 September 1921, Hunter Scrapbook 1887–1929, Hunter Papers.

3. Hunter, "Story of a Check, Dated October 27, 1913"; Hunter to C. A. Ashby, 30 May 1919; *Haywood School Register*, October 1922, Hunter Scrapbook 1902–29; Hunter to Hubert Haywood, 10 September 1928, Hunter Papers.

4. Hunter to C. A. Ashby, 30 May 1919; Hunter to Ernest Haywood, 18 October 1920; Hunter to Hubert Haywood, 10 September 1928; Hunter to Jannis G. Trapin, 27 April 1931, Hunter Papers.

5. Hunter to Ernest Haywood, 10 November 1929, Hunter Papers.

6. *Raleigh Times*, 20 June 1916, Hunter Scrapbook 1891–1911, Hunter Papers.

7. Mary Ellen Hedrick to B. S. Hedrick, 12 May 1865, Hedrick Papers; Vance, *Speech Delivered in the Senate of the United States on the Negro Question*.

8. *The Land We Love* 6 (February 1869):305; Jonathan Worth to S. Whitaker, 15 September 1865, in Hamilton, *Correspondence of Jonathan Worth*, 1:417, 421–22.

9. Don MacRae to Hugh MacRae, 4 September 1865, MacRae Papers; Olsen and McGrew, "Prelude to Reconstruction," p. 47.

10. Nathan O'Berry to Mina Weil, 20 April 1928, Weil Papers.

11. *Nation*, 28 September 1865, p. 395; 2 November 1865, p. 559; 9 November 1865, p. 585.

12. Rippy, *F. M. Simmons*, p. 5; *Nation*, 2 November 1865, p. 557; E. J. Thompson to B. S. Hedrick, 24 June 1866, Hedrick Papers.

13. E. J. Thompson to B. S. Hedrick, 24 June 1866, Hedrick Papers; *Raleigh Daily Record*, 19 September 1867; *Nation*, 2 November 1865, p. 557; Andrews, *The South since the War*, p. 177.

14. Reid, *After the War*, pp. 44–45; *Nation*, 21 September 1865, p. 366; 28 September 1865, p. 396; 2 November 1865, pp. 557–58; 9 November 1865, p. 585.

15. John A. Hedrick to B. S. Hedrick, 13 June 1865, Hedrick Papers; Don MacRae to Hugh MacRae, 4 September 1865, MacRae Papers; *Nation*, 21 September 1865, p. 368; 12 October 1865, p. 457; Andrews, *The South since the War*, p. 178.

16. *Nation*, 28 September 1865, p. 396.

17. James, *Annual Report of the Superintendent of Negro Affairs*, pp. 3–4.

18. Ibid., pp. 44–46.

19. Ibid., pp. 45–47, 54–59; Payne to B. S. Hedrick, 20 June 1865, Hedrick Papers.

20. *Raleigh Daily Record*, 13 June 1865.

21. Ibid., 1 June 1865.

22. *Nation*, 21 September 1865, pp. 367–68; 28 September 1865, p. 396; Reid, *After the War*, pp. 51–52.
23. Hunter to Editor of the *Ossippee Valley News*, 7 July 1882, Hunter Scrapbook 1900–1924, Hunter Papers.
24. Reid, *After the War*, p. 50; Moore, *To the Voters of Wake County*, 12 September 1865; *Raleigh Semi-Weekly Record*, 2 September 1865; *Journal of Freedom*, 21 October 1865; *Nation*, 5 October 1865, p. 427.
25. *Raleigh Semi-Weekly Record*, 2 September 1865.
26. *Nation*, 19 October 1865, p. 492; *Greensboro Daily News*, 24 July 1932; Raper, *Holden*, p. 74; McKitrick, *Andrew Johnson*, pp. 7–9.
27. *Christian Recorder*, 28 October 1865; Jones, "An Opportunity Lost," pp. 47–48.
28. *Nation*, 19 October 1865, p. 493; Andrews, *The South since the War*, p. 120.
29. *Christian Recorder*, 28 October 1865; Hunter, "An Appeal for Friendly Race Relations," *Fayetteville Observer*, 31 January 1927; Hunter, "The Position of the Negro," *Raleigh Gazette*, 23 April 1892, Hunter Scrapbook, 1891–1911, Hunter Papers; Jonathan Worth to B. G. Worth, 11 September 1865, in Hamilton, *Correspondence of Jonathan Worth*, 1:417.
30. *Christian Recorder*, 28 October 1865.
31. Ibid.; Olds, "First Convention of Negroes in North Carolina," 1:142; Ashe, *History of North Carolina*, 2:1027.
32. Hunter, "The Position of the Negro," *Raleigh Gazette*, 23 April 1892, Hunter Scrapbook 1891–1911; Hunter, "Does the Negro Seek Social Equality? [ca. 1921]," Hunter Papers; Hunter, "An Appeal for Friendly Race Relations," *Fayetteville Observer*, 31 January 1927.
33. *Journal of Freedom*, 30 September 1865; *Christian Recorder*, 28 October 1865.
34. *Nation*, 26 October 1865, p. 526; Andrews, *The South since the War*, pp. 157, 177.
35. Olds, "First Convention of Negroes in North Carolina," 1:142; Hamilton, *Reconstruction in North Carolina*, p. 526.
36. *Nation*, 26 October 1865, p. 526; *Christian Recorder*, 28 October 1865; *Raleigh Signal*, 19 August 1888; Andrews, *The South since the War*, p. 154.
37. Browning, "The North Carolina Black Code," pp. 461–73; U.S. Congress, House, H. Doc. 118, 39th Cong., 1st sess., 1866; Phillips, *Remarks in the House of Commons, January 1866*; Miller, "Samuel F. Phillips," pp. 269–70; Hamilton, *Reconstruction in North Carolina*, pp. 172–77.
38. Whitener, "Public Education in North Carolina," p. 73; *Nation*, 5 October 1865, p. 482; Hunter, "St. Augustine Protestant Episcopal Church," Undated Papers, Hunter Papers.
39. Hunter to Editor of the *Ossippee Valley News*, 17 July 1882, Hunter Scrapbook 1900–1924; Hunter to J. L. Peacock, 6 June 1931, Hunter Papers.
40. *Minutes of the Freedmen's Convention of October 1866*.

41. Ibid.
42. Ibid.
43. Hunter to Editor of the *New National Era*, n.d., Hunter Scrapbook 1866–74, Hunter Papers; Hunter, "The Position of the Negro," *Raleigh Gazette*, 23 April 1892.
44. Harris, *Speech Delivered before the Grant and Wilson Ratification Meeting, June 26, 1872*, in Busbee Scrapbooks, 2:88.
45. Undated Manuscript, Hunter Papers.
46. Jacob F. Chur to Hunter, 27 May 1869, 6 April 1870; Hunter to G. A. Edwards, 15 February 1927, Hunter Papers.
47. W. W. Holden to S. A. Ashe, 6 December 1881, in *Raleigh News and Observer*, 9 December 1881.
48. Mary Ellen Hedrick to dear Husband [B. S. Hedrick], 15 May 1867; Perrin Busbee to Prof. Hedrick, 8 January 1866, Hedrick Papers; *Minutes of the Freedmen's Convention of October 1866*; "Petition to the Congress of the United States of America," 8 July 1867, Harris Papers; Harris, "W. W. Holden," p. 364.
49. *Raleigh Daily Progress*, 19 September 1867, Hunter Scrapbook 1896–1921, Hunter Papers; *Christian Recorder*, 19 August 1865; "Charter to Establish a State Grand Council of the Union League in Raleigh," 26 March 1867, Harris Papers; Jonathan Worth to Thomas Ruffin, 29 March 1867, in Hamilton, *Correspondence of Jonathan Worth*, 2:923–24; Perrin Busbee to B. S. Hedrick, 8 January 1866, Hedrick Papers; "The Duty of the Republican Party towards One of Its Most Faithful and Trusted Leaders,"23 April 1874, Busbee Scrapbooks, 1:923–25.
50. Edmunds to Harris, 26 March 1867, Harris Papers; W. C. Ken to B. S. Hedrick, 27 March 1867, Hedrick Papers; *Raleigh Weekly Republican*, 29 June 1867; Worth to Thomas Ruffin, 29 March 1867,in Hamilton, *Correspondence of Jonathan Worth*, 2:923–25; Raper, *Holden*, pp. 91–96.
51. Mary Ellen Hedrick to dear Husband [B. S. Hedrick], 7 June 1867, Hedrick Papers; Raper, *Holden*, p. 94.
52. Perrin Busbee to B. S. Hedrick, 8 January 1866, Hedrick Papers; *Raleigh Republican*, 30 November 1867, Hunter Scrapbook 1867–1928, Hunter Papers; *Raleigh Daily Progress*, 4 January 1868.
53. Wilson to Harris, 8 November 1867, Hunter Scrapbook 1867, Hunter Papers.
54. *Journal of the Constitutional Convention of the State of North Carolina at Its Session of 1868*, pp. 162–75, 216, 473; Noble, *History of the Public Schools of North Carolina*, pp. 286–87; Hoffman, "The Republican Party in North Carolina," p. 51.
55. Worth to Hedrick, 2 June 1868, Hedrick Papers.
56. Chur to Hunter, 27 May 1869; Hunter to Chur, 21 October 1869, Hunter to S. A. Ashe, 9 February 1927, Hunter Papers.

57. Hunter, "Manuscript Prepared for the *New National Era*," 24 April 1872, Hunter Papers.

58. Hamilton, *Reconstruction in North Carolina*, p. 453; *Raleigh News and Observer*, 30 October 1920; [Holden], *Memoirs of W. W. Holden*, pp. 139–41; *North Carolina Standard*, 18 August 1869; "Testimony of John W. Long in State v. Thomas W. Gray; Testimony of William Tickel in State v. Wm. Rowe et al.; Testimony of Sandy Sellars, James E. Boyd, and John A. Moore in State v. William Andrews et al.," Ku Klux Klan Papers; U.S. Congress, Senate, *Senate Report 693*, 1:398–400.

59. Hunter to Chur, 21 October 1869, Hunter Papers.

60. U.S. Congress, *Senate Report 693*, 1:146–47.

61. Ibid.

62. Hunter, "Manuscript Prepared for the *New National Era*," 24 April 1872; Hunter, "Some of the Evils of Reconstruction"; Hunter, Undated Manuscript, Hunter Papers.

63. Hunter, "Manuscript Prepared for the *New National Era*," 24 April 1872; Hunter, Undated Manuscript, Hunter Papers.

64. Ex-Senator John Pool, "The Convention in North Carolina," *Republic* 4 (May 1875): 157–65.

# Chapter 2

1. *North Carolina Standard*, 25 June 1869; Hunter to the *North Carolina Standard*, 25 June 1869; Hunter to Chur, 5 July 1869, Hunter Papers; *North Carolina Daily Standard*, 7 July 1869.

2. *Raleigh Weekly Telegram*, 8 July 1871.

3. Pike, *Address at the Celebration of Emancipation Day*, pp. 1–2; *North Carolina Daily Standard*, 4 January 1871.

4. Hunter to Sumner, 22 December 1871; Sumner to Dear Sir, 29 December 1871; Moore to Messrs Friday Jones and Others, 1 January 1872, Hunter Papers.

5. *Raleigh Weekly Republican*, 29 June 1871; *A Mistake Somewhere*, Hunter Scrapbook 1866–74, Hunter Papers.

6. *The Blasting Powder*, 10 July 1872; Harris, *Speech Delivered before the Grant and Wilson Ratification Meeting, June 26, 1872*, Busbee Scrapbooks, 2:88.

7. Hunter to the Editor of the *New National Era*, 24 April 1872, Hunter Papers.

8. Ibid.

9. Hunter to S. A. Ashe, 9 February 1927, Hunter Papers.

10. *Daily Crescent*, 29 March 1874; Hunter, *A Card to the Voters of the Eastern Ward*, 17 April 1874, Hunter Papers.

11. Hunter, *A Card to the Voters of the Eastern Ward*, 17 April 1874, Hunter Papers.

12. Hunter to S. A. Ashe, 9 February 1927; Hunter to F. L. Meritt, 19 December 1898, Hunter Papers.

13. J. A. Gladd to Hunter, 30 September 1871; Undated Manuscript by Hunter for the *Banner of Temperance*, Hunter Scrapbook 1866–74, Hunter Papers.

14. Undated Newspaper Clippings, Hunter Scrapbook 1866–74, Hunter Papers.

15. "Petition to the Right Worthy Grand Lodge of North America, June 1873," Hunter Papers; *Raleigh Weekly Era*, 26 June 1873.

16. Hunter, "Speech to Members of the Queen of the South Lodge, Grand Order of Good Templars, May 31, 1873," Hunter Papers.

17. Hoyle, *The Negro Question and the I.O.G.T.*, pp. 22–23.

18. Ibid., pp. 15–23; *Monthly Elevator*, April 1877, Hunter Scrapbook 1875–1924, Hunter Papers.

19. Olson, *The Logic of Collective Action*, pp. 60–61.

20. *Raleigh Weekly Era*, n.d., Hunter Scrapbook 1886–1921, Hunter Papers; Hunter to Holden, 28 May 1873, in *Raleigh Weekly Era*, 5 June 1873.

21. Friday Jones, *A Card*, 1 May 1873, Busbee Scrapbooks, 1:13.

22. *Weekly Republican*, 2 June 1874.

23. "The Civil Rights Bill and Public Schools," *Our Living and Our Dead*, 1:93–94; *Report [1877] of the Board of Directors and Superintendent of the Insane Asylum*.

24. *Raleigh Sentinel*, quoted in *Charlotte Weekly News*, 15 January 1870, Busbee Scrapbooks, 3:103; *Congressional Record*, 2:565.

25. *House Journal of the North Carolina General Assembly. Session of 1873–74*, p. 296.

26. Hunter to the Editor of the *New National Era*, 24 April 1872; *New National Era*, June 1874, Hunter Scrapbook 1866–74, Hunter Papers.

27. Hunter to the Editor of the *New National Era* [1874], Hunter Scrapbook 1866–74, Hunter Papers.

28. *Raleigh Weekly Republican*, 13 June 1874.

29. Dollard, *Caste and Class in a Southern Town*, p. 255; Litwack, *Been in the Storm So Long*, p. x.

30. Hunter to the Editor of the *New National Era* [1874], Hunter Scrapbook 1866–74, Hunter Papers.

31. *New National Era*, 1874, Hunter Scrapbook 1866–74, Hunter Papers; "Protest. An Address to the People of North Carolina by the Republican Members of the Late Constitution Convention [1875]," Busbee Scrapbooks, 2:263.

32. Richard T. Greener to My dear Prof., 12 September 1874; Hunter to W. R. Davis, 9 November 1875; Hunter to Brodie, 7 March 1876; Hunter to J. C. Pritchard, 21 April 1902; Hyman to Hunter, 14 July 1875, Hunter Papers.

33. Brandon, "Carpetbaggers in North Carolina," p. 76; Balanoff, "Negro Legislators," p. 35; Noble, *History of the Public Education of North Carolina*, pp. 290–91.

34. *Tri-Weekly Era*, 10 April 1873.

35. *First Annual Catalogue and Circular of the Biddle Memorial Institute*; *Raleigh News and Observer*, 27 October 1919.

36. O. Hunter, *Essay*, pp. 6–8; Knight, *Public School Education in North Carolina*, pp. 257–58.

37. Hunter, *Review of Negro Life in North Carolina*, pp. 18–24.

38. Hunter to Holden, 25 March 1876, Hunter Papers.

39. Ibid.

40. *Tri-Weekly Era*, 4 April 1876, Hunter Scrapbook 1875–1924, Hunter Papers.

41. *Wide Awake*, 26 September 1876.

42. Hunter to J. C. Scarborough, 7 April 1877; *Monthly Elevator*, April 1877, Hunter Scrapbook 1875–1924, Hunter Papers.

43. *House Resolution 58. North Carolina General Assembly*, p. 411; Logan, "The Movement of Negroes from North Carolina," pp. 45–46.

44. *Raleigh Observer*, 28 December 1876; *Raleigh News and Observer*, 3 January 1877.

45. Hunter to Scarborough, 7 April 1877; Hunter, "Letter from North Carolina," 30 March 1877, Hunter Scrapbook 1866–74, Hunter Papers.

46. *Monthly Elevator*, April, May 1877, Hunter Scrapbook 1875–1924, Hunter Papers.

47. *Raleigh Register*, 20 September 1877; *Session Laws and Resolutions of the General Assembly, 1876–77*, pp. 589–90.

48. *New York Times*, quoted in *Raleigh Register*, 28 October 1877; *Proceedings of the State Convention of Colored Citizens, October 1877*, pp. 4–5; Norfleet, "The Convention of Colored Men a Great Mistake," Hunter Scrapbook 1866–74, Hunter Papers.

49. *Proceedings of the State Convention of Colored Citizens, October 1877*, pp.6–13.

50. Ibid.

51. *Raleigh Weekly Observer*, 8 January 1878; *New York Times*, 2 January 1878.

52. *Raleigh Register*, 31 January 1878; U.S. Congress, *Senate Report 693*, 1:405.

53. Johnson, "The Ideology of White Supremacy," pp. 149–50.

54. *Raleigh News and Observer*, 27 October 1919.

55. "An Act to Incorporate the North Carolina Industrial Association," 14 March 1879; "Constitution of the North Carolina Industrial Association," 1879, Hunter Papers.

56. Polk to O. Hunter, 8 April 1879, Hunter Papers; *Journal of Industry*, April 1879; Osborne Hunter to Vance, 11 June 1879, Vance Papers.

57. *Journal of Industry*, April 1879.
58. Ibid.; *Raleigh News and Observer*, 27 October 1919.
59. Executive Committee of the North Carolina Industrial Association, "Announcement to the Colored People, 1897," Hunter Scrapbook, 1879–83, Hunter Papers.
60. Hunter to L. L. Gravely, 5 February 1931, Hunter Papers.
61. *Journal of Industry*, 19 November 1879; *Raleigh Signal*, 23 September 1880.
62. Taylor, "The Great Migration from North Carolina in 1879," pp. 20–31.
63. U.S. Congress, *Senate Report 693*, 1:xiv–xvii, 107, 285–97, 303, 313, 401–5, 423–33.
64. Ibid., 1:285, 299, 397–410.
65. Ibid., 1: 49–70, 101–132.
66. Ibid., 1:viii, xv–xvii.

# Chapter 3

1. *Raleigh Times*, 2 January 1880.
2. "Mr. Otey's Oration," Manuscript in Hunter Papers; *Raleigh News*, 2 January 1880; *Raleigh Observer*, 2 January 1880; Taylor, "The Great Migration from North Carolina in 1879," p. 29.
3. *Raleigh Signal*, 21 January 1880; Logan, "The Movement of Negroes from North Carolina," pp. 46–47.
4. "Frederick Douglass' Speech at 2d Fair of Colored Persons of North Carolina, October 1, 1880," Hunter Papers. The original manuscript of the speech was presented to Hunter.
5. Ibid.; *Indianapolis Sentinel*, cited in *Fayetteville Examiner*, 14 October 1880.
6. *Raleigh News and Observer*, 2 October 1880.
7. *Raleigh Register*, 22 October; 19 November 1884.
8. *Raleigh Signal*, 21 January 1880.
9. *The Banner* [1881], Hunter Scrapbook 1886–1921, Hunter Papers; *Wilmington Post*, 12 February 1882.
10. [Holden], *Memoirs of W. W. Holden*, p. 179; *Banner* [1881], Hunter Scrapbook 1886–1921, Hunter Papers.
11. *Raleigh News and Observer*, 21 September 1881; *Goldsboro Enterprise*, 16 February 1881, Hunter Scrapbook 1888–1905, Hunter Papers; *Wilmington Post*, 22 January 1882.
12. *Wilmington Post*, 12 February 1882.

13. Ibid., 2, 9 April 1882; *Ossippee Valley News*, 7 July 1882, Hunter Scrapbook 1900–1924, Hunter Papers.

14. *Wilmington Post*, 6, 13 November; 18 December 1881.

15. *Journal of the Fourth Annual Meeting of the North Carolina State Teachers' Association*, pp. 17–31.

16. *Ossippee Valley News*, 7 July 1882, Hunter Scrapbook 1900–1924, Hunter Papers.

17. Logan, "The Legal Status of Public School Education for Negroes," p. 348; Noble, *A History of Public Schools in North Carolina*, p. 407; *Smithfield Herald*, 25 January 1883; *Clinton Caucasian*, n.d.; *State Press*, n.d.; *Newton Enterprise*, n.d.; *Charlotte Home Democrat*, n.d.; *Asheville Citizen*, n.d., Hunter Scrapbook 1883, Hunter Papers.

18. *Statesville American*, 30 June 1884, Hunter Scrapbook 1900–1924; Hunter, "Education in North Carolina," Hunter Papers.

19. *Journal of the Fourth Annual Meeting of the North Carolina State Teachers' Association*, p. 25; Puitt v. Gaston County County Commissioners, 94 NC 709 (1886); Riggsbee v. Town of Durham, 94 NC 800 (1886); Hunter, "Education in North Carolina," Hunter Papers.

20. Hunter to Dear Sir, n.d., Hunter Papers. This letter was written to Senator Zebulon B. Vance and it describes some of his activities while governor of North Carolina. At that time Vance was the only member of the Senate who had also been governor of North Carolina.

21. Ibid.; *Journal of the Fourth Annual Meeting of the North Carolina State Teachers' Association*, pp. 8–11; *Outlook*, 15 January 1887, Hunter Scrapbook 1887–1928, Hunter Papers.

22. Bingham, *"The New South,"* pp. 13–15.

23. Finger, *Educational and Religious Interests of the Colored People of the South*.

24. *Afro-American Presbyterian*, 9 July 1885, Hunter Scrapbook 1887–1928, Hunter Papers; Logan, "The Movement to Establish a State Supported College for Negroes," p. 167.

25. Aptheker, *A Documentary History of the Negro*, 2:191–94.

26. *Outlook*, 25 February 1887, Hunter Scrapbook 1885–1929, Hunter Papers; Logan, "The Movement to Establish a State Supported College for Negroes," p. 168.

27. Buxton, *Address Delivered on Thursday November 15, 1883*, Hunter Scrapbook 1883, Hunter Papers.

28. *Raleigh Register*, 27 August 1884.

29. *Wilmington Messenger*, 14 July 1888.

30. *Raleigh Register*, 15, 22 October 1884.

31. Ibid., 22 October 1884.

32. Hunter, "Interview, New York Sun," n.d., Hunter Papers. This document was written between the time of Cleveland's election on 6 November 1884 and his inaugural on 4 March 1885.
33. Hunter to the Postmaster General of the United States, 15 August 1889; Henry Edward Brown to Hunter, 11 April 1885; Notice of Applicant's Standing—Special Examiner Pension Office, 18 August 1884; Robert D. Graham to Hunter, 20 September 1884, Hunter Papers.
34. Hunter to Albert L. Cox and Brother, 29 December 1919; Hunter to Willis B. Crawford, 19 November 1921; *Enfield Progress*, 5 August 1887, Hunter Scrapbook 1888–1905, Hunter Papers; Hunter to Clarence Poe, 11 March 1924, Aycock Papers.
35. *Enfield Progress*, 5 August 1887, Hunter Scrapbook 1888–1905; *Goldsboro Argus*, 26 February 1886; 16 October, 11 November 1887, Hunter Scrapbook 1887–1929, Hunter Papers; Hunter to Poe, 11 March 1924, Aycock Papers; Orr, *Charles Brantley Aycock*, p. 77.
36. *Enfield Progress*, 5, 12 August 1887, Hunter Scrapbook 1888–1905, Hunter Papers.
37. Ed to Hunter, 18 January 1887; Osborne Hunter to Hunter, 18 November 1887; Hunter, "A Great White Southerner's Tribute to a Great Negro," 1919, Hunter Papers; *Durham Daily Recorder*, 4 November 1887.
38. Hunter, "Some of the Evils of Reconstruction" [1887]; Hunter to F. L. Meritt, 19 December 1898, Hunter Papers; *Raleigh News and Observer*, 13 January 1904.
39. Hunter, "Some of the Evils of Reconstruction," Hunter Papers.
40. Ibid.; Hunter to the Editor of the *Southern Christian Recorder*, n.d., Hunter Papers.
41. *Detroit Plaindealer*, 27 January 1888; *New York Freeman*, 21 January 1888; *Cleveland Gazette*, n.d., Hunter Scrapbook 1888–1905, Hunter Papers.
42. *Southern Christian Recorder*, 2 March 1888, Hunter Scrapbook 1888–1905, Hunter Papers; *Raleigh News and Observer*, 13 January 1904.
43. *Raleigh Signal*, 9 February; 14 June; 5 July; 8 September 1888.
44. Ibid., 19 January; 9 February; 16 June 1888.
45. *State Chronicle*, 12 October 1888.
46. Ibid., 9, 13, 16, 27 November; 18 December 1888; *Daily Tobacco Plant*, 7, 8, 14 November 1888; *Raleigh Signal*, 24 January 1889.
47. *State Chronicle*, 18 December 1888; *Raleigh Signal*, 24 January 1889.
48. *Raleigh Signal*, 8 December 1888.
49. *State Chronicle*, 3 May 1889; *Wilmington Messenger*, 14 July 1888; *Raleigh Signal*, 7 March 1889; *Independent* (New York), 14 November 1889, p. 12. The article in the *Independent* was unsigned, the author having asked to remain anonymous. There is a clipping of this article bearing the initials "C.N.H." in

the Hunter Scrapbook 1891–1911 which contains Hunter's writings for the press.

50. *Raleigh Signal,* 14 March 1888; Steelman, "Republican Party Strategists and the Issue of Fusion with Populists," p. 248; Daniels, *Tar Heel Editor,* p. 485; *North Carolina Weekly Intelligencer,* 15 October 1890.
51. *State Chronicle,* 19 March; 10 May 1890.
52. *Raleigh News and Observer,* 27 April 1889.
53. *State Chronicle,* 19 March 1890.
54. *Raleigh Signal,* 18 April 1889; *Enfield Progress,* 5 August 1887, Hunter Scrapbook 1888–1905, Hunter Papers.
55. Hunter to R. P. Porter, 10 June 1889, Hunter Papers.
56. *Republican Magazine,* January 1885, pp. 782–83.
57. Form Letter to Dear Sir, 17 January 1889; Blair to My dear Sir, 23 February 1889, Hunter Papers.
58. Nichols to Hunter, 22 February 1889; A. S. Barnes Company to Hunter, 3 May 1889; Haywood to Hunter, 6 July 1889; Cheatham to Hunter, 22 February 1889, Hunter Papers.
59. Hunter to the Postmaster General, 15 August 1889, Hunter Papers.
60. *Independent* (New York), 14 November 1889, Hunter Scrapbook 1891–1911, Hunter Papers.
61. Hunter to Fowle, 14 November 1889, Hunter Papers; *State Chronicle,* 10 May 1889.

# Chapter 4

1. *Raleigh Gazette,* 3 October 1891, Hunter Scrapbook 1902–27, Hunter Papers.
2. Price, "Does the Negro Seek Social Equality?" p. 563.
3. *Chicago Record,* 5 November 1898.
4. Ed to Hunter, 11, 30 September; 29 December 1890, Hunter Papers.
5. *Raleigh Gazette,* 26 March 1892, Hunter Scrapbook 1887–1929, Hunter Papers.
6. Ibid., 3, 24 October 1891, Hunter Scrapbook 1902–27, Hunter Papers. Williamson was a member of the Constitutional Convention of 1868 and he had served four terms in the state legislature. He was also a delegate to the Republican National conventions of 1877, 1884, and 1888. Penn, *The Afro-American Press,* pp. 180–82; *Raleigh Signal,* 26 September 1891.
7. *Raleigh Gazette,* 7 November 1891, Hunter Scrapbook 1871–1928, Hunter Papers.

8. Ibid.

9. *Raleigh Gazette*, quoted in *Raleigh Signal*, 10 October 1891.

10. *Raleigh Gazette*, 9 April 1892, Hunter Scrapbook 1891–1911, Hunter Papers. Some of the editorials did not appear in the *Gazette* under Hunter's or anyone's name, but the rhetoric and reasoning are clearly his. Clippings of these editorials are also contained in his Scrapbook labeled "Writings for the Press."

11. Ibid., 23 April 1892.

12. Ibid.

13. Ibid., 30 April; 23 July 1892.

14. Ibid., 23 April 1892; Hicks, "The Farmers' Alliance in North Carolina," p. 182.

15. "The Present Nightmare in the South," pp. 310–13; *Raleigh Gazette*, 23 April 1892, Hunter Scrapbook 1891–1911, Hunter Papers; Page, "The Hold of the Southern Bully," p. 304.

16. Vance, *Speech on the Negro Question*.

17. *Raleigh Gazette*, 30 May 1891, Hunter Scrapbook 1891–1911, Hunter Papers; Brown, "The White Man's Problem," pp. 268–74; Price, "Does the Negro Seek Social Equality?" p. 564.

18. Schenck Journal vol. 12, Schenck Papers; Keith, *Memories of B. F. Keith*, pp. 75–77; Winston, *It's a Far Cry*, p. 218; Crow, "Fusion, Confusion and Negroism," p. 364; Ingle, "A Southern Democrat at Large," p. 190; Trelease, "Fusion Legislatures of 1895 and 1897," pp. 282–94. For general discussions of Fusion politics in North Carolina, see Edmonds, *The Negro and Fusion Politics*, and Hunt, "The Making of a Populist," pp. 317–43.

19. *Raleigh Register*, 27 August 1884; *Raleigh News and Observer*, 30 October 1896.

20. *Raleigh Gazette*, 15 October 1891; *Raleigh Signal*, 22 October; 19 November 1891.

21. Durden, *The Climax of Populism*, p. 152; *Raleigh News and Observer*, 18, 23 October 1896.

22. *Raleigh News and Observer*, 18–25 October 1896.

23. Ibid., 24, 25 October; 1 November 1896.

24. Crow and Durden, *Maverick Republican in the Old North State*, pp. 54–55; Thomas Settle to Hunter, 14 August 1898, Hunter Papers.

25. Hunter to Clarence Poe, 22 March 1924, Aycock Papers.

26. Ibid.; Edmonds, *The Negro and Fusion Politics*, pp. 97–103; *Norfolk Journal and Guide*, 23 April 1921.

27. *Raleigh News and Observer*, 13 January 1904.

28. Hunter to F. L. Meritt, 19 December 1898; Hunter to E. C. Brooks, 24 October 1919, Hunter Papers.

29. Crow, "Fusion, Confusion, and Negroism," p. 383; Hunter to S. A. Ashe, 9 February 1927, Hunter Papers.

30. *Raleigh Gazette*, 19 December 1896; 9 January 1897.
31. Ibid., 21, 28 November 1896; 6, 16 January; 6 February; 20 March 1897; *Raleigh News and Observer*, 11 November 1896; 11 March 1897.
32. *Raleigh Gazette*, 6 March 1897.
33. Ibid., 9, 16 January 1897.
34. *Raleigh News and Observer*, 14 November 1896; 10 July 1897; *Raleigh Gazette*, 31 July; 23,30 October 1897.
35. Knight, *Public School Education in North Carolina*, p. 325; *Raleigh Gazette*, 7 August 1897.
36. *Raleigh Gazette*, 23, 30 October; 6, 20 November 1897.
37. *Charlotte Observer*, 7 November 1897.
38. Ibid., 7, 14 November 1897; *Raleigh Gazette*, 13 November 1897; *Raleigh News and Observer*, 3 November 1897.
39. *Raleigh News and Observer*, 4 November 1897.
40. *Raleigh Gazette*, 13 November 1897; *Biblical Recorder*, 17 November 1897.
41. *Charlotte Observer*, 12 March 1899.
42. *Raleigh Gazette*, 6 November 1897; *History of the General Assembly of North Carolina January 9–March 13, 1895*, p. 62.
43. *Raleigh News and Observer*, 31 October 1897; 8 October 1898; *Biblical Recorder*, 16 February 1898.
44. *Biblical Recorder*, 10 November 1897; 16 February 1898.
45. Miller, *The Effects of the Emancipation upon the Mental and Physical Health of the Negro*.
46. *Raleigh Gazette*, 6, 20 November 1897.
47. *Raleigh News and Observer*, 21 February 1897; *Biblical Recorder*, 6 October 1897; Hunter to Dear Sir, 10 March 1897, Hunter Papers.
48. *Raleigh Gazette*, 11 December 1897; 8 January 1898; *Raleigh News and Observer*, 2 January 1898.
49. *Raleigh Gazette*, 8 January 1898; *Raleigh News and Observer*, 2 January 1898.
50. *Colored American*, 30 April 1898; *Raleigh News and Observer*, 22 May 1898; *Washington Bee*, 28 May 1898.
51. *Congressional Record*, 31:25–26; *Colored American*, 19 March; 30 April 1898; *Washington Bee*, 28 May 1898.
52. Howell to Hunter, 23 June 1898; Pritchard to Hunter, 24 June 1898; White to Hunter, 25 June 1898; Dancy to Hunter, 28 June 1898; Strowd to Hunter, 2 July 1898, Hunter Papers.
53. *Raleigh News and Observer*, 25 December 1898; Gossett, *Race*, p. 265.

# Chapter 5

1. *Charlotte Observer*, 12 March 1899.
2. Connor and Poe, *Charles Brantley Aycock*, p. 15; Daniels, *Editor in Politics*, p. 623.
3. Connor and Poe, *Charles Brantley Aycock*, p. 69.
4. Nunn, "Speech at Memorial Exercises under the Auspices of Craven County Bar Association, May 13, 1946," Nunn Papers; Simmons, "Address at City Auditorium, October 25, 1928," Simmons Papers.
5. Daniels, *Tar Heel Editor*, pp. 147, 255, 293–95; Edmonds, *The Negro and Fusion Politics*, pp.141–42.
6. *Five Lessons for North Carolina Voters* [1898]. For a survey of campaign propaganda, see *Raleigh News and Observer*, August through November 1898.
7. Nunn, "Speech at Memorial Exercises under the Auspices of Craven County Bar Association, May 13, 1946," Nunn Papers.
8. Keith, *Memories of B. F. Keith*, p. 76; Kilgo, "Our Duty to the Negro," pp. 369–70.
9. *Raleigh News and Observer*, 20 September 1898; *Raleigh Visitor*, 19 September 1898.
10. Ibid., 21, 22 September 1898.
11. *Raleigh Morning Post*, 21 September 1898, Hunter Scrapbook 1888–1905, Hunter Papers; *Raleigh News and Observer*, 22 October 1898.
12. *Raleigh News and Observer*, 23, 24, 25 September 1898; *Wilmington Messenger*, 25 September 1898.
13. *Raleigh News and Observer*, 22, 29 October 1898; Prather, "The Red Shirt Movement," pp. 174–84.
14. *Raleigh News and Observer*, 4 October 1898.
15. Daniels, *Editor in Politics*, p. 301; Hamilton, *North Carolina since 1860*, 3:284–88.
16. *Chicago Record*, 2, 5, 9 November 1898; *Wilmington Messenger*, 14 July 1898.
17. "Race Troubles in the Carolinas," p. 624; Grundy and Weinstein, *The Ideologies of Violence*, pp. 2–16.
18. Dancy, *Sand against the Wind*, p. 69; Edmonds, *The Negro and Fusion Politics*, pp. 173–74. For contemporary accounts of the Wilmington incident, see: *Raleigh News and Observer*, November 1898; *Washington Post*, November 1898; Connor, "Memorandum of My Personal Recollections of the Election of 1898," Connor Papers; Daniels, *Editor in Politics*, pp. 307–10; Waddell, "The Story of Wilmington North Carolina Race Riots," pp. 4–16; West, "The Race War in

North Carolina," pp. 578–99. For historians' interpretations of the event, see: Edmonds, *The Negro and Fusion Politics*, pp. 150–77; Wooley, "Race and Politics," pp. 160–94; McDuffie, "Politics in Wilmington and New Hanover County," pp. 662–768; Prather, *We Have Taken a City*, pp. 136 ff., 147–52.

19. *New York Herald Tribune*, quoted in *Raleigh News and Observer*, 16 November 1898; Cronly, "Wilmington White Revolution," Cronly Papers; *Charlotte People's Paper*, 25 November 1898.

20. Mebane, *"The Negro Problem"*, pp.7–8.

21. *Raleigh News and Observer*, 15 November 1898; "Condition of Affairs in Wilmington" [ca. 1900], Edmund Smithwick and Family Papers.

22. *Biblical Recorder*, quoted in *Raleigh News and Observer*, 16 November 1898; *North Carolina Presbyterian Review*, 17 November 1898; J. E. Bunting to J. Van B. Metts, 2 January 1906, transmitting the Minutes of a meeting of the Wilmington Light Infantry, 14 December 1905.

23. Worth [Walter Hines Page], *Southerner*, p. 166; Thomas, "The Psychology of Race Prejudice," pp. 610–11; Eustis, "Race Antagonism in the South," p. 145; Young, "What Is Race Prejudice?" p. 136; Morales, "The Collective Preconscious and Racism," pp. 289–90; *Raleigh News and Observer*, 13 November 1898; *Wilmington Morning Star*, 15 November 1898.

24. *Raleigh News and Observer*, 15 November 1898.

25. Ibid., 13 November 1898; Gay, "Crisis of Identity," p. 81; Andrews, *John Merrick*, pp. 152–53.

26. Daniels, *Editor in Politics*, pp. 311–12.

27. *Raleigh News and Observer*, 18 November 1898; Hunter to Meritt, 19 December 1898, Hunter Papers.

28. *Raleigh News and Observer*, 20 November 1898; *Wilmington Messenger*, 13 December 1898.

29. Ibid.; Newbold, *Five Negro Educators*, p. 41.

30. *Raleigh Press-Visitor*, 27 March 1896; *Raleigh News and Observer*, 13 December 1898.

31. *Raleigh News and Observer*, 26 November 1898; *Five Lessons for North Carolina Voters* [1898]; *Southern Workman*, 27:239–40.

32. Fuller, *Twenty Years in Public Life*, pp. 60–61.

33. *Raleigh News and Observer*, 13, 14, 16 November 1898.

34. Ibid., 3 January 1899.

35. *Richmond Planet*, 7 January 1899.

36. Steelman, "The Progressive Era in North Carolina," p. 198; Poland, *The Glorious Victory 1898*, p. 9; A.C., "The Passing of the Negro from Politics," p. 227; "Nomination Address of Charles B. Aycock" [11 April 1900], Aycock Papers.

37. Hunter to J. C. Pritchard, 21 April 1902; Hunter, "Education in North Caro-

lina," Undated Manuscript, Hunter Papers; Newbold, *Five Negro Educators*, p. 31; *Raleigh Morning Post*, 31 December 1898; *Raleigh News and Observer*, 13 December 1898; 3 January 1899.

38. Johnson, *Light Ahead for the Negro*, pp. 63–64.

39. *New York Tribune*, 11 December 1898; *Raleigh News and Observer*, 19 January 1899; *Concord Times*, 16 January 1899.

40. *Charlotte Observer*, 29 January 1899; *Union Republican* (Winston), 19 January 1899.

41. *Charlotte Observer*, 29 January 1899; *Southern Workman*, 28:44–45.

42. Weeks to Benehan Cameron, 2 January 1899, Cameron Papers.

43. *Charlotte Observer*, 18 February 1899; Rountree, *The Great Speech of George Rountree*.

44. *Raleigh News and Observer*, 10 January; 18, 19 February 1899; Fuller, *Twenty Years in Public Life*, p. 89.

45. *Charlotte Observer*, 16 February 1899; *Raleigh News and Observer*, 18 February 1899; Fuller, *Twenty Years in Public Life*, p. 91.

46. *Charlotte Observer*, 12 March 1899; Jones, *Memories and Speeches of Locke Craig*, p. 53.

47. Tourgée, "Shall White Minorities Rule?" pp. 143–44.

48. *Proceedings and Debates of the Convention of North Carolina Called to Amend the Constitution, June 4, 1835*, pp. 61–76; Helper, *The Negroes in Negroland*, pp. 237–47.

49. Jones, *Memoirs and Speeches of Locke Craig*, pp. 32–55; Haller, *Outcasts from Evolution*, p. 52. For a survey of contemporary attitudes regarding disfranchisement, see: Avent, Scrapbook of Literature on the Amendment Proposed to the Constitution of North Carolina 1899; Underwood, "The Struggle for White Supremacy"; Steelman, "The Progressive Movement in North Carolina."

50. Fortune to Hunter, 21 March 1899, Hunter Papers.

51. Director of the Twelfth Census to Hunter, 12 May 1899; White to Hunter, 16 May 1899; Thomas Rollings to Hunter, 16 May 1899; Ed to Hunter, 5 July 1899, Hunter Papers.

52. Hunter to Clarence Poe, 22 March 1924, Aycock Papers; *Raleigh News and Observer*, 2 January; 19 July 1900; Hunter to Washington Duke, 30 June 1899, Duke Papers.

53. *Raleigh News and Observer*, 2 January 1900.

54. Ibid.

55. Ibid.

56. Ibid.

57. Cheatham to Hunter, 24 January 1900; Johnson to Hunter, 12 January 1900, Hunter Papers.

58. Fortune, "Good Niggers and Good Indians," p. 189.

59. Pritchard to Hunter, 26 January 1900, Hunter Papers.
60. Broughton to Hunter, 26 July 1900, Hunter Papers.
61. Winston, "The Relation of the Whites to the Negroes," p. 115; Hamilton, *North Carolina since 1860*, p. 313; *Views of Distinguished Statesmen of South Carolina and North Carolina on White Supremacy*, pp. 5–7.
62. Hunter to Clarence Poe, 22 March 1924, Aycock Papers; Hunter to S. A. Ashe, 9 February 1927; Hunter to Aycock, 3 August 1900; Hunter to Aycock, 9 January 1905, Hunter Papers.
63. Poe to Josephus Daniels, 3 March 1924; Aycock to Edwin Mims, 20 November 1903, Aycock Papers; *Views of Distinguished Statesmen of South Carolina and North Carolina on White Supremacy*, p. 8; *Raleigh News and Observer*, 25 March 1900; *Raleigh Times Visitor*, 22 August 1900.
64. Pepitone, *Attraction and Hostility*, p. 11; Winston, *It's a Far Cry*, p. 238.
65. Ed to Hunter, 7 March 1901; Broughton to Hunter, 7 February 1900; 13 March 1902, Hunter Papers.
66. Rosenthal to Hunter, 28 June 1900; Moses to Hunter, 29 June; 2 July 1900, Hunter Papers.
67. Ed to Hunter, 23 November; 7 December 1900; 9 April 1901, Hunter Papers; Hunter to Clarence Poe, 22 March 1924, Aycock Papers.

# Chapter 6

1. White, *Defense of the Negro Race*, p. 4.
2. Barringer, *The American Negro, His Past and Future*, pp. 5–15; Barringer, *Speech before the Tri-State Medical Society*, p. 7.
3. McNair, *The Race Crisis*, pp. 9–10; Lilly, "The Attitude of the South to the Colored People," pp. 271–73; Bingham, "An Ex-Slave Holder's View," pp. 8–15; Winston, "The Relation of the Whites to the Negroes," pp. 108–9.
4. Winston, "The Relation of the Whites to the Negroes," pp. 115–16; Bingham, "An Ex-Slave Holder's View," pp. 8–15; Poe, "Lynchings: A Southern View," p. 156; Kilgo, "An Inquiry concerning Lynchings," p. 7.
5. Poe, "Should Southern Whites Aid Negro Schools?" p. 1012; A.C., "The Passing of the Negro from Politics," pp. 227–28.
6. L. T. Christmas, *An Evil Router from All the Walks of Life*, pp. 4–17; Mebane, "Have We an American Race Question?" pp. 451–67.
7. Lacy to Hunter, 30 March 1901, Unaddressed Letter from J. E. King, 17 June 1901; Dudley to Whom It May Concern, 24 December 1901; Boyd to John W. Griggs, 19 December 1901, Hunter Papers.

8. Hunter to My dear daughter, 26 November 1901; Hunter to the Reverend H. Schuyler, 20 February 1902, Hunter Papers.

9. S. H. Hardwick to Hunter, 2 December 1901; R. E. L. Branch to Hunter, 9 December 1901; Wm. G. Wheeler to Hunter, 8 March 1902; John H. Lewis to Hunter, 25, 30 March; 25 April 1902, Hunter Papers.

10. Broughton to Hunter, 13 March 1902; Battle to Hunter, 17 January 1902, Hunter Papers.

11. Hunter, "The Negro Problem at Last Solving Itself," *Raleigh Morning Post*, 20 April 1902; Manuscript for the *North American*, 12 May 1902, Hunter Papers.

12. Ibid.

13. Ibid.

14. Hunter to Pritchard, 21 April 1902, Hunter Papers.

15. Ibid.; Pritchard to Hunter, 24 April 1902, Hunter Papers.

16. Broughton to Hunter, 13 March 1902; Aycock to Hunter, 4 April 1901; Hunter to Lacy, 21 March 1903; G. Rosenthal to Hunter, 19 June 1902, Hunter Papers; Hunter to Clarence Poe, 22 March 1924, Aycock Papers.

17. *Raleigh News and Observer*, 5 October 1902.

18. Ibid., 31 August; 29 October; 30 November 1902; *Raleigh Morning Post*, 2, 30 August; 7 October 1902.

19. *Raleigh News and Observer*, 8 October 1902; *Raleigh Morning Post*, 7 October 1902.

20. *Raleigh News and Observer*, 1, 8, 27 October 1902.

21. Ibid., 28, 29 October; 4 November; 25 December 1902.

22. *Biblical Recorder*, 5 November 1902; 4 March 1903.

23. *Raleigh Morning Post*, 28 November 1902; *Raleigh News and Observer*, 12 November 1902.

24. *Raleigh Morning Post*, 11 November 1902; *Raleigh News and Observer*, 28 November 1902; *Biblical Recorder*, 3 December 1902.

25. *Biblical Recorder*, 3 December 1902; *Raleigh News and Observer*, 2 January 1903.

26. North Carolina Teachers' Association, *Proceedings of the Twentieth Annual Session*, pp. 15–16; *Raleigh News and Observer*, 2 January 1903; 2 January 1907.

27. Aycock, "Address at the Negro State Fair, 29 October 1901," Aycock Papers; Strange, *Church Work among the Negroes*, pp. 20–24; *Raleigh News and Observer*, 31 May 1903; 14 February 1905; *Biblical Recorder*, 4 November 1903; Simmons, "The Political Future of the Negro," p. 1522.

28. *Raleigh News and Observer*, 4 November 1905; *Baptist Sentinel*, 9 January 1908; Hunter to Edward P. Moses, 25 June 1903; Hunter to Benjamin R. Lacy, 21 March 1903, Hunter Papers.

29. Hunter, Notebook for the Oberlin School, 1902–1903 Session, Hunter Papers; Winston, "An Unconsidered Aspect of the Negro Question," pp. 264–68.

30. *Raleigh Morning Post*, 18 January 1903.

31. Ibid.; Hunter to the Editor of the *Independent* (New York), 30 January 1904, Hunter Papers.

32. *Raleigh News and Observer*, 1 November 1905; *Raleigh Morning Post*, 21 May 1905.

33. *Raleigh Morning Post*, 30 August 1903; Hunter to J. R. Poole, 14 August 1903; Hunter to J. Y. Joyner, 19 January 1903; Form Letter from Hunter, 3 January 1903, Hunter Papers; *Raleigh Times*, 13 June 1903.

34. Broughton to Hunter, 26 August 1903, Hunter Papers; *Raleigh Morning Post*, 1 September; 4 October 1903.

35. Otey to Hunter, 5 October 1903, Hunter Papers; Whitener, *Prohibition in North Carolina*, p. 143.

36. *Raleigh Morning Post*, 31 October 1903.

37. Ibid.; *Raleigh News and Observer*, 2 January 1904; Byrd, *Reasons Why the Negro Should Remain in the South*, pp. 1–12.

38. *Raleigh News and Observer*, 13 January 1904.

39. Ibid.

40. Ibid.; Hunter to Jarvis, 19 January 1904, Hunter Papers.

41. *Raleigh News and Observer*, 2 January 1904; Hunter to Aycock, 9 January 1905, Hunter Papers.

42. Aycock to Hunter, 10 January 1905, Hunter Papers.

43. *Raleigh News and Observer*, 14 February 1905.

44. Hunter to Mr. President, Hunter Papers. This is a draft of a letter that was to have been passed to the president by John C. Dancy. There is no evidence to indicate whether or not Roosevelt received it. *Raleigh Liberator*, 18 March 1905, Hunter Scrapbook 1888–1905, Hunter Papers.

45. *Raleigh News and Observer*, 17 November 1906; 2 January 1907; *Raleigh Evening Times*, 11 August 1906, Hunter Scrapbook 1886–1921, Hunter Papers.

46. *Richmond Criterion* (Virginia), 17 November 1906, Hunter Scrapbook 1886–1921, Hunter Papers.

47. *Raleigh News and Observer*, 2 January 1907.

48. Jenkins, *James B. Duke*, pp. 145–47; Houck, "A Newspaper History of Race Relations in Durham," pp. 75–83; *State Journal*, 8 May 1918, p. 8; Hunter to Spaulding, 3 January 1907, Hunter Papers.

49. J. H. Garner to Whom It May Concern, 2 September 1908; C. C. Spaulding to Whom It May Concern, 22 September 1908. See also correspondence between Hunter and Spaulding 1905–10, Hunter Papers. Hunter, "Address on the Occa-

sion of the 44th Anniversary of the Proclamation of Emancipation," Hunter Papers; *Raleigh News and Observer*, 2 January 1907.

50. Hunter, "An Address on the Occasion of the 44th Anniversary of the Proclamation of Emancipation," Hunter Papers; *Raleigh News and Observer*, 2 January 1907.

51. *Salisbury Post*, cited in *Raleigh News and Observer*, 6 January 1907.

# Chapter 7

1. Hunter to Giles B. Jackson, 22 August 1906, Hunter Papers.
2. Ibid.; C. H. Williamson et al. to Honorable School Committee of Raleigh Township, 29 January 1907; Williamson to Hunter, 9 October 1907, Hunter Papers.
3. Secretary, N.C. State Organization to Dear Sir, n.d.; Hunter to Jackson, 22 August 1906, Hunter Papers.
4. Williamson et al. to Honorable School Committee of Raleigh Township, 29 January 1907; Hunter to Drewry, 2 February 1907, Hunter Papers.
5. Hunter to Graham, 31 January 1907; "A Joint Resolution concerning the Jamestown Exposition February 16, 1907"; Hunter to A. F. Hilyer, 30 April 1907; "Governor Glenn at the Negro Building [1907]," Hunter Papers.
6. Hunter to Pogue, 3 March 1907; Pogue to Hunter, 4 March 1907; Ed to Hunter, 15 February; 4 March 1907, Hunter Papers.
7. Hunter to Honorable School Committee, Raleigh Township, 11 April 1907; Hunter to Broughton, 16 April 1907, Hunter Papers.
8. Hunter to Pogue, 24, 30 April 1907; Hunter to Ed, 10 May 1907; Pogue to Hunter, 5 May 1907, Hunter Papers.
9. Pogue to Hunter, 24 July 1907; Hunter to G. W. Hinshaw, 22 June 1907, Hunter Papers.
10. Hunter to Reynolds, 2 June 1907; Hunter to Carr, 10, 25 May 1907; Hunter to A. W. Wheeler, 15 May 1907; Hunter to J. O. O'Daniels, 7 May 1907; Hunter to D. W. Ashley, 23 May 1907, Hunter Papers.
11. Hunter to S. G. Atkins, 11 May 1907; Hunter to J. A. Dodson, 27 May 1907; Hunter to W. Saunders, 16 March 1907; Hunter to Kemp P. Battle, 9 April 1907; Hunter to A. W. Pegues, 20 May 1907; Hunter to A. J. Wilson, 20 May 1907, Hunter Papers.
12. Hunter to Battle, 9 April 1907; Hunter to Goler, 10 May 1907, Hunter Papers.
13. "Jamestown Exposition Notes [1907];" C. H. Gattis to Hunter, et al., 12 July 1907, Hunter Papers.

14. Hunter to Tucker, 11, 18 July 1907; Bolles to Hunter, 26 July 1907; "Jamestown Exposition Notes [1907]," Hunter Papers.

15. Hunter to Pogue, 24 July 1907; Hunter to Glenn, 29 July 1907; Glenn to Hunter, 30 July 1907, Hunter Papers.

16. "North Carolina in a Class Alone [1907]"; "Governor Glenn at the Negro Building"; Hunter to Daniels, 23 March 1907; Glenn to Hunter, 24 August 1907, Hunter Papers.

17. *True Reformer*, 29 May 1907; Williamson to Hunter, 19 May 1907; Hunter to Executive Committee, North Carolina State Fair, 1 August 1930; "North Carolina in a Class Alone [1907]"; Pogue to Hunter, 3 January 1908, Hunter Papers; Schenck, "Negro Participation in Three Southern Expositions," pp. 65–72.

18. *Raleigh News and Observer*, 24 October 1907.

19. Joe Brenan to Hunter, 24 July 1907, Hunter Papers.

20. Hunter to Aycock, 29 July 1907; Hunter to W. A. Guthrie, 29 July 1907; Hunter to B. R. Lacy, 29 July 1907; Hunter to W. M. Russ, 29 July 1907; Hunter to N. B. Broughton, 29 July 1907; Hunter to Hubert Haywood, 29 July 1907; Hunter to A. A. Thompson, 29 July 1907, Hunter Papers.

21. Hunter to J. E. Ray, 29 July; 2, 6 September 1907; Hunter to J. E. Pogue, 29 July 1907; Hunter to Honorable Board of Trustees, School of the Blind and Deaf, 6 September 1907, Hunter Papers.

22. *Raleigh News and Observer*, 2 January 1907; Hunter to Foraker, 13 January 1907; Foraker to Hunter, 14 January 1907; Hunter to Dear Sir [Foraker], 24 February 1908, Hunter Papers.

23. Ed to Hunter, 5 May 1908, Hunter Papers.

24. *Raleigh News and Observer*, 24 April; 6, 10, 13 May 1908.

25. J. Milton Waldron to Hunter, 15 May 1908, Hunter Papers.

26. Open Letter from Waldron and William Monroe Trotter, 10 July 1908, Hunter Papers.

27. Ed to Hunter, 16 March; 5 April 1909. Hunter Papers; U.S. Congress, House, *Inaugural Addresses of the Presidents of the United States*, pp. 196–97.

28. Hunter to the President, 3 April 1909; Fuller to Hunter, 14 April 1909, Hunter Papers; *New York Age*, 10 June 1909; Steelman, "Republicans in North Carolina," pp. 160–61.

29. Hunter to E. Dana Durand, January 1910; Hunter to Overman, 15 February 1910; Durand to Overman, 3 February 1910; Acting Director of the Census to Hunter, 4 February 1910, Hunter Papers.

30. *Raleigh News and Observer*, 20 October 1909; Hunter to "The People of North Carolina," 21 January 1910; Spaulding to Hunter, 4 October 1910; George Clinton to Hunter, 7 October 1910, Hunter Papers; *Independent* (New York), 69:1169–70.

31. *Raleigh News and Observer*, 27 November 1911.

32. J. H. Branch to Hunter, 20 November 1911; Hunter, "Oration Delivered on the Occasion of the Celebration of the Proclamation of Emancipation, January 1912," Hunter Papers.
33. Hunter, "Oration Delivered on the Occasion of the Celebration of the Proclamation of Emancipation, January 1912," Hunter Papers.
34. Ibid.; *Raleigh Times*, 1 January 1912; *Searchlight* [1912], Hunter Scrapbook 1887–1927, Hunter Papers.
35. Undated Manuscript, Hunter Papers. The contents of this document date it after 1910. *Raleigh Times*, 15 April 1912.
36. *Raleigh Times*, 15 April 1912; *Raleigh News and Observer*, 26 March 1912.
37. *Raleigh News and Observer*, 4 June 1912; J. W. Bailey, "Simmons—Organizer for Victory," *Carolina Democrat*, 8 June 1912, Simmons Papers; Nunn, "To the Voters of Craven County [1912]," Nunn Papers.
38. Hunter to Daniels, 22 March 1913; *Raleigh Times*, 26 December 1912, Hunter Scrapbook 1900–1924, Hunter Papers.
39. *Raleigh Times*, 26 December 1912, Hunter Scrapbook, 1900–1924, Hunter Papers.
40. Poe, "Rural Land Segregation between Whites and Negroes," pp. 208–9; Stephenson, "The Segregation of the White and Negro Race in Cities," pp. 2–4; Poe to Dear Brother, 12 September 1913; *Progressive Farmer*, 30 August 1913, quoted in *Crisis*, 8:68; *State Journal*, 26 September 1913; 26 February 1915; *Greensboro Daily News*, 30 May 1914.
41. *Greensboro Daily News*, 30 May 1914.
42. Dudley to C. L. Coon, 4 June 1913, Coon Papers; Dudley to Hunter, 13 January 1914, Hunter Papers.
43. *Crisis*, 7:170; *Raleigh News and Observer*, 31 October 1914.
44. *Raleigh Times*, 22 December 1913; *Fayetteville Observer*, 31 January 1927.
45. A Southern Woman, "Black and White in the South," pp. 538–46.
46. Hunter, "A Negro's Hopeful Views of the Race Problem," *State Journal*, 10 April 1914.
47. Ibid.

# Chapter 8

1. Hunter to J. Y. Joyner and Others, n.d.; Hunter to the School Committee of Raleigh Township, 21 August 1915, Hunter Papers.
2. W. B. T. Williams, "Report on Wake County Training Schools—25 March 1915," Department of Public Instruction Papers.

3. Hunter to B. T. Washington, 2 July 1914; Washington to Zebulon Judd, 17 July 1914; Washington to Hunter, 7 July 1914; Zebulon Judd to Whom It May Concern, 7 July 1914; Zebulon Judd to Hunter, 18 July 1914, Hunter Papers; W. B. T. Williams, "Report on Wake County Schools—25 March 1915," Department of Public Instruction Papers.

4. Alvord, *Sixth-Annual Report on Schools for Freedmen*, p. 75.

5. "East Raleigh School—Second Session 1879–1880," Hunter Papers; Newbold, "Negro County School Commencements."

6. *Raleigh News and Observer*, 24 May 1916.

7. Hunter to B. F. Montague, 10 August 1915; "Petition to the Honorable School Committee of Raleigh Township," 21 August 1915, Hunter Papers.

8. Montague to Hunter, 19 August; 9 September 1915, Hunter Papers.

9. *State Journal*, 17 December 1915.

10. Moore to Hunter, 11 May 1915; *Raleigh Times*, 24 May 1915, Hunter Scrapbook 1891–1911, Hunter Papers.

11. A. M. Moore to Dear Friend, 10 August 1915; Form Letter from A. M. Moore to ———, 7 June 1916, Hunter Papers; *Norfolk Journal and Guide*, 4 November 1916; *Report of Professor Charles H. Moore*, pp. 6–7.

12. *Report of Professor Charles H. Moore*, p. 4; Coon, "Who Pays for Negro Education?" Lyon to Coon, 30 September 1909; R. D. W. Connor to Coon, 29, 30 September 1909, Coon Papers; *Nation*, 89:244. Also see: Coon, *Public Taxation and Negro Schools*; *Raleigh News and Observer*, 25, 28 September 1909. A recent quantitative study using data similar to Coon's tends to support the conclusion that blacks did indeed pay for their education. See Kousser, "Progressivism—For Middle Class Whites Only," pp. 169–94.

13. Emmett J. Scott to Hunter, 23 November 1915; D. F. Giles to Hunter, 22 December 1915; "Resolutions Adopted by the Negro Teachers of Wake County in Honor of Dr. B. T. Washington," 15 January 1916; Mrs. Booker T. Washington to Hunter, 11 February 1916, Hunter Papers.

14. *State Journal*, 17 December 1915.

15. Ibid.

16. Ibid., 25 June 1915; J. R. Evans to Hunter, 23 March 1916; James Henderson to Hunter, 28 March 1916; North Carolina Republican Executive Committee, *To the Colored Republicans of North Carolina March 11, 1916*, Hunter Scrapbook 1871–1928, Hunter Papers.

17. *Raleigh News and Observer*, 26 April 1916; Taylor to Hunter, 30 October 1916, Hunter Papers.

18. *Raleigh News and Observer*, 2 January 1916; *Raleigh Times*, 3 November 1916, Hunter Scrapbook 1902–27, Hunter Papers.

19. *Greensboro Daily News*, 29 October 1916; *Raleigh Times*, 4 November 1916, Hunter Scrapbook 1902–27, Hunter Papers.

20. *Greensboro Daily News*, 29 October 1916; Hunter to Bickett, 11 November 1916; Bickett to Hunter, 16 November 1916; Hunter to Lacy, 11 November 1916; Lacy to Hunter, 13 November 1916, Hunter Papers.

21. Lott Mason to Hunter, 9 October 1916; Giles to F. D. Haywood, 16 June 1916; Howell to Hunter, 24 June 1916; Hunter to Giles, 11 October 1916, Hunter Papers.

22. *Manufacturer's Record*, 12 April 1917.

23. Hunter to B. F. Lacy, 19 May 1917; Hunter to Marshall DeLancey Haywood, 16 June 1917, Hunter Papers.

24. Hunter to Marshall DeLancey Haywood, 16 June 1917; M. D. Haywood to Hunter, 18 June 1917; F. D. Haywood to J. Y. Joyner, 20 June 1917; Lacy to Hunter, 19 May 1917, Hunter Papers.

25. Hunter to Edgar W. Knight, 6 August 1917; Knight to Hunter, 6 September 1917, Hunter Papers.

26. Martin and House, *Papers of Thomas Walter Bickett*, p. 270; *Raleigh Times*, 17 July 1917, Hunter Scrapbook 1886–1921, Hunter Papers; *Greensboro Daily News*, 17 July 1917.

27. *Raleigh Times*, 17 July 1917; *Greensboro Daily News*, 17 July 1917.

28. Ibid.; Jordan to Hunter, 30 July 1917; Hunter to Bickett, 20 July 1917, Hunter Papers.

29. Editor of the (Raleigh) *Independent* [Hunter] to Pou, 15 August 1917, Hunter Papers.

30. Knight to Hunter, 3, 6 August 1917; National League on Urban Conditions among Negroes to Dear Sir, 5 April 1917; Paul G. Prayer to Hunter, 24 April 1917; Dancy to Hunter, 16 August 1917, Hunter Papers.

31. *Norfolk Journal and Guide*, 14 April 1917; *Raleigh News and Observer*, 5, 17 August 1917; Stephenson to Hunter, 16 August 1917, Hunter Papers.

32. *Raleigh News and Observer*, 19 August 1917.

33. Ibid.; Moore to Hunter, 20 August 1917, Hunter Papers.

34. Hunter to Johnson, [10 December 1917]; Johnson to Hunter, 17 December 1917; Editor of the (Raleigh) *Independent* [Hunter] to the Butterworth-Judson Company, n.d., Hunter Papers.

35. Hunter, "The Negro's Call to World Service, an Address Delivered at the Johnston County Fair, November 15, 1917," Hunter Papers.

36. Walker to Hunter, 19, 21 November 1917; Martin to Walker, 19 November 1917, Hunter Papers.

37. Hunter to Page, 9 November 1917; Lucas to Hunter, 12 November 1917, Hunter Papers.

38. Hunter to Page, 19 November 1917; Hunter to Lucas, 26 January 1918, Hunter Papers.

39. Hunter to Lucas, 22 May 1918; Page to Hunter, 20 February 1918; Lucas to Hunter, 27 May 1918; Jane S. McKimmon to Hunter, 19 February 1918;

Francis H. Fries to Hunter, 1 February 1918; Hunter to Page, 30 March 1918, Hunter Papers.
40. Hunter to Craig, 1 May 1918; Hunter to Doughton, 15 May 1918, Hunter Papers.
41. Hunter to Lucas, 14 May 1918, Hunter Papers.
42. Ibid.; Lucas to Hunter, 16 May 1918; Hunter to Lucas, 22 May 1918, Hunter Papers.
43. Hunter to Ramsey, 15 May 1918; Ramsey to Hunter, 7 June 1918, Hunter Papers.
44. Hunter to Simmons, 6 May 1918; Hunter to Doughton, 7 May 1918, Hunter Papers.
45. Ibid.; Simmons to Hunter, 8 May 1918; Doughton to Hunter, 9 May 1918; Hunter to Doughton, 15 May 1918, Hunter Papers.
46. *Raleigh News and Observer*, 12 July 1918.
47. Ibid.; Pou to Hunter, 1, 12 June 1918, Hunter Papers; *Congressional Record*, 56:7237.
48. Julian B. Clark to Pou, 13 June 1918; Pou to Hunter, 20 June 1918; Hunter to Satterwhite, 27 June 1918; Hunter to L. E. McCauley, 27 June 1918; Hunter to Berry O'Kelly, [1918]; Hunter to J. Y. Joyner, [1918]; Hunter to Newbold, 17 May 1918; Hunter to D. F. Giles, July 1919, Hunter Papers.
49. Hunter to Johnson, 27 May 1918; Hunter to Eugene K. Jones, 27 May 1918, Hunter Papers; U.S. Department of Labor, *The Negro at Work during the World War*, pp. 20, 98–104, 287.

# Chapter 9

1. Hunter to Lucas, 26 June 1918; Hunter to E. E. Britton, 24 June 1918; Hunter to B. R. Lacy, 10 November 1918, Hunter Papers.
2. Hunter to Britton, 24 June 1918; Hunter to Sanford, 13 July 1918; Hunter to Daniels, 22 August 1918; Hunter to E. A. Johnson, 4 March 1921; Hunter to W. P. Wright, 7 April 1921; Daniels to Hunter, 1 August 1918, Hunter Papers.
3. Hunter to Giles, July 1919; Hunter to Judd, 12, 20 August 1920; Hunter to J. A. Amee, 1919; Hunter to C. H. Talem, 11 April 1921, Hunter Papers.
4. *Portsmouth Star*, 17 October 1918, Hunter Scrapbook 1887–1929; Hunter to Daniels, 28 October 1918; Daniels to Hunter, 24 October; 5 November 1918, Hunter Papers.
5. J. E. McCulloch to Hunter, 2 November 1918; Hunter to Daniels, 27 December 1918; Daniels to Hunter, 2 January 1919, Hunter Papers.
6. Chase to Hunter, 22 February 1919, Hunter Papers; *New York Age*, 1 March

1919; *Eighth and Ninth Annual Report of the National Association for the Advancement of Colored People*, pp. 31–35.

7. *Raleigh News and Observer*, 2 January 1919.

8. Ibid.; *New York Age*, 18 January 1919.

9. *New York Age*, 18 January 1919.

10. *Baltimore Afro-American*, 18 April 1919; *Raleigh News and Observer*, 27 May 1919; *Raleigh Times*, undated clipping in Hunter Scrapbook 1886–1921; Hunter to John Love, 17 March 1919; W. H. Ancrum to Hunter, 14 May 1919, Hunter Papers.

11. Hunter to James K. Satterwhite, 25 March 1919, Hunter Papers; *Raleigh News and Observer*, 26 April 1919.

12. Hunter to Satterwhite, 25 March 1919; Hunter to C. A. Ashby, 20 May 1919, Hunter Papers.

13. Hunter to Chase, 19 March 1919, Hunter Papers.

14. *Raleigh News and Observer*, 13 April 1919.

15. Hunter to Ashby, 30 May; 11 June 1919, Hunter Papers.

16. Ibid.

17. Ibid.

18. Ibid.

19. Ibid.

20. Ibid.

21. Ibid.; Johnson, "A Sociological Interpretation of the New Ku Klux Klan," pp. 442–44.

22. Martin and House, *Papers of Thomas Walter Bickett*, pp. 189–92.

23. Hunter to Miss Faulk, 30 September 1919; Hamlin to Hunter, 26 July 1919, Hunter Papers; *Raleigh News and Observer*, 8 August 1919.

24. *Raleigh News and Observer*, 25, 30 July; 5, 8 August; 21 October 1919.

25. Martin and House, *Papers of Thomas Walter Bickett*, pp. 291–92.

26. Ibid.; *Raleigh News and Observer*, 6 August 1919.

27. *Raleigh News and Observer*, 29, 30 May 1919.

28. Ibid.

29. Ibid.; Martin and House, *Papers of Thomas Walter Bickett*, pp. 297–98.

30. *Raleigh News and Observer*, 26 September 1919; *Baltimore Afro-American*, 1 August 1919.

31. *Greensboro Daily News*, 29 April 1920; *Crisis*, 19:330–31; *Biblical Recorder*, 15 September 1920.

32. *A Declaration of Principles by Representative Negroes, September 26, 1919*, pp. 3–5.

33. Ibid.; *New York Age*, 31 July 1920; *Biblical Recorder*, 15 September 1920; *Southern Women and Race Cooperation*.

34. Hunter to Brooks and Newbold, 22 October 1919, Hunter Papers; *Raleigh News and Observer*, 27 October 1919.

35. Brooks to Hunter, 28 October 1919; Hunter to Julian S. Carr, 1 December 1919; Hunter, "A Great White Southerner's Tribute to a Great Negro [1919]," Hunter Papers.

36. Hunter to Page, 1919, Hunter Papers.

37. *New York Age*, 20 March; 23 October 1920; *Twenty-first Annual Report of the National Association for the Advancement of Colored People*, pp. 7–8.

38. *New York Age*, 22 April; 1 May 1920; *Greensboro Daily News*, 11, 29 April 1920; *Raleigh News and Observer*, 29 April 1920; Scurlock to Hunter, 14 April 1920, Hunter Papers.

39. Hunter to Scurlock, 29 April 1920; Hunter to George H. Moses, 29 April 1920, Hunter Papers.

40. Hunter to Moses, 29 April 1920, Hunter Papers.

41. Ibid.

42. *New York Age*, 22 May 1920; *Greensboro Daily News*, 11 April 1920.

43. *New York Age*, 12 June 1920.

44. Ibid., 1 May 1920.

45. Corbitt and Richardson, *Papers and Letters of Cameron Morrison*, pp. xxii–xxiii; Persons to Hunter, 16 June 1920, Hunter Papers.

46. Hunter to Persons, 10 July 1920; Wright to Hunter, 19 July 1920; Wright to Hunter, n.d., Hunter Papers. There are several undated letters from Wright to Hunter addressing the race question, in Hunter's Papers.

47. Wright to Hunter, 12 January 1921; Wright to Hunter, n.d., Hunter Papers.

48. Wright to Hunter, 19 July 1920; Hunter to Wright, 12 January 1921, Hunter Papers.

49. *Raleigh News and Observer*, 15 August 1920.

50. Hunter to C. J. Lewis, 30 August 1920; Hunter to Wright, 7 April 1921; Hunter to William A. Lee, 13 May 1921; Hunter to W. N. Huggins, 17 February 1921, Hunter Papers.

51. Hunter to Persons, 10 July 1920, Hunter Papers; *Greensboro Daily News*, 3 October 1920; Mewborn to Weil, 26 August 1920, Weil Papers.

52. *Eleventh Annual Report of the National Association for the Advancement of Colored People*, p. 25; *New York Age*, 16 October 1920.

53. *Greensboro Daily News*, 6 October 1920; *New York Age*, 16, 23 October 1920.

54. *Twenty-first Annual Report of the National Association for the Advancement of Colored People*, pp. 7–13.

55. Hunter to W. E. L. Sanford, 13 November 1920; Scurlock to Hunter, 26 February 1921; Hunter to J. T. Fisher, 10 December 1920, Hunter Papers.

56. *Raleigh News and Observer*, 2 January 1921; *Greensboro Daily News*, 29 April 1920.

57. *Raleigh News and Observer*, 2 January 1920.

58. Ibid., 3 January 1922; 2 January 1923; Hunter to Editor of the Norfolk, Virginia, *Pilot*, 30 March 1921, Hunter Papers.

59. Hunter to Editor of the Norfolk, Virginia, *Pilot*, 30 March 1921; Jaffee to Hunter, 14 April 1921, Hunter Papers.

60. Hunter to Charles J. Lewis, 21 January 1921; Hunter to S. G. Atkins, 14 March 1921, Hunter Papers.

61. Ibid.; Hunter to Johnson, 4 March 1921; Johnson to Hunter, 8 March 1921; Hunter to Roosevelt, 18 March 1921, Hunter Papers.

62. Hunter to Roosevelt, 21 March 1921; Roosevelt to J. H. Love, 11 April 1921; Roosevelt to E. H. Hunter, 11 April 1921; Dudley to Roosevelt, 16 March 1921; Roosevelt to Dudley, 19 March 1921; Levi C. Brown to Roosevelt, 25 March 1921; E. H. Hunter to Roosevelt, 19 March 1921; E. H. Hunter to Hunter, 29 March 1921; Hunter to R. H. Kyles, 1 April 1921, Hunter Papers.

63. Hunter to W. E. L. Sanford, 23 March 1921; Hunter to Newbold, 21 March 1921; Hunter to Daniels, 21 March 1921, Hunter Papers.

64. Typescript of telegram from Hunter to Daniels, 5 March 1921; Hunter to Daniels, 21 March 1921; Daniels to Hunter, 9 March 1921, Hunter Papers.

65. Hunter to Atkins, 14 March 1921; Atkins to Hunter, 19 March 1921; Hunter to Roosevelt, 18, 21, 24 March 1921, Hunter Papers.

66. Hunter to Roosevelt, 18, 21, 24 March, 1921; Hunter to Hays, 23 March 1921; Perry W. Howard to Hunter, 26 March 1921, Hunter Papers.

67. Hays to Hunter, 30 March 1921; Hunter to Pou, 16 April 1921; Pou to Hunter, 19 April 1921; Hunter to Roosevelt, 2 May 1921, Hunter Papers.

68. Denby to Hunter, 6 May 1921; Hunter to Newbold, 21 March 1921; Hunter to Daniels, 21 March 1921; Hunter to W. H. Watson, 4 April 1921, Hunter Papers.

# Chapter 10

1. Hunter to Harding, 20 April 1921; Charles M. Stedman to Hunter, 25 April 1921, Hunter Papers.

2. *Raleigh News and Observer*, 21 May; 25, 29 June 1921.

3. *Greensboro Daily News*, 17 May 1921.

4. Ibid.; Overman to D. C. Suggs, 18 May 1921; Overman to S. J. Ervin, 21 May 1921; Overman to Plummer Stewart, 21 May 1921; Overman to A. M. Matheson, 6 June 1921; Overman to T. H. Taylor, 14 June 1921; E. F. Vandiver to Overman, 21 May 1921; J. O. Guthrie to Overman, 21 May 1921, Overman Papers.

5. Walter White to Hunter, 23 May 1921, Hunter Papers; *Greensboro Daily News*, 17 May 1921.

6. *Greensboro Daily News*, 18 May 1921.

7. Ibid.; Overman to Suggs, 18 May 1921; Suggs to Overman, 19 May 1921, Overman Papers; *Raleigh News and Observer*, 21 May 1921.

8. *Raleigh News and Observer*, 21 May 1921.

9. Telegram from E. E. Britton to *News and Observer*, 29 May 1921, Hunter Papers; *Raleigh News and Observer*, 21 May 1921.

10. Ed to Hunter, 30 May 1921; J. K. Satterwhite to Hunter, 4 June 1921; Taylor to Hunter, 22 May 1921; Spaulding to Hunter, 21 May 1921; Avery to Hunter 24, 31 May 1921, Hunter Papers.

11. White to Hunter, 23 May 1921; Johnson to Hunter, 6 June 1921; Hunter to Alford Robinson, 14 June 1921, Hunter Papers.

12. Amelia J. Hunter to Hunter, 19 June 1921; Satterwhite to Hunter, 16 June 1921; Williams to Hunter, 11 June 1921; Reid to Hunter, 20 June 1921; Hunter to Reid, 15 June 1921; Avery to Hunter, 15 June 1921, Hunter Papers.

13. Suggs to Hunter, 18 June 1921, Hunter Papers; *Norfolk Journal and Guide*, 25 June 1921; *Raleigh News and Observer*, 21, 24 June 1921.

14. *Raleigh News and Observer*, 25 June 1921.

15. Ibid.

16. "The Highlights of the Linney Testimony," Simmons Papers.

17. Ibid.; *Raleigh News and Observer*, 25, 29 June 1921.

18. Eppes to Overman, 4 June 1921; A. G. Harper to Overman, 11 June 1921, Overman Papers; *Norfolk Journal and Guide*, 25 June 1921; *Raleigh News and Observer*, 27 June 1921.

19. *Raleigh News and Observer*, 21, 29 June; 6 July 1921; 3 January 1922; Wade H. Ancrum to Hunter, 8 July 1921, Hunter Papers.

20. *Norfolk Journal and Guide*, 2 July 1921; *Raleigh News and Observer*, 18 July 1921; Ancrum to Hunter, 8 July 1921, Hunter Papers.

21. *Raleigh News and Observer*, 26 June; 9, 11 August 1921.

22. *Norfolk Journal and Guide*, 19 November 1921.

23. Hunter to Elder L. M. Mason, 7, 8 July 1921; Hunter to Willis D. Crawford, 19 November 1921, Hunter Papers; *Raleigh News and Observer*, 17 September; 25 October 1921.

24. R. W. Winston to Hunter, 5 October 1921; A. H. Mooneyhan to Hunter, 29 September 1921; H. Clarkson to Hunter, 5 October 1921; S. A. Ashe to Hunter, 5 October 1921; W. B. Merrimon to Hunter, 1 October 1921; J. M. Broughton to Hunter, 28 September 1921; R. H. Lewis to Hunter, 11 October 1921; M. A. Barber to Hunter, 28 September 1921; J. B. Cheshire to Hunter, 30 September 1921; I. R. Humphreys to Hunter, 6 October 1921; J. C. Caddell to Hunter, 2 October 1921; J. R. Chamberlain to Hunter, 3 October 1921; C. B. Edwards to Hunter, 10 October 1921; H. L. Stevens to Hunter, 4 October 1921; Connor to Hunter, 30 September 1921, Hunter Papers; *Raleigh News and Observer*, 25 October 1921.

25. *Norfolk Journal and Guide*, 24 September 1921.

26. *Raleigh News and Observer*, 29 November 1921.

27. Ibid., 27 October 1921; 3 January 1922; *Norfolk Journal and Guide*, 5 November 1921.

28. *Norfolk Journal and Guide*, 5 November 1921; Hunter to G. B. Christian, 15 November 1921, Hunter Papers; *Raleigh News and Observer*, 28 October 1921.

29. *Raleigh News and Observer*, 28 October; 8 November 1921.

30. Ibid., 28 October; 8, 15 November 1921.

31. Crawford to Hunter, 15 November 1921; Hunter to Crawford, 19 November 1921, Hunter Papers.

32. *Norfolk Journal and Guide*, 19 January 1921.

33. London to W. R. Thompson, 7 September 1922, Hunter Papers.

34. Shaw to J. R. Hudson, 3 April 1923; Ernest Haywood to Hunter, 19 October 1922; Edgar Haywood to Hunter, 23 November 1922; James B. Dudley to Hunter, 9, 26 January 1923; Sanford to Hunter, 11 October 1922; Johnson to Hunter, 24 July; 3 August 1923; Mary B. Palmer to Hunter, 12 June 1923, Hunter Papers; *Siler City Weekly Herald*, 19 April 1923.

35. Hunter, "Oration on the Occasion of the Celebration of the Sixtieth Anniversary of the Proclamation of Emancipation, January 1923," Hunter Papers.

36. *Raleigh News and Observer*, 3 January 1923.

37. Ibid.; Hunter to L. M. Mason, 8 July 1921, Hunter Papers.

38. *Congressional Record*, 64:1509; Hunter to Stedman, 24 January 1923; Stedman to Hunter, 29 January 1923; Hunter to Haywood, 7 November 1923, Hunter Papers.

39. Hunter to Willis B. Crawford, 19 November 1921; Hunter to F. P. Haywood, 7 November 1923, Hunter Papers; *Norfolk Journal and Guide*, 12 May 1923.

40. *Greensboro Daily News*, 26 June 1923.

41. Ibid., 4 July 1923; Moore to Hunter, 4 July [1923]; Cochran to Hunter, 11 July 1923, Hunter Papers.

42. *Chatham Record*, 31 January 1924, Hunter Scrapbook 1875–1924; Hunter to the Honorable School Committee, District No. 2, 12 September 1923; "Opening of George M. Horton Public School, October 1923," Hunter Papers.

43. *Norfolk Journal and Guide*, 26 January 1924.

44. Shaw to Hunter, 9 September 1924; Hunter to S. B. Underwood, 10 May 1922; Hunter to Clarence Poe [26 July 1923]; 31 July 1923, Hunter Papers.

45. Hunter to Poe, 26 July 1923; Poe to Hunter, 31 July 1923; 2 July 1924; H. F. Srygley to Hunter, 8, 22, July 1924, Hunter Papers.

46. Hunter to Roscoe C. Simmons, 25 July 1924; *Norfolk Journal and Guide*, 10 February 1924.

47. Hunter to Simmons, 25 July 1924; Overman to Hunter, 16 April 1924; A. V. Dockery to Hunter, 5 May 1924; Moore to Hunter, 29 July [1924], Hunter Papers.

48. Hunter to William M. Butler, 24 July 1924; Hunter to Simmons, 25 July 1924, Hunter Papers.
49. Ibid.; J. H. Love to Simmons, 26 July 1924; A. Myron Cochran and W. J. Latham to Simmons, 2 August 1924; P. B. Young to Simmons, 7 August 1924; Satterwhite to Simmons, 18 August 1924; Simmons to Hunter, 23 July 1924; Eva to Hunter, 1 November 1924, Hunter Papers.
50. Miller to Hunter, 1 August 1924, Hunter Papers.
51. Hunter, "What Shall the Negro Do?" 18 August 1924; Hunter to McLean, 5 November 1924, Hunter Papers.
52. Hunter to Clarkson, 5 November 1924; Hunter to Lacy, 5 November 1924, Hunter Papers.
53. Sanford to Hunter, 3 August 1924, Hunter Papers; Bryan to Nunn, 10 September; 11 November 1924, Nunn Papers.
54. Hunter to Briggs, 27 November 1924; Moore to Hunter, 22 November; 16 December 1924, Hunter Papers.
55. Hunter to the President of the United States with a Copy to the Attorney General, December 1924, Hunter Papers; *Raleigh News and Observer*, 30 December 1924.

# Chapter 11

1. Laura J. A. King to Hunter, 4 June 1926; Hunter to H. B. Marrow, 14 February; 5, 22 June 1926, Hunter Papers.
2. Hunter to Marrow, 5, 22 June; 1 September 1926; Marrow to Hunter, 5 September 1926; Laura J. A. King to Hunter, 9 October 1926, Hunter Papers.
3. Noble to Hunter, 1 January 1926; Marrow to H. F. Srygley, 14 January 1927, Hunter Papers.
4. Lacy to H. F. Srygley, 14 June 1926; Lacy to Hunter, 14 June 1926; S. J. Betts to Hunter, 26 July 1926; W. H. Easterling to Editor of the *Raleigh Times*, n.d., Hunter Papers. Although the letter to the *Times* bore Easterling's signature, evidence indicates it was written by Hunter. The letter is in Hunter's handwriting and the phraseology and logic are his. Also at the time the letter was written, Easterling was renting Hunter's house in Raleigh.
5. Newbold to Hunter, 30 July 1926; Easterling to the Editor of the *Raleigh Times*, n.d., Hunter Papers.
6. Chesnutt to Hunter, 12 October 1926; Hunter to B. F. McBryde, 13 December 1926; Hunter to Newbold, 4 February 1927, Hunter Papers.
7. Hunter to Newbold, 7 February 1927; Hunter to R. R. Nimmocks, April 1927, Hunter Papers.

8. Allen to Hunter, 24 June 1927; C. D. Douglas to Hunter, 24 June 1927, Hunter Papers.

9. Hunter to Ashe, 9 February 1927; J. H. Love to Hunter, 30 March 1925; Barnes to Hunter, 23 March 1927, Hunter Papers; *Norfolk Journal and Guide*, 28 May 1927.

10. *Raleigh News and Observer*, 3 May 1927; *Norfolk Journal and Guide*, 28 May 1927.

11. Hunter to Edwards, 9 September 1927; W. P. Hawfield to Hunter, 16 August 1928, Hunter Papers.

12. Newbold to Hunter, 29 April 1922; Noble to Hunter, 15 September; 3 December 1925; 1 January 1926; Amelia J. Hunter to Hunter, 16, 25 February 1926; Berry O'Kelly to Hunter, 17 February 1926, Hunter Papers.

13. Olds to Hunter, 22 June 1925; 6, 8, 16 April 1926; Edmonds to Hunter, 14 July 1925, Hunter Papers.

14. Hunter to S. A. Ashe, 9 February 1927, Hunter Papers.

15. *Fayetteville Observer*, 13 January 1927; Hunter to Ashe, 2 February; 9 November 1927, Hunter Papers.

16. *Fayetteville Observer*, 13, 31 January 1927; *Raleigh News and Observer*, 23 November 1927; Hunter to Olds, 5 November 1927; Hunter to Ashe, 9 February 1927, Hunter Papers.

17. *Raleigh News and Observer*, 23 November 1927; *Fayetteville Observer*, 13 January 1927.

18. *Fayetteville Observer*, 31 January 1927; Olds to Hunter, 17 March 1927, Hunter Papers.

19. Dunston to Hunter, 17 February 1927, Hunter Papers.

20. Hunter, *Review of Negro Life in North Carolina with My Recollections*, pp. 6–7.

21. Hunter to E. E. Smith, 10 January 1927; Hunter to Dunston, 5 November 1927, Hunter Papers.

22. Ashe to Hunter, 3 February; 7, 27 November 1927; Hunter to Ashe, 13 September 1929, Hunter Papers; *Raleigh Times*, 24 November 1927.

23. Hunter to Olds, 5 November 1927; Olds to Hunter, 12 November, 6 December 1927; Clarence S. Bringham to Hunter, 5 December 1927; Burton Stevenson to Hunter, 31 January 1928; Library Committee, University of Pennsylvania to Hunter, 8 September 1928; Hunter to Carter G. Woodson, 30 September 1929; Hunter to E. E. Smith, 10 January 1931; Cotten to Hunter, 21 July 1928; Litchford to Hunter, 26 October 1929, Hunter Papers.

24. Hunter to Woodson, 30 September 1929; Hunter to Smith, 10 January 1931, Hunter Papers.

25. *Fayetteville Observer*, 13 January 1927; *Norfolk Journal, and Guide*, 17 March 1928.

26. *Raleigh Times*, 3 January 1928, Hunter Scrapbook 1887–1929, Hunter Papers.

27. *Norfolk Journal and Guide*, 17 March; 7 April 1928.

28. *Raleigh Times*, 3 January 1928, Hunter Scrapbook 1887–1929, Hunter Papers.

29. Hunter to Work, July 1928, Hunter Papers.

30. Ibid.; Hawkins to Hunter, 14 September 1928, Hunter Papers.

31. Hunter, "What Shall the Negro Do?" 24 July; 8 August 1928, Hunter Papers.

32. Ibid.

33. Ibid.

34. W. P. Beazell to Hunter, 25 July 1928; A. R. Holcombe to Hunter, 27 July 1928; Gray to Hunter, 31 August 1928, Hunter Papers.

35. Simmons, "Address at City Auditorium, October 25, 1928"; Simmons, *Exposure and Denunciation of the Tammany-Smith-Raskob-DuPont Coalition, October 12, 1928*, White Family Papers; Puryear, *Democratic Party Dissension in North Carolina*, pp. 16–17; *Raleigh News and Observer*, 26 October 1928.

36. Taylor and Hunter, "To the Voters of North Carolina," 8 September 1928; Hunter, "What Shall the Negro Do?" 24 July; 28 August 1928, Hunter Papers.

37. Briggs to Hunter, 1 September 1928; Hunter, "What Shall the Negro Do?" 28 August 1928; Hunter to H. H. Taylor, 20 September 1928; Taylor and Hunter, "To the Voters of North Carolina," 20 September 1928, Hunter Papers.

38. Hunter to My Dear Sir [H. H. Taylor], 8 September 1928, Hunter Papers.

39. Ibid.; Taylor and Hunter, "To the Voters of North Carolina," 8 September 1928, Hunter Papers.

40. Ibid.

41. Hunter to My Dear Sir [H. H. Taylor], 8 September 1928; Hunter to Dear Taylor, 28 September 1928, Hunter Papers; Puryear, *Democratic Party Dissension in North Carolina*, p. 17; Simmons, "Address at City Auditorium," 25 October 1928, Simmons Papers; *Raleigh News and Observer*, 26 October 1926.

42. Jennie to Hunter, 28 June 1929; *Raleigh Times*, 8 July 1929, Hunter Scrapbook 1877–1924, Hunter Papers.

43. *Raleigh News and Observer*, 26 June 1929; *Carolina Times*, quoted in *Raleigh Times*, 8 July 1929, Hunter Scrapbook 1877–1924, Hunter Papers.

44. *Carolina Times*, quoted in *Raleigh Times*, 8 July 1929, Hunter Scrapbook 1877–1924, Hunter Papers.

45. Ibid.

46. *Union Reformer*, 30 June 1928, Hunter Scrapbook 1877–1924; "Minutes of the Conference on July 16, 1928 of Negro Citizens to Consider the Feasibility of Continuing the Holding of a Negro State Fair in North Carolina," Hunter Papers.

47. Hunter to F. A. Olds, 29 June 1928; T. L. Love to Hunter, 29 June 1928; Hunter to L. G. Gravely, 5 February 1931, Hunter Papers.

48. Hunter to Olds, 29 June 1928; Olds to Hunter, 30 June; 30 July 1928; Hunter to

Broughton, [5] February 1929; Broughton to Hunter, 18 February 1929, Hunter
Papers.

49. Hunter to O. Max Gardner, 17 December 1929; Tyre C. Taylor to Hunter, 26
December 1929; "Minutes of the Meeting of the Executive Committee of the
North Carolina Industrial Association July 19, 1930"; Hunter to the Executive
Committee, North Carolina State Fair, 2 August 1930; Hunter to C. R. Hudson,
4 July 1930, Hunter Papers.

50. Hunter to the Executive Committee, North Carolina State Fair, 2 August 1930;
Hunter to T. B. Smith, 20 January 1931; Hunter to R. B. Whitley, 12 February
1931; Executive Committee, NCIA to L. G. Gravely, 5 February 1931, Hunter
Papers.

51. Hunter to Hinsdale, 12 February 1931; "Proceedings of the Executive Committee, North Carolina Industrial Association June 17th 1931," Hunter Papers;
*Raleigh News and Observer*, 5 September; 11 October 1931.

52. Hunter to Peacock, 6 June 1931, Hunter Papers.

53. *Raleigh News and Observer*, 5 September 1931; Moore to Hunter, 4 July
[1923], Hunter Papers.

# Conclusion

1. Saunders, "Race Attitudes of County Officials [1933]."
2. Sorel, *Reflections on Violence*, pp.32–34.

# Selected Bibliography

## Primary Sources

### Manuscript Collections

J. Y. Joyner Library, East Carolina University, Greenville
    White Family Papers.
North Carolina Department of Archives and History, Raleigh
    Charles Brantley Aycock Papers.
    Department of Public Instruction Papers.
    James H. Harris Papers.
    David S. Reid Papers.
    Edmund Smithwick and Family Papers.
    Zebulon B. Vance Papers.
    Gertrude Weil Papers.
Perkins Library, Duke University, Durham
    Cronly Family Papers.
    Washington Duke Papers.
    Benjamin Sherwood Hedrick Papers.
    Charles N. Hunter Papers.
    Ku Klux Klan Papers.
    Hugh MacRae Papers.
    Romulus A. Nunn Papers.
    Furnifold M. Simmons Papers.
Southern Historical Collection, University of North Carolina, Chapel Hill
    Benehan Cameron Papers.
    Henry Groves Connor Papers.
    Charles L. Coon Papers.

Lee S. Overman Papers.
David A. Schenck Papers.
Alfred Moore Waddell Papers.


## Contemporary Accounts

A.C. "The Passing of the Negro from Politics." *Trinity Archive* (February 1903): 223–28.

Andrews, Sidney. *The South since the War*. Introduction by David Donald. Boston: Ticknor and Fields, 1866; Sentry ed., Boston: Houghton Mifflin, 1971.

Ashe, Samuel A'Court. *History of North Carolina*. 2 vols. Raleigh: Edwards and Broughton, 1927.

A Southern Woman. "Black and White in the South. The Basis of Adjustment." *Outlook* 108 (March 1914): 538–46.

Barringer, P.B. *The American Negro, His Past and Future*. Raleigh: Edwards and Broughton, 1900.

Bingham, Robert. "An Ex-Slave Holder's View of the Negro Question in the South." *Harpers Monthly Magazine*, European ed. (July 1900): 8–15.

Brown, David. "The White Man's Problem." *African Methodist Episcopal Zion Quarterly* 4 (April 1894): 268–74.

Byrd, John W. *Reasons Why the Negro Should Remain in the South*. Wilson, N.C.: P. D. Gold Publishing Company, 1904.

Christmas, L. T. *An Evil Router from All the Walks of Life—From the Cradle to the Grave, a Panacea for Racial Friction and a Crowning Benediction to Humanity*. Raleigh: Edwards and Broughton, 1900.

Corbitt, D. L., and William H. Richardson, eds. *Public Papers and Letters of Cameron Morrison, Governor of North Carolina 1921–25*. Raleigh: Edwards and Broughton, 1927.

Daniels, Josephus. *Editor in Politics*. Chapel Hill: University of North Carolina Press, 1941.

————. *Tar Heel Editor*. Chapel Hill: University of North Carolina Press, 1939.

DuBois, W. E. Burghardt. "The Twelfth Census and the Negro Problem." *Southern Workman* 29 (May 1900): 305–9.

Fortune, T. Thomas. "Good Niggers and Good Indians." *Independent* (New York) 51 (June 1899): 1689–90.

Fuller, Thomas O. *Twenty Years in Public Life 1890–1910*. Nashville: National Baptist Printing Board, 1919.

Hamilton, J. G. de Roulhac, ed. *The Correspondence of Jonathan Worth*. 2 vols. Raleigh: Edwards and Broughton, 1909.

Helper, Hinton Rowan. *The Negroes in Negroland; The Negroes in America and*

*Negroes Generally. Also: The Several Races of White Men Considered as the Evolutionary and Predestined Supplanters of the Black Men.* New York: G. N. Carleton, 1868.

*History of the General Assembly of North Carolina January 9–March 13, 1895.* Raleigh: E. M. Uzelle, Printer and Binder, 1895.

Holden, William Woods. *Memoirs of W. W. Holden.* John Lawson Monographs of the Trinity College Historical Society, vol. 2. Durham: Seeman Printery, 1911.

Hood, J. W. "The Fifteenth Amendment." *Independent* (New York) 65 (September 1908): 651–52.

Hoyle, William. *The Negro Question and the I.O.G.T. An Historical Disquisition.* London: E. Curtice and Company, 1876.

Hunter, Charles N. *Review of Negro Life in North Carolina with My Recollections.* Raleigh: N.p., [1927].

Jones, Mary F. *Memoirs and Speeches of Locke Craig, Governor of North Carolina, 1913–1917: A History Political and Otherwise from Scrapbooks and Old Manuscripts.* Asheville: Hackney and Moale Company, 1923.

Keith, B. F. *Memoirs of B. F. Keith.* Raleigh: Bynum Printing Company, 1922.

Kilgo, John Carlisle. "An Inquiry concerning Lynchings." *South Atlantic Quarterly* 1 (January 1902): 4–13.

———. "Our Duty to the Negro." *South Atlantic Quarterly* 2 (October 1903): 369–85.

Lilly, Clay D. "The Attitude of the South to the Colored People." *Union Seminary Magazine* 16 (February-March 1905): 270–87.

Martin, Santford, and R. B. House, eds. *Public Letters and Papers of Thomas Walter Bickett, Governor of North Carolina 1917–1921.* Raleigh: Edwards and Broughton, 1923.

McNair, Colin. *The Race Crisis.* N.p., 1904.

Mebane, George Allen. "Have We an American Race Question? 1. The Negro Vindicated." *Arena* 24 (November 1900): 449–67.

———. *"The Negro Problem" as Seen and Discussed by Southern White Men in Conference at Montgomery, Alabama, with Criticisms by the Northern Press.* New York: Alliance Publishing Company, 1900.

Newbold, N. C. "Common Schools for Negroes in the South." *Annals of the American Academy of Political and Social Sciences* (November 1928), reprint in North Carolina Collection, University of North Carolina at Chapel Hill.

———. "Negro County-School Commencements." *Southern Workman* (December 1916), reprint in North Carolina Collection, University of North Carolina at Chapel Hill.

Odum, Howard W. "Fundamental Principles Underlying Inter-Racial Co-operation." *Journal of Social Forces* 1 (March 1923): 282–85.

## Selected Bibliography

Page, Walter Hines. "The Last Hold of the Southern Bully." *Forum* 16 (November 1893): 303–14.

Penn, I. Garland, and J. W. E. Brown, eds. *The United Negro: His Problems and His Progress*. Atlanta: D. E. Luther Publishing Company, 1902.

Poe, Clarence H. "Rural Land Segregation between Whites and Negroes: A Reply to Mr. Stephenson." *South Atlantic Quarterly* 13 (January 1914): 207–12.

————. "Suffrage Restriction in the South; Its Causes and Consequences." *North American Review* 175 (October 1902): 534–43.

Poland, C. Beauregard. *The Glorious Victory 1898*. Raleigh: By the Author, 1898.

Pool, [John]. "The Convention in North Carolina." *Republic* 4 (May 1875): 257–65.

"The Present Nightmare in the South." *African Methodist Episcopal Zion Quarterly* 4 (April 1894): 310–13.

Price, J. C. "Does the Negro Seek Social Equality?" *Forum* 10 (January 1891): 558–64.

"Race Troubles in the Carolinas." *Literary Digest* 17 (November 1898): 624.

Reid, Whitelaw. *After the War*. Edited by C. Vann Woodward. New York: Harper and Row, 1965.

Simmons, F. M. "The Political Future of the Negro." *Independent* (New York) 60 (June 1906): 1521–26.

Stephenson, Gilbert T. "The Segregation of the White and Negro Races in Cities." *South Atlantic Quarterly* 13 (January 1904): 1–18.

Strange, Robert. *Church Work among the Negroes in the South*. Hale Memorial Sermon No. 2. Chicago: Western Theological Seminary, 1907.

Tourgée, Albion W. "Shall White Minorities Rule?" *Forum* 27 (April 1899): 143–55.

Waddell, Alfred Moore. "The Story of the Wilmington, North Carolina Race Riots." *Collier's Weekly* 22 (November 1898): 4–16.

West, Harry L. "The Race War in North Carolina." *Forum* 26 (January 1899): 578–99.

Winston, George T. "The Relations of the Whites to the Negroes." *Annals of the American Academy of Political and Social Sciences* (July 1901): 105–18.

Winston, Robert W. "An Unconsidered Aspect of the Negro Question." *South Atlantic Quarterly* 1 (July 1902): 264–68.

————. *It's a Far Cry*. New York: Henry Holt and Company, 1937.

# Selected Bibliography

## Official Publications

Alvord, J. W. *Sixth Semi-Annual Report on Schools for Freedmen July 1, 1868.* Washington, D.C.: Government Printing Office, 1868.

*House Journal of the North Carolina General Assembly, Session of 1873–74.*

James, Horace. *Annual Report of the Superintendent of Negro Affairs in North Carolina 1864 with an Appendix Containing the History of the Freedmen in the Department up to June 1st, 1865.* Boston: W. F. Brown and Company, n.d.

*North Carolina General Assembly House Resolution 58, 1876–77 Session.*

*North Carolina General Assembly Session Laws and Resolution 1876–77.*

U.S. Congress. House. *Inaugural Address of the Presidents of the United States from George Washington 1789 to John F. Kennedy 1961.* H. Doc. 218, 87th Cong., 1st sess. Washington, D.C.: Government Printing Office, 1961.

——. *Message from the President of the United States in Answer to a Resolution of the House of 27th Ultimate. Relative to the Provisions in the Constitutions of Several Southern States.* H. Doc. 118, 39th Cong., 1st sess. Washington, D.C.: Government Printing Office, 1866.

——. Representative Cain Speaking on Civil Rights, 43d Cong., 1st sess., 10 January 1874. *Congressional Record*, vol. 2.

——. Representative Pou Speaking on Behalf of Loyalty of Negro Americans, 65th Cong., 1st sess., 9 January 1923. *Congressional Record*, vol. 64.

——. Representative White Speaking on Duty of Negro to Defend the Nation. 55th Cong., 2d sess., 7 March 1898. *Congressional Record*, vol. 31.

U.S. Congress. Senate. *Report and Testimony of the Select Committee of the U.S. Senate to Investigate the Causes of the Removal of the Negro from the Southern States to the Northern States. In Three Parts.* S. Rept. 693. Washington, D.C.: Government Printing Office, 1883.

U.S. Department of Labor. Division of Negro Economics. *The Negro at Work during the World War and during the Reconstruction.* Washington, D.C.: Government Printing Office, 1921.

## Addresses and Proceedings

*A Declaration of Principles by Representative Negroes of North Carolina, Raleigh, September 26, 1919.* Raleigh: Office of the Superintendent of Public Instruction, n.d.

Barringer, P. B. *Speech before the Tri-State Medical Society, 20 February 1900.* N.p., n.d.

Bingham, Robert. *"The New South": An Address in the Interest of National Aid to*

# Selected Bibliography

*Education Delivered Feb. 15, 1884, in Washington, D.C., before the Superintendents' Department of the National Education Association and Repeated in Madison, Wisconsin before the National Educational Association on the 16th of July 1884.* N.p., n.d.

Coon, Charles L. *Public Taxation and Negro Schools—Paper Read before the Twelfth Annual Conference for Negro Education in the South Held at Atlanta, Georgia, April 14, 15, and 16, 1909.* Cheney, Pa.: Committee of Twelve for the Advancement of the Interest of the Negro Race, 1909.

*Eighth and Ninth Annual Report of the Association for the Advancement of Colored People for the Years 1917 and 1918.* New York: National Association for the Advancement of Colored People, 1919.

*Eleventh Annual Report of the National Association for the Advancement of Colored People for the Year 1920.* New York: National Association for the Advancement of Colored People, 1921.

Finger, S. M. *The Educational and Religious Interests of the Colored People of the South. An Address Delivered to the North Carolina Teachers' Association (Colored) on November 11th 1885.* N.p., n.d.

*First Annual Catalogue and Circular of the Biddle Memorial Institute, Charlotte, North Carolina, 1867–8.* N.p., n.d.

*Five Lessons for North Carolina Voters.* N.p., [1898].

Hunter, O. *Essay Delivered at the Second Annual Meeting of the North Carolina Educational Association in the House of Representatives at Raleigh, N.C. July 9, 1874.* Raleigh: John Nichols and Company, 1874.

*Journal of the Constitutional Convention of the State of North Carolina at Its Sessions 1868.* Raleigh: J. W. Holden, Convention Printer, 1868.

*Journal of the Fourth Annual Meeting of the North Carolina State Teachers' Association Held in the First Congregational Church in the City of Raleigh, November 10th and 11th 1885.* Raleigh: A. Williams and Company, 1886.

Miller, J. F. *The Effects of Emancipation upon the Mental and Physical Health of the Negro in the South. Paper Read before the Southern Medico-Psychological Association at Asheville, N.C. September 16, 1896.* N.p., n.d.

"Minutes of a Meeting of the Wilmington Light Infantry Held at the Lumina, Wrightsville Beach, 14 December 1905." North Carolina Collection, University of North Carolina at Chapel Hill.

*Minutes of the Freedmen's Convention, Held in the City of Raleigh on the 2nd, 3rd, 4th, and 5th of October, 1866.* Raleigh: Standard Book and Job Company, 1866.

Moore, B. F. *To the Voters of Wake County, 12 September 1865.* N.p., n.d.

North Carolina Teachers' Association. *Proceedings of the Twentieth Annual Session Held at Kittrell College, Kittrell, North Carolina, June 12, 13, 14, 15, 16, 17th, 1901.* Elizabeth City: E. F. Snakenberg, 1903.

# Selected Bibliography

Phillips, S. F. *Remarks in the House of Commons at the Called Session of the Legislature, January 1866, in Committee of the Whole Upon the Question of Admitting Negro Evidence in Courts of Justice.* N.p., n.d.

Pike, H. L. *Address at the Celebration of Emancipation Day at Raleigh January 1870.* Raleigh: Standard, 1870.

*Proceedings and Debates of the Convention of North Carolina Called to Amend the Constitution of the State Which Assembled at Raleigh, June 4, 1835 to Which Are Subjoined the Convention Act and the Amendments to the Constitution Together with the Votes of the People.* Raleigh: Joseph Gales and Sons, 1836.

*Proceedings of the State Convention of Colored Citizens Held in the House of Representatives in the City of Raleigh, N.C. on the 18th and 19th Days of October 1877.* Raleigh: Edwards, Broughton and Company, 1877.

*Report of Professor Charles H. Moore, State Inspector of Negro Schools Made before the North Carolina State Teachers' Association Assembled at Greensboro, June 23, 1916.* Durham: Durham Reformer Press, n.d.

*Report of the Board of Directors and Superintendent of the Insane Asylum of North Carolina for the Official Year Ending November 30th 1877.* Raleigh: Edwards, Broughton and Company, 1878.

Rountree, George. *The Great Speech of George Rountree, Esq., Delivered in the House of Representatives of North Carolina on the Subject of the Constitutional Amendment.* N.p., n.d. [17 February 1899].

*Southern Women and Race Cooperation. A Story of the Memphis Conference, October 6 and 7th 1920.* Atlanta: Commission on Interracial Cooperation, 1920.

*Twenty-first Annual Report of the National Association for the Advancement of Colored People.* New York: National Association for the Advancement of Colored People, 1931.

Vance, Z. B. *Speech Delivered in the Senate of the United States on the Negro Question, Thursday January 30, 1890.* Washington, D.C.: N.p., 1890.

White, George H. *Defence of the Negro Race—Charges Answered, Speech in the House of Representatives, January 29, 1901.* Washington, D.C.: N.p., 1901.

## Newspapers

*Asheville Gazette*, 1902.
*Baltimore Afro-American*, 1918–19.
*Baltimore Manufacturer's Record*, 1917.
*Charlotte Observer*, 1897–99.
*Charlotte People's Paper*, 1898.
*Charlotte Weekly News*, 1870.

# Selected Bibliography

*Chicago Record*, 1898.
*Concord Times*, 1899.
*Detroit Plaindealer*, 1888.
*Durham Daily Recorder*, 1887.
*Durham Daily Tobacco Plant*, 1888.
*Fayetteville Examiner*, 1880.
*Fayetteville Observer*, 1927–31.
*Fayetteville Wide Awake*, 1876.
*Greensboro Daily News*, 1914–32.
*Littleton True Reformer*, 1902–07.
*New York Age*, 1909–21.
*New York Freeman*, 1888.
*New York Times*, 1878.
*New York Tribune*, 1898.
*Norfolk Journal and Guide*, 1917–28.
*North Carolina Christian Advocate*, 1928.
*North Carolina Daily Standard*, 1870.
*North Carolina Presbyterian*, 1898.
*North Carolina Republican*, 1880.
*North Carolina Standard*, 1869.
*North Carolina Weekly Intelligencer*, 1890.
*North Carolina Weekly Standard*, 1869.
*Philadelphia Christian Recorder*, 1865.
*Raleigh Banner Enterprise*, 1883.
*Raleigh Baptist Sentinel*, 1905.
*Raleigh Biblical Recorder*, 1897–20.
*Raleigh Blasting Powder*, 1872.
*Raleigh Daily Crescent*, 1874.
*Raleigh Daily Record*, 1865–67.
*Raleigh Daily Sentinel*, 1868.
*Raleigh Gazette*, 1891–98.
*Raleigh Journal of Freedom*, 1865.
*Raleigh Journal of Industry*, 1879.
*Raleigh Morning Post*, 1898–05.
*Raleigh News*, 1880.
*Raleigh News and Observer*, 1881–1931.
*Raleigh Observer*, 1876–80.
*Raleigh Press-Visitor*, 1896.
*Raleigh Semi-Weekly Record*, 1865.
*Raleigh Signal*, 1880–91.
*Raleigh State Chronicle*, 1888–89.

*Raleigh State Journal*, 1913–18.
*Raleigh Times*, 1912–29.
*Raleigh Tri-Weekly Era*, 1873.
*Raleigh Weekly Era*, 1873.
*Raleigh Weekly Observer*, 1878.
*Raleigh Weekly Republican*, 1867–74.
*Raleigh Weekly Telegram*, 1871.
*Richmond* (Virginia) *Planet*, 1899.
*Siler City Weekly Herald*, 1923.
*Union Republican* (Winston), 1899.
*Washington* (D.C.) *Bee*, 1898.
*Washington* (D.C.) *Colored American*, 1898.
*Washington* (D.C.) *Post*, 1898–1903.
*Wilmington Messenger*, 1881–98.
*Wilmington Morning Star*, 1898.
*Wilmington Post*, 1881–84.

### Periodicals

*Crisis*, 1913–20.
*Independent* (New York), 1889–1910.
*Land We Love*, 1869.
*Nation*, 1865, 1909.
*Our Living and Our Dead*, 1874.
*Republic*, 1885.
*Southern Workman*, 1898–99.

# Secondary Sources

### Books

Andrews, R. McCants. *John Merrick: A Biographical Sketch*. Durham: Seeman Printer, 1920.
Aptheker, Herbert A., ed. *A Documentary History of the Negro People in the United States*. 2 vols. New York: Citadel Press, 1951.
Chafe, William H. *Civilities and Civil Rights*. New York: Oxford University Press, 1980.

# Selected Bibliography

Connor, R. D. W., and Clarence Poe. *The Life and Speeches of Charles Brantley Aycock*. Garden City, N.J.: Doubleday, Page and Company, 1912.

Crow, Jeffrey J., and Robert Durden. *Maverick Republican in the Old North State: A Political Biography of Daniel L. Russell*. Baton Rouge: Louisiana State University Press, 1979.

Dancy, John C. *Sand against the Wind: The Memoirs of John C. Dancy*. Detroit: Wayne State University Press, 1966.

Dollard, John. *Caste and Class in a Southern Town*. New Haven: Yale University Press, 1937.

Drake, St. Clair, and Horace R. Cayton. *Black Metropolis: A Study of Negro Life in a Northern City*. New York: Harcourt, Brace and Company, 1945.

Durden, Robert F. *The Climax of Populism in the Election of 1896*. Louisville: University of Kentucky Press, 1965.

Edmonds, Helen G. *The Negro and Fusion Politics in North Carolina 1894–1901*. Chapel Hill: University of North Carolina Press, 1951.

Frederickson, George M. *The Black Image in the White Mind: The Debate on Afro-American Character and Destiny, 1817–1914*. New York: Harper and Row, 1971.

Gaston, Paul M. *The New South Creed*. Baton Rouge: Louisiana State University Press, 1970.

Geyl, Pieter. *Use and Abuse of History*. New Haven: Yale University Press, 1955.

Gossett, Thomas F. *Race: The History of an Idea in America*. Dallas: Southern Methodist University Press, 1963.

Grundy, Kenneth W., and Michael A. Weinstein. *The Ideologies of Violence*. Columbus: Charles E. Merrill Publishing Company, 1974.

Haller, John S., Jr. *Outcasts from Evolution, Scientific Attitudes of Racial Inferiority, 1859–1900*. Urbana: University of Illinois Press, 1971.

Hamilton, J. G. de Roulhac. *North Carolina since 1860*, vol. 3, *History of North Carolina*. Chicago: Lewis Publishing Company, 1919; reprint, Spartanburg, S.C.: Reprint Company, 1973.

————. *Reconstruction in North Carolina*. New York: Columbia University Press, 1914; reprint, Gloucester, Mass.: Peter Smith, 1964.

Jenkins, John Wilbur. *James B. Duke, Master Builder*. New York: George H. Doran Company, 1927.

Johnson, E. A. *Light Ahead for the Negro*. New York: Grafton Press, 1904.

Johnson, Guion Griffis. "The Ideology of White Supremacy 1876–1918." In *Essays in Southern History*, pp. 124–56. Edited by Fletcher Melvin Green. James Sprunt Studies in History and Political Science, vol. 31. Chapel Hill: University of North Carolina Press, 1949.

Knight, Edgar W. *Public School Education in North Carolina*. Boston: Houghton Mifflin, 1916; reprint, New York: Negro Universities Press, 1969.

# Selected Bibliography

Litwack, Leon F. *Been in the Storm So Long: The Aftermath of Slavery.* New York: Alfred A. Knopf, 1979.

Logan, Frenise A. *The Negro in North Carolina 1876–1894.* Chapel Hill: University of North Carolina Press, 1964.

Mabry, William Alexander. *The Negro in North Carolina Politics since Reconstruction.* Historical Papers of the Trinity College Historical Society, no. 23. Durham: Duke University Press, 1940; reprint, New York: A.M.S. Press, 1970.

McKitrick, Eric L. *Andrew Johnson and Reconstruction.* Chicago: University of Chicago Press, 1960.

Newbold, N. C. *Five North Carolina Negro Educators.* Chapel Hill: University of North Carolina Press, 1939.

Noble, M. C. S. *A History of the Public Schools of North Carolina.* Chapel Hill: University of North Carolina Press, 1930.

Olson, Alan M., ed. *Myth, Symbol, and Reality.* South Bend: Notre Dame Press, 1980.

Olson, Mancur, Jr. *The Logic of Collective Action.* Cambridge, Mass.: Harvard University Press, 1965.

Orr, Oliver H., Jr. *Charles Brantley Aycock.* Chapel Hill: University of North Carolina Press, 1961.

Page, Walter Hines [Nicholas Worth]. *The Southerner. A Novel Being the Autobiography of Nicholas Worth.* New York: Doubleday, Page and Company, 1909.

Penn, I. Garland. *The Afro-American Press and Its Editors.* Springfield, Mass.: Wiley and Company, 1891.

Pepitone, Albert. *Attraction and Hostility.* Atherton Press Behavioral Science Series. Chicago: Atherton Press, 1964.

Prather, H. Leon. *We Have Taken a City.* Cranbury, N.J.: Associated University Presses, 1984.

Puryear, Elmer L. *Democratic Party Dissension in North Carolina 1928–1936.* James Sprunt Studies in History and Political Science, vol. 44. Chapel Hill: University of North Carolina Press, 1962.

Raper, Horace W. *William Woods Holden, North Carolina's Political Enigma.* James Sprunt Studies in History and Political Science, vol. 59. Chapel Hill: University of North Carolina Press, 1985.

Rippy, J. Fred, ed. *F. M. Simmons, Statesman of the New South: Memoirs and Addresses.* Durham: Duke University Press, 1936.

Sorel, Georges. *Reflections on Violence.* Translated by T. E. Hulme. New York: Peter Smith, 1941.

Tindall, George B. *The Ethnic Southerners.* Baton Rouge: Louisiana State University Press, 1976.

———. "Mythology: A New Frontier in Southern History." In *The Idea of the South: Pursuit of a Central Theme*, pp. 1–15. Edited by Frank E. Vandiver. Chicago: University of Chicago Press, 1964.

Whitener, Daniel J. *Prohibition in North Carolina 1715–1945*. James Sprunt Studies in History and Political Science, vol. 27. Chapel Hill: University of North Carolina Press, 1945.

———. "Public Education in North Carolina during Reconstruction 1865–1876." In *Essays in Southern History*, pp. 67–90. Edited by Fletcher Melvin Green. James Sprunt Studies in History and Political Science, vol. 31. Chapel Hill: University of North Carolina Press, 1949.

Woodward, C. Vann. *American Counterpoint*. Boston: Little, Brown and Company, 1964.


## Articles

Balanoff, Elizabeth. "Negro Legislators in the North Carolina General Assembly, July 1868–February 1872." *North Carolina Historical Review* 49 (January 1972): 22–54.

Browning, James B. "The North Carolina Black Code." *Journal of Negro History* 15 (October 1930): 461–73.

Crow, Jeffrey J. "Fusion, Confusion, and Negroism: Schisms among Negro Republicans in the North Carolina Election of 1896." *North Carolina Historical Review* 53 (October 1976): 364–84.

Gatewood, Willard B. "North Carolina's Negro Regiment in the Spanish-American War." *North Carolina Historical Review* 48 (October 1971): 370–87.

Gay, Dorothy A. "Crisis of Identity: The Negro Community in Raleigh, 1890–1900." *North Carolina Historical Review* 50 (April 1973): 121–40.

Eustis, J. B. "Race Antagonism in the South." *Forum* 6 (October 1888): 144–54.

Harris, William C. "William Woods Holden: In Search of Vindication." *North Carolina Historical Review* 59 (October 1982): 354–72.

Hicks, John D. "The Farmers' Alliance in North Carolina." *North Carolina Historical Review* 2 (April 1925): 162–87.

Hunt, James L. "The Making of a Populist: Marion Butler, 1863–1895." *North Carolina Historical Review* 62 (July 1985): 317–43.

Ingle, Larry. "A Southern Democrat at Large: William Hodge Kitchen and the Populist Party." *North Carolina Historical Review* 45 (April 1968): 178–94.

Johnson, Guy B. "A Sociological Interpretation of the New Ku Klux Klan Movement." *Journal of Social Forces* 1 (May 1923): 440–45.

Kousser, J. Morgan. "Progressivism—For Middle Class Whites Only: North Carolina Education, 1880–1910." *Journal of Southern History* 46 (May 1980): 169–94.

# Selected Bibliography

Logan, Frenise A. "Black and Republican: Vicissitudes of a Minority Twice Over in the North Carolina House of Representatives, 1876–1877." *North Carolina Historical Review* 61 (July 1984): 311–46.

———. "The Legal Status of Public School Education for Negroes in North Carolina, 1877–1894." *North Carolina Historical Review* 32 (July 1955): 346–57.

———. "The Movement of Negroes from North Carolina 1876–1894." *North Carolina Historical Review* 33 (January 1956): 45–65.

———. "The Movement to Establish a State Supported College for Negroes." *North Carolina Historical Review* 35 (April 1958): 167–80.

Martin, Everett Dean. "Some Mechanisms Which Distinguish the Crowd from Other Forms of Social Behavior." *Journal of Abnormal Psychology and Social Psychology* 18 (October–December 1923): 187–203.

Miller, Robert D. "Samuel Field Phillips: The Odyssey of a Southern Dissenter." *North Carolina Historical Review* 58 (July 1981): 263–80.

Morales, Armando. "The Collective Preconscious and Racism." *Social Casework* (May 1971): 285–93.

Olsen, Otto H., and Ellen Z. McGrew. "Prelude to Reconstruction: The Correspondence of State Senator Leander Sams Gash, 1866–1867." *North Carolina Historical Review* 60 (January 1983): 37–83.

Prather, H. Leon. "The Red Shirt Movement in North Carolina, 1898–1900." *Journal of Negro History* 62 (April 1977): 174–84.

Steelman, Joseph F. "Republican Party Strategists and the Issue of Fusion with Populists in North Carolina 1893–1894." *North Carolina Historical Review* 47 (July 1970): 244–69.

———. "Republicans in North Carolina: John Motley Morehead's Campaign to Revive a Moribund Party, 1908–1910." *North Carolina Historical Review* 42 (April 1965): 153–68.

Taylor, Joseph H. "The Great Migration from North Carolina in 1879." *North Carolina Historical Review* 31 (January 1954): 18–33.

Thomas, William I. "The Psychology of Race Prejudice." *American Journal of Sociology* 9 (March 1904): 593–611.

Trelease, Allen W. "The Fusion Legislatures of 1895 and 1897: A Roll Call Analysis of the North Carolina House of Representatives." *North Carolina Historical Review* 57 (July 1980): 280–309.

Watson, Elgiva D. "The Election Campaign of Governor Jarvis, 1880: A Study of the Issues." *North Carolina Historical Review* 48 (July 1971): 276–300.

Woodward, C. Vann. "The Antislavery Myth." *American Scholar* 31 (Spring 1962): 312–28.

Young, Erle Fiske. "What Is Race Prejudice?" *Journal of Applied Sociology* 10 (1925–26): 135–40.

# Selected Bibliography

## Unpublished Materials

Anderson, Eric Douglas. "Race and Politics, 1872–1901: The Black Second Congressional District." Ph.D. dissertation, University of Chicago, 1978.

Avent, Joseph E. "Scrapbook of Literature on the Amendment Proposed to the Constitution of North Carolina 1899." North Carolina Collection, University of North Carolina at Chapel Hill.

Brandon, Betty Jane. "Carpetbaggers in North Carolina: Emphasis on Social Attitudes and Contributions of Non-Natives in Economics, Politics, and Education." M.A. thesis, University of North Carolina at Chapel Hill, 1964.

Busbee, Quentin. Scrapbooks. 3 vols. North Carolina Collection, University of North Carolina at Chapel Hill.

Gay, Dorothy A. "Crisis of Identity: The Negro Community in Raleigh 1890–1900." M.A. thesis, University of North Carolina at Chapel Hill, 1970.

Hoffman, Richard Lee. "The Republican Party in North Carolina, 1867–1871." M.A. thesis, University of North Carolina at Chapel Hill, 1960.

Houck, Thomas H. "A Newspaper History of Race Relations in Durham 1910–1940." M.A. thesis, Duke University, 1941.

Jones, Bobby Frank. "An Opportunity Lost: North Carolina Race Relations during Presidential Reconstruction." M.A. thesis, University of North Carolina at Chapel Hill, 1961.

McDuffie, Jerome A. "Politics in Wilmington and New Hanover County, North Carolina, 1865–1900: The Genesis of a Race Riot." Ph.D. dissertation, Kent State University, 1979.

"Negroes in North Carolina." 4 vols. Clipping File. North Carolina Collection, University of North Carolina at Chapel Hill.

Saunders, Wiley B. "Race Attitudes of County Officials (1933)." North Carolina Collection, University of North Carolina at Chapel Hill.

Schenck, William Ziegler. "Negro Participation in Three Southern Expositions." M.A. thesis, University of North Carolina at Chapel Hill, 1970.

Steelman, Joseph Flake. "The Progressive Era in North Carolina, 1894–1917." Ph.D. dissertation, University of North Carolina at Chapel Hill, 1955.

Underwood, Evelyn W. "The Struggle for White Supremacy in North Carolina." M.A. thesis, University of North Carolina at Chapel Hill, 1943.

Wooley, Robert Howard. "Race and Politics: The Evolution of the White Supremacy Campaign of 1898 in North Carolina." Ph.D. dissertation, University of North Carolina at Chapel Hill, 1977.

# Index

# Index

# Index

# Index

# Index

# Index

# Index

# Index

# Index